THE SOCIAL EXPERIENCE OF CHILDHOOD IN ANCIENT MESOAMERICA

MESOAMERICAN WORLDS: FROM THE OLMECS TO THE DANZANTES

General Editors: Davíd Carrasco and Eduardo Matos Moctezuma

After Monte Albán | JEFFREY P. BLOMSTER, EDITOR

The Apotheosis of Janaab' Pakal | GERARDO ALDANA

Carrying the Word | SUSANNA ROSTAS

Commoner Ritual and Ideology in Ancient Mesoamerica | NANCY GONLIN AND JON C. LOHSE, EDITORS

Conquered Conquistadors | FLORINE ASSELBERGS

Empires of Time | ANTHONY AVENI

Encounter with the Plumed Serpent | MAARTEN JANSEN AND GABINA AURORA PÉREZ JIMÉNEZ

Fanning the Sacred Flame | EDITED BY MATTHEW A. BOXT AND BRIAN D. DILLON

In the Realm of Nachan Kan | MARILYN A. MASSON

Invasion and Transformation | REBECCA P. BRIENEN AND MARGARET A. JACKSON, EDITORS

The Kowoj | PRUDENCE M. RICE AND DON S. RICE, EDITORS

The Lords of Lambityeco | MICHAEL LIND AND JAVIER URCID

The Madrid Codex | GABRIELLE VAIL AND ANTHONY AVENI, EDITORS

Maya Creation Myths | TIMOTHY W. KNOWLTON

Maya Daykeeping | JOHN M. WEEKS, FRAUKE SACHSE, AND CHRISTIAN M. PRAGER

Maya Worldviews at Conquest | LESLIE G. CECIL AND TIMOTHY W. PUGH, EDITORS

Mesoamerican Ritual Economy | E. CHRISTIAN WELLS AND KARLA L. DAVIS-SALAZAR, EDITORS

Mesoamerica's Classic Heritage | DAVÍD CARRASCO, LINDSAY JONES, AND SCOTT SESSIONS, EDITORS

Mexico's Indigenous Communities | ETHELIA RUIZ MEDRANO, TRANSLATED BY RUSS DAVIDSON

Mockeries and Metamorphoses of an Aztec God | GUILHEM OLIVIER, TRANSLATED BY MICHEL BESSON

Negotiation within Domination | ETHELIA RUIZ MEDRANO AND SUSAN KELLOGG, EDITORS; TRANSLATED BY RUSS DAVIDSON

Networks of Power | BY EDWARD SCHORTMAN AND PATRICIA URBAN

Rabinal Achi | ALAIN BRETON, EDITOR; TRANSLATED BY TERESA LAVENDER FAGAN AND ROBERT SCHNEIDER

Representing Aztec Ritual | ELOISE QUIÑONES KEBER, EDITOR

Ruins of the Past | TRAVIS W. STANTON AND ALINE MAGNONI, EDITORS

Skywatching in the Ancient World | CLIVE RUGGLES AND GARY URTON, EDITORS

Social Change and the Evolution of Ceramic Production and Distribution in a Maya Community | DEAN E. ARNOLD

The Social Experience of Childhood in Mesoamerica | TRACI ARDREN AND SCOTT R. HUTSON, EDITORS

Stone Houses and Earth Lords | KEITH M. PRUFER AND JAMES E. BRADY, EDITORS

The Sun God and the Savior | GUY STRESSER-PÉAN

Sweeping the Way | CATHERINE DICESARE

Topiltzin Quetzalcoatl | H. B. NICHOLSON

The World Below | JACQUES GALINIER

The Social Experience of Childhood in Ancient Mesoamerica

---

edited by

Traci Ardren & Scott R. Hutson

UNIVERSITY PRESS OF COLORADO
Denver

Published by University Press of Colorado
1580 North Logan Street, Suite 660
PMB 39883
Denver, Colorado 80203-1942

First paperback edition 2025

The University Press of Colorado is a proud member of the Association of University Presses.

The University Press of Colorado is a cooperative publishing enterprise supported, in part, by Adams State University, Colorado State University, Fort Lewis College, Metropolitan State University of Denver, University of Alaska Fairbanks, University of Colorado, University of Denver, University of Northern Colorado, University of Wyoming, Utah State University, and Western Colorado University.

ISBN: 978-0-87081-827-1 (hardcover)
ISBN: 978-1-60732-463-8 (paperback)

Library of Congress Cataloging-in-Publication Data

The social experience of childhood in ancient Mesoamerica / edited by Traci Ardren and Scott Hutson.
p. cm. — (Mesoamerican worlds)
Includes bibliographical references and index.
ISBN: 978-0-87081-827-1 (hardcover : alk. paper)
ISBN: 978-1-60732-463-8 (paperback : alk. paper)
1. Indian children—Anthropometry—Central America. 2. Indian children—Anthropometry—Mexico. 3. Human remains (Archaeology)—Central America. 4. Human remains (Archaeology)—Mexico. 5. Social archaeology—Central America. 6. Social archaeology—Mexico. 7. Central America—Antiquities. 8. Mexico—Antiquities. I. Ardren, Traci. II. Hutson, Scott. III. Series.
F1435.2.C44S63 2006
972.8—dc22

2005037321

Support for the publication of the hardcover edition was generously provided by the Eugene M. Kayden Fund at the University of Colorado.

To Marty and Bob Ardren and Jim and Kathy Hutson

CONTENTS

FIGURES

TABLES

FOREWORD

Davíd Carrasco and
Eduardo Matos Moctezuma

The publication of *The Social Experience of Childhood in Mesoamerica* greatly enhances the empirical range and theoretical engagement of Mesoamerican studies in general and of the Mesoamerican Worlds series in particular. Drawing on the creative currents of gender studies, feminist scholarship, archaeology, and ethnohistory, the book's editors, Traci Ardren and Scott R. Hutson, have integrated a wide range of essays into a new general vision of why and how children mattered in Mesoamerican families and society. Through their scholarship, the contributors bring the experiences of Mesoamerican children to life.

As Traci Ardren argues in her impressive introduction, this book "attempts to remedy more than a century of study that systematically overlooked at least half of ancient Mesoamerica's population" (i.e., the children who were ubiquitous in Mesoamerica's villages, towns, fields, and cities). By uncovering the lives of children in social and ritual contexts, the contributors focus attention on local contexts and knowledge about the human family, while keeping in mind the limits of Eurocentric definitions of childhood when studying Mesoamerican varieties of engendering and raising children. With topics ranging across space and time—from the Olmecs to the Aztecs and beyond—these well-written essays reveal how Mesoamerican peoples defined, practiced, sanctified, and symbolized children within the contexts of family, house, neighborhood, temple, and cosmos. We learn how children occupied and moved through social spaces and were trained for adulthood, how they were sometimes ornamented or sacrificed, and how they were valued in death and symbolized in the afterlife. In the process, we fortunate readers can see how new directions in scholarship, including health studies, family theory, local histories, and ritual studies, allow us to discover the tense, tender, and reciprocal relationships among children, adults, culture, the state, and the gods. Mesoamerican peoples profoundly valued their children, as displayed in this greeting to a newborn, which was reported by Sahagún:

> "O my grandson, O master, O our lord, O precious one, O precious person, O precious green stone, O bracelet, O precious turquoise, O precious feather, O hair, O fingernail, thou hast endured fatigue, though hast endured weariness, thou wert formed in the place of duality (which is above) the nine heavens in tiers."

This book reminds us that children are both our individual pasts and our collective futures and beckons us to give greater attention and study to their lives and roles.

DAVÍD CARRASCO AND
EDUARDO MATOS MOCTEZUMA

CONTRIBUTORS

TRACI ARDREN, Professor, Department of Anthropology, University of Miami, Coral Gables, Florida

XIMENA CHÁVEZ BALDERAS, Office of the Attorney General, Quintana Roo, Mexico

BILLIE FOLLENSBEE, Professor, Department of Art and Design, Missouri State University, Springfield, Missouri

BYRON ELLSWORTH HAMANN received a joint PhD from the departments of Anthropology and History at the University of Chicago.

SCOTT R. HUTSON, University Research Professor, Department of Anthropology, University of Kentucky

ROSEMARY A. JOYCE, Professor Emerita, Department of Anthropology, University of California, Berkeley, California

STACIE M. KING, Professor, Department of Anthropology, Indiana University, Bloomington, Indiana

JEANNE LOPIPARO, Associate Professor, Rhodes College, Memphis, TN

PATRICIA A. MCANANY, Kenan Eminent Professor Emerita, Department of Anthropology, University of North Carolina, Chapel Hill.

GEOFFREY G. MCCAFFERTY, Professor emeritus, Department of Archaeology, University of Calgary, Calgary, Alberta

SHARISSE D. MCCAFFERTY, Adjunct Professor, Department of Archaeology, University of Kentucky, Lexington, KY

JUAN ALBERTO ROMÁN BERRELLEZA, Director, Museo del Templo Mayor, Mexico City, Mexico

REBECCA STOREY, Professor emerita, Department of Anthropology, University of Houston, Houston, Texas

RISSA M. TRACHMAN, Professor, Department of Anthropology, Elon University , Elon, NC

FRED VALDEZ JR., Professor, Department of Anthropology, University of Texas, Austin, Texas

THE SOCIAL EXPERIENCE OF CHILDHOOD IN ANCIENT MESOAMERICA

Part I

INTRODUCTION

1

SETTING THE TABLE

Why Children and Childhood Are Important in an Understanding of Ancient Mesoamerica

Traci Ardren

The title of this chapter is a deliberate reference to Western notions of childhood and the role of children in society. Many Western adults have left behind the time when they performed household chores or spoke only when spoken to for the independence and privilege of adult life. Their memories and experiences of childhood seem far removed from knowledge production in the academy or the rigors of professional scholarship. Yet the intellectual walls constructed between childhood and adulthood in the West are not only a relatively recent convention but also a culturally specific one, a device for the organization of social activity in a society where industrialization and technology have lessened labor demands on certain sectors of the population and created opportunities for large-scale leisure. In short, the Western notion of a carefree childhood is a specific cultural artifact, and yet it has become naturalized to the extent that many scholars find it hard to conceptualize how children or the young would have contributed meaningfully in ancient societies.

An interesting social convergence is responsible for challenging this assumption and focuses new attention on questions about the role children played in the ancient world. Scholarship, much of it explicitly feminist, on the role of gender and especially the experiences of women highlights the importance of illuminating other "invisible populations," including children. Simultaneously, as scholars increasingly examine their own personal motivations for research agendas, the role of parenthood within the academy has been destigmatized and incorporated into intellectual debates. Many of the authors contributing to this scholarship have personally reevaluated their preconceptions of the role of children in ancient societies as they become parents and raise their own children. This self-reflection is embraced within feminist scholarship as an honest assessment of the unavoidable connections between the personal and the political in academic research.

In a tradition not unlike the apologetics who finally saw more to human evolution than "man the hunter" models allowed, those of us working on child kings and their regent mothers, or child sacrifice in places such as Tenochtitlan, wonder how we approached the past *without* an awareness of the fundamental importance of children. This volume is an attempt to remedy more than a century of study that systematically overlooked at least half of ancient Mesoamerica's population. From the frequent depiction of children in Olmec figurines (Chapter 10) to Classic Maya burials where children wear gender-specific ornaments (Chapter 7) to the role of Aztec young people in the machinations of the empire (Chapter 9), children are everywhere in the record of ancient Mesoamerica, and not as appendages or silent apprentices, but often as innovators and repositories of sacred knowledge and power, and at the very juncture of cultural change and evolution that characterizes the heart of anthropological research.

The lack of attention paid to studies of children in ancient societies is obvious; one only has to try and find "child" or "children" in most published indices of the past 100 years to graphically demonstrate that this large segment of the population was systematically overlooked. Explanation of this fact is significantly more difficult, given the goals and objectives of the anthropological enterprise. The Western conception of childhood is certainly partially to blame; in addition to the disconnect between who we were as children and who we are today as scholars, the current practice in our own society of protecting children from labor and most other meaningful, productive activity has ensured that childhood is often vigorously defended as a period without significant responsibility or obligation. The emphasis on play (such as highly organized playgroups), the overabundance of toys (such as McDonald's Happy Meals), and Western legal codes (for example, set ages to work, vote, or serve in the military) are but a few of the current cultural practices used by Western culture to preserve childhood as carefree. Not surprisingly, a biological rationale has been used to justify these practices, and today in the West most adults believe children are physically less capable of labor or other productive activities. This perception has, in turn, significantly constrained our models of ancient societies by eliminating from our minds one sector of society that certainly could have been more actively engaged in cultural production and reproduction than children in the West are today. Ethnographic literature is replete with examples of children performing heavy labor, holding ceremonial or political offices, and creating art. Just as feminist scholarship has shown that biology does not determine women's roles cross-culturally or throughout time, scholarship has now shown that biological factors are not a significant limitation on the roles of children.

Mary Baker (1997) says it is the relationship of children to women, their close association when children are infants, and their shared use of domestic space that is responsible for the invisibility of children in anthropological research. Baker equates children with women and the domestic sphere, lumping all of them into the "non-male" and thus traditionally invisible components of culture. Like many other feminist critiques of previous scholarship, Baker asserts that attention has historically been paid only to male spheres of activity and that only male activities are visible to academics. Thus her explanation is that the academic study of children is inherently uninteresting because the subjects are invisible. This critique has much to commend it of course, especially as an explanation of early research trends, but it still operates within a Western conceptual framework that believes children are domestic creatures. Certainly infants spend a good deal of time with their mothers, but the duration of this period is highly variable and each subsequent phase is also highly culturally dependent. In modern Yucatán and Chiapas, children are expected to help with household chores by about age three, leaving the house for errands and even to tend fields by the time they are eight (Redfield and Villa Rojas 1934:71; McGee 1990:26). We cannot impose an easy equation of children and the domestic upon the ancient record, and we cannot explain the absence of children from our archaeological models simply because they were always in the home.

A similar critique posits that children are simply seen as incomplete humans, inactive receivers of culture and knowledge, thus they are less important or interesting as subjects of study (Burman 1994). Besides

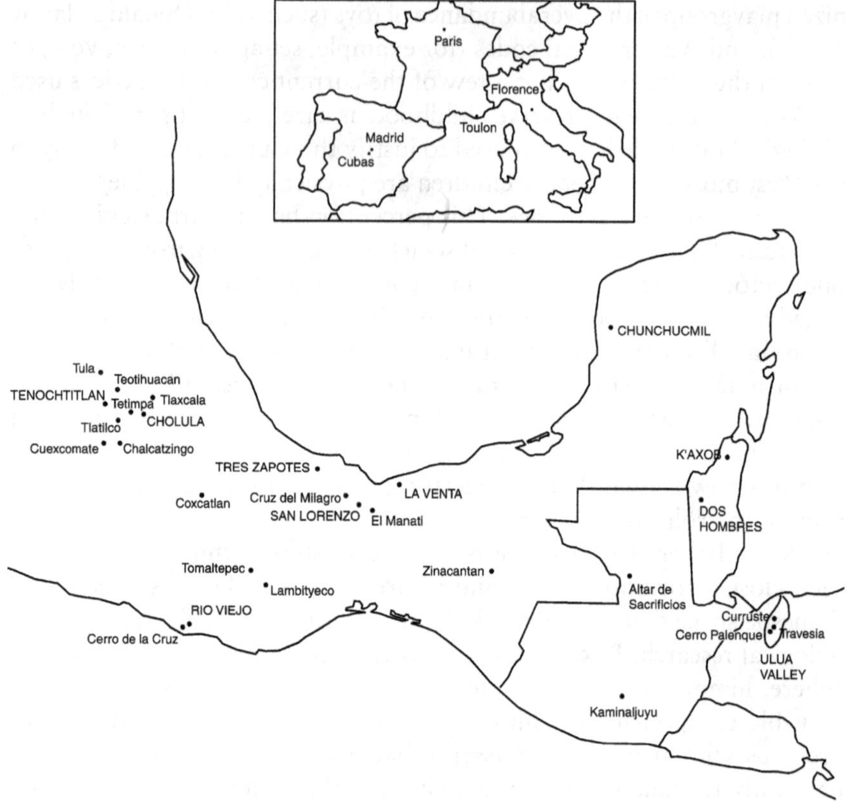

1.1: Map of Mesoamerica showing the locations of major sites mentioned in this book.

being completely dependent upon a Western model of childhood as a passive stage of life, this view of childhood begs the question why the process of knowledge transference or acculturation was considered unimportant. Throughout the history of anthropology, the process of transmission of cultural values has been central to understanding cultural reproduction and perpetuation (Baxter 2005). If indeed children are little sponges waiting to be filled with information, why haven't archaeologists observed the processes by which these repositories are filled? Furthermore, cultural transmission implies a materialization of cultural ideals—the toy tea set given to little girls or the uniform worn by Boy Scouts. These materialized values are essential for the reproduction of the state and should be everywhere for archaeologists to recover. Rosemary Joyce wrote a key early article on these very objects within the

Aztec state—the miniaturized representations of discrete gender roles, given to infants and recorded not only in the archaeological record but in ethnohistoric documents as well (Joyce 2000). Many of the authors in this volume return to her work for inspiration and confirmation that the rituals of childhood were also key rituals of the state and, as such, windows to the cultural values anthropologists strive to illuminate.

In reference to the concept that children were passive receivers of culture, Andrew Chamberlain noted, "[C]hildren contribute to the archaeological record whether or not we are competent to recognize them" (Chamberlain 1997:249). This observation underscores the point that Western notions are not universally applicable, but also the perspective that in many societies (and even our own?) children are innovators. When play is not rigidly defined as toy specific, or located only on playgrounds, the natural curiosity and fearlessness of children can play a key role in cultural innovation. Artifact analyses have been the primary arena where archaeologists have demonstrated the experimentation of children—through fingerprint studies of clay vessels, miniature or less-sophisticated lithic points, and reuse of discarded objects—to prove that children are present in the archaeological record as experimenters who may have pushed the boundaries of adult conceptions of style and substance (Chapter 5; see also Spector 1993; Park 1998; Crown 1999; Kamp et al. 1999; Wilson 1999; Grimm 2000). One can imagine that children may have also discovered new resources or locations within the cultural landscape through a similar process of experimentation and exploration.

As with the study of other invisible populations, the archaeological research on children and childhood has proceeded along two complementary avenues. One seeks to identify children in the archaeological record to find the voices that have been overlooked or ignored. The other approach discusses and examines the process of cultural transmission through the lens of childhood, using the stages or experiences of childhood as a clue to cultural values.

FINDING CHILDREN

In one of the first edited volumes dedicated to the study of children in the ancient New World, Nan Rothschild argues that childhood is a socially constructed experience and cannot be assumed to exist in every culture (Rothschild 2002). Using historical studies of childhood in Western Europe, Rothschild argues that the modern conception of childhood embraced by Western scholars developed over the past few hundred years as a result of class changes, especially the rise of a middle class (Rothschild 2002:2). Yet from the few earlier studies and especially ethnohistoric accounts, we know that a concept of childhood did exist in precontact Mesoamerica.

Each society has its own definition of significant age categories, which are integral to social organization. Kathryn Kamp (2001) suggests an important first step in research on ancient childhood is to attempt to define significant age categories and their basic characteristics. This exercise is fundamental to answering Rothschild's concern that childhood must not be assumed to exist and also to moving closer toward a local definition of childhood, free of imposed modern or Western notions of biological "realities." In Mesoamerica, significant work has already been done on the perception of childhood age grades by archaeologists and ethnographers. In an examination of Aztec ethnohistoric records, Rosemary Joyce (2000) found evidence for three age grades of approximately four years each. Bodily markings were performed at the transition between each grade, and costuming was used to cement the transition. To Joyce, the Aztec materials suggest a child was perceived as without individual identity at birth, but then one was given to her by her culture/family/state at key moments in her early lifecycle. Joyce's findings correlate well with one of the other rare archaeological analyses relevant to a reconstruction of age grades, Rebecca Storey's osteological analysis of the human mortuary population from Copan (Storey 1992). Storey found mortality patterns of juveniles ages 1–15 at Late Classic Copan contained four significant divisions (Storey 1992:164). Mortality was highest in ages 1–4, then dropped significantly in the ages 5–9, and dropped again in the ages 10–14. She suggests these differences reflect real demographic dynamics, as opposed to illusions of sampling error, in the patio compounds in the 9N-8 group at Copan. Although the explanation of these dynamics must be complex and consider such factors as overall fertility rates, disease risks, and genetic health, there is a suggestion that these distinctions between age groups may have resulted from nutritional changes that accompanied lifestyle transitions that occurred when an individual child moved from one age grade to another.

These tentative age-grade findings are remarkably consistent with Evon Vogt's ethnographic studies of the highland Maya area, in which he noticed three discrete phases of childhood. Since an infant is susceptible to soul loss after birth, protective ceremonial practices are performed after an initial period of confinement for mother and child (Vogt 1970:62). From this time until the mother's next birth (usually 3 to 4 years later) the infant is carried, nursed on demand, and little differentiated from its mother. Upon the birth of a younger sibling, the infant is quickly weaned and put into the care of older siblings who run around the house and houselot performing small tasks without significant responsibility. Vogt noted that this transition was often quite difficult for a three- or four-year-old accustomed to constant attention, who now becomes the smallest member of a busy domestic world. Around age nine, children who had previously played together since weaning were expected to differentiate themselves along strict gender-based lines and segregate themselves from one another for much of the day. Boys began to accompany their fathers to agricultural fields; girls began to haul water, prepare food, and weave. This phase lasted until age 12 or 13, when young people assumed adult levels of responsibility and began to form their own identities apart from their families. Significantly, Vogt's data identifies three stages of approximately four years each, a pattern which, in its similarity to that observed by Joyce for the Aztecs and Storey for the Classic Maya at Copan, suggests the *longue durée* of Mesoamerican civilization. Although the tremendous changes that have occurred in Maya society since contact must be acknowledged, elements of precontact cultural values are still present in modern Maya society (Vogt 1970; Broda 1971; Tedlock 1982; McGee 1990). Perhaps the perception of childhood as consisting of three general stages—infancy, youngster, and preadult—is one of the core elements of self-identity and cultural organization present in related forms throughout Maya history.

Understanding a local definition of childhood also means being attentive to the definition of economic and social roles for children. Again the ethnographic record attests that archaeologists have demonstrated an extraordinary amount of ageism by not factoring child labor into our economic models and by not allowing children to be significant social actors. In the literature from studies of ancient Mesoamerica, children are almost completely absent from most archaeological models, even though the ancient states of Mesoamerica demanded enormous amounts of labor from their supporting populations. As mentioned earlier, Vogt documented a role in household and supra-household economic activities starting around age nine in the Maya highlands. This ethnographic fact is borne out across modern Mesoamerica, where children continue to provide substantial amounts of labor in the domestic sphere, in marketplaces, on urban streets, and elsewhere. Certain tasks performed today by young people, such as water hauling, spinning, small livestock tending, fishing, fuel gathering, and food preparation, were certainly as demanding in the ancient period as they are today.

Cheryl Claassen's important study of early agricultural societies of North America is easily applicable to much of agriculturally dependent ancient Mesoamerica. Through analysis of bioarchaeological data from the Middle Woodland period of the American Midwest, Claassen (2002) surmises that the transition from foraging to agriculture was accompanied by a markedly increased workload for women, which in turn was mitigated by increased work expectations for small children. Assumptions about the gendered nature of agricultural work aside, Claassen's conclusion raises an important question about ancient agricultural practices in Mesoamerica. If production was substantially higher than modern levels throughout much of the ancient period, as was warranted by the significant urban populations of places such as Teotihuacan, lowland Maya cities, and Cholula, then surely labor demands upon household farmers were much greater as well. These demands must have been met by work parties comprising adults and children, given that children were such a large portion of the ancient population. Comparative studies worldwide have shown that most prehistoric populations had childhood mortality rates so high that at least half the overall population must have been under eighteen in order for stability to exist (Chamberlain 2000:207; Sobolik 2002:135; Storey and McAnany, Chapter 3).

A correlated effect of this model is the need for child-care when adults have a heavy burden of labor away from the domestic area. Children too young to labor in the fields may have become the primary caretakers for infants and other children. Grete Lillehammer suggests that in many ancient societies where life expectancy was relatively low and labor demands high, children were raised by other children while their parents satisfied huge labor obligations (Lillehammer 2000:23). When one is sensitized to the presence of children in prehistory, the population explosions long associated in the literature with fully agricultural societies translate into huge numbers of children everywhere who require care as infants and supervision as youngsters. For agricultural peoples, this burden (and pleasure, to be fair) was added to the household production responsibilities already operational in foraging societies. Ethnographers have commented that agricultural societies often value obedient and responsible children more than other societies precisely because their labor contributions are essential to the success of a household (Draper and Cashdan 1988).

We are only beginning to identify the significant contributions of children to the social and ceremonial events that served in part to solidify and reify the ancient states of Mesoamerica. Several of the contributions in this volume (see Hamann, Chapter 8; Román and Chávez,

Chapter 9; and Follensbee, Chapter 10) significantly advance our understanding of the numinous state of early infancy and its cooptation by the state or ruling sectors through ceremonies of sacrifice. Scattered artistic and epigraphic references to child kings who participated in rituals of royal accession in the Maya area indicate that age was not a barrier to certain kinds of power. Likewise, age does not seem to have been a significant barrier to artistic expression, especially when directed to the service of the state. The often quoted *Cantares Mexicanos* of Aztec period poetry and song include a famous cradlesong composed for Ahuitzotl, who became the lord of the Mexica. The cradlesong is widely believed to have been composed by a young girl who lived in a royal palace complex, who describes herself only as "the little maid, [who] conceived my song in the interior of the house of flowers" (Leon-Portilla 1992: 175).

CULTURAL TRANSMISSION THROUGH LIVED EXPERIENCE

One of the most fascinating aspects of this subject is that once one identifies the presence of children in the archaeological record or as significant social agents in prehistory, the examination of cultural transmission is unavoidable. Grete Lillehammer suggests one way to bridge these questions is to attempt a definition of the "world of children," a locally specific set of linkages between children and aspects of time, space, culture, and identity (Lillehammer 2000:20). Once defined, this world of children illuminates the "interconnected relationships between being children in mind and action and the diverse spheres in which children actively move" (Lillehammer 2000:20). It is clear that the specific details of childhood are always embedded in ongoing experiential negotiations—between child and parent, between child and child, between individual and state. As Joyce says in the conclusion to this volume, "the physical traces of young people do not equal the cultural construct of childhood," and at times it is much more challenging to tease out the local perception of "child" than it is to identify the biological status of being young. But identification of the social experiences of children helps us move in the direction of understanding social transmission, as does an attention to the linkages between being a child in mind and the circulations such a status allows.

Perhaps one of the most plentiful bodies of data from which to explore the processes of cultural transmission are health studies of ancient populations, most of them based on osteological data. Such analyses in Mesoamerica have always shown evidence of pervasive nutritional stress in childhood in the form of paleopathological markers such as enamel defects, which indicate physiological stress during the time of enamel formation in early childhood (see, for example, Whittington 1991; Storey 1992; Danforth 1997; Saul and Saul 1997). Enamel hypoplasia, one of the most pronounced and consistent markers of such nutritional stress, is widely believed to correlate with or derive from weaning, when young children switch from a diet based on nutrient-rich breast milk and some supplemental foods, to one based on carbohydrate- and sugar-rich corn dough (Danforth 1997; Saul and Saul 1997). Many studies further suggest that this nutritional stress in childhood was shared unequally between boys and girls, although there is disagreement about the degree to which girls were deprived (see Ardren 2002 for a summary of this debate). These patterns suggest a culture in which childhood nutritional needs were not elevated above those of adults, and in fact children may have been responsible for a certain degree of foraging or self-directed food procurement. It further suggests that in periods when the nutritional needs of entire populations were only barely satisfied, such as the periodic but consistent episodes of urbanism in ancient Mesoamerica, citizens learned at an early age to internalize a culture of minimum needs. The implications of huge populations raised since infancy on barely sufficient food are enormous, both from a biological perspective but also significantly from a cultural or social perspective where nutritional vulnerability could have played a major role in the ability of the state to foster a sense of dependency and obligation.

Much of this nutritional stress was borne by ancient Mesoamericans living in urban environments. The 200,000 inhabitants of urban Tenochtitlan, crowded into an area approximately the size of Classical Rome, may have lived in cleaner and healthier conditions than their European contemporaries, but they certainly experienced the universal characteristics of urban life—crowding, pollution, noise, and crime. Children raised within this physical environment would have been accustomed to such factors, and certainly ancient urban centers were largely sustained by young populations of citizens who didn't question the conditions of urban life. But these same children would have suffered lifelong health compromises from poor water and pollution, from increased exposure to disease and crime. These experiences, in addition to nutritional stress, were certainly fundamental to each child's negotiation of the embodied experience of life in the urban parts of ancient Mesoamerica. Models of the rise of urbanism have overlooked the contribution of citizens who internalize the hardships of urban life in order to serve the monarch or participate in ritual performances of the state.

An almost unimaginable exertion of the state upon the bodies and lives of ancient Mesoamericans was the apparently widespread use of human infants for ritual sacrifice. It is difficult to think about the degree to which children were aware of this practice and internalized its occurrence but scholarship demonstrates the certainty that adults performed this act frequently and in a context consistent with other forms of human sacrifice. Philip Arnold's careful study of one Aztec year-opening ceremony known as Atl Caualo explores the complex and conflicting emotional responses that participants in these ceremonies experienced. In the Atl Caualo, participants visited seven different hilltop shrines within a 120-kilometer area surrounding Tenochtitlan and, at each one, sacrificial blood was offered to ensure the return of the rains. "The bodies of children served as food for the tlalocs who reciprocated by releasing elements from the opening of the earth. Tlaloc's flesh and a child's body constituted a correspondence whose relationship was physically circumscribed by the sacrificial event" (Arnold 1991:226). The identification of the child's body with the earth's body made children appropriate sacrificial offerings and demonstrated the principle that, as the earth sustained human life, children sustained the earth.

Arnold's translation goes even further to illuminate Aztec attitudes toward this practice. Section 17 of the passage recorded by Sahagún states, "[V]ery much it would let them show compassion, it would make people cry, it made one break down crying, it caused them great pain, which indeed resulted in much sighing" (Arnold 1991:223). Far from being emotionally immune to the practice of ritualized human offerings, sacralized weeping and sorrow over the deaths of these children was an essential component of the ceremony. The high cost of sacrificing children was expressed and even foregrounded through ritualized tears seen to encourage the return of rain. The tears of the dying children were also perceived as magically effective in drawing rain (Arnold 1991:228). The spiritual contracts between human and deity in ancient Mesoamerica were often not a comfortable or comforting experience; they were a set of obligations and reciprocal understandings that required severe personal sacrifice or deprivation. Within this context, the loss of a child is no less monstrous on a personal level but becomes consistent with other deeply personal losses that citizens of the Aztec state experienced frequently.

The topic of human sacrifice in Mesoamerica can be described as normalized violence, violence practiced within a complex framework of interdependency between human and divine, individual and state, adult and child. We do not know the ways an individual who grew to adulthood within this cultural milieu internalized or experienced the practice of child sacrifice, but Davíd Carrasco (1999) has shown that such extreme demands on the part of the Aztec state (to choose only one example) created a form of social cohesion that was central to the exercise of elite power. Further research will illuminate whether this principle also underscores earlier practices of human and child sacrifice in ancient Mesoamerica.

Finally, the experience of substantial labor demands in early childhood also reinforced the power of the state or ruling powers. The tasks and experiences discovered through finding children in the archaeological record of other complex societies demonstrate that children could have performed labor in ancient Mesoamerica and must have grown up understanding such expectations (Finlay 1997; Crown 1999; Kamp 2001). The experience of laboring in service to others, the expectation that such labor demands were nonnegotiable, and the ability of the state to extract or define that labor, from even its smallest members, all contributed to the strongly internalized experience of an all pervasive state power that reached deep into the lives of its citizens to define them in ways that were productive and meaningful to itself.

Recently deciphered hieroglyphic inscriptions allow us to reconstruct a partial biography of one child whose life demonstrates many of the themes of cultural transmission and internalization discussed earlier. Aj Wosal (Double Comb) is one of the earliest kings from the polity of Naranjo, located in the eastern Maya lowlands not far from Tikal. In 546 CE, Aj Wosal was only twelve years old, but he acceded to the royal throne of Naranjo under the supervision or patronage of a Calakmul king named Tuun K'ab Hix, an early proponent of the expansion of Calakmul as a regional power (Martin and Grube 2000:72). Aj Wosal names his mother and father on his stone monuments and describes himself as thirty-fifth in line from the royal deity who founded their dynastic lineage, even though he is the first Naranjo king to erect a monument or engrave his name in hieroglyphic writing. He reigned for sixty-nine years and throughout his life remained loyal to his patron from Calakmul.

This brief biography of Aj Wosal illustrates certain key elements of the local Mesoamerican conception of childhood, as well as certain vital processes of cultural transmission in elite Maya culture of the Classic period. Although very young for accession, twelve years of age correlates with some of the other available data for a Maya conception of age grades and may have marked a culturally appropriate point for the transition to adult responsibility. A few Maya kings acceded at an even younger age, although their mothers often ruled as regents. Many Maya kings acceded not long after their twelfth birthday, and this pattern indicates something vital about the perception of status transformation and adulthood.

The ritual of accession is certainly one of status transformation. We know these ceremonies were performed in elite residential areas with key family members and political allies present and in the presence of ancestral powers and dynastic deities. Certainly such a ceremony would have had a profound effect upon the individual undergoing this socially sanctioned transformation as he or she moved from a largely private life to one of public responsibility and visibility. Participation in the accession of a young king by members of the court and family validated their expectations and experiences of age-based status transitions, as well as the means by which young people were incorporated into the body politic.

At twelve years of age, Aj Wosal pushes the boundaries of what Westerners might consider the functional capacities of adolescent people. But by historical accounts his was a successful and stable reign, free from overt manipulations of either the historical record or common rules of succession that took place when child kings acceded only because of the absence of any other suitable heir. In other words, the accession of Aj Wosal proceeded normally, within the patterns of acceptable behavior for Maya elites during the Classic period, and thus demonstrates to us a profoundly different understanding of the thirteenth year of life. With accession came untold obligations of court life that more than likely brought to an end any vaguely carefree phase of Aj's life, and in turn replaced it with obligations not of heavy physical labor but of service to a state or hegemonic power with which Aj was clearly invested as well as identified. We do not know if the young king resisted this transition, but the discussion earlier of the cumulative effect of lifelong labor expectations suggests that he did not. Aj was incorporated into a larger power or corporate entity, visible at various scales as his dynastic line, the Naranjo polity, the larger Calakmul political realm, and perhaps even the overarching culture of elite prestige and power experienced during feasts, ballgames, and royal visits throughout the lowlands. From an external perspective these demands defined Aj's life as a young king, although we cannot tell for certain what elements he chose to internalize as part of his personal identity. Perhaps further research at Naranjo will some day provide more information about the choices Aj made as king, and the way in which he expressed his royal identity.

CONCLUSION

Other disciplines such as history and geography have also recently rediscovered the social category of childhood as an important and previously invisible component of the study of historical processes (see, for example, Holloway and Valentine 2000; Heywood 2001). The intellectual stance that categories such as female, male, old, and young are socially and historically specific constructions has greatly enriched anthropological studies of ancient societies by charging scholars with the responsibility to see the social actor in populations often marginalized within our own culture. Children are historical agents who have voices and agency in any civilization, however muted; but particularly in prehistoric preindustrial societies, children and the processes by which children were constructed are fundamental components of the social landscape.

The state is a key factor in understanding the experience and conceptualization of childhood in ancient Mesoamerica. The consistent transmission of cultural values and ideals is especially important for ancient states, and this goal was accomplished in a particularly forceful manner (Silverblatt 1987; Brumfiel 1991; Dean 2001). Maya literature describes young people installed in political office, Aztec ethnohistoric documents detail severe punishments for inappropriate behavior by children, and excavations show the infant body carried a numinous power that could be the salvation of a people. One might argue that there is no more graphic example of the force with which a state perpetuates itself than a careful examination of the lives of its youngest members.

As those who understand material culture to be actively used in the construction of social identities, archaeologists have an obligation to examine such processes on many levels within a population. Decades of scholarship on the materialization of gender in the ancient New World show the expression of complementarity and the definition of power-based hierarchies grounded in the human body. In this volume we shift to a closely related question about how age was materialized and how age-based identities shaped the experiences of an ancient population. Our goal is to advance the discourse concerning a culturally specific definition of childhood for ancient Mesoamerica and, in the process, uncover life experiences of the young that are a fundamentally overlooked component of current models of ancient life.

One of the major themes to surface in this volume is an emerging dialogue over the definition of children and childhood in relation to adulthood. Is childhood just preparation for adulthood and a set of cumulative experiences, or is it a truly separate and distinct social category? The authors in *The Social Experience of Childhood in Ancient*

Mesoamerica bring different data to bear on this issue and find resolution of the question to be difficult. The three chapters that deal with the numinous state of infancy and its relationship to sacrifice (Chapters 8, 9, and 10) would certainly suggest that childhood (or a sub-category such as infancy) is a distinct identity with specific privileges and obligations, and Stacie King's data from Postclassic Oaxaca (Chapter 7) suggest a segregation of children and adults in the funerary realm that may correspond to separate identities. Others, such as Geoffrey McCafferty and Sharisse McCafferty (Chapter 2), Rissa Trachman and Fred Valdez (Chapter 4), see miniature people in the data on children and argue that in ancient Mesoamerica childhood was preparation for the responsibilities and sensibilities of adulthood. We do not believe these differing interpretations are inconsistent but rather reflect the emergence of serious theoretical concerns within childhood studies and signal directions for future research and consideration.

We organized this volume into three related sections. The first is "Defining the Child," in which Geoffrey McCafferty and Sharisse McCafferty (Chapter 2), Rebecca Storey and Patricia McAnany (Chapter 3), and Rissa Trachman and Fred Valdez (Chapter 4) examine the differential treatment of children and adults, especially as seen through the lens of mortuary data. In a detailed study of the large Postclassic burial sample from Cholula and early Colonial records from central Mexico, McCafferty and McCafferty suggest that mortuary offerings should be seen as an indication that juvenile death "interrupted" gendered processes of enculturation. Storey and McAnany find the intersection of age and class differentiation represented in the Formative period architectural burials of children from K'axob. In a close application of ethnographic and ethnohistoric literature from the Maya area to archaeological interpretation, Trachman and Valdez suggest patterns of age- and gender-specific bodily ornamentation known from the Colonial and modern periods are significant clues to an interpretation of the Classic period burials found at Dos Hombres.

The second section is "Practicing Childhood," in which Scott Hutson (Chapter 5), Jeanne Lopiparo (Chapter 6), and Stacie King (Chapter 7) explore the production of conceptions of childhood through processes of materialization. Hutson takes on the notion that "direct" evidence is necessary to examine the role children played in ancient Chunchucmil and problematizes the assumption that the study of children can be isolated from the study of other past populations. Through examination of Terminal Classic household sites and craft production in the Ulúa Valley, Lopiparo is able to envision a society in which children were instrumental to social reproduction as participants in domestic production industries. King suggests that the absence of children from domestic mortuary rituals at Río Viejo reflects the importance of age-related identities and a social conceptualization of "child" as quite distinct from "adult."

Finally, the third section is "The Sanctity of Children," in which Byron Hamann (Chapter 8), Juan Alberto Román Berrelleza and Ximena Chávez Balderas (Chapter 9), and Billie Follensbee (Chapter 10) explore the power of children as a sacred category, especially through their role in sacrifice and violence. Using early historical documents from Europe and the New World, Hamann explores how Aztec conceptualizations of childhood authority shaped stories of child martyrs told by early Spanish friars. Román and Chávez demonstrate childhood was a period of utmost ritual purity and explore the interrelated conditions of illness and sanctity in an illumination of the practice of Aztec child sacrifice. In an examination of Olmec Formative period figurines, Follensbee explores the range of child depictions and concludes sacrifice was only one avenue through which a distinct and socially meaningful role for children was expressed. A concluding chapter by Rosemary Joyce identifies the ways scholars have defined children and understood childhood, then suggests future directions for investigating the archaeology of children in the Mesoamerican past.

We anticipate that *The Social Experience of Childhood in Ancient Mesoamerica* will inspire scholars working on the construction of social identities to reexamine the roles of children and the child in some of the most dynamic and complex ancient societies of the New World. There is ample evidence for at least ten such volumes, and the further development of this field is only dependent upon the recognition of questions about age-based identities as central to the anthropological endeavor. The growing literature in childhood studies from other ancient societies and the related fields of history and art history promise a rich and fruitful future for inquiry into the means by which identity is shaped by age and experience. Now we have set the table.

ACKNOWLEDGMENTS

Many scholars and colleagues contributed to the ideas presented in this volume. The original participants in the session "The Social Experience of Childhood in Ancient Mesoamerica," organized for the Annual Meeting of the American Anthropological Association held November 2002 in New Orleans, Louisiana, as well as the final participants in this volume are all thanked for their intellectual curiosity and commitment to collaboration. My coeditor, Scott Hutson, has been a valued friend and colleague for many years and brought intellectual depth to this project. The scholarship of Rosemary Joyce paved the way for this volume. Darrin Pratt and the staff of University Press of Colorado were instrumental in convincing me of the need for this volume, and I thank Darrin for his support throughout. Other friends and colleagues who have contributed significantly to this project include Rebecca Biron, Davíd Carrasco, Patricia L. Crown, Martha Few, Susan Gillespie, Anthony Krupp, Aline Magnoni, J. Bryan Page, Anne Pyburn, Matthew Restall, and Gabrielle Vail. I thank them all for their contributions but retain all responsibility for the material presented.

REFERENCES CITED

Ardren, Traci
2002 Death Became Her: Images of Female Power from Yaxuna Burials. In *Ancient Maya Women,* ed. T. Ardren, 68–88. Walnut Creek: Altamira Press.

Arnold, Philip P.
1991 Eating Landscape: Human Sacrifice and Sustenance in Aztec Mexico. In *To Change Place: Aztec Ceremonial Landscapes,* ed. D. Carrasco, 219–232. Boulder: University Press of Colorado.

Baker, Mary
1997 Invisibility as a Symptom of Gender Categories in Archaeology. In *Invisible People and Processes: Writing Gender and Childhood into European Archaeology,* ed. J. Moore and E. Scott, 248–250. London: Leicester University Press.

Baxter, Jane Eva
2005 *The Archaeology of Childhood.* Walnut Creek: Altamira Press.

Broda, Johanna
1971 Las fiestas aztecas de los dioses de la lluvia: Una reconstrucción según las fuentes del siglo XVI. *Revista Española de Antropologia Americana* 6:245–327.

Brumfiel, Elizabeth M.
1991 Weaving and Cooking: Women's Production in Aztec Mexico. In *Engendering Archaeology: Women and Prehistory,* ed. J. Gero and M. Conkey, 224–251. Oxford: Basil Blackwell.

Burman, Erica
1994 *Deconstructing Developmental Psychology.* London: Routledge.

Carrasco, Davíd
1999 *City of Sacrifice: The Aztec Empire and the Role of Violence in Civilization.* Boston: Beacon Press.

Chamberlain, Andrew T.
1997 Commentary: Missing Stages of Life: Towards the Perception of Children in Archeology. In *Invisible People and Processes: Writing Gender and Childhood into European Archaeology,* ed J. Moore and E. Scott, 248–250. London: Leicester University Press.
2000 Minor Concerns: A Demographic Perspective on Children in Past Societies. In *Children and Material Culture,* ed. J. Sofaer Derevenski, 206–212. London: Routledge.

Claassen, Cheryl
2002 Mother's Workloads and Children's Labor During the Woodland Period. In *Pursuit of Gender: Worldwide Archeological Approaches,* ed. S. M. Nelson and M. Rosen-Ayalon, 225–238. Walnut Creek: Altamira Press.

Crown, Patricia L.
1999 Socialization in American Southwest Pottery Decoration. In *Pottery and People: A Dynamic Interaction,* ed. J. M. Skibo and G. M. Feinman, 25–43. Salt Lake: University of Utah Press.

Danforth, Marie E.
1997 Late Classic Maya Health Patterns: Evidence from Enamel Micro-defects. In *Bones of the Maya,* ed. S. Whittington and D. Reed, 127–137. Washington, DC: Smithsonian Institution Press.

Dean, Carolyn
2001 Andean Androgyny and the Making of Men. In *Gender in Pre-Hispanic America,* ed. C. Klein, 143–182. Washington, DC: Dumbarton Oaks.

Draper, Patricia, and Elizabeth Cashdan
1988 Technological Change and Child Behavior Among the !Kung. *Ethnology* 27:339–365.

Finlay, Nyree
1997 Kid Knapping: The Missing Children in Lithic Analysis. In *Invisible People and Processes,* ed. J. Moore and E. Scott, 203–212. London: Leicester University Press.

Grimm, Linda
2000 Apprentice Flintknapping: Relating Material Culture and Social Practice in the Upper Paleolithic. In *Children and Material Culture,* ed. J. Sofaer Derevenski, 17–26. London: Routledge.

Heywood, Colin
2001 *A History of Childhood.* Cambridge: Polity Press.

Holloway, Sarah L., and Gill Valentine, eds.
2000 *Children's Geographies: Playing, Living, Learning.* New York: Routledge.

Joyce, Rosemary
2000 Girling the Girl and Boying the Boy: The Production of Adulthood in Ancient Mesoamerica. *World Archaeology* 31(3):473–483.

Kamp, Kathryn
2001 Where Have all the Children Gone? The Archaeology of Childhood. *Journal of Archaeological Method and Theory* 8(1):1–34.

Kamp, Kathryn, Nichole Timmerman, Gregg Lind, Jules Graybill, and Ian Natowsky
1999 Discovering Childhood: Using Fingerprints to Find Children in the Archaeological Record. *American Antiquity* 64(2):309–316.

Leon-Portilla, Miguel
1992 *Fifteen Poets of the Aztec World.* Austin: University of Texas Press.

Lillehammer, Grete
2000 The World of Children. In *Children and Material Culture,* ed J. Sofaer Derevenski, 17–26. London: Routledge.

McGee, R. Jon
1990 *Life, Ritual, and Religion Among the Lacandon Maya.* Belmont, CA: Wadsworth Publishing.

Martin, Simon, and Nikolai Grube
2000 *Chronicle of the Maya Kings and Queens.* London: Thames and Hudson.

Park, Robert W.
1998 Size Counts: The Miniature Archeology of Childhood in Inuit Societies. *Antiquity* 72(276):269–282.

Redfield, Robert, and Alfonso Villa Rojas
1934 *Chan Kom: A Maya Village.* Prospect Heights, IL: Waveland Press.

Rothschild, Nan
2002 Introduction. In *Children in the Prehistoric Puebloan Southwest,* ed. K. Kamp, 1–13. Salt Lake City: University of Utah Press.

Saul, Julie M., and Frank Saul
1997 Preclassic Skeletons from Cuello. In *Bones of the Maya,* ed. S. Whittington and D. Reed, 28–50. Washington, DC: Smithsonian Institution Press.

Silverblatt, Irene
1987 *Moon, Sun, and Witches: Gender Ideologies and Class in Inca and Colonial Peru.* Princeton: Princeton University Press.

Sobolik, Kristin D.
2002 Children's Health in the Prehistoric Southwest. In *Children in the Prehistoric Puebloan Southwest,* ed. K. Kamp, 125–151. Salt Lake City: University of Utah Press.

Spector, Janet
1993 *What This Awl Means: Feminist Archaeology at a Wahpeton Dakota Village.* St. Paul: Minnesota Historical Society Press.

Storey, Rebecca
1992 The Children of Copan: Issues of Paleopathology and Paleodemography. *Ancient Mesoamerica* 3:161–167.

Tedlock, Barbara
1982 *Time and the Highland Maya*. Albuquerque: University of New Mexico Press.

Vogt, Evon Z.
1970 *The Zinacantecos of Mexico: A Modern Maya Way of Life*. New York: Holt, Reinhart, and Winston.

Whittington, Stephen L.
1991 Detection of Significant Demographic Differences between Subpopulations of Prehispanic Maya from Copan, Honduras, by Survival Analysis. *American Journal of Physical Anthropology* 85(2): 167–184.

Wilson, Samuel M.
1999 When We Were Very Young. *Natural History* 108(9):58–62.

Part II

DEFINING THE CHILD

2

BOYS AND GIRLS INTERRUPTED

Mortuary Evidence of Children from Postclassic Cholula, Puebla

Geoffrey G. McCafferty

Sharisse D. McCafferty

INTRODUCTION

Just as women were left out of historical reconstructions of ancient Mesoamerican culture a mere ten years ago, children have also been consistently overlooked. Ethnohistorical accounts by chroniclers such as Bernardino de Sahagún (1950–1982) provide faint glimpses of Aztec child-rearing practices, and the *Codex Mendoza* (1992) outlines the process by which children were introduced to adult roles (Calnek 1992; Joyce 2000, 2001). These vague hints parallel the minimal representation that women had in Colonial sources (Hellbom 1967; Nash 1978; Brown 1983; McCafferty and McCafferty 1988, 1991, 2000a; Rodríguez 1988; Brumfiel 1991, 2001; Burkhart 1997; Joyce 2000, 2001).

The goal of this chapter is to flesh out the skeletal outline of sub-adults in pre-Hispanic Cholula. Our study focuses on mortuary remains from Cholula (Puebla, Mexico), an urban center that reached its maximum size in the Post-classic period (900–1520 CE) (see Figure 1.1). Extensive excavations in the ceremonial precinct around the Great Pyramid recovered over 400 interments (Noguera 1937; Romero 1937; López, Lagunas, and Serrano 1976), most of which date to the Postclassic. Additionally, eighteen skeletons from the Early Postclassic UA-1 house offer a domestic perspective on Cholula mortuary practices (McCafferty 1992).

Mortuary data is presented on age, sex, position, orientation, and grave goods. These statistics are used to reconstruct patterns for Infants (less than one year old), Children (1–13 years old), and Juveniles (14–21 years old). The combined study group of Infants, Children, and Juveniles might be better termed "sub-adults." We prefer, however, to stick with a more vernacular "children," making the distinction between lowercase "children" when referring to sub-adults, but capitalizing "Children" when referring to the 1–13-year age group. The mortuary patterns for children are then compared with those of adult males and females in order to infer the process by which the normative social identities of "man" and "woman" were attained. Based on Sahagún's (1950–1982) extensive accounts, information is available for stereotypical male and female gender roles, including descriptions of ambiguous and alternative identities (McCafferty and McCafferty 2000a). Following Sahagún, Aztec males were characteristically engaged in farming, hunting, fishing, warfare, and commercial craft production. Adult females were more closely associated with domestic tasks, such as cooking, child-care, spinning, and weaving. These stereotypes are more closely linked to elite practice with greater fluidity of occupation probably found among commoners and servants.

Very little is said about children and their associated roles in the ethnohistoric records. In several accounts newborns are referred to as a "precious necklace, precious feather, precious greenstone, precious bracelet, [or] precious turquoise" (e.g., Sahagún 1950–1982, 6:176). The *Codex Mendoza* (1992) describes the process by which children grew to adulthood, taking on progressively more complex responsibilities: cooking, spinning, and weaving for girls; and hunting, fishing, and warfare for boys (Calnek 1992; Figure 2.1). Following Rosemary Joyce (2000, 2001), childhood is a process of enculturation during which adult identities are learned and achieved. The death of a child, then, could be construed as a case of "girl (or boy) interrupted," with the mortuary ritual reflective of a stage in the "girling" or "boying" process (after Joyce 2001). Mortuary ritual is obviously more complex than simple reflection, so the patterns apparent in the archaeological record must be interpreted carefully in relation to the normative patterns of adults or alternative identities perhaps indicative of age grades associated with

2.1: Children in the process of learning adult skills (drawn by S. McCafferty after Codex Mendoza, *1992, 3:60r).*

childhood or adolescence or even other socially meaningful categories (Crawford 2000; Sofaer Derevenski 2000). The Cholula burial data provide an exceptional basis for studying these processes.

DEATH IN POSTCLASSIC MEXICO

Postclassic Cholula was a multicultural society that was likely dominated by the Nahua ethnic group and, therefore, probably shared many cultural attributes with the better documented Aztecs of the Basin of Mexico. At the same time, Cholula's archaeological record allows for the empirical evaluation of ethnohistorical data and can serve as a caution against overly simplistic generalizations. The Aztecs believed that different fates awaited the deceased depending on the cause of death (McKeever Furst 1995). The most common burial practice was cremation. Sahagún (1950–1982, 3:44–45) describes the actual cremation:

> And then it came to pass that [the old men] had ornamented [the dead one], then they took him to the fire. And the little dog they first slew; thereupon [the dead one and the dog] burned. Two sextons took great care of [the dead one]. And some of the sextons were gathered singing. And when the body of [the dead one] already was burning, they took great pains with it; they kept packing it down. And the body crackled and popped and smelled foul. And when it had come to pass that they burned it, thereupon

> they placed it in a heap[;] they piled up the embers. And they said: "Let him be bathed"; thereupon they bathed him—they threw water on him, they kept wetting him, they made a slush. When it cooled, once again they placed the charcoal in a heap. Thereupon they dug a round hole in which to place it: a pit. This they called a cave. . . . And likewise [it was done with] the noblemen as well as the commoners. When they had burned [the body], they sorted out, they gathered up all [his] bones. Into an earthen vessel, into a pot, they put them. Upon the bones they placed a green stone. They buried [the pot] in the home.

The deceased was burned along with his/her worldly possessions in preparation for the journey to Mictlan, the land of the dead located in the distant north.

> [W]hen men died, [their kin] burned with them all their baskets with insignia, their shields, their obsidian-bladed swords, and all the things [they had wrested] from their captives, and all their capes, and all which had been their various clothing. . . . Likewise, [if it was] a woman, all her baskets, her waist bands, her divided cords [for holding up the textile], her skeins, her shuttles, her battens, her cane stalks, her combs also all burned with her. (Sahagún 1950–1982, 3:43)

Other goods, including wooden figures, smoking tubes, and clothing, were bundled up and burned at intervals after the funeral as offerings to Mictlantecuhtli, the lord of the underworld (ibid., 43–44). If the deceased was a noble, then slaves were killed and cremated to accompany him to the afterlife (ibid., 45):

> And some became the companions [of the dead one]—the beloved slaves, perchance a score of the men as well as so many of the women. Thus they said: as they had taken care of their lord, they yet made chocolate for him, they yet prepared food for him. And the men who had served them as messengers just so would care for them in the place of the dead.

Diego Durán (1971:121–122) also described the Aztec burial practices:

> Some people were buried in the fields; others, in the courtyards of their own homes; others were taken to shrines in the wood; others were cremated and their ashes were buried in temples. No one was interred without being dressed in his mantles, loincloths, and fine stones. In sum, none of his possessions [was] left behind; and if he was cremated, the jar which received his ashes was filled with jewelry and stones, no matter how costly. Dirges similar to

> our responses were chanted, and [the dead] were mourned, great ceremonies taking place in their honor. At these funerals [people] ate and drank; and if [the deceased] had been a person of quality, lengths of cloth were presented to those who had attended the funeral. [The dead man] was laid out in a room for four days until [mourners] arrived from the places where he had friends. Gifts were brought to the dead man; and if the deceased was a king or chieftain of a town, slaves were killed in his honor to serve him in his afterlife. His priest or chaplain was slain. . . . He was killed so that he might perform the ceremonies in the afterlife. They slew the chief steward who had served him, the cup bearer, the male and female humpbacks, and the dwarfs who had been in his service. . . . They killed the grinders of corn so that these women might grind and prepare tortillas in the other world. The deceased was not to suffer poverty; therefore, he was buried with immense riches: gold, silver, jewels, precious stones, fine mantles, earplugs, bracelets, and feathers. If he was cremated, together with his body were burned those who had been slain to serve him [in the after-life]. The ashes [of the victims] were mixed together and thus stirred [and] were buried with great solemnity. The funeral rites lasted for ten days filled with sorrowful, tearful chants.

Mortuary ritual from the early Colonial period is described by Bartolomé de Alva in his *A Guide to Confession Large and Small in the Mexican Language, 1634* (Alva 1999:83): "When someone died . . . did you accompany, bury, and wrap each one of them up with henequen cloaks, tobacco, tumplines, sandals, money, water, food, [and all] unbeknownst to the priest?"

This practice is illustrated in the *Codex Magliabechiano* (Boone 1983; Codex Magliabechiano 1983:56), where the deceased is wrapped in a cloak and tied with rope. Offerings that accompany the burial include precious stones, a metal bell, and a ceramic vessel. These are shown attached to the wrapped bundle and might also be within the wrappings. A feather headdress rests on top of the bundle.

In contrast to these Aztec practices, Gabriel de Rojas (1927:164, translation by author) described the indigenous burial practice at Cholula: "When they died they were buried in front of an idol, in a round hole, not lying extended but rather drawn up or squatting." The distinction between cremation among the Aztec and direct, primary interment as at Cholula is one likely distinction between the two Postclassic cultures. For example, numerous pots each containing cremated remains and usually a single greenstone bead were found by Sisson at Late Postclassic Coxcatlan Viejo (1974:31–33), part of the Aztec empire to the south of Cholula. Otherwise, however, relatively few Aztec cremation burials have been found. Non-cremation burials have occasionally been found in Postclassic residential areas, as at Cihuatecpan in the Valley of Mexico (Evans and Abrams 1988), Tetla-11 at Chalcatzingo (Norr 1987) and Cuexcomate and Capilco (Smith 2002) in the Valley of Morelos, Tula (Healan 1989), and Coxcatlan in the Tehuacan Valley (Sisson 1973, 1974). In part because of the scarcity of Postclassic burials, especially of adults, Michael Smith (2002:108–109) suggests that there may have been cemeteries perhaps associated with public buildings or with older parts of sites. In this sense, the hundreds of Postclassic burials found at Cholula's Great Pyramid (López, Lagunas, and Serrano 1976), largely abandoned during the Middle and Late Postclassic, may constitute such a cemetery.

In contrast to the mortuary ritual of adults, Aztec children were believed to have a different destiny. Sahagún's *Primeros Memoriales* (1993, 2:151n42) noted:

> And he who died when he was a rather young child, and indeed still a babe in the cradle, it was said, did not go to Mictlan, but only went to Xochitlalpan. It was said that there stood a tree of udders, there [at which] the babies suckled. Underneath it the babies were opening and closing their mouths; the milk dripped into their mouths.

This paradise was located in the heavens and was presided over by Tonacatecuhtli, the lord of all created things, who gave life to all animate creatures (Sahagún 1950–1982, 6:115). Jill Leslie McKeever Furst (1995:25–26) writes that these young souls took the form of birds or butterflies while they awaited the chance to return to earth to repopulate during the next world age.

Diego Durán (1971:441) describes the Feast for the Little Dead, Micailhuitontli, which took place in August and "commemorated innocent, dead children. . . . In the solemn ceremonies of this day offerings and sacrifices were made to honor and venerate these children." Offerings of chocolate, candles, and food were made during this festival. Live children were incorporated in the rites as "a thousand diabolical inventions" were used to protect them, including haircuts; anointing with tar, feathers, and soot; beads; and little bones. From the list of confession questions (Alva 1999:85), women were asked:

> When your child died, did you put your breast milk on him with a reed? Did you bury it with him? Or where you buried him: do you go there to spill and pour your breast milk on him?

Based on this survey of ethnohistorical information on mortuary practices in Postclassic central Mexico, cremation was clearly identified with the Aztecs. Grave offerings, including both material objects and sacrificed attendants, were burned to accompany the deceased to the land of the dead. These offerings represented the same goods used in life and therefore reflect, at least to some degree, the status and occupation of the deceased. Young children, who "had not reached the age of reason" (McKeever Furst 1995:26), faced a different fate upon death, and this would be potentially reflected in distinct burial practices, although the sources do not comment on this. Since most of the previously mentioned information was recorded about the Aztecs, it should not be assumed that all cultures of central Mexico shared these practices. In the case study to be discussed, Cholula was a multiethnic community that shared some religious practices with the Aztecs, but also had its own unique patterns that reflected a distinctive cultural mix.

INTRODUCTION TO CHOLULA

Cholula is located in the Puebla/Tlaxcala valley of the central highlands, east of the Basin of Mexico. The site was founded in the Middle Formative period (ca. 1000 BCE), and at least by the Late Formative it was developing as a regionally important ceremonial center (McCafferty 1996). The Great Pyramid of Cholula, known as the Tlachihualtepetl ("artificial mountain"), evolved over at least fifteen centuries to become the largest pyramid in the world, with a palimpsest of accruing symbolic meanings (Figure 2.2; McCafferty 2001). The Great Pyramid was abandoned at the end of the Early Postclassic period (ca. 1200 CE) when Nahua Tolteca-Chichimeca took control of the city and created a new ceremonial center in what is still the civic-administrative center of San Pedro Cholula. Although the city developed around the "new" Pyramid of Quetzalcoatl, the old Tlachihualtepetl pyramid retained ritual importance as the center for mountain worship dedicated to Tonacatecuhtli and a rain deity called Chiconauquahuitl (Rojas 1927; Durán 1971; see also McCafferty 2001). The old ceremonial precinct also continued as a prominent place for ritual interments (López, Lagunas, and Serrano 1976) as hundreds of Postclassic burials were placed in and around the abandoned buildings.

Although there has been extensive exploration of the ceremonial precinct around the Great Pyramid, minimal archaeological exploration has been done in the surrounding urban zone. Consequently, little is known of domestic patterns from any period of the city's history. One

2.2: Great Pyramid of Cholula, view from the south.

exception is a house dating to the Middle and Late Tlachihualteptl phase of the Early Postclassic period (900–1200 CE), roughly contemporary with the final stage of the Great Pyramid (McCafferty 1992, 1996). The Structure 1 house was discovered during the UA-1 excavations on the campus of the University of the Americas (Wolfman 1968; McCafferty 1992). It comprises four rooms, a sweatbath, and porch areas immediately outside of the structure. Evidence of burning and in situ deposits on the house floor suggest a cataclysmic destruction and rapid abandonment of the structure (McCafferty 2003). Included with occupation and immediate post-abandonment contexts were skeletal remains of eighteen individuals, mostly children.

CHOLULA MORTUARY DATA

Between the 1930s and the 1970s, extensive excavations were conducted at the Great Pyramid under the direction of Ignacio Marquina (Marquina 1951, 1970, 1975; Messmacher 1967). Known as the Proyecto Cholula, the project sought to discover the architectural history of the pyramid by digging tunnels into the interior of the mound and clearing exterior surfaces, especially on the south and west sides. In the course of these excavations, hundreds of human skeletons were recovered (Romero 1937; López, Lagunas, and Serrano 1970, 1976). By far the most comprehensive publication on these remains was that of Sergio López, Zaid Lagunas, and Carlos Serrano in their monograph *Enterramientos Humanos de la Zona Arqueológica de Cholula, Puebla* (1976). This volume presents the methods used for skeletal analysis, results of the analyses grouped by chronological period, and a discussion of ceremonial interments. Tables identify the age, sex, burial position, and orientation of each burial and list grave goods by individual.

The original report distinguished between a group including unborn, neonatals, and perinatals, and a group including infants (1–13 years), juveniles (14–21 years), and adults. For the purpose of our present analysis, the unborn, neonatal, and perinatal categories have been collapsed into a single "Infant" group, and the Proyecto Cholula's "infant" category will be termed "Children." Juveniles were occasionally identified by sex, as were adults, although no rationale was given for how these determinations were made.

In adapting the Proyecto Cholula data for the current reanalysis, we have combined those burials from periods Cholulteca II and III. According to the chronology used by the original investigators (Müller 1970, 1978), these would date to after the abandonment of the Great Pyramid, or roughly 900–1520 CE. Problems with the Postclassic chronology used by the Proyecto (discussed in McCafferty 1996), however, blur the distinctions used to separate these two phases. Consequently, burials from the two phases are considered together.

The Proyecto Cholula recovered 440 burials (López, Lagunas, and Serrano 1976:24, table 4), of which 1 dated to the Preclassic, 17 were from the Classic period (Cholula II and III), 55 were Epiclassic (Cholula IV and Cholulteca I), 346 were Postclassic (Cholulteca II and III), 19 dated to the Contact period (Cholulteca IV), and 2 were of undetermined date. Classic period burials were generally buried in a flexed position on the side, with males more often oriented east to west and females buried north to south (based on the head-to-foot axis). The burial pattern during the Epiclassic period was radically different, suggesting larger cultural changes. Individuals were nearly all cremated with their remains placed in large ceramic vessels. Most of the burials were of adults. Mortuary patterns for the Postclassic are distinctive with most individuals buried in a flexed seated position and oriented to the north. This varied pattern suggests a dynamic cultural landscape, as is indicated by ethnohistorical accounts (McCafferty 2003).

Although plans of the ceremonial zone indicate the general location of burials from each time period, they are at a large scale and therefore not useful for understanding much about burial contexts. Photos do show particular burials, so additional information is available in these cases.

Skeletal remains of nineteen individuals were found at UA-1, eighteen of which were associated with the Early Postclassic Structure 1 house. Preliminary identification of the skeletons was prepared by Dr. Arturo Romano of the Museo Nacional de Antropología and reported in Wolfman's preliminary report (1968; also McCafferty 1992:143–157, 207–220). An isolated mandible of an adult (individual 13) was found on the surface, but the remaining burials were found in and around Structure 1 (Figure 2.3). Burials 1, 2, and 15 were fetuses all interred together in a Torre Polychrome bowl associated with a large trash midden. Burials 4, 5, 6, 7, 11, and 12 were buried together in a pit dug through the floor of Room 4; since some of the cranial remains projected above the floor level it is speculated that they were interred a short time after the house was abandoned but before the adobe walls began to collapse (Figure 2.4). An adobe retaining wall enclosed four of the individuals, but Burials 11 and 12 were placed outside that wall. Burials 9, 10, 14, 16, 17, and 18 were buried together against an exterior adobe wall that connected with the north/south wall of Structure 1 and, based on seriation analysis of associated ceramics, these burials were probably interred before the abandonment of Structure 1 (McCafferty 1992:463). Single burials included Burial 3, found against the exterior wall and covered by wall collapse; Burial 8, which was placed in a pit through the stucco floor before the construction of a wall connecting Rooms 3 and 4; and Burial 19, found above the floor level near the intersection of two interior walls. Since all of these individuals were buried during the occupation or shortly after the abandonment of the house, it is likely that they were members of the household group.

Results of the Proyecto Cholula analysis were used by Michelle Hayward in her dissertation (1986) that constructed life tables for Postclassic and early Colonial Cholula. Baptismal records from sixteenth-century San Andrés Cholula provided the database for the Colonial period. One conclusion of this study was that there was a surprisingly low incidence of infant and child burials in the Great Pyramid burial assemblage, which resulted in a suspiciously low infant mortality rate, at least as compared with other preindustrial cities (compare with demographic profiles presented by Storey and McAnany, Chapter 3, this volume).

Michael Smith (2002) has also commented on the general infrequency of burials at Postclassic sites in central Mexico and proposes

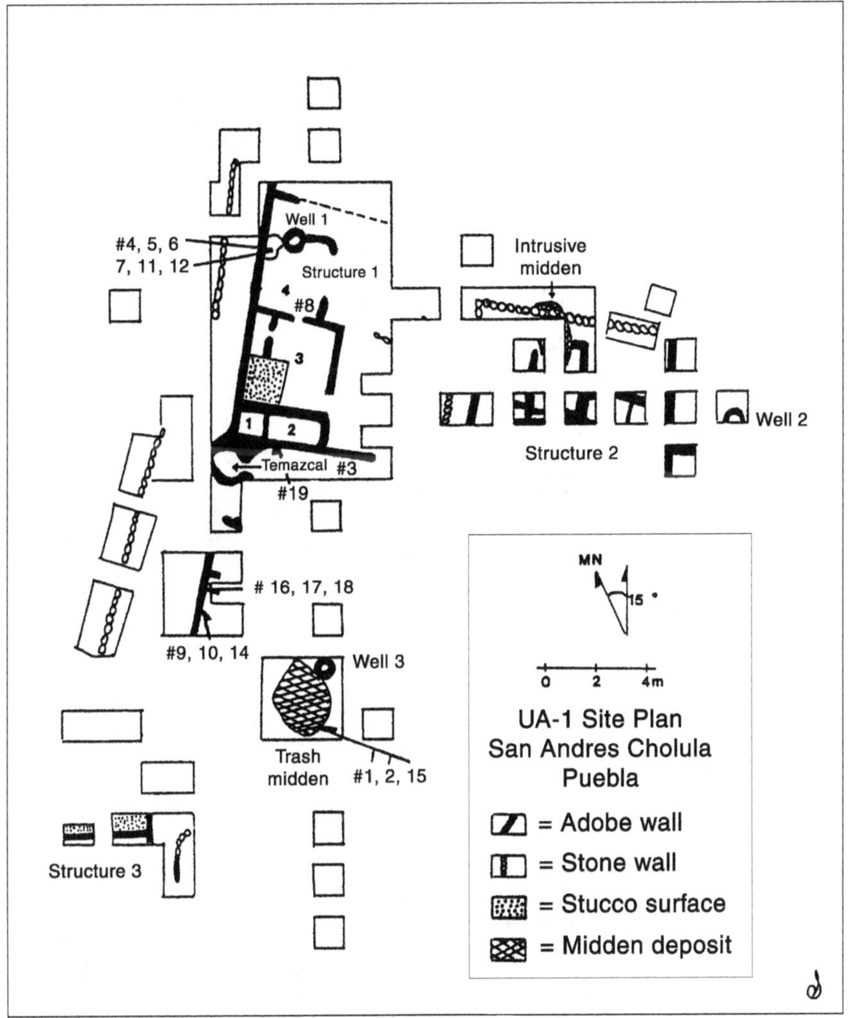

2.3: *Plan of UA-1, indicating location of burials (drawn by S. McCafferty).*

that cemeteries must have existed, perhaps in abandoned portions of sites. The ceremonial precinct of the Great Pyramid may constitute such a cemetery, but it still presents the problem of potential underrepresentation of infants and children. The UA-1 household context suggests that infants and children may have been buried more often in residential areas. Thus the UA-1 context offers a means of correcting for the biased sample recovered by the Proyecto Cholula.

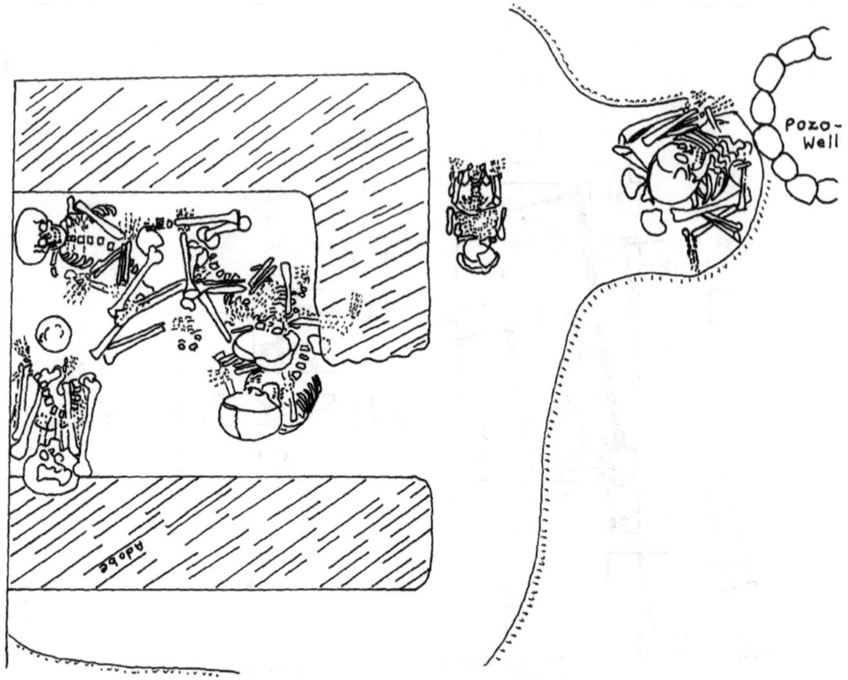

2.4: Group burial in Structure 1, room 4 (drawn by Sharisse McCafferty after Elena Eritta).

RESULTS OF THE MORTUARY ANALYSIS, PROYECTO CHOLULA

Combining the individuals from Cholulteca II and Cholulteca III (López, Lagunas, and Serrano 1976), there were 12 Infants, 103 Children (ages 1–13), 11 Juveniles (ages 14–21), and 176 Adults, of which 99 were males and 77 were females. Individuals who could not be identified as to age and adults whose sex could not be identified were not included in this analysis.

Of the Infants with good contextual information, two were secondary interments and eight were primary (Table 2.1). Five of the primary burials were in the flexed dorsal position (63 percent), and two were flexed seated and one was flexed on its right side. Five of the burials (63 percent) were oriented in a northerly direction. Infants were never accompanied by grave goods (Table 2.2).

Children were present as primary interments in 83 percent of the cases (n = 81). The flexed seated position was most common (53 percent, n = 43), although the dorsal flexed position was also found in 24 cases (30 percent). Children were buried in a northerly orientation in 55 percent of the cases (n = 45), but this group had the greatest variability in burial orientation.

Children were accompanied by grave goods 34 percent of the time. Ceramic vessels were the most common offering found with children (n

Table 2.1. Proyecto Cholula Burial Position and Orientation

	Infants	*Children*	*Juveniles*	*Males*	*Females*
PRIMARY	8 (80%)	81 (83%)	8 (73%)	76 (81%)	54 (73%)
SECONDARY	2 (20%)	17 (17%)	3 (27%)	18 (19%)	20 (27%)
SEATED FLEXED	2 (25%)	43 (53%)	5 (63%)	58 (76%)	36 (67%)
North	—	17 (21%)	2 (25%)	33 (43%)	18 (33%)
Northeast	1 (12%)	5 (6%)	1 (12%)	15 (20%)	11 (20%)
Northwest	—	3 (4%)	—	2 (3%)	1 (2%)
South	—	1 (1%)	—	1 (1%)	1 (2%)
Southeast	—	2 (2%)	—	2 (2%)	—
Southwest	—	3 (4%)	—	—	—
East	—	6 (7%)	—	3 (4%)	3 (6%)
West	1 (12%)	6 (7%)	2 (25%)	—	2 (4%)
DORSAL FLEXED	5 (63%)	24 (30%)	2 (25%)	14 (17%)	11 (20%)
North/South	—	—	—	1 (1%)	—
Northeast/Southwest	1 (12%)	2 (2%)	—	—	—
Northwest/Southeast	—	1 (1%)	1 (12%)	—	—
South/North	3 (38%)	11 (14%)	—	10 (13%)	6 (11%)
Southeast/Northwest	—	—	—	—	—
Southwest/Northeast	1 (12%)	5 (6%)	—	3 (4%)	2 (4%)
East/West	—	5 (6%)	1 (12%)	—	—
West/East	—	—	—	—	3 (6%)
VENTRAL FLEXED	0 (0%)	1 (1%)	0(0%)	0(0%)	0(0%)
North/South	—	—	—	—	—
Northeast/Southwest	—	—	—	—	—
Northwest/Southeast	—	—	—	—	—
South/North	—	—	—	—	—
Southeast/Northwest	—	1 (1%)	—	—	—
Southwest/Northeast	—	—	—	—	—
East/West	—	—	—	—	—
West/East	—	—	—	—	—
RIGHT SIDE FLEXED	1 (12%)	3 (4%)	0(0%)	2 (3%)	4 (7%)
North/South	—	2 (2%)	—	1 (1%)	—
Northeast/Southwest	—	—	—	—	1 (2%)
Northwest/Southeast	—	—	—	—	—

continued on next page

Table 2.1—*continued*

	Infants	*Children*	*Juveniles*	*Males*	*Females*
South/North	—	—	—	—	3 (6%)
Southeast/Northwest	—	—	—	—	—
Southwest/Northeast	—	—	—	—	—
East/West	1 (12%)	—	—	1 (1%)	—
West/East	—	1 (1%)	—	—	—
LEFT SIDE FLEXED	0 (0%)	7 (9%)	1 (12%)	1 (1%)	3 (6%)
North/South	—	—	—	—	1 (2%)
Northeast/Southwest	—	—	1 (12%)	—	—
Northwest/Southeast	—	2 (2%)	—	—	—
South/North	—	1 (1%)	—	—	1 (2%)
Southeast/Northwest	—	—	—	—	—
Southwest/Northeast	—	2 (2%)	—	1 (1%)	1 (2%)
East/West	—	—	—	—	—
West/East	—	2 (2%)	—	—	—

Table 2.2. Proyecto Cholula Mortuary Data

Artifact Class	*Infants*	*Children*	*Juveniles*	*Female*	*Male*
No Offering	12 (100%)	6 (66%)	7 (64%)	37 (48%)	49 (49%)
Offering	0 (0%)	35 (34%)	4 (36%)	40 (52%)	50 (51%)
Vessels	—	20 (19%)	2 (18%)	33 (43%)	36 (36%)
Figurines	—	2 (2%)	—	2 (3%)	—
Clay balls	—	6 (6%)	—	1 (1%)	2 (2%)
Beads	—	7 (7%)	—	—	1 (1%)
Lithics	—	2 (2%)	1 (9%)	1 (1%)	3 (3%)
Whistles/Flutes	—	3 (3%)	—	—	—
Carved bone "J"	—	1 (1%)	—	—	—
Obsidian lip plug	—	1 (1%)	—	—	1 (1%)
Tortoise shell	—	1 (1%)	—	—	1 (1%)
Dog mandible	—	1 (1%)	—	1 (1%)	—
Jadeite fragments	—	1 (1%)	—	1 (1%)	—
Sahumadores	—	4 (4%)	1 (9%)	—	8 (8%)
Shell	—	—	1 (9%)	3 (4%)	6 (6%)
Spindle whorls	—	—	—	4 (5%)	3 (3%)
Bone needles	—	—	—	2 (3%)	—
Bone awl	—	—	—	1 (1%)	1 (1%)
Human bone fragments	—	—	—	3 (4%)	2 (2%)
Paint remains	—	—	—	1 (1%)	3 (3%)
Mano	—	—	—	1 (1%)	—
Ceramic disk	—	—	—	1 (1%)	1 (1%)
Human face, stone	—	—	—	1 (1%)	—
Clay mold	—	—	—	1 (1%)	—
Deer antler	—	—	—	—	1 (1%)
Armadillo shell	—	—	—	—	1 (1%)

Table 2.3. Distribution of Vessel Forms

Vessel Form	*Infants*	*Children*	*Juveniles*	*Females*	*Males*
Comal/*comal*	—	1	—	—	—
Small comal	—	—	—	—	3
Plate/*plato*	—	4	—	8	8
Small plate	—	3	—	4	4
Tripod Plate	—	—	—	2	3
Bowl/*cajete*	—	8	3	8	15
Small bowl	—	1	—	4	3
Tripod bowl	—	—	—	1	3
Basin/*escudilla*	—	1	—	—	1
Shoepot/*patojo*	—	—	—	1	—
Jar/*olla*	—	—	—	1	—
Small olla	—	—	—	1	1
Pitcher/*cantaro*	—	—	—	1	1
Small pitcher	—	—	—	1	—
Cup/*copa*	—	1	—	—	—
Constricted mouth basin/*tecomate*	—	—	—	1	—
Unspecified vessel/*vasija*	—	1	—	3	2
Small vessel	—	2	—	—	1
Tripod vessel	—	—	—	—	1
Small zoomorphic vessel (turtle)	—	1	—	—	—
Vessel fragments	—	4	—	5	3

= 20, 19 percent); other repeated offerings included beads (n = 7, 7 percent), clay balls (n = 6, 6 percent), *sahumador* incense burners (n = 4, 4 percent), whistles/flutes (n = 3, 3 percent), figurines (n = 2, 2 percent), and lithics (n = 2, 2 percent). Bowls and plates were the most common of the ceramic vessels recovered (Table 2.3).

Juveniles were buried as primary interments in 73 percent of cases (n = 8). The seated flexed position was most common, found in 63 percent of cases (n = 5). No consistent burial orientation was observed in the small sample. Juveniles were buried with grave goods in 36 percent of the cases. Two interments included ceramic vessels (18 percent), and lithics, *sahumadores,* and a shell were each present in one burial (9 percent each). Bowls were the only vessel form found with juvenile burials.

RESULTS OF THE MORTUARY ANALYSIS, UA-1

Of the eighteen burials associated with Structure 1, nine were either fetuses or infants (Table 2.4), defined as less than one year of age by Romano, the physical anthropologist who conducted the initial analysis (Wolfman 1968:34). This age group is roughly equivalent to the Infant group from the Proyecto Cholula, and accounts for 50 percent

Table 2.4: UA-1 Burial Data (after Wolfman 1968:table 4)

Burial #	*Orientation*	*Position*	*Age*	*Grave Goods*
#1	—	—	fetus	none
#2	—	—	fetus	none
#3	north	seated flexed	infant	bowl rim, obsidian frag, copper ring
#4	north	seated flexed	adult	bowl, red seeds[a]
#5	northwest	dorsal flexed	child	[a]
#6	east	dorsal flexed	child	[a]
#7	north	seated flexed	child	beads, a ceramic ball, greenstone celt, shell, shell whistle, obsidian eccentric "m," obsidian eccentric butterfly[a]
#8	north	seated flexed	child	obsidian blade
#9	north	seated flexed	child	bowl[b]
#10	north	dorsal flexed	infant	bowl[b]
#11	north	dorsal flexed	infant	[a]
#12	northeast	ventral flexed	child	[a]
#13	—	—	adult	none
#14	north	seated flexed	infant	2 large sherds[b]
#15	—	—	fetus	none
#16	north	seated flexed	infant	bowl[b]
#17	?	seated flexed	child	obsidian blade, large sherds[b]
#18	?	?	infant	obsidian blade, large sherds[b]
#19	north	seated flexed	child	carved bone, polishing stone, chert projectile point

[a] Several objects were found in proximity to Burials #4, #5, #6, #7, #11, and #12 but could not be clearly associated with individual skeletons, nor are they clearly grave goods. These included a chert point, obsidian scraper, a spindle whorl, and a figurine head.

[b] Objects were also found with Burials #9, #10, #14, #16, #17, and #18 that could not be associated with any individual skeleton. This included a high frequency of obsidian blades and scrapers, two projectile points, two figurines, a spindle whorl, and numerous ceramic balls.

of the UA-1 Structure 1 mortuary assemblage. Children ranged in age from 1 to 12 years of age, with Burials 5, 7, 8, 9, 12, 17, and 19 falling into the 4–6 years category, while Burial 6 was in the 7–12 age range (Wolfman 1968:34, table 4). Only Burial 4 was identified as an adult, a female aged 21–35 years.

With the exception of three fetuses found in a single polychrome bowl, all of the individuals were buried in the flexed position. Nine were seated (50 percent), four (22 percent) were dorsal, and one was ventral (6 percent); burial position could not be determined for Burial 18.

For the purposes of comparison with the Proyecto Cholula data, McCafferty (1992:146–147) modified the orientations originally reported in Wolfman's preliminary report. All but one were buried in a northerly direction (92 percent).

Romano reported that Burials 4, 5, 6, 7, 8, 12, and 17 all exhibited evidence of cranial modification of the tabular erect variety (Wolfman 1968:34, table 4).

In contrast to the Proyecto Cholula data, Infants were accompanied by grave goods and Children had grave goods in higher frequencies. Notably, some objects of exotic material or manufacture, suggesting value, were included, such as a copper ring, greenstone celt, and obsidian eccentrics. Vessels and vessel fragments continued as the most common offering.

COMPARISON WITH ADULT PATTERNS

The child burials can be compared with the norms established from the adult burials of the Proyecto Cholula, where adult males were interred as primary burials in 81 percent of the cases, and females were primary burials 73 percent of the time.[1] Sub-adults therefore conform to this general pattern of primary interment.

Adult males appear in the seated flexed position in 76 percent of cases, the highest frequency of any group in the Proyecto Cholula population, and adult females are in the seated flexed position 67 percent of the time, the second highest frequency. This evidence suggests that the seated flexed position was the Postclassic norm and, although most sub-adults conformed to that norm, it was less standardized. In fact, the frequency of sub-adults in the flexed position increased from the Infant (25 percent) through Juvenile (63 percent) groups, suggesting that with age the likelihood of a child burial conforming to the adult pattern increased. Conversely, the younger the sub-adult, the more likely it was to be buried in a non-adult manner, with the dorsal flexed position most common among Infants and found with 30 percent of Children.

Similarly, burial orientation among adult males and females was consistently to the north (83 percent and 78 percent, respectively). These frequencies are again much more regular than the orientation of sub-adults, suggesting that the cultural norms were less restrictive for children or that alternative beliefs may have influenced sub-adult burials.

Adult males and females were about equally likely to be buried with offerings (51 percent and 52 percent, respectively). Ceramic vessels were again the most typical grave good, and were slightly more common among females (43 percent) than males (36 percent). After vessels, *sahumador* incense burners were the next most common object buried with men (n = 8, 8 percent), followed by a shell (n = 6, 6 percent), lithics (n = 3, 3 percent), spindle whorls (n = 3, 3 percent), paint remains (n = 3, 3 percent), clay balls (n = 2, 2 percent), and human bone fragments (n = 2, 2 percent).

Four spindle whorls (5 percent) were found with female burials and were the most common grave good after ceramic vessels. Other objects found with females included shells (n = 3, 4 percent), human bone fragments (n = 3, 4 percent), figurines (n = 2, 3 percent), and bone needles (n = 2, 3 percent).

There was no great difference in the vessel forms associated with males and females, although males were about twice as likely to be accompanied by bowls (males = 15, females = 8). Males were uniquely buried with small comales. The strongest gendered association found in the grave goods is *sahumador* incense burners, which were found with males but never with females. Spindle whorls, often associated with female identity (McCafferty and McCafferty 1991, 2000b) were found with both females and males (females = 4, males = 3), in contrast to the gender stereotype of women as textile producers (see discussion in McCafferty and McCafferty 2000b). Bone needles, however, were only found with adult females and so may indicate specialized production that was more rigorously associated with female gender identity.

In comparing sub-adults' grave goods with those of adults, Children and Juveniles were less often accompanied by offerings; about half of adults had grave goods as opposed to only about one-third of Children and Juveniles. The major difference in the class of grave good is in the lower incidence associated with sub-adults of ceramic vessels, which, although still the most common offering, occurs roughly half as often as with adults. Other duplicated adult offerings that did not appear with sub-adults were spindle whorls, bone needles, and human bone fragments. The lack of sub-adults buried with spindle whorls is contrary to the expectation based on the depictions from the *Codex Mendoza* (1992), since according to that source girls began learning to spin during childhood and spinning was considered an important aspect of female identity even at a young age.

Offerings that showed up in association with Children more often than with adults include whistles/flutes, beads, and ceramic balls. The presence of beads could be related to the Feast for the Little Dead ceremonies described by Durán (1971:441), although it seems unlikely that this ceremony would be the only explanation for the presence of beads as mortuary goods. Elsewhere, we have suggested that the clay balls were used as blowgun projectiles, perhaps used to hunt waterfowl or lizards (McCafferty 1992; McCafferty and McCafferty 2000b), and so may have been among a sub-adult's activities. Also it should be noted that four Children and one Juvenile were buried with *sahumadores*, which may indicate a male identity or a specialized ritual for children.

DISCUSSION AND CONCLUSION

The results of this analysis indicate only minimal variation in the cultural norm of Postclassic mortuary ritual, at least as represented in the Proyecto Cholula population. Flexed seated burials oriented to the north are most common among adults, but are also the predominant type for all other age groups except Infants. This position and orientation conforms with the ethnohistorical account of the deceased being placed in a hole in a seated position oriented toward Mictlan (Rojas 1927). The increasing frequencies among older Children and Juveniles suggest that as the "girling" and "boying" process increased, so did the likelihood that burials would conform to the normative burial position and orientation of adults.

The Infant class showed the least amount of conformity with overall patterns. The dorsal flexed position occurs most frequently, in contrast to all other age classes. There was a lack of grave offerings with Infants in the Proyecto Cholula assemblage, although most Infants from UA-1 were accompanied with offerings. This discrepancy may suggest a cultural distinction between those Infants interred in the more public cemetery at the Great Pyramid, as opposed to those buried in the UA-1 domestic precinct. The lack of offerings with Infants from the Proyecto Cholula population may indicate an age grade in which the very young were not yet considered gendered or even "human." (See Scott [2001] for a crosscultural perspective on the archaeology of infanticide.) A similar situation occurs in contemporary Cholula, where infants are not considered complete individuals worthy of their full baptismal name until after their third year. This belief goes against Sahagún's (1950–1982, 6:201–204) description of the bathing and naming ceremonies that took place soon after birth. It may explain, however, the accompanying depiction, which shows a toddler-sized child in the ritual (Figure 2.5). Once again, Sahagún's descriptions may represent an idealized situation, more applicable to the elite, but the illustrations could depict social practices more typical of commoners (see also Brown 1983; McCafferty and McCafferty 1988).

Additional age-related variation occurs with Children's grave offerings, where some differences may be associated with sub-adult/adult distinctions as opposed to adult male or female identities. The incidence of Children with whistles and flutes may suggest that these were toys.

2.5: Bathing ceremony in which gendered goods are presented to newborns; note that distinct male and female items are identified (drawn by S. McCafferty after Sahagún 1950–1982, Book 6).

The relatively high presence of clay balls might also be the result of these objects being toys if they were used as marbles or gaming pieces, as has been suggested, or as blowgun projectiles as we believe (see also contributions by Lopiparo and King in this volume, Chapters 6 and 7, respectively, discussing children's toys, and especially Storey and McAnany, Chapter 3, on Maya blowguns). It is interesting that Children were more likely to be buried with beads than any other group. Figurines, an artifact class that may have functioned at least in part as toys, were found exclusively with Children and adult females. In a contextual analysis of Postclassic household ritual, again based on UA-1 data, Geoffrey McCafferty (n.d.) has demonstrated that figurines were often found in non-ceremonial contexts such as porch areas, where it is likely that children played. Other figurines and particularly those with female attributes, however, were found in wells where they were possibly deposited as offerings to the earth/fertility goddess complex in relation to prayers. These dual functions of figurines (and there were undoubtedly even more) could correspond to their presence with Child and adult female burials in the Proyecto Cholula data. Another possible gender marker would be the *sahumador* incense burner, which was only found with adult males and Children; it is plausible that the unsexed children with *sahumadores* may have been boys, although this inference remains speculative.

In reference to the ceramic vessels found as grave offerings, Children were relatively less likely to be buried with vessels than were adults. A category of small/*pequeña* vessels was indicated in the Proyecto Cholula inventory, but these did not appear with sub-adults to any notable degree. Unlike other areas of central Mexico, particularly Oaxaca, miniature vessels are rare in Cholula and have not been found in ritual context. Thus it is unlikely that miniature, or "toy," vessels were part of children's mortuary ritual.

Although children from the ceremonial center were somewhat less likely to be buried with offerings than were adults, some were buried with numerous offerings and in fact some of the richest burials were those of children (López, Lagunas, and Serrano 1976). For example, Individual 134 was accompanied by two tortoise shells (probably drums), a whistle, and a *sahumador*. This burial may relate to what Sahagún (1950–1982, 2:79) described as a "little offering priest," a child who took part in processions at the calmecac in honor of Tlaloc. Individual 175 had nine vessels. Individual 209 had a bowl covering the head, a miniature vessel, and fourteen beads of obsidian and chert. Individual 238 was buried with a polychrome bowl, two anthropomorphic figurine fragments, and fragments of flutes.

The relative wealth associated with child burials is also indicated at the UA-1 site, where nearly all of the Infant and Child burials had some grave goods. Burial 7 was exceptional, with beads, a ceramic ball, a greenstone celt, a shell, a shell whistle, and two obsidian eccentrics—one in the shape of an M, usually interpreted as a blood glyph, and the other of red obsidian in the form of a butterfly, also a symbol associated with death and rebirth (Berlo 1983).

In conclusion, the sub-adult burials of Postclassic Cholula show minor quantitative and little qualitative distinction with those of adults. The same cosmological principles seem to have dictated burial position and orientation, although burial of Infants and Children may not have conformed to these as rigorously as those of adults did, perhaps because of the belief that young children went to a separate paradise after death. Children were buried with grave goods of value, possibly related to childhood activities such as making noise, hunting small animals, and playing with figurines. We see this evidence as supporting the idea that children were progressively indoctrinated into the gendered roles of adulthood. This trajectory was interrupted in death, with the mortuary context reflecting the deceased's stage in the boying or girling process. A more detailed determination of the age at death would be useful in refining possible age grades.

Distinctions exist between the burial practices of the Great Pyramid cemetery and those of the UA-1 domestic context. Whereas sub-adults constituted a lower than expected proportion of the Great Pyramid burial population, leading Hayward (1986) to postulate a low level of infant mortality, they were the predominant age group at UA-1. This discrepancy suggests that the Great Pyramid should not be used as a representative sample for demographic interpretation, but also suggests that cultural distinctions may have determined the specific burial practices associated with different classes of individuals. Were high status individuals buried at the pyramid? Does the relative number of adults indicate achievement? Were Infants and Children more likely to have been buried within the house compound because they had not yet attained a more public status? Or, since the UA-1 Infants and Children were more often buried with grave goods, did their death evoke greater emotional response within the private sphere? The ethnohistorical sources recount some glimpse of the grieving that accompanied death, including the idea of a mother pouring breast milk on the grave of her newborn (Alva 1999:85).

The Cholula mortuary data offer a rich basis for inferring pre-Columbian burial practices, including the treatment of sub-adults. This information presents a valuable tool for evaluating the ethnohistorical sources, which, because they are more specifically related to Aztec practices from the Basin of Mexico, highlight differences with the Cholula patterns. For example, the high incidence of primary burial is a striking contrast to the importance of cremation among the Aztecs. On the other hand, the Postclassic burials from the Great Pyramid cemetery represent a period of at least 600 years, encompassing profound ethnic changes in the resident population. Differences between the Great Pyramid and UA-1 practices may simply relate to these temporal distinctions.

We believe that the comparison between the cemetery and household contexts provides a meaningful insight into different scales of social practice and performance. Playing off of the insights of Aubrey Cannon (2002), cemeteries associated with monumental architecture may instill a sense of community identity where burials are melded into group memory. In contrast, household-scale burials preserve individual memories and corporate identity. Susan Gillespie (2002) suggests that the burial of family members within the household compound serves to reify ties to the landscape, where the house signifies both material and social manifestations of the corporate unit. In Maya society, both adults and children were buried beneath and around the house in order to recycle the souls, or *ch'ulel,* of the ancestors into the spirits of the living. This concept is reminiscent of the Aztec concept of Xochitlalpan, the paradise of deceased children awaiting reincarnation, and therefore may relate to the predominance of child burials within the UA-1 Structure 1 compound.

Children are an important component of any society, since they represent the transmission of cultural patterns into the future. The children of Cholula were buried in accordance with adult patterns but only to a degree. Following the ethnohistorical example of adults buried with grave goods associated with their life, children were often buried with objects such as clay balls, flutes/whistles, and figurines as possible toys. If clay balls were used as blowgun pellets, then their presence with child burials would conform to the *Codex Mendoza*'s depictions of young boys learning to hunt and fish, but the lack of spinning and weaving tools with children goes against similar representations of girls learning these female tasks.

Thus, as is so often the case, the Cholula burial data both support and contrast with ethnohistorical information, further demonstrating the utility of archaeology in exploring past cultural practices. To quote Cannon (2002:197):

> [T]he spatial narratives of death are among the most complete and most commonly available records of archaeological history. They are conscious creations that were meant to tell a story of relevance and value from the perspective of past peoples' perceptions and interests. When read with the same critical care applied to any historical documentation, the long-term histories written in treatments of the dead can provide archaeology with a record of social and political change and an unusual source of insight into the nature of past perceptions of life and death, and of history itself.

ACKNOWLEDGMENTS

We thank Traci Ardren for organizing this important session on Mesoamerican children and thereby giving us the opportunity and impetus to write this chapter. Traci, Scott Hutson, Darrin Pratt, and two anonymous reviewers provided valuable commentary. We appreciate the challenge to think outside the coffin.

Over the years several students have worked with the Cholula mortuary data in course work directed by Geoffrey McCafferty, and we acknowledge discussions about the collection with Beth Hrchuck, Kerry Larkin, and David Cooper; this chapter represents an entirely independent analysis of the materials. Jocelyn Williams read a draft of this chapter and provided several suggestions, including the recommendation that "sub-adult" be used as a general term for children. A Spanish version of this chapter was presented at the Tercer Congreso sobre el Género Prehispanico, organized by Maria Rodríguez-Shadow, in Mexico City; as a result of that presentation we received valuable comments from Lourdes Marquez and Ernesto Gonzalez Licón. We thank all who have shown interest in this project but take full responsibility for any errors in interpretation that remain.

NOTE

1. The distinction between primary and secondary interments was made by López, Lagunas, and Serrano (1976) based on whether the skeleton was articulated at the time of burial, or rather disarticulated and therefore probably de-fleshed. Since the majority of the Cholula burials are direct interments (i.e., buried directly in the ground without benefit of a crypt or tomb), subsequent disturbance could only be caused by inadvertent natural or cultural transformation processes. These disturbances may include tree roots, rodent activity, or later excavations, but do not include such processes as tomb reentry (see McCafferty 1996 for an example of this type of disturbance). Consequently, the distinction between primary and secondary interment implies a very different treatment of the deceased, probably relating to the individual's status in life or the conditions of his/her death. Although there is no ethnohistorical information useful for understanding this distinction, it might relate to the difference between a free person and a slave, or perhaps a sacrificial victim.

REFERENCES CITED

Alva, Bartolomé de

1999 *A Guide to Confession Large and Small in the Mexican Language, 1634*. Ed. B. D. Sell and J. F. Schwaller, with L. A. Homza. Norman: University of Oklahoma Press.

Berlo, Janet Catherine

1983 The Warrior and the Butterfly: Central Mexican Ideologies of Sacred Warfare and Teotihuacan Iconography. In *Text and Image in Pre-Columbian Art: Essays on the Interrelationship of the Verbal and Visual Arts*, ed. J. C. Berlo, 79–118. Oxford: BAR International Series 180.

Boone, Elizabeth Hill

1983 *The Codex Magliabechiano and the Lost Prototype of the Magliabechiano Group*. Berkeley: University of California Press.

Brown, Betty Ann

1983 Seen But Not Heard: Women in Aztec Ritual—The Sahagun Texts. In *Text and Image in Pre-Columbian Art: Essays on the Interrelationship of the Verbal and Visual Arts*, ed. J. C. Berlo, 119–138. Oxford: BAR International Series 180.

Brumfiel, Elizabeth

1991 Weaving and Cooking: Women's Production in Aztec Mexico. In *Engendering Archaeology: Women and Prehistory*, ed. J. M. Gero and M. W. Conkey, 224–251. Oxford: Basil Blackwell.

2001 Asking about Aztec Gender: The Historical and Archaeological Evidence. In *Gender in Pre-Hispanic America*, ed. C. F. Klein,

57–86. Washington, DC: Dumbarton Oaks Research Library and Collection.

Burkhart, Louise M.
1997 Mexica Women on the Home Front: Housework and Religion in Aztec Mexico. In *Indian Women in Early Mexico,* ed. S. Schroeder, S. Wood, and R. Haskett, 25–54. Norman: University of Oklahoma Press.

Calnek, Edward E.
1992 The Ethnographic Content of the Third Part of the *Codex Mendoza.* In *The Codex Mendoza, Volume I: Interpretation, Appendices,* ed. F. F. Berdan and P. R. Anawalt, 81–93. Berkeley: University of California Press.

Cannon, Aubrey
2002 Spatial Narratives of Death, Memory, and Transcendence. In *The Space and Place of Death,* ed. H. Silverman and D. B. Small, 191–199. Arlington, VA: Archaeological Papers of the American Anthropological Association, Number 11.

Codex Magliabechiano
1983 *The Book of the Life of the Ancient Mexicans, Containing an Account of Their Rites and Superstitions.* Berkeley: University of California Press.

Codex Mendoza
1992 *The Codex Mendoza.* 4 vols. Ed. F. F. Berdan and P. R. Anawalt. Berkeley: University of California Press.

Crawford, Sally
2000 Children, Grave Goods, and Social Status in Early Anglo-Saxon England. In *Children and Material Culture,* ed. J. Sofaer Derevenski, 169–179. New York: Routledge.

Durán, Diego
[1576–1579] 1971 *The Book of the Gods and Rites and the Ancient Calendar.* Trans. F. Horcasitas and D. Heyden. Norman: University of Oklahoma Press.

Evans, Susan T., and Elliot M. Abrams
1988 Archaeology at the Aztec Period Village of Cihuatecpan, Mexico: Methods and Results of the 1984 Field Season. In *Excavations at Cihuatecpan: An Aztec Village in the Teotihuacan Valley,* ed. S. T. Evans, 50–234. Nashville, TN: Vanderbilt University Publications in Anthropology, No. 36.

Gillespie, Susan D.
2002 Body and Soul among the Maya: Keeping the Spirits in Place. In *The Space and Place of Death,* ed. H. Silverman and D. B. Small, 67–78. Arlington, VA: Archaeological Papers of the American Anthropological Association, Number 11.

Hayward, Michelle H.

1986 A Demographic Study of Cholula, Mexico, from the Late Postclassic and the Colonial Period of 1642–1738. Ph.D. dissertation, Department of Anthropology, Pennsylvania State University, University Park, PA.

Healan, Dan, ed.

1989 *Tula of the Toltecs: Excavations and Survey.* Iowa City: University of Iowa Press.

Hellbom, Anna-Britta

1967 *La Participación Cultural de las Mujeres: Indias y Mestizas en el México Precortesiano y Postrevolucionario.* Monograph Series, Publication No. 10. Stockholm, Sweden: The Ethnographical Museum.

Joyce, Rosemary A.

2000 *Gender and Power in Prehispanic Mesoamerica.* Austin: University of Texas Press.

2001 Girling the Girl and Boying the Boy: The Production of Adulthood in Ancient Mesoamerica. *World Archaeology* 31(3):473–483.

López Alonso, Sergio, Zaid Lagunas R., and Carlos Serrano

1970 Sección de Antropología Física. In *Proyecto Cholula,* ed. I. Marquina, 143–152. Serie Investigaciones 19. Mexico D.F.: Instituto Nacional de Antropología e Historia.

1976 *Enterramientos Humanos de la Zona Arqueológica de Cholula, Puebla.* Colección Científica 44, Departamento de Antropología Física. Mexico, D.F.: SEP-INAH.

Marquina, Ignacio

1951 *Arquitectura Prehispanica.* Memorias del Instituto Nacional de Antropología e Historia, No. 1. Mexico, D.F.: SEP-INAH.

1975 Cholula, Puebla. In *Los Pueblos y Senorios Teocráticos: El Período de las Ciudades Urbanas, primera parte,* by E. Matos M. et al., 109–122. Mexico, D.F.: Departamento de Investigaciones Historicas, SEP-INAH.

Marquina, Ignacio, ed.

1970 *Proyecto Cholula.* Serie Investigaciones 19. Mexico, D.F.: Instituto Nacional de Antropologia e Historia.

McCafferty, Geoffrey G.

1992 The Material Culture of Postclassic Cholula, Mexico: Contextual Analysis of the UA-1 Domestic Compounds. Ph.D. dissertation, Department of Anthropology, State University of New York at Binghamton, Binghamton, NY.

1996 The Ceramics and Chronology of Cholula, Mexico. *Ancient Mesoamerica* 7(2):299–323.

2001 Mountain of Heaven, Mountain of Earth: The Great Pyramid of Cholula as Sacred Landscape. In *Landscape and Power in Ancient Mesoamerica,* ed. R. Koontz, K. Reese-Taylor, and A. Headrick, 279–316. Boulder, CO: Westview Press.

2003 Ethnic Conflict in Postclassic Cholula, Mexico. In *Ancient Mesoamerican Warfare,* ed. M. K. Brown and T. W. Stanton, 219–244. Walnut Creek, CA: Altamira Press.

n.d. Altar Egos: Domestic Ritual and Social Identity in Postclassic Cholula. In *Commoner Ritual, Commoner Ideology: A View from Households and Beyond Across Mesoamerica,* ed. N. Gonlin and J. Lohse. Boulder: University Press of Colorado. Forthcoming.

McCafferty, Sharisse D., and Geoffrey G. McCafferty

1988 Powerful Women and the Myth of Male Dominance in Aztec Society. *Archaeological Review from Cambridge* 7:45–59.

1991 Spinning and Weaving as Female Gender Identity in Post-Classic Central Mexico. In *Textile Traditions of Mesoamerica and the Andes: An Anthology,* ed. M. Schevill, J. C. Berlo, and E. Dwyer, 19–44. New York: Garland Publishing.

2000a Alternative and Ambiguous Gender Identities in Postclassic Central Mexico. Paper presented at the Annual Meeting of the Society for American Archaeology, Philadelphia, PA.

2000b Textile Production in Postclassic Cholula, Mexico. *Ancient Mesoamerica* 11:39–54.

McKeever Furst, Jill Leslie

1995 *The Natural History of the Soul in Ancient Mexico.* New Haven, CT: Yale University Press.

Messmacher, Miguel, ed.

1967 *Cholula, Reporte Preliminar.* Mexico D.F.: Editorial Nueva Antropología.

Müller, Florencia

1970 La Cerámica de Cholula. In *Proyecto Cholula,* ed. I. Marquina, 129–142. Serie Investigaciones 19. Mexico D.F.: Instituto Nacional de Antropología e Historia.

1978 *La Alfarería de Cholula.* Serie Arqueología. Mexico, D.F.: Instituto Nacional de Antropología e Historia.

Nash, June

1978 The Aztecs and the Myth of Male Dominance. *Signs: Journal of Women in Culture and Society* 4(2):349–362.

Noguera, Eduardo

1937 *El Altar de los Cráneos Esculpidos de Cholula.* Mexico, D.F.: Talleres Gráficos de la Nación.

Norr, Lynette

1987 The Excavation of a Postclassic House at Tetla. In *Ancient Chalcatzingo,* ed. D. Grove, 400–408. Austin: University of Texas Press.

Rodríguez-Shadow V., Maria J.
1988 *La Mujer Azteca.* Toluca, Mexico: Universidad Autonoma del Estado de México.

Rojas, Gabriel de
[1581] 1927 Descripción de Cholula. *Revista Mexicana de Estudios Históricos* 1(6):158–170.

Romero, Javier
1937 Estudio de los Enterramientos de la Pirámide de Cholula. *Anales del Museo Nacional de México* (Epoch 5a) 2:5–36.

Sahagún, Bernadino de
[1547–1585] 1950–1982 *Florentine Codex: General History of the Things of New Spain,* 13 vols. Ed. and trans. A.J.D. Anderson and C. E. Dibble. Salt Lake City and Santa Fe: University of Utah Press and School of American Research.
1993 *Primeros Memoriales.* Norman, OK, and Madrid: University of Oklahoma Press and the Patrimonio Nacional and the Real Academia de la Historia.

Scott, Eleanor
2001 Killing the Female? Archaeological Narratives of Infanticide. In *Gender and the Archaeology of Death,* ed. B. Arnold and N. L. Wicker, 3–21. Walnut Creek, CA: Altamira Press.

Sisson, Edward B.
1973 *First Annual Report of the Coxcatlán Project.* Andover, MA: Robert S. Peabody Foundation for Archaeology.
1974 *Second Annual Report of the Coxcatlán Project.* Andover, MA: Robert S. Peabody Foundation for Archaeology.

Smith, Michael E.
2002 Domestic Ritual at Aztec Provincial Sites in Morelos. In *Domestic Ritual in Ancient Mesoamerica,* ed. P. Plunket, 93–114. Monograph 46. Los Angeles, CA: The Cotsen Institute of Archaeology, University of California, Los Angeles.

Sofaer Derevenski, Joanna
2000 Material Culture Shock: Confronting Expectations in the Material Culture of Children. In *Children and Material Culture,* ed. J. Sofaer Derevenski, 3–16. New York: Routledge.

Wolfman, Daniel
1968 Preliminary Report on Excavations at UA-1, July 1968. Report submitted to the Departamento de Monumentos Prehispanicos. Manuscript on file at the Department of Anthropology, Universidad de las Américas, Santa Catarina Martir, Puebla, Mexico.

3

CHILDREN OF K'AXOB

Premature Death in a Formative Maya Village

Rebecca Storey

Patricia A. McAnany

In an archaeological search for children and childhood in ancient Mesoamerica, mortuary evidence is considered one of the prime sources of potential information (see Joyce, Chapter 11). So what can we learn about children and childhood at the Formative Maya village of K'axob from the juvenile burials? Obviously, the skeleton can tell us the age (but not sex without DNA analysis for prepubertal individuals) of the individual at death and something about his/her life from health indicators. The mortuary treatment is likely to reflect mostly adult valuation of individual children, as well as communal ideas regarding the proper way to commemorate a child's death and to prepare him/her for the afterlife. Other children may have participated in the mortuary rituals but are not likely to have directed them. As for childhood quality of life, mortuary data cannot really tell us about daily activities and pleasures of childhood, nor can it do more than suggest how the Maya of K'axob conceived of childhood and related to children. Information about what childhood involved and its salience can be gleaned from a few ethnohistorical studies of the sixteenth century and ethnographic studies of contemporary Maya children, as have been detailed in other chapters in this volume (see Trachman and Valdez, Chapter 4, and Lopiparo, Chapter 6). These conceptions could have been quite different in the Formative period as there is quite a time gap, and K'axob is not exactly equivalent to modern Maya villages, as will be discussed later in this chapter.

Various ethnographers of contemporary Maya people stress the affection that parents display toward their children but also the importance of children's obedience and helpfulness. The prevailing sentiment from these accounts is aptly summed up by Robert Redfield (1950:149), who noted, "The prevailing view in the village is that children should be useful to their parents, while the parents teach industry, sobriety, and obedience." Children often are put to work in domestic tasks at young ages and males are involved in farming and other adult tasks by the time they are 10–13 years old (Vogt 1969; Daltabuit 1992). By the time they are six or seven years old, children—especially females—have become important to household maintenance. By the time children are young adolescents, they are almost adults in terms of productivity and their position within the family economic unit. There is really no such thing as adolescence but rather a progressive accumulation of responsibilities until adulthood is reached (Daltabuit 1992; Burns 1993). Marriage for females occurs at 13–15 years in many Maya communities (Daltabuit 1992), but males tend to marry a few years later. Because of this relatively early onset of adult social roles in traditional Maya societies, only individuals who died before reaching approximately fifteen years of age can be perceived as children. At that age, an individual was likely treated as an adult even if her/his body had not reached full biological maturation.

From colonial and ethnohistorical sources, it appears that strict gender differentiation and division of labor probably date from preconquest times (Restall 1997; Sigal 2000). Ethnographically, the practice of giving tools to babies that are indicative of their gender and future work load has been noted (Vogt 1969). Based on ethnohistorical accounts of Yucatán, Roys (1972) observed that after puberty or a little before, males did not live in their natal households but in large communal houses; during the day, they assisted with agricultural work and other male tasks. Females remained in their homes, assisting with household chores. As discussed by Trachman and Valdez (Chapter 4), puberty at age twelve to fourteen marks when individuals would be able to be married, and it is likely that these individuals were considered adults soon after. Many of the patterns noted in the ethnohistorical accounts find definite similarities among the contemporary Maya.

Within the ancient village of K'axob were children given more and more responsibilities strictly divided by gender as they got older? Probably so, although one can never be sure about projecting such patterns deep into the past. By the time a child of K'axob reached fifteen years of age, he/she likely would have been treated as an adult and considered a fully productive member of the community.

The site of K'axob (see Figure 1.1), situated in the wetland zone of northern Belize, provides an important glimpse into Formative Maya life, one that is too often obscured by the later size and monumentality of Classic Maya civilization. K'axob was one of many large villages in an area that attracted Formative Maya agriculturalists because of its rich soil and varied protein resources. Between 1990 and 1993, the K'axob Project conducted large-scale excavations in several platforms that revealed highly stratified sequences of Formative-period residential construction with associated mortuary contexts. These deposits have yielded unique insights into lifeways and deathways of the Formative period and provide a stark contrast to later developments of the Classic period (McAnany and Varela 1999; McAnany 2004).

The Formative-period deposits of K'axob are highly relevant to an investigation of ritual behavior, especially that surrounding death and burial. The interment of children at the Maya site of K'axob clearly was part of a general burial program for the village. The sample is small and not representative of all juvenile deaths, just those interred within architectural contexts. Out of 98 Formative-period individuals, only 26 (26 percent) are juveniles under the age of fifteen. This fraction likely is an underestimate of the actual proportion of juvenile deaths within the population, especially if K'axob was a dynamic and growing village, as it probably was during this period. As demographic studies have shown, a growing population tends to be a young one, and juveniles found in a death sample from a growing population should be the majority (see Waldron 1994).

Archaeologically, excavations at K'axob were concentrated in a few structures and the plazas in front of residences; thus, not all possible mortuary locations were investigated. Given the rapid rate of biological decay in humid tropical environments, however, any off-mound mortuary interments would be less likely to be preserved archaeologically without the protection of architecture. Thus, if the missing proportion of expected child interments were off-mound, they are probably not recoverable. In the end, the sample we have collected, although biased, probably represents the only preserved fraction of the child burial population.

Child burials span 800 BCE to 250 CE, a time usually defined as the Middle, Late, and Terminal Formative periods. Because of the well-stratified deposits of K'axob, a fine-grained ceramic chronology could be constructed (López Varela 1996); this seriation aids in the interpretation of the burials that can be dated securely to one of the defined ceramic complexes (see McAnany and López Varela 1999 for more information on the chronology). Chaakk'ax, the earliest complex—dated from around 800 to 400 BCE—has been subdivided into two facets (early and late) and is followed by the K'atabche'k'ax complex, which is divided into three facets (early, late, and terminal) that span a time period from 400 BCE to 250 CE. The child burials are most common in the Early and Late K'atabche'k'ax.

The site of K'axob is separated into northern and southern sectors, each containing a pyramid complex surrounded by satellite residences. The southern sector was the focus of investigations reported here. One large excavation unit (Operation 1), located on the eastern side of the pyramidal Structure 18, yielded the greatest time depth, containing early Chaakk'ax deposits (see Figure 3.1). This location appears to have been the focus of ritual and a place of high-ranking residences throughout much of K'axob's history. Burials also were recovered from excavations at five other mounded locales (presumed to have been satellite residences) but only two contained child burials (Operations 11 and 12). The sample likely is biased toward higher-ranking individuals, as 20 of the 26 children (77 percent) came from Operation 1, whereas the other six had been interred in two of the surrounding satellite residences. In-depth analysis of the Formative and Early Classic deposits of K'axob can be found in McAnany (2004) and McAnany and López Varela (1999); comprehensive analyses of the burial population of K'axob are available in McAnany, Storey, and Lockard (1999) and Storey (2004). The digital accompaniment to Storey 2004 contains two comprehensive databases relevant to this study: the Burial database, which presents detailed information on the context and accouterments of each burial context, and the Skeletal Elements database, which contains an inventory of the presence and condition of skeletal elements for each individual.

At K'axob, the proportion of juvenile burials steadily decreased within each of the two Formative-period ceramic complexes. In the earlier complex, children declined from 56 percent of burials during Early Chaakk'ax times to none during the Late Chaakk'ax (but only three burials date to this facet anyway). During the Early K'atabche'k'ax complex, juveniles make up 48 percent of the sample but drop to 25 percent during Late K'atabche'k'ax times and finally to 4 percent dur-

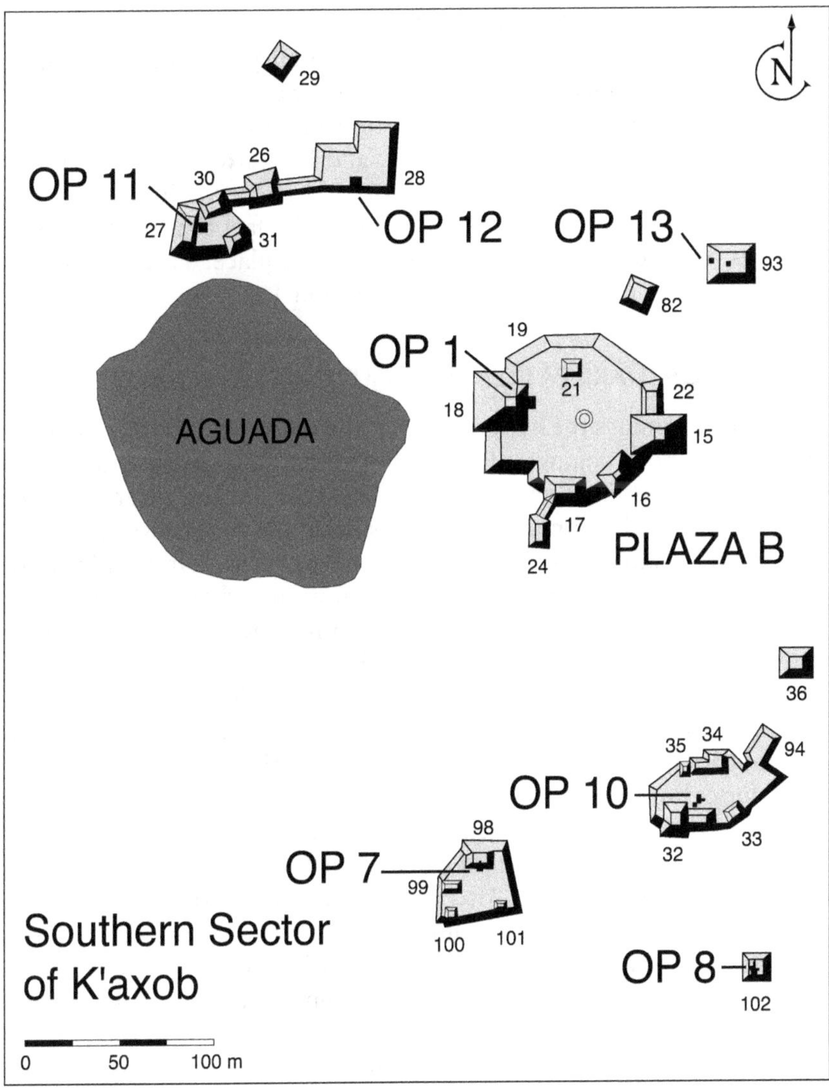

3.1: Map of southern sector of K'axob, showing location of Operations 1, 11, and 12.

ing the terminal facet of the K'atabche'k'ax complex. The complexes containing the highest overall number of burials are Late and Terminal K'atabche'k'ax, although the representation of children is lower during this time. The declining representation of juvenile burials probably reflects changes in mortuary treatment in the excavated locations and in the types of individuals considered properly buried there; it does not necessarily indicate a decreasing tendency to bury juveniles around the residence. For instance, within Operation 1 the excavation area changed through time from a residential area to a plaza area with a probable ancestral shrine (see McAnany, Storey, and Lockard 1999). Sub-adults are also underrepresented in the Cholula cemetery (McCafferty and McCafferty, Chapter 2), which could reflect the fact that relatively few juveniles merited commemoration in that focal place, as seems to have been the case in the upper levels of Operation 1.

MORTUARY PATTERNS FOR JUVENILES AT K'AXOB

This study examines the hypothesis that the mortuary treatment of children reflects both demographic realities about child death and the importance of children of various ages in the daily life and future plans of their families and community. We consider these two factors to be related. One variable in a society's mortuary patterns that usually is not considered involves the age pattern of mortality that is specific to a particular time and place. Joyce (2001), for instance, has referred to the potential of demography to inform us about mortuary treatment in the past, but few mortuary analyses are conducted in light of known demographic patterns of mortality. Here, the characteristic pattern of mortality in subadult populations in a non-modern setting provides the framework for cultural responses to premature death. Generally, mortality is high among infants and, in prehistoric and many historic populations, it remains relatively elevated until age four or five, when a child has successfully survived weaning. After five, the risk of mortality lowers and rises only gradually in young adults (see, for example, Waldron 1994). All juvenile mortality is premature mortality in that an individual is lost too soon to a family and population, but some losses are more predictable than others. The people of K'axob probably hoped for the best but would have expected to lose some babies and small children. Children ages four to fifteen, however, should survive. Children in this subadult category could already be of economic importance and, moreover, would be groomed and valued as the future adults of their families and communities. In light of these age-sensitive demographic trends and cultural roles, one can examine whether there are any differences in how children were treated posthumously based on the age at which they died.

Bogin and Smith (1996) describe four universal stages for human sub-adults: infancy, childhood, juvenile, and adolescence. These stages are defined by growth and development patterns, dependence on adults for food and care, and sexual maturation. Of course, there are cross-cultural differences in how many years are spent in each stage and the conceptualization of abilities and behavior proper to each stage, but the underlying human patterns of development make it logical that ethnographic, ethnohistorical, and ancient lifecycle stages among the Maya would have many similarities. For example, Vogt (1969:182–192) defines the following lifecycle stages for Zinacantan, a Tzotzil Maya community of Chiapas, Mexico: birth to weaning; small boys and girls (ages 2–3 to 9–10); big boys and girls (ages 9–10 to 12–13); and, finally, full-grown boys and girls (ages 12–13 until marriage). During each of these stages, more and more responsibilities are given to children until they are seen as able to work on their own. This sequence is similar to the stages proposed by Bogin and Smith (1996), because the abilities of children to carry out various tasks will be influenced by their stage of development and autonomy from direct adult supervision. One cannot be sure that the Formative Maya of K'axob would have thought of children in the same four stages. K'axob was also an autonomous agricultural village with some stratification, which seems to have increased through time, and not a marginalized village within a larger state polity like Zinacantan. Both villages, however, subsisted on agriculture, and households had various tasks to maintain themselves, which means that the labor of children within households and in fields would have been as valuable at K'axob, as it is in Maya communities today. It is possible that high-ranking children would have experienced different expectations and perhaps enjoyed a more formal education. Regardless, as the children matured, the future potential of these individuals would have become more important to their families and community.

It is probable that Maya parents of ancient times distinguished between unweaned and weaned children because the need to nurse would keep an individual close to mother. The age of weaning at K'axob, however, presently is unknown. Even today, in many pre-modern and poorer countries, children are vulnerable to higher mortality rates during the time of weaning (Waldron 1994). Skeletal studies of prehistoric Maya childhood from Kaminaljuyú indicate that maize was eaten by age two, but also that weaning was a protracted process with breastfeeding serving as a complementary source of nutrition until age five or six (Wright and Schwarcz 1998). Of course, there was individual variation and some children were probably completely weaned as soon as another baby arrived, as is the pattern today in Zinacantan (Vogt 1969:185).

Although the same pattern may not have been present at K'axob, it is possible that children ages 3–5 may not have been completely weaned but would be treated as more capable and self-reliant than younger children. As Vogt says of Zinacantan small children, "[L]ife becomes more trying for a boy or girl between three and nine. Other household members can be expected to offer little affection, many commands to perform errands" (Vogt 1969:189). Children ages 11–13 should be considered on the cusp of puberty and adulthood. As discussed previously, with increasing age came increasing responsibilities and Maya parents probably distinguished minimally among unweaned infants and toddlers, weaned children from around age three to nine, and older children on the cusp of puberty and adulthood. Mortality rates should be elevated only for the earliest stage and the beginning of the second stage.

In the K'axob sample, there are eight infants who probably were not yet walking, seven children who were 1–3 years old and probably unweaned toddlers, seven weaned children (4–9 years old), and two 11–13 year old sub-adults who likely were nearing puberty and adulthood (Table 3.1). Additionally, two individuals can be aged only as a child and probable older child, but no finer aging is possible at this point. Sub-adults were aged by dental development, so the assigned ages are likely to be accurate to within a year or two (Ubelaker 1989). Thus, 58 percent of the twenty-six children died during the years of expected high mortality for very young children, which still leaves a hefty 42 percent who died at low-mortality ages.

Only nine (35 percent) of the child burials are single interments; the other seventeen are part of multiple interments. Fourteen (54 percent) of the sub-adult interments were secondary, because the skeletal elements are disarticulated, meaning that the remains were curated in some fashion and then given final interment. Secondary interment was a common burial mode at K'axob, so a slight majority of children had been moved to a final place of interment and given the extra processing of a corpse that secondary interment requires (see McAnany, Storey, and Lockard 1999; Storey 2004). We suspect that there were probable temporary burial facilities as part of the ritual landscape of K'axob, but at this point there is no evidence of how remains were curated. Of the fourteen secondary interments, twelve occurred with other individuals. Across the entire burial population of K'axob, secondary burial became more prevalent during the latter part of the Formative period. Thus, children usually were buried with other individuals and often as secondary interments.

Eleven sub-adults were interred with no perceptible accouterments, but of these eleven only two were single interments of infants. The other nine might be considered to share the offerings of the individuals with whom they were buried. Since the interments of these nine all occurred

Table 3.1. Description of the children of K'axob

Burial	*Age*	*Burial Position*	*Number within Interment*	*Ceramic Complex*
1-35	2–3	Secondary, scattered	1	Early Chaakk'ax
1-37a	11–13	Primary, extended	2	Early Chaakk'ax
1-37b	newborn	Probably primary?	2	Early Chaakk'ax
1-39	<1	Primary, extended	1	Early Chaakk'ax
1-40	5–7	Primary, extended	1	Early Chaakk'ax
1-18	4–5	Secondary, bundle	3	Early K'atabche'k'ax
1-27	5–6	Primary, extended	1	Early K'atabche'k'ax
1-32	12–13	Primary, extended	1	Early K'atabche'k'ax
1-34b	2–3	Probably secondary?	3	Early K'atabche'k'ax
1-44	child	Secondary, bundle	1	Early K'atabche'k'ax
11-7	5–8	Primary, seated	2	Early K'atabche'k'ax
11-8	<1	Primary, seated	2	Early K'atabche'k'ax
11-9	<1	Primary, flexed	1	Early K'atabche'k'ax
11-11	<1	Primary, seated	1	Early K'atabche'k'ax
11-12b	newborn	Probably primary?	2	Early K'atabche'k'ax
1-4	older child	Secondary, bundle	3	Late K'atabche'k'ax
1-6b	1–2	Secondary, bundle	4	Late K'atabche'k'ax
1-6c	3–5	Secondary, bundle	4	Late K'atabche'k'ax
1-6d	newborn	Secondary, bundle	4	Late K'atabche'k'ax
1-12b	5–7	Secondary, bundle	3	Late K'atabche'k'ax
1-14	2–3	Primary, extended	1	Late K'atabche'k'ax
1-15b	2–3	Secondary, bundle	3	Late K'atabche'k'ax
1-17b	3–4	Probably secondary?	3	Late K'atabche'k'ax
1-17c	<1	Probably secondary?	3	Late K'atabche'k'ax
12-16b	7–9	Secondary, bundle	2	Late K'atabche'k'ax
1-2c	7–10	Secondary, scattered	9	Term. K'atabche'k'ax

at the same time as that of the other individuals, this interpretation is possible. It is also possible, however, that in several of the cases these children, who were all under the age of five, might actually be considered part of the offering. As discussed in more detail later, these children are all buried with an older individual, probably a family member, who might be considered the main interment. The reunion of family was probably part of the mortuary ritual.

Most juveniles (85 percent) were buried inside structures rather than in more public plaza areas—a fact that provides support for an interpretation of their death as a focus of concern primarily among household members and close kin. Three children not buried within a residence are part of a multiple interment, and the fourth is a single, secondary interment. Only two of these children are older; the other two are probably around weaning age, so there is no real age pattern. Interestingly, this situation contrasts with that seen elsewhere in Mesoamerica, where only adults are found buried within structures (see King, Chapter 7). Burial within a structure does not necessarily mean that there was not also a public performance associated with the mortuary ritual (Joyce and Hendon 2000). Joyce and Hendon (2000) indicate that it is probably better to think of the differences in mortuary locations in terms of differences of intimacy. Burial inside a structure, with the burial generally not being otherwise marked for later commemoration, would likely have involved relatively few individuals when children were involved. Yet, King (Chapter 7) has a different interpretation for a pattern that seems to exclude children from burial within a structure, so there are probably very different meanings attached to locations of burials by age across Mesoamerica.

Furthermore, how public was the plaza area of Operation 1, the location of the only non-structure burials? This locale certainly became increasingly public through time, culminating with pyramid construction during the Classic period. During the Middle and Late Formative periods, it was a residential locale, likely that of the most influential family of K'axob. As such, there were probably lots of ritual and political events (including mortuary observances) that were staged near or at the residence and likely involved the entire community of K'axob. Thus, the burials of the four children in the patio area might have been public affairs, especially those three buried in multiple interments with adults.

What of our hypothesis—namely, that age at death might affect the mortuary treatment of children? All juveniles over the age of four were buried with accouterments or showed some evidence of special treatment; for example, extra processing of the corpse to create a secondary burial. But then the same can be said of practically all the infants and younger children. That pattern derives from the fact that there exists, in our opinion, a strong pattern of family interments of multiple individuals in the residential areas of Formative K'axob. In fact, fifteen (58 percent) of the juveniles belong to family interments in which several individuals were placed very close together in the same pit. All but three of these individuals were placed as part of a single interment episode, indicating a onetime creation of a family interment. The other three were part of a more protracted period of interment. All were eventually closed to further additions, but these also appear to be more like family mausolea than random accumulations of individuals. Most interestingly, in eleven of the cases, the juveniles were secondary interments that were associated with an adult—usually a female. These children were curated for some time after death, but we do not know whether this involved temporary burial, charnel house storage, or another practice. However stored, the individual was then moved so as to be part of a final interment, thus indicating special and prolonged burial treatment. Secondary interments of sub-adults as well as adults often have been interpreted as evidence of sacrificed individuals (Welsh 1988; Robin 1989), but these skeletons show no evidence of cut marks or other violence.

Secondary interments at K'axob are found in two forms—bundled and scattered—and neither seems likely to represent sacrificed individuals but rather represent curated community (and probably family) members. The secondary remains of two children had been scattered and the remains of nine bundled. Additionally, three children were found as secondary remains but poor preservation precludes an identification of form. Bundle burials contain a variety of skeletal elements and only a portion of the skeleton; both small and large bones are present as if the bundles were prepared from whichever skeletal elements were present among the curated remains. Scattered secondary interments predictably contain only a portion of the skeleton. At K'axob, there are multiple scattered individuals (sub-adults and adults) who were accompanied by offerings or a scattering of shell or pigment. Both scattered child interments included offerings. These secondary interments represent de-fleshed individuals, not dismembered pieces of intact bodies. Secondary burial is a common cross-cultural pattern for treatment of honored dead (Hertz 1960), and so it appears at K'axob, where all ages and both sexes are found as secondary interments.

For the ten children buried as primary interments, seven were placed alone in a pit. Additionally, two newborns, both probably buried with their mothers, were only identified after excavation, and so primary interment is only probable. Two of the ten primary interments were buried with each other and the third with one of the newborns who may or may not have been a primary interment. Seven of the primary interments had offerings, and only one of these did not include some shell, a relatively valuable item. Interment in this mode would have occurred soon after death and the individual was not moved at a later date (although a couple of primary interments were disturbed by later construction activities). All juvenile ages are represented in both primary and secondary interments and, although seven of the primary interments can be classified as termination burials (i.e., placed within a structure immediately before it was rebuilt), the others were placed in structures that continued to be occupied for some time. Thus, there is no simple rule by age or timing of death that determined whether a child was buried as a primary interment or destined to be curated and reburied.

AGE CLASS DIFFERENCES IN MORTUARY TREATMENT

A difference in the pattern of treatment by age is visible, however, if the K'axob children are compared within age groups (defined earlier) that probably held salience as developmental indicators for the residents of the village. The main difference between children who died during the lower mortality ages and those who died during the peak mortality ages is that the former generally have offerings and evidence of a more elaborate interment ritual than the latter. Comparisons begin with those closest to adulthood and end with infants and newborns.

Both from 11 to 13 years of age, Burials 1-37a and 1-32 are similar in how they were positioned in death—primary, extended, and supine. This position was common for adults during the periods in which they were interred (Early Chaakk'ax and Early K'atabche'k'ax, respectively). Poignantly, Burial 1-37a was found with the skeletal parts of a newborn. Because excavators were not aware that these bones belonged to a second individual, the exact position of the baby is unclear (i.e., whether within or next to the body of the juvenile). This lack of information hampers interpretation, but the perinate was fragmentary and small. The age of the juvenile (sex is not determinable given preservation conditions) seems to be somewhat young for motherhood, but it is certainly biologically possible. On the other hand, it could be that these two deaths took place in quick succession and the family decided to inter them together. A complete marine shell had been placed over the heart of juvenile Burial 1-37a and a shell bead, likely from a bracelet, was found near the right hand. Burial 1-32, although similar in age grade, differed greatly in burial accouterments. Notably, this juvenile was interred with a *yuntun* (a shaped limestone sphere used as a *bola* stone). A *yuntun* generally forms part of a young boy's tool inventory, as it is used to thwart the incursion of unwanted wildlife into maize fields (an important responsibility of young boys in contemporary Maya villages). At Cholula, similar balls, but of clay, were associated only with children (McCafferty and McCafferty, Chapter 2). McCafferty and McCafferty have suggested that these may have been used with blowguns for the hunting of small animals, so some commonalities to the artifacts of childhood across Mesoamerica is indicated. A shell bead and three *Pomacea* shells completed the offerings placed with this youngster.

The older children ages 4–10 years (see Table 3.2) can be contrasted both with the two near-adults just discussed and the infant/toddlers (ages 0–4 years) who probably were newly weaned or unweaned at death (Table 3.3). Only one interment, Burial 1-44, is excluded from consid-

Table 3.2. Mortuary Treatment of Older Children at K'axob

Burial No.	*Age*	*Offerings*	*Other Treatment*
Bur 1-37a	11–13	Complete marine shell, shell bead	Termination burial of structure
Bur 1-32	11–13	*Yuntun*, shell bead, 3 *Pomacea* shells	
Bur 1-2c	7–10	Small ribbed bowl and jade bead shared with others	Partially covered by bowl and area sprinkled with hematite, at top of series of interments in shrine
Bur 12-16b	7–9	Bowl, cache of *Pomacea* shells, macroblade	Inside bowl with evidence of burning ritual at time of placement
Bur 1-4	older child	Small bowl with restricted orifice	Placed over legs of adult, last individual placed in possible family group
Bur 11-7	5–8	Fragments of a vessel, shell pendant, shell blank	Buried with infant Bur 11-8, termination burial of structure
Bur 1-40	5–7	3 *Pomacea* shells at feet	Semicircle of stones around head
Bur 1-12b	5–7	None	Charcoal and burnt limestone from burning ritual closing family group
Bur 1-27	5–6	1 small bowl with restricted orifice, 1 fragmentary vessel, shell pendant, *Pomacea* shell	Termination burial of structure
Bur 1-18	4–5	Small bowl with restricted orifice as head-covering, five shell beads of headdress	Probable family group pit sprinkled with hematite

eration here. A secondary bundle with no offerings, Burial 1-44 contained the remains of an individual, which had been placed under a thin plaster cap—evidence of special mortuary treatment. Unfortunately, the poor preservation of the skeleton precludes identification beyond the gross category of child and so this burial is omitted from the following discussion.

Evidence of some type of protracted mortuary treatment is present in five of the eight interments of older children. Such treatment was also present among half of the interments of K'axob adults. In two cases (Burials 1-4 and 1-12b), the remains of these older children were placed as secondary bundles within a sequence of three separate interment episodes that occurred within two separate pits over some period of time. In both cases, the child was the last to be placed within the pit. Burial 1-4 was positioned (along with a small Sierra Red, restricted-orifice bowl) over the legs of a female. In Burial 1-12b, the mortuary facility appears to have been closed with some sort of termination ritual involving burn-

Table 3.3. Mortuary Treatment of Probable Weaning Age and Unweaned Children

Burial No.	*Age*	*Offerings*	*Other Treatment*
Bur 1-6c	3–5	None	Part of probable family group
Bur 1-17b	3–4	None	Part of probable family group
Bur 1-35	2–3	3 shells, 11 shell tinklers	Skeleton and offerings scattered in Pit
Bur 1-34b	2–3	None	Part of probable family group
Bur 1-15b	2–3	2 shell beads	Part of probable family group
Bur 1-14	2–3	Small bowl with everted rim, 6 shark vertebrae, 2 shell beads, shell tinkler carved with death deity	Single interment into ongoing residence
Bur 1-6b	1–2	None	Part of probable family group
Bur 1-39	<1	None	Termination burial in structure
Bur 11-8	<1	None	Buried with older child
Bur 11-9	<1	fragments of a vessel	
Bur 11-11	<1	None	Termination burial of structure
Bur 1-17c	<1	None	Part of probable family group
Bur 1-6d	newborn	None	Part of probable family group
Bur 1-37b	newborn	None	Buried with mother?
Bur 11-12b	newborn	None	Buried with mother?

ing after the placement of the child (see Figure 3.2). Burial 1-18 is also part of a multiple interment, but in this case the three individuals appear to have been buried simultaneously. The child, a secondary bundle, was placed in the lap of a female; the small skull was covered with a diminutive Sierra Red bowl (again, a form with a restricted orifice). This entire interment was sprinkled with hematite as it was closed (see Figure 3.3). Burial 12-16b, part of a secondary interment composed of two fragmentary skulls, was placed in a bowl with other offerings and evidence of a burning ritual at closure. In fact, this burial appears more in the nature of a dedicatory cache than an interment. Burial 1-2c, on the other hand, is part of a large set of secondary interments that were successively positioned in layers within a pit that was covered by what we have interpreted as an ancestral shrine (McAnany, Storey, and Lockard 1999). Whereas all other interments were adults, this child was one of four individuals whose remains were scattered across the top of the pit along with a small, ribbed Society Hall Red bowl, a jadeite bead, and a sprinkling of hematite. It appears that the inclusion of older children in these elaborate mortuary treatments was appropriate and, in the case of Burials 1-4 and 1-12b, may have been considered an important element of the termination rituals. The death of these children, when

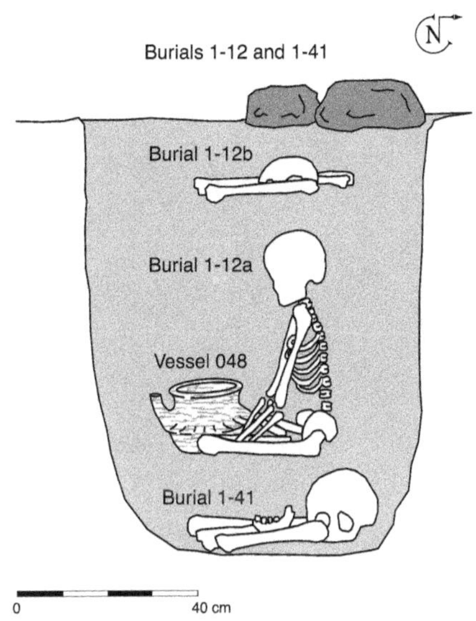

3.2: Plan of Burials 1-12 and 1-41 with the bundled remains of the child at the top of the pit with burned limestone rocks and charcoal above from the termination ritual.

they were more likely to survive to adulthood, may have been felt keenly by the families.

Infants/toddlers generally lacked offerings and, for ten of the fifteen who died before reaching the age of five, the only elaboration or special treatment consisted of inclusion within a probable family group, usually as a secondary interment. Infants and newborns, especially, reveal scant preserved evidence of resources expended or ritual complexity at the time of interment. Some of the infant remains do appear as termination burials; that is, as last burials placed before reconstruction of a structure. In this situation, the burial pit is not closed but covered by architectural fill. Individuals of all ages, however, whether interred as single or multiple burials (and richly endowed or not), were found interred as termination burials. It is probable that the death of family members may have affected the timing of reconstructing residential structures, but half the structural interments took place during the use-life of a structure. Only in a few of the instances discussed do the ritual and situation of the interment seem to indicate that a special termination event was practiced, and none of these involved infants. That does not mean there was no particular mortuary ritual for infants or that grief was not felt, but that less archaeological evidence has accumulated for infant burials than for older children.

Interestingly, one of the richest juvenile burials is that of a 2–3-year-old, Burial 1-14 (see Table 3.3). Regardless of the general pattern for an age set, one should always expect idiosyncratic cases that reflect the particular situation of the individual involved. This child may or may not have been partially weaned and can be considered to have died during a vulnerable age. This fact does not seem to have dampened the family's desire to invest this interment with distinctive burial accouterments,

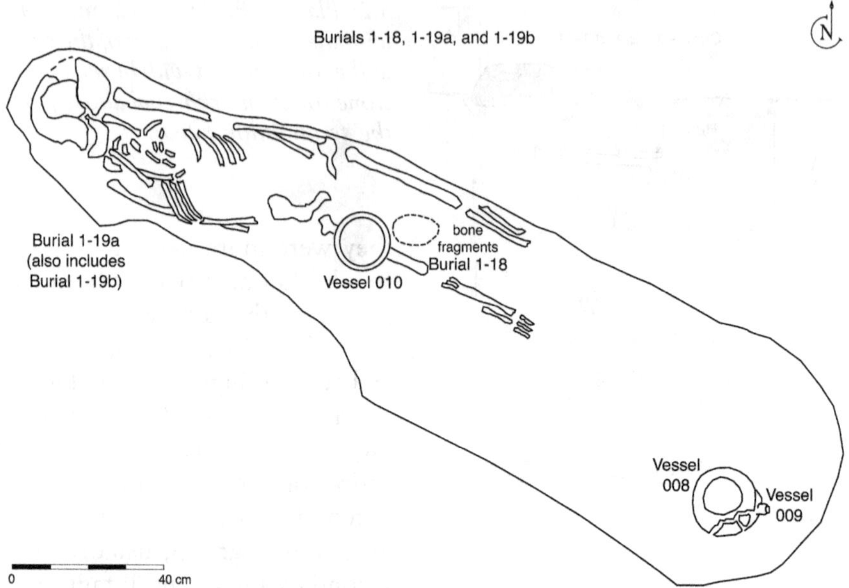

3.3: Plan of Burials 1-18 and 1-19 where the head of the child was under the inverted ceramic vessel in the lap of the female primary interment.

including the following items: a small Sierra Red bowl (with an everted rim), six shark vertebrae, two shell beads, and an *Oliva* sp. shell tinkler carved with the face of the death deity. Such burial goods probably reflect both the social standing of the child and the disappointment of the family that he/she did not survive. This individual was buried as a single interment inside a residential structure during its use-life. In spite of the intimacy of the interment setting, it is possible that a quite elaborate ritual surrounded the interment of this particular child.

CONCLUSION

Among the children of K'axob, there are four mortuary patterns that reveal age differentiation. First, only one of the eight infant burials included offerings—sherds from a portion of a vessel. All other infants were placed in a multiple burial context with probable family members or within a termination burial with no offerings or other evidence of particular ritual. Second, the only neonates in the sample likely were buried with their mothers. Neonates whose mothers did not also die during childbirth, or who were not placed ultimately with the family group, were not buried in the structures or associated plazas. Third, of those who were toddlers at the time of their death and were buried in simultaneous interments with adults, only one has associated offerings. On the other hand, the two who were buried singly were associated with distinctive offerings. Fourth, all older children and near-adults were distinguished by being part of a protracted and episodic burial context, usually with both offerings and termination rituals. Thus, there is a gradient of mortuary involvement that tends to become more elaborate with age at death.

These trends in mortuary treatment provide support for the notion that families handled infant death with a certain amount of acceptance, given the demographic reality associated with this vulnerable age class and the shorter period of parental investment that had transpired. On the other hand, protracted interment rituals for older children were much more common, and these burials often contained artifacts that were rarely found with adult interments. Examples include the *yuntun* of Burial 1-32 and the many small bowls (most shaped like tecomates with a restricted mouth) found with older children. Spouted jars and large open bowls, common accouterments among adult burials at K'axob, were never placed near the remains of children. The pattern of distinctive offerings is similar to that found by McCafferty and McCafferty (Chapter 2) for Cholula. Several other chapters in this volume stress that children are qualitatively different from adults in Mesoamerica in a ritual sense (see Hamann, Chapter 8, and Román and Chávez, Chapter 9). Children are also "adults in training" (see McCafferty and McCafferty, Chapter 2, and Lopiparo, Chapter 6), and so one would expect to find some distinctions at K'axob.

Another trend, however, crosscuts the pattern of increasing mortuary elaboration as a function of age class. Regardless of age, some children were curated for burial with other individuals at a later date. Despite their premature death, even infants and unweaned children continued to be considered family members and part of the family interment program. This pattern, which modified a strict model of age-based parental investment in mortuary ritual, may be attributable to the relatively good general health of the K'axob Formative-period population (see Storey 2004). This fact likely depressed the rate of premature deaths and heightened the sense of loss associated with a child's death, regardless of the child's age. In such a situation, even infant fatalities might not have been very common, and thus it is not surprising that the remains of infants as well as younger and older children were curated and incorporated into protracted family-based mortuary ritual. This apparent variability, in spite of some general patterns, suggests to us that during the Formative Period there were no strictly prescribed burial practices for children. Rather, families maintained the prerogative to commemorate premature death in the manner deemed most appropriate to those who had endured the loss of a child.

ACKNOWLEDGMENTS

Field research at K'axob was conducted under permit from the Government of Belize, Department of Archaeology, during 1990, 1992, and 1993. We express our gratitude to those who wore the hat of commissioner during the "old" days of the Department of Archaeology, particularly the late Mr. Harriot Topsey. We thank the many Belizeans who facilitated this research, especially Mr. Concepcion Campos, landowner of K'axob. For those Belizeans who worked side-by-side with us in the field—swinging a machete or a shovel or meticulously excavating a burial—we owe a very special debt of gratitude. We also acknowledge the contribution of the many Boston University field school students and volunteers. Finally, we are grateful to the following agencies that provided funding for this field research: Ahau Foundation, Boston University Division of International Programs, and the National Science Foundation (SBR-9112310).

REFERENCES CITED

Bogin, Barry, and B. H. Smith
1996 Evolution of the Human Lifecycle. *American Journal of Human Biology* 8:703–716.

Burns, Allan F.
1993 *Maya in Exile: Guatemalans in Florida.* Philadelphia: Temple University Press.

Daltabuit G., Magali
1992 *Mujeres Mayas: Trabajo, Nutricíon, y Fecundidad.* Mexico City: Universidad Nacional Autónoma de México.

Hertz, Robert
1960 *Death and the Right Hand*, trans. R. Needham and C. Needham. Glencoe: The Free Press.

Joyce, Rosemary
2001 Burying the Dead at Tlatilco: Social Memory and Social Identities. In *Social Memory, Identity, and Death,* ed. M. S. Chesson, 12–26. Washington, DC: Archeological Papers of the American Anthropological Association, Number 10.

Joyce, Rosemary A., and Julia Hendon
2000 Heterarchy, History, and Material Reality: "Communities" in Late Classic Honduras. In *The Archaeology of Communities,* ed. M. A. Canuto and J. Yaeger, 143–169. New York: Routledge.

López Varela, Sandra L.
1996 The K'axob Formative Ceramics: The Search for Regional Integration through a Reappraisal of Ceramic Analysis and Classification in Northern Belize. Ph.D. dissertation, University of London.

McAnany, Patricia A, ed.
2004 *K'axob: Ritual, Work, and Family in an Ancient Maya Village.* Monumenta Archaeologica 22. Los Angeles: Cotsen Institute of Archaeology at UCLA.

McAnany, Patricia A., and Sandra L. López Varela
1999 Re-creating the Formative Maya village of K'axob: Chronology, Ceramic Complexes, and Ancestors in Architectural Context. *Ancient Mesoamerica* 10:147–168.

McAnany, Patricia A., Rebecca Storey, and Angela K. Lockard
1999 Mortuary Ritual and Family Politics at Formative and Early Classic K'axob, Belize. *Ancient Mesoamerica* 10:129–146.

Redfield, Robert
1950 *A Village That Chose Progress: Chan Kom Revisited.* Chicago: The University of Chicago Press.

Restall, Matthew
1997 *The Maya World: Yucatec Culture and Society, 1550–1850.* Stanford: Stanford University Press.

Robin, Cynthia
1989 *Preclassic Maya Burials at Cuello, Belize.* BAR International Series 480. Oxford: British Archaeological Reports.

Roys, Ralph L.
1972 *The Indian Background of Colonial Yucatan.* Norman: University of Oklahoma Press.

Sigal, Pete
2000 *From Moon Goddess to Virgins: The Colonization of Yucatecan Maya Sexual Desire.* Austin: University of Texas Press.

Storey, Rebecca
2004 Ancestors: Bioarchaeology of the Human Remains. In *K'axob: Ritual, Work and Family in an Ancient Maya Village,* ed. P. A. McAnany, 109–138. Monumenta Archaeologica 22. Los Angeles: Cotsen Institute of Archaeology at UCLA.

Ubelaker, Douglas
1989 *Human Skeletal Remains,* 2nd ed. Washington, DC: Taraxacum Press.

Vogt, Evon Z.

1969 *Zinacantan: A Maya Community in the Highlands of Chiapas.* Cambridge, MA: The Belknap Press of Harvard University Press.

Waldron, Tony

1994 *Counting the Dead.* London: John Wiley and Sons.

Welsh, W.B.M.

1988 *An Analysis of Classic Lowland Maya Burials.* BAR International Series 409. Oxford: British Archaeological Reports.

Wright, Lori E., and Henry P. Schwarcz

1998 Stable Carbon and Oxygen Isotopes in Human Tooth Enamel: Identifying Breastfeeding and Weaning in Prehistory. *American Journal of Physical Anthropology* 106:1–18.

4

IDENTIFYING CHILDHOOD AMONG THE ANCIENT MAYA

Evidence Toward Social Reproduction at the Dancer Household Group in Northwestern Belize

Rissa M. Trachman

Fred Valdez Jr.

INTRODUCTION

Partially because of preservation issues, children are under-represented in the archaeological record, which often causes archaeologists to overlook them in reconstructions of the past (Sofaer Derevenski 1994, 1997a). Some of this underrepresentation is the result of issues of variable preservation in mortuary contexts, especially in certain environmental settings, and the fragility of skeletal remains of smaller human bodies. Consequently, recovering a mortuary sample that includes children can be problematic. Theoretically it can be challenging to derive a culturally and historically meaningful definition of child or childhood in context. It is as difficult as defining any other social construct we may endeavor to investigate archaeologically, such as *household* or *gender*. Additionally, our ability as archaeologists to recognize the material residue or patterns of non-mortuary remains associated with children and childhood activities requires a greater ability to perceive and interpret certain data. Even our Western categorization of age distinctions, which compartmentalizes life-cycle experiences, can bias our ability to approach an investigation of childhood (Sofaer Derevenski 1994).

In this chapter we attempt to go beyond some of these difficulties with the hope that this previously marginalized, yet significant, group of people can be thoughtfully investigated. Archaeologists are only beginning to make inroads into understanding children and the part they played in home life as well as in society (see Ardren, Chapter 1). Previously the activities of ancient children were seen merely as a site formation process that distorted the remains of the patterned behavior of other actors (Hammond and Hammond 1981). Today we recognize that children are social beings. Children were obviously present in the past and highly capable of interaction with the people and circumstances of their daily lives, communities, and societies. Their behavior is as likely to leave patterns or traces in the archaeological record as any adult or group.

We propose that given a practical theoretical notion, additional lines of evidence may be used in order to attempt to define age divisions culturally and historically, if they existed. The primary lines we employ are derived from excavated data, ethnohistory, and ethnography. Ethnohistory and ethnography for the historic and modern Maya have great potential for informing us about social identities. Excavated data are an important opportunity to view the way that social identities may have been expressed materially and spatially for the ancient Maya. Further, the difficulties of accessing data regarding age divisions in the early part of the life cycle may be overcome by directing ethnohistorically and ethnographically informed efforts toward recognizing the potential archaeological signs of childhood.

Here we attempt to address the issue of the ways in which gender may have been socialized symbolically through the use of material culture as a means of social reproduction. In addition to ethnohistory, we present comparative archaeological data that aids in the interpretation of a set of domestic remains found outside the site of Dos Hombres in northwestern Belize. The result is a solid interpretation of symbolic material culture from this small household through the lens of continuity of historical practice.

A QUESTION OF IDENTITY: DEFINING CHILD AND CHILDHOOD

As illustrated by the variety of topics and research approaches thus far surrounding children and childhood, children participated at some level in almost every aspect of social life. Certainly, which or how particular biological life stages are categorized or treated is socially constructed. Children might then be defined by the cultural perception of a person's life stages. Philippe Ariès's (1965) work emphasized the significance of considering historical context when attempting to define conceptions of children (see Hamann, Chapter 8, for an extended discussion of Ariés's work). It follows then that age divisions are socially constructed within the context of a particular social history (Sofaer Derevenski 1997a:194; Gilchrist 1999:89).

Defining the concept of childhood follows. The experience of particular age divisions derived from historically specific contexts conceivably constitutes the concept of childhood. Children are undoubtedly active participants in the negotiation of their experience (Sofaer Derevenski 2000:8).

Social Reproduction and Socializing Gender

Our argument for the need to explore children and their experiences derives from Henrietta Moore's (1988, 1994) concept of social reproduction. Moore (1994:90) has stated that we cannot assume that the reproduction of society follows unproblematically from the biological reproduction of individuals. As important as biological reproduction, and crucial for maintaining society, is the production of individuals who hold particular social identities and are differentiated socially in appropriate ways. Moore (1988:48; 1994) has established that social reproduction (or the social relations of reproduction) is a set of arrangements that reproduce human groups from generation to generation. These arrangements include, but are not limited to, the means of constructing and organizing sex, gender, procreation, and domestic labor. Social reproduction does not take place solely at the domestic level. Many other social institutions participate in the process. The result is that society is reproduced so that specific kinds of people have specific social identities (Moore 1994:93). In essence, society is reproduced by the proper socialization of individuals.

The construction and organization of gender and other kinds of difference related to identity are central to social reproduction (Moore 1994:92). Gender, as Gilchrist (1999:1) defines it, is the cultural construction of sexual difference in historical context. Gender-specific behavior may be perceived as "learned behavior, resulting from historically specific processes of socialization" (Gilchrist 1999:9). Johanna Sofaer Derevenski (1997b:487) has suggested that gender and age should be studied together because gendered identities are subject to change over the course of life. Evidence from mortuary analysis can help identify such changes in gender identities as ancient subjects progress through age grades (1997b:489).

Material Culture and Childhood

Of specific importance to archaeology, in terms of gendered divisions or identities of people and the reproduction of culturally and historically relevant people, are the material consequences of such identities. Marie Louise Stig Sørensen (2000:94) argues that "the physicality of objects, which gives them the ability to transcend the life of individuals and the limits of events, is seen as providing the material environment for the reproduction of society, including its gender ideologies."

Gender, adulthood, childhood, and other social ideals can be encoded in items of material culture, both portable and non-portable. Children learn about gender through the material world around them (Sofaer Derevenski 1997a:196, 2000:8; Gilchrist 1999:90; Sørensen 2000:9; see also Joyce 2000a, 2000b; Joyce and Hendon 2000) and through personal interactions. Buildings, monuments, temples, and other structures may be inscribed with information about certain events and people seeking legitimacy. They are also encoded with acceptable, normal expectations of behavior that are habitually reinforced by repetitive action (Bourdieu 1977). Portable items are imbued with relevant cultural information and present a special way of communicating because they can be produced, utilized, and enjoyed in more private settings. Interaction with these items is often more personal. Creativity and critical decision-making become important factors in whether particular (encoded) information is passed along or particular items reproduced. Material objects connect generations to one another and are essential for arbitrating or reconciling tradition (Sørensen 2000:9).

Bodily adornment, for example, is a fundamental mechanism for reproducing and communicating role distinctions and position among interacting members of a group (Dietler and Herbich 1998:242; see also Joyce 1999; Sørensen 2000). Joyce (1999, 2000a, 2000b) has successfully highlighted the importance of costume in expressing both social and individual difference in ancient Mesoamerica.

Toys and child's play are other exceptional examples of the ways in which childhood, identity, and socialization are expressed materially. Artifacts associated with child's play are more than just irrelevant playthings, as they are often imbued with concepts of identity such as age, gender, class, ethnicity, and socially accepted ideas of beauty (Wilkie

2000). As Laurie Wilkie notes (2000:101), child-specific artifacts often signify attempts by adults to communicate behavioral norms. Child-specific items created by adults present an interesting opportunity for children to negotiate an understanding of the messages communicated and their ultimate acceptance (or not) of these ideas. Jeanne Lopiparo (Chapter 6) has made an important contribution to our understanding of playthings in the ancient past and their role in reproducing society.

ETHNOHISTORY AND ETHNOGRAPHY OF MAYA CHILDREN

Data from ethnohistoric and ethnographic sources are essential in defining the child and recognizing parameters for the experience of childhood within ancient Maya culture (Trachman and Valdez 2001). Ethnohistoric accounts of early colonial contact in the Americas can be a valuable source of information about the practices of societies present at that time because some aspects of cultural ideology and practice do not leave a material residue or only leave an ambiguous one. Although the documentation of colonial contact peoples is of obvious value, some vigilance in its consideration is prudent. In this study we utilize historic documentation of Postclassic- to Colonial-period Maya, written from the point of view of colonial authorities. Our primary source is Alfred M. Tozzer's 1941 translation of Diego de Landa's memoirs. Landa was a Spanish priest who resided for a time in Yucatán. Given the conditions of the current and most popular translations, it is important to acknowledge some issues or problems surrounding the use of Landa's writings. Matthew Restall and John F. Chuchiak IV (2002) have traced the derivation of the two most common translations of Landa's writings. They noted that the actual origin and authorship of the original writings are problematic. After the original writings were lost or forgotten, what was thought to be Landa's writing was rediscovered in 1861 and translated into French. The first of the two most cited versions of Landa is a translation by William Gates (Landa [1566] 1978) published in 1937 and based on the problematic and biased French translation (Restall and Chuchiak 2002). The most recent and first truly scholarly publication of Landa is the translation by Alfred Tozzer published in 1941. Restall and Chuchiak (2002) consider this translation to have some of the same problems since it is based on the collection of writings assumed to have been Landa's but these writings are clearly problematic. Regardless of its enigmatic nature, Landa's *Relación de las Cosas de Yucatán* "is nevertheless an authentic product of lost or as-yet-undiscovered late-sixteenth-century observations and writings by Landa (or by Landa and his contemporaries).

As such, it remains an invaluable primary source on sixteenth-century Yucatán and on Maya civilization" (Restall and Chuchiak 2002:664). Tozzer's translation of Landa has proven to be an inestimable contribution and is extremely useful for our purposes here.

In addition to the complications with Landa's writings, we cannot presume cultural continuity between northern Yucatán in the sixteenth century, as described by Landa, and the Classic and Preclassic Maya of other regions. The practices recorded by Landa at the time cannot be taken as direct indicators of ancient actions. Careful consideration and material evidence are necessary to corroborate historical observations. We apply some of the ethnohistory and ethnography presented here to a set of excavated data in order to better understand material remains. The goal is to demonstrate a measure of continuity with respect to a specific practice related to socializing the gender of ancient Maya children with verification of additional evidence.

According to J. Eric S. Thompson's (1970:283) interpretation of early historic accounts, Maya birth ceremonies included a form of union between newborns and maize (i.e., each became the counterpart of the other). These ceremonies entailed cutting the umbilical cord over an ear of maize, using an obsidian blade, which was thrown into a nearby river afterward. The maize grains were prepared and planted twice in succession. After tribute was paid, the resulting crop was considered the basis for the child's support until the child was old enough to support him- or herself (Thompson 1970:283). A modern example of this ceremony also exists among the Tzotzil in which the blood stained grains of maize are saved, planted, and carefully tended as the crop may prognosticate the child's future (Guiteras H. 1960). The harvest thus served as a unifying meal connecting all members of the family to the new child (Thompson 1970:284). We find no account of this infant birth ceremony in Landa's *Relación.* Landa (Tozzer 1941:129), however, did mention that women prayed to the goddess of childbearing, Ix Chel, for help in childbirth and placed a figurine of her image under the bed of the laboring mother.

Thompson gives a detailed account of a ceremony in which children are carried astride the hip for the first time among the modern Maya of Yucatán. Landa (Tozzer 1941:88) noted only that children were carried on the hip habitually by their mothers, which he believed made them bowlegged. In a footnote to the Landa text, Tozzer references a particular passage about the modern Maya ceremony called the *hetzmek,* which relates to this practice of carrying astride the hip. The ceremony would take place when girls were three months of age and boys were four months (Thompson 1970:166). For girls, the significance in timing for this event is related to the Maya hearth's having three stones. The hearth in this case is explicitly associated with the activities of women as a contemporary gender construct. For boys, the cornfield has four corners and is representative of the gendered agricultural activity that boys will engage in.

Landa makes no mention of children being carried astride the hip during or in association with a life-cycle ceremony nor does he use the term *hetzmek* to describe any of the other ceremonies. Apparently Landa's reference in the text to children habitually being carried on the hip is simply his explanation for the biological phenomena of bowed legs, which more likely resulted from a vitamin deficiency or disease pathology such as treponemal disease (see Saul and Saul 1997).

It is also possible that researchers such as Thompson later conflated the *hetzmek* ceremony with another ceremony that Landa described in detail. Landa (Tozzer 1941:159) documented the *Yolob u dzab kam yax,* "ceremony of receiving the blue color," commonly referred to as the "ceremony of the occupations," in a separate section of the *Relación* concerning rites that were specific to various calendar months. Landa documented this ceremony in which occupational or artisanal implements and tools of adulthood were involved. He explains that the ceremony of the occupations was performed by an *Ix Mol,* or an old female "conductress" (Tozzer 1941:159). The first step in the process was to anoint all of the implements that the children would use in adulthood with a blue substance. Once all the boys and girls were gathered together,

> instead of smearings and ceremonies, they struck each of them on the joints of the backs of the hands, nine slight blows; and to the little girls, the blows were given by an old woman, clothed in a dress of feathers, who brought them there. . . . [T]hey gave them these blows, so that they might become skilful workmen in the professions of their fathers and mothers. (Tozzer 1941:159)

Children were generally not clothed at all until the age of four or five years, probably around or just after the time they were weaned (Tozzer 1941:125). According to Landa, at this time children received an overgarment for wearing at night along with a loincloth for the boys and a below-the-waist covering, likely a skirt, for the girls. Important gender symbolic ornaments were also worn by children.

> They had then this custom in preparing for baptism: the Indian women brought up the children till they were three years old, and in the case of the little boys they used always to put on their heads

> a little white bead, stuck to the hair on the top of the head. And the little girls wore a thin cord about their loins, very low, and to this was fastened a small shell which hung just over the sexual parts; and it was thought a sin and a very dishonorable thing to take off these two things from the little girls before their baptism, which was always administered between the ages of three and twelve, and they were never married before being baptized. (Tozzer 1941:102)

It is difficult to discern from this passage the actual age(s) that the gender specific ornaments were initially put on by children. It seems that it may have been at three years of age, but it remains unclear since later Landa states that they were not removed before the "baptism" ceremony, which took place between the ages of three and twelve.

The "baptism" ceremony that Landa (Tozzer 1941:102) referred to as a prerequisite for marriage was actually called *caput sihil* (see Joyce, Chapter 11, for additional discussion of the *caput sihil* ceremony). The ritual was interpreted through the eyes of Spanish friars as a form of baptism. Literally translated, *caput sihil* means "to be born anew" (Tozzer 1941:102), and this name may be one reason for the parallel in meaning seen by Spanish priests. It was during this ceremony that the gender symbols of the bead and shell were removed. After a long series of activities in which children were gathered in an area especially cordoned off while a priest burned herbs and incense, a white cloth was placed on their heads (Tozzer 1941:105). Then an appointed person took a bone and shook it in front of each child's forehead and wet it with special water and sprinkled the children on their foreheads, faces, and between their fingers and toes. Once the water was sprinkled on the children, the gender-specific ornaments were removed:

> And immediately the priest cut off with a stone knife the bead which the little boys wore stuck on their heads. . . . [T]he young girls were first dismissed; and their mothers went up to them to take off the cords, which they had worn up to that time tied around their loins, and the little shell, which they wore as a token of their purity. This was, as it were, a license allowing them to marry whenever it should please their fathers. (Tozzer 1941:106)

The parallel to Christian baptism is undeniable and obviously the reason Landa described this ceremony in great detail.

One of Tozzer's footnotes acknowledges some discrepancy in ethnohistoric documents about the age at which this ceremony was actually performed. Landa reported that it took place at the ages of three to twelve, but the *Relación* of Motul states it may have taken place at the ages of fourteen or fifteen (Tozzer 1941:102). Other Maya researchers have interpreted the various accounts to mean that children received their gender-symbolic items at a very early age, possibly at an earlier ceremony, and then removed them at the rebirth ceremony (see Sharer 1994:482; 1996:118). Landa wrote of the gender symbols just before he began to describe a life-cycle ceremony that was similar to what he knew as baptism. It is possible he mentioned it only briefly in order to set the stage for what he thought was much more important. There is little way to tell exactly what Landa meant in terms of the age of the children when they received the gender-encoded symbol or when it was removed. We will address this question again after our presentation of the archaeological data.

The *caput sihil* was clearly a transitional ceremony. Although when the children emerged they were considered marriageable, according to Landa, they often did not marry right away. Rather they went through another period of preparation. Girls were trained in their households of origin, but boys of marriageable age went to live together in a communal house until they were married (Tozzer 1941:124).

The age of marriage, Landa (Tozzer 1941:100) noted, was twenty years in "olden times," which presumably meant before Spanish contact. He went on to say that at the time of his observance, they married at the age of twelve or fourteen. Tozzer attributed this change to a colonial law that forced girls to marry at age twelve. The law was passed after the conquest of Bacalar in order to increase the population (Tozzer 1941:100).

CASE STUDY: HOUSEHOLD DATA FROM DOS HOMBRES

Our interest in the preceding ethnohistoric and ethnographic reading concerning the Maya life cycle resulted from the recovery of a set of archaeological remains at a household in a settlement area outside Dos Hombres in northwestern Belize (see Figure 1.1). The investigations presented here were done under the auspices of the Programme for Belize Archaeological Project (PfBAP), a long-term research effort in northwestern Belize (Figure 4.1). The Rio Bravo Conservation and Management area includes more than 250,000 acres of land in northwestern Belize. The PfBAP began research in 1992, directed by R.E.W. Adams, as an extension of the Río Azul and Ixcanrio Projects in northwestern Petén, Guatemala (Valdez and Adams 1995). The goals of the PfBAP are to define the political, economic, and social structures that gave rise to and supported the cities of the region, with attention to middle- and

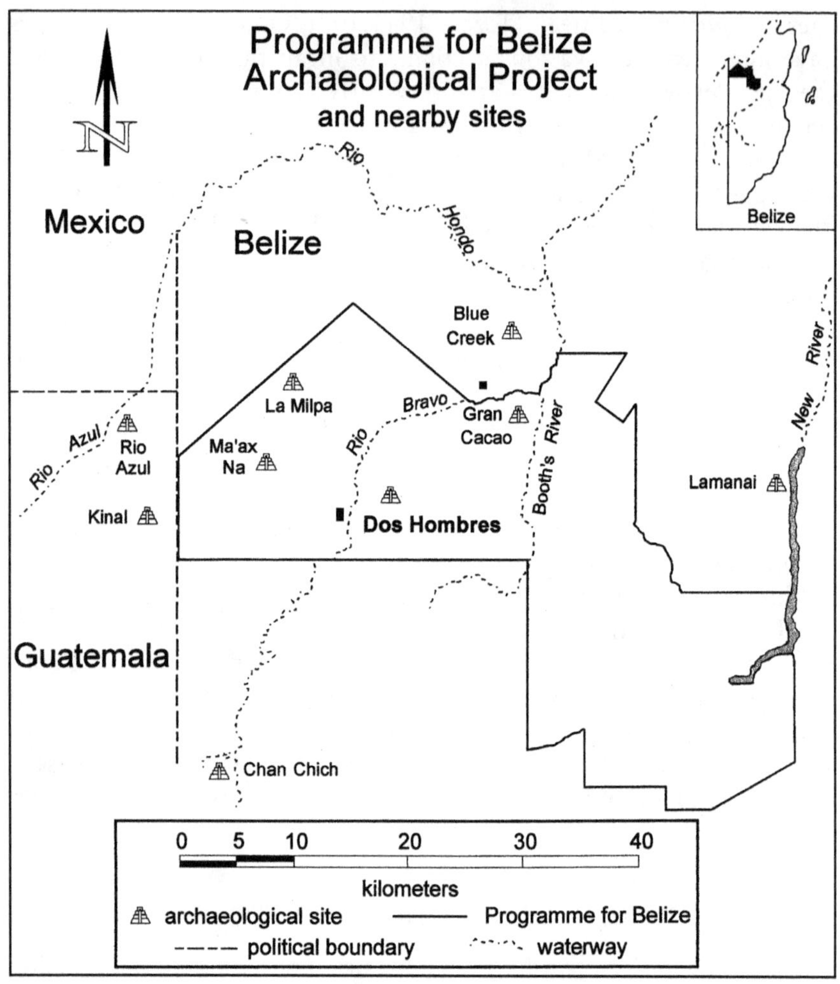

4.1: *Map of northwestern Belize (drawn by Jon Lohse).*

small-sized sites (Valdez and Adams 1995). This study is concerned with a specific set of data retrieved from a household group excavation carried out during the 1999, 2000, and 2001 field seasons of the PfBAP.

Within the PfBAP area, the site of Dos Hombres is situated approximately 1.5 kilometers east of the foot of the Rio Bravo escarpment in the Rio Bravo Embayment (Brokaw and Mallory 1993). The Rio Bravo, running north-south, is located just west of the Dos Hombres site center at the bottom of the escarpment. Mapping at Dos Hombres took place with two different transect surveys (Lohse 2001; Hageman

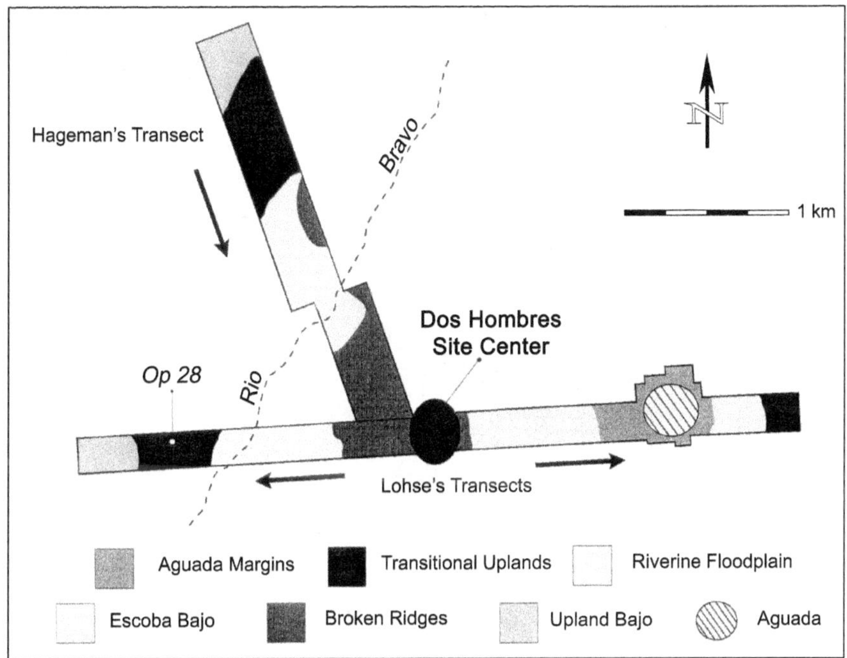

4.2: The Dos Hombres settlement transects and their environmental subzones with location of Operation 28 (Op 28) noted (drawn by Jon Lohse).

and Lohse 2003; Figure 4.2). Six different environmental subzones were established across the settlement near Dos Hombres, specifically within the transect survey research areas (Lohse 2001; Hageman and Lohse 2003). Rissa Trachman (2003) undertook a household investigation in two of the established environmental subzones. This study utilizes data retrieved from one of the household groups investigated in the transitional uplands subzone of the western transect, originally designated Operation 28, herein referred to as the Dancer Household Group (Figure 4.2).

The Dancer Household Group lies approximately 1.75 kilometers west of the ball court of the Dos Hombres site center and may be part of a separately organized community. It comprises an L-shaped low platform with two structures (Figure 4.3) resting on a residential terrace. Excavations established at least two phases of occupation at this household—Late Preclassic (300 BCE–150 CE) buried by Late Classic (650–850 CE)—as determined by ceramic chronology. The two structures visible on the surface are from the Late Classic phase, and wall remnants from

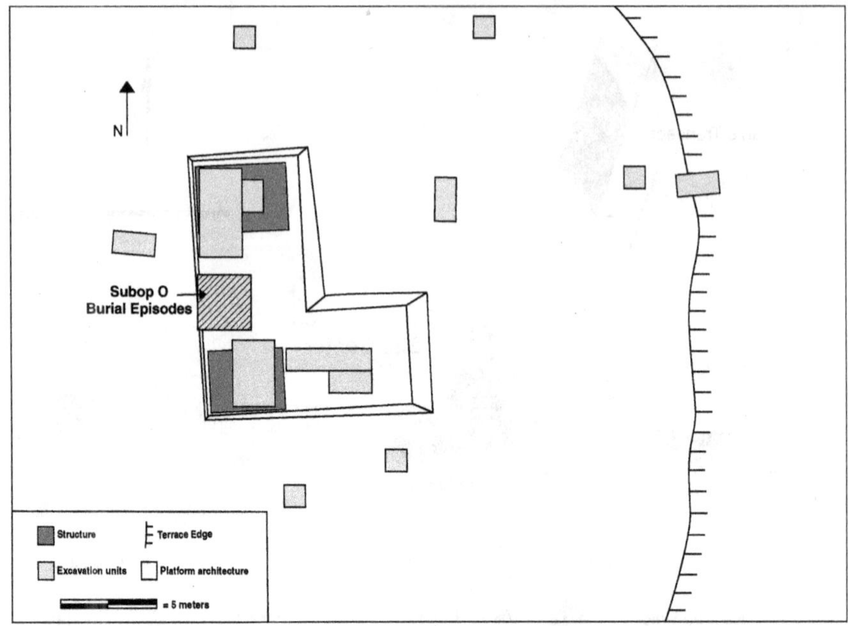

4.3: Plan overview of Operation 28 with location of burial episodes noted (drawn by R. Trachman).

an earlier building, probably the Late Preclassic phase, were also documented some 40–50 centimeters below Structure 2.

During the excavation of the platform, a series of burials was discovered in fill between the two Late Classic–phase structures (Figure 4.3). The burials were in three sets, each consisting of multiple burials, which will be presented here as "episodes" (Saul and Saul 2003) and numbered as they were encountered (as opposed to their relative age or depth) in the excavations (Figure 4.4). Each of these episodes has several individuals associated with it, and together they represent the two previously noted time periods. The skeletal remains were poorly preserved, as is common in shallow household deposits of the Maya region. Yet, for several reasons, including their placement in dense clay and gravel matrix and their very shallow depth with little construction or plaster overlying them, these sets of burials were particularly difficult to excavate and analyze. We acknowledge that since episodes 2 and 3 are both from the Late Preclassic period, it is possible that they were placed in the same interment event. Because they are spatially distinct, we will consider them separately for the analytical purposes of this paper.

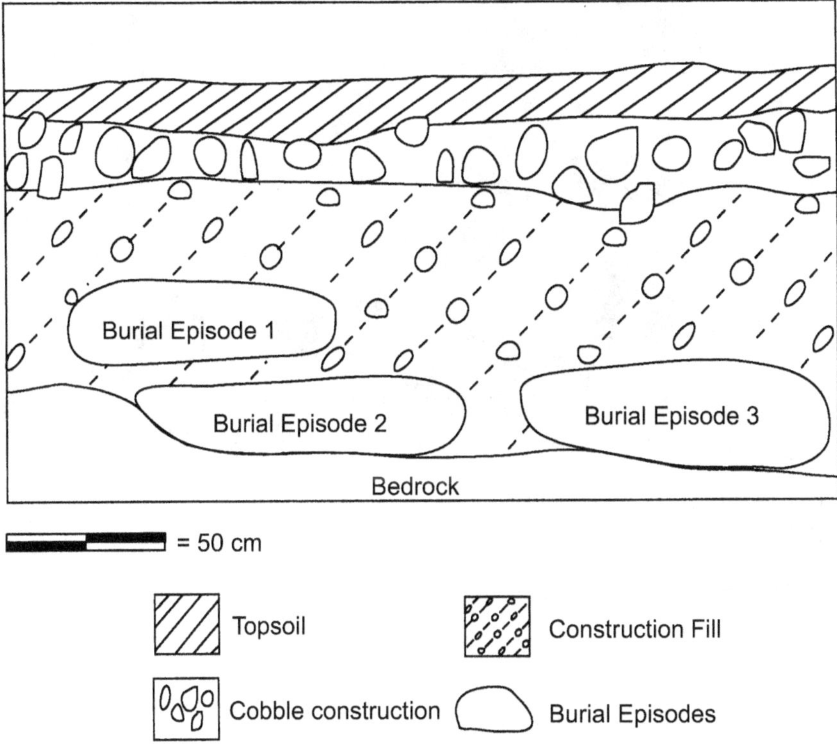

4.4: Schematic profile of excavation unit in which all three burial episodes occurred (drawn by R. Trachman).

Lauren Sullivan (2003) carried out the ceramic analysis for the Dancer Household Group, and Julie and Frank Saul (2003) performed the skeletal analysis. We present preliminary findings from both of these analyses along with additional artifact analysis and interpretations of mortuary remains.

Burial episode 1 is from the Late Classic, dating to the Tepeu 2-3 phase, and is associated with two whole vessels (Sullivan 2003). Skeletal data shows that episode 1 has a minimum number of individuals (MNI) of four, classified as one young adult (possible female), two other adults with no teeth recovered (therefore age was unassigned), and one child approximately twelve years in age (± 2½ years).

In addition to the two whole vessels, we recovered a shell ornament engraved with human features (Figure 4.5). The positioning of drill holes suggests that if the ornament was to be displayed so that the human

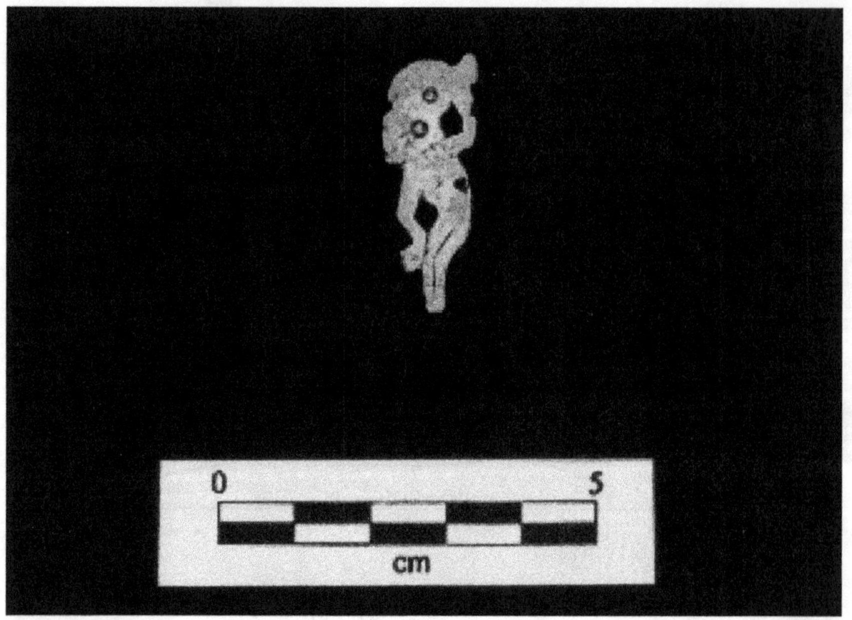

4.5: Anthropomorphic engraved shell ornament (photo by R. Trachman).

features would be upright, it was most likely sewn to a piece of cloth, clothing, or blanket (Figure 4.6).

In association with episode 2, two whole vessels were found dating to the Chicanel phase of the Late Preclassic (Sullivan 2003). An MNI of three was determined for episode 2, two of which are young adults and one is a young/middle adult (Saul and Saul 2003). Four greenstone beads were found in association with cranial fragments and the mandible of one of these adults.

Episode 3 also dates to the Chicanel phase with four whole vessels recovered (Sullivan 2003). This episode has the highest MNI with six individuals, consisting of two young adults and four children. One child died at age 2–4, two at age 3–4, and one at age 5–7 (Saul and Saul 2003). A high quantity of grave goods was recovered in episode 3, likely related to the greater number of people interred. These include one greenstone bead and an array of marine shell artifacts: three small shell disc beads (Figure 4.7), one irregular shell bead, seven tinklers (Figure 4.8), a small bivalve (pelecypod) with a drilled hole (Figure 4.9), a relatively unmodified univalve (gastropod) (Figure 4.9), and finally a larger bivalve (pelecypod) with at least two holes (Figure 4.10). The larger bivalve (Figure 4.11) is likely of the genus Spondylus and has a natural

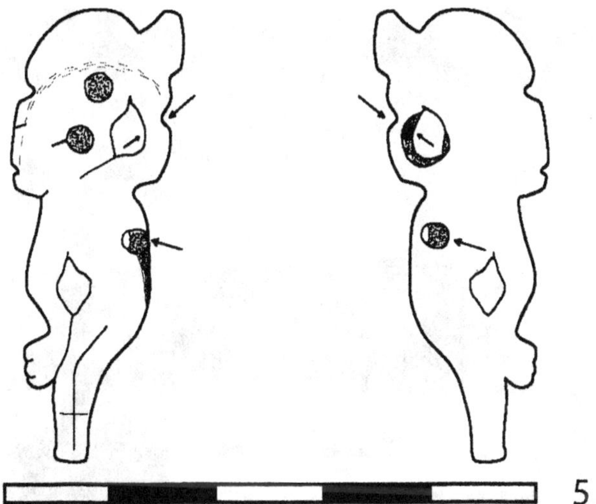

4.6: Engraved shell ornament with location and orientation of drilled holes noted (drawn by R. Trachman).

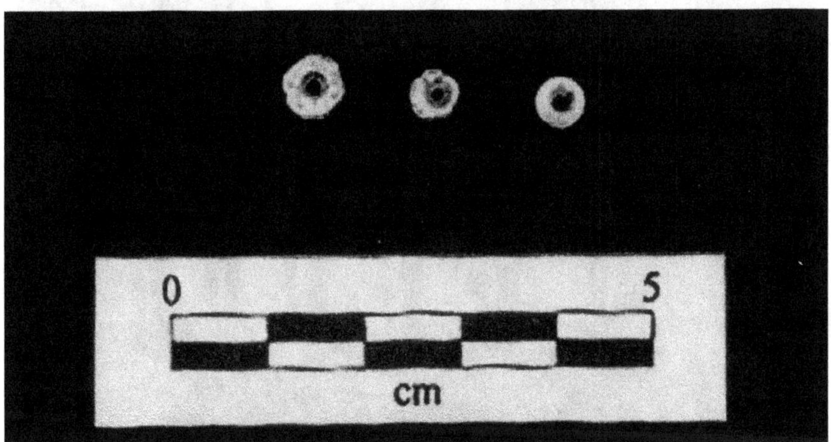

4.7: Three disc shell beads (photo by R. Trachman).

red band present around its rim. There are at least two drill holes discernable and two engraved lines on the inside of the shell rim (ventral side). The position of the drill holes and engraved marks indicates the likelihood that it hung as a pendant. It is this specific artifact along with its mortuary context that we will interpret. We believe this may be the gender symbol that Landa described girls' wearing on a cord around

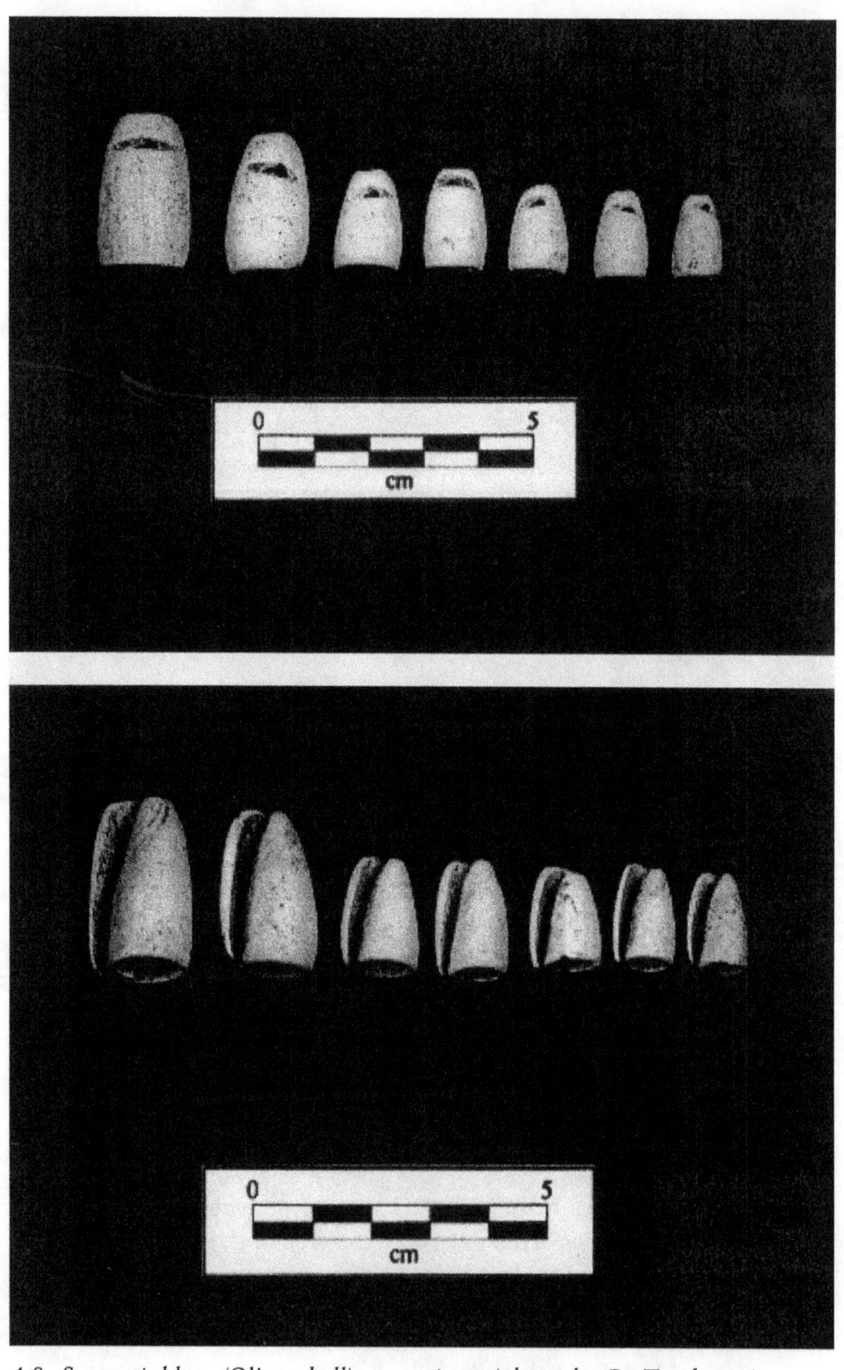

*4.8: Seven tinklers (*Oliva *shell), two views (photo by R. Trachman).*

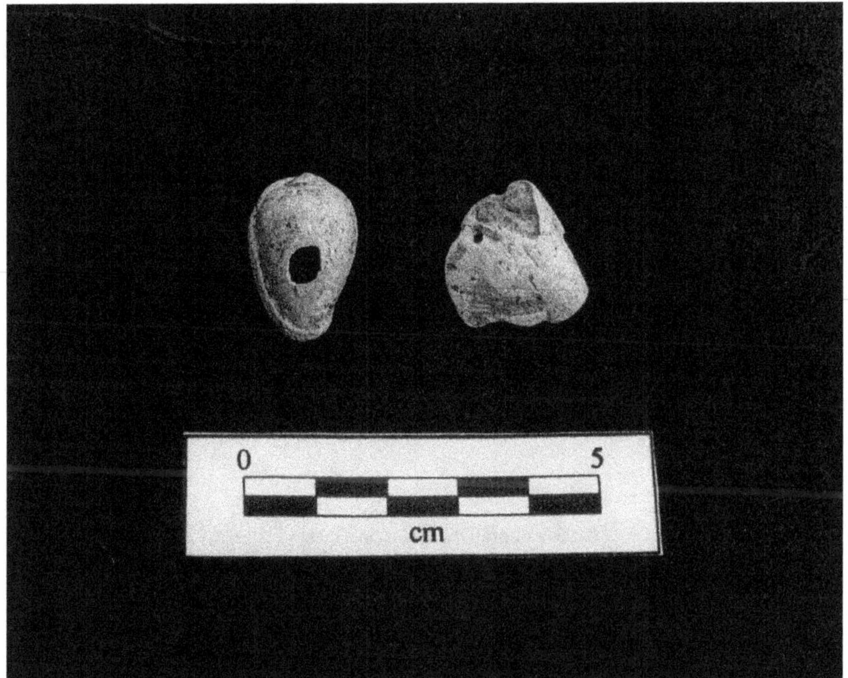

4.9: Left: *a univalve that is relatively unmodified;* right: *a small bivalve with one drilled hole (photo by R. Trachman).*

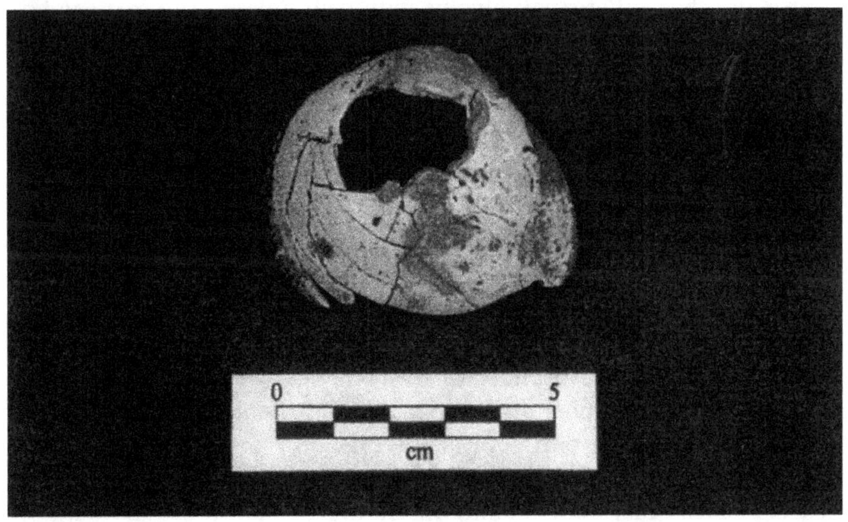

4.10: Larger bivalve Spondyllus (photo by R. Trachman).

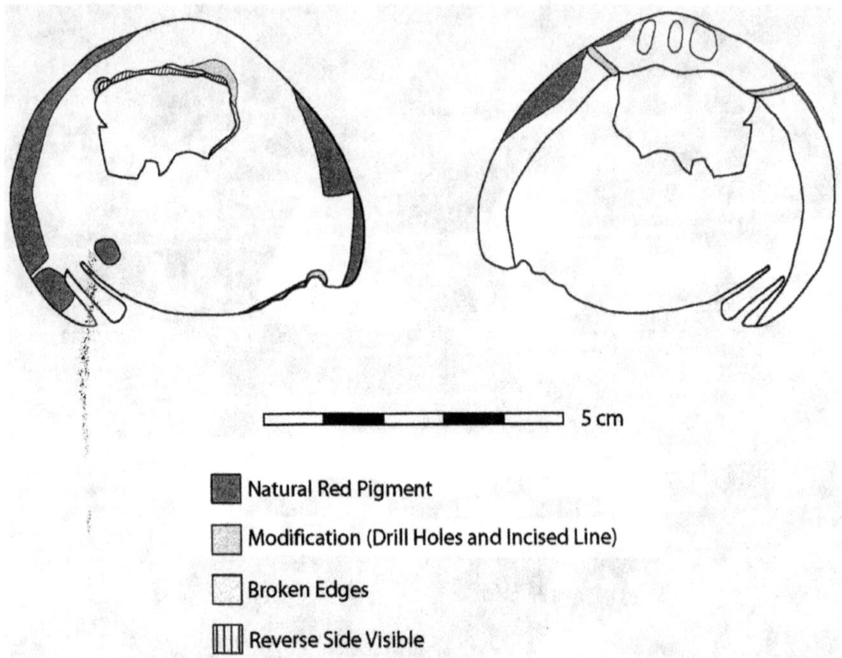

4.11: Line drawing of the larger bivalve Spondyllus; note the position of the drilled holes and the engraved lines on reverse side (figure drawn by R. Trachman).

their waist. The other small bivalve with drill holes found in episode 3 may also prove significant.

EXPRESSIONS OF GENDER IN LOWLAND MORTUARY DATA

It is tempting to make a direct interpretation of the data from the Dancer Household Group using the ethnohistoric record. A comparative analysis, however, may prove to be an important line of evidence in ascertaining or establishing the possibility of continuity in the specific practice of Maya children wearing gendered symbols. If the practice did indeed exist, then we can enhance our understanding of this single household deposit, address the continuity of this practice, and possibly begin to resolve some of the ambiguity in Friar Diego de Landa's work. With this in mind we turn to several published works on mortuary data from the Maya Lowlands. We consulted two site-specific sets of data from Cuello, Belize, and Yaxuna, Mexico, and one compilation of mortuary data for sixteen sites gathered from across the Maya Lowlands prior to 1988. For the purpose of analysis we examined data for all of those buried at these sites who fit the category of sub-adult, defined as all those under the age of twenty. Within this sample, sub-adult burials that contained offerings of shells similar to the Spondylus from the Dancer Household Group interested us the most. Since Landa describes a shell hanging from the waist, we specifically looked for marine shell pendants documented within the context of the pelvis of sub-adults in these studies.

The Children of Cuello

The Cuello mortuary data we consulted were published by Cynthia Robin (1989; Robin and Hammond 1991) in conjunction with the osteological analyses of Frank and Julie Saul (1991) gathered from 1975 to 1987. The sample comprises 142 people, the vast majority alive during the Preclassic period (Robin 1989:1; Saul and Saul 1991:134). The archaeology of Cuello, directed by Norman Hammond (1991), revealed occupation that began as early as the Middle Preclassic and lasted at least until the Late Classic. A systematic field recording system was used in excavation of the burials at Cuello (Robin 1989:5), and the detailed illustrations of grave goods proved to be a crucial factor in our considerations of children and gender symbols. The Sauls' osteological analysis both in the field and in the lab played a critical role in our examination, specifically in terms of age assessments.

Of the 142 people in the Cuello burial sample, approximately 17 percent (n = 24) are sub-adults. They range in age from only a few months old to nineteen years of age. A variety of materials accompanied these sub-adults in their interments, such as jade beads, shell in many forms, and ceramic vessels. Copious shell beads of several varieties were found with both adults and sub-adults. Other shell artifacts included engraved shell pendants and Spondylus bivalve pendants. In three cases marine bivalves with drill holes for pendant use were documented to have been on or very near the pelvises of sub-adults. Two of these were child burials: one age 2–4 years at death and one age 8–9 at death. Both of these children had Spondylus bivalve pendants identified at the pelvis and both are Late Preclassic in date. The third person with a bivalve pendant in this location was not a child and was sexed as male. This person was 55–59 years at the time of their death in the Late Preclassic. From drawings it appears that the three bivalve pendants are very similar in form to one another and to the Spondylus bivalve pendant found at the Dancer Household Group. A fourth possible individual from Cuello with a marine univalve pendant was 2–4 years old at death and dated to the Middle Preclassic. The exact location of the univalve pendant within the burial is not known, but it exhibits a form similar to the Spondylus pendants described earlier.

Child Burials at Yaxuna

The site of Yaxuna in Yucatán, Mexico, was investigated from 1986 to 1996 (Ardren 2002:71) under the direction of David Freidel (Freidel 1993). The site was occupied from the Middle Preclassic through the Postclassic periods (Ardren 2002:71). The research conducted during that time at Yaxuna revealed the remains of forty-two individuals (Ardren 2002:71). Twenty-nine of these date to the Late to Terminal Classic, providing some contrast in time to the evidence from Cuello. Once again, excellent field records and osteological analysis prove an important factor in the consideration of age determinations, burial goods, and their associations. The data presented here are derived primarily from final field reports and the osteological analysis of Sharon Bennett (Bennett 1992, 1993, 1994).

There are thirteen sub-adults from Yaxuna, which represent approximately 30 percent of the sample. They range in age from a few months to 15–21 years. Marine shell is abundant among the sub-adult Yaxuna burials, sometimes in the form of Spondylus or other marine bivalve shell pendants. As Ardren (2002:76) observed, juvenile females in the Yaxuna burial sample are accompanied by marine shell pendants. In four sub-adult burials the bivalve pendants were located on or near the pelvis, each dating to the Terminal Classic. Two of these four children died at 4+ years, one at 5–6 years, and one at 5–7. One additional marine bivalve pendant was found just above the disturbed crypt of a child 4–6 years of age, also from the Terminal Classic. Two additional sub-adult burials may have female gender symbols associated with them. One is a Terminal Classic burial of a fifteen-year-old with an undefined shell ornament. The other is an Early Classic burial of an infant within the age category of birth to 6 months. The infant is accompanied by a univalve pendant.

Welsh's Study

The third source for our comparative data is a compilation of burial data by W.B.M. Welsh (1988). The nature of the data presented is vastly different from that of Cuello and Yaxuna. Instead of data presented by the investigators themselves, Welsh gathered existing burial data from sixteen sites in the Maya Lowlands. The data were not gathered or recorded uniformly in the original reports. Welsh had the daunting task of trying to amass a diverse set of documents created by various investigators, each with his or her own set of research agendas.

In order to use Welsh's data in the present study we must overcome two problematic issues. The first concerns age categorizations for sub-adults. Since the research itself was not compiled specifically with regard to research questions about children or sub-adult age grades, the sub-adult age categories are quite broad. Welsh (1988:250) used three age groups for sub-adults: *infants* (less than two years of age at death); *child* (2–12 years of age at death); and *youth* (12–17 years of age at death). Therefore, rather than giving a specific age or range of age at death for each sub-adult, they were put into one of those three broad categories. This contrasts with the previous two data sets in which ages at death or an age range at death, as determined by osteological analyses, spanned only a few years.

A second issue has to do with the generalization of categories of shell artifacts found with each sub-adult. Welsh (1988:247) stated the number and type of artifacts found by each researcher but reported that these "should only be considered as approximate for some burials because the precise number of a specific type of grave good was not always provided by the original excavators." Often "shell," "bivalve," or "shell pendant" was used to describe a shell artifact found in a burial. Artifact illustrations verifying the actual type or form of shell artifacts were not included. Our interest concerns a very specific type of artifact, which required strict reliance on its presence or absence in burial contexts with good association information. As Welsh (1988:247) noted, the data that he presented did not include the provenience or association of each artifact because it was not always indicated in the excavation reports. As a result, we are unable to determine if the specific type of artifacts we are interested in occurred in clear association with sub-adult burials. The result is that in the frequent circumstance of multiple burials, specific artifacts are not associated with specific individuals.

What we can say about sub-adult burials from the Welsh study is somewhat limited yet interesting nonetheless. There were a total of 1,327 individuals represented in the study and, of those, 26 percent are sub-adults (n = 342). Only 14 of the sub-adults (4 percent) were able to be sexed by the analysts. The majority (n = 10) of those that were sexed fell in the *youth* category, 12–17 years of age at death. Interestingly, 70 percent (n = 7) of these sexed sub-adult *youths* had no shell buried with them. A total of 68 of the sub-adults (20 percent) in Welsh's study were buried with some kind of shell artifact, a surprisingly low number. This is also somewhat skewed by the fact that 45 percent of these occurred in multiple burials both with other children and other adults and no clear association is noted for the shell.

SEX, GENDER, AND MATERIAL CULTURE

If we consider only the most solid evidence from the comparative data, the forms of bivalve pendants at Cuello and Yaxuna are consistent with our case study as well as Landa's documentation. At both sites shell pendants were found clearly associated with specific individuals and located at the pelvis. The comparative data therefore reflects a likelihood of continuity in the practice of placing gender symbols on children. Specifically it reflects the practice of placing shell bivalve pendants at the waists of young females possibly as far back as the Preclassic (although admittedly few in numbers) and then again in the Terminal Classic period.

At Cuello two children clearly had female gender symbols and can be considered to be gendered female. They were 2–4 years and 8–9 years at the time of their deaths. No other shell pendants, bivalve or univalve, were found on or near the pelvises of sub-adults or adults, with the one male exception. The 2–4-year-old child with an unprovenienced marine univalve pendant could have also been a female child, even though the form is slightly different.

The 55–59-year-old man from Cuello with the Spondylus pendant is a bit of an enigma. Since the ancient Maya seem to have culturally constructed and intentionally imbued costume elements with specific gendered meaning, however, this person might have been of the male sex but gendered female.

The existence of female gender signifiers in the Preclassic may not be surprising given the discovery of the San Bartolo murals by William Saturno. Karl Taube (2005) recently discussed the distinct possibility that the murals serve as a text for the Maya creation myth that was later recorded in the Popol Vuh. The north wall mural, Taube (2005) offers, is the maize god in his resurrection coming out of the flower mountain accompanied by several young women. We further suggest that one of these young women is wearing a cord or belt around her waist with a red shell hanging in the front of her pelvis. She could have been a young prepubescent female, or she could have been performing as a young prepubescent female.

Given that the four shell pendants associated with Terminal Classic sub-adult burials at Yaxuna had the same form as those discussed earlier and were also placed near the pelvic regions of these individuals, the use of shell as a gender-marking adornment was also practiced in the Terminal Classic. Although recovered in a disturbed context, a fifth burial from Yaxuna is also very likely to be gendered female because of the presence of the shell by the pelvis. Therefore, at least five children, and possibly as many as seven, could be considered female in the Yaxuna sample. The five most clearly female children according to their material symbols were all in the cumulative age range of 4–7 years at the time of death.

The Dancer Household Group mortuary data, when viewed in light of ethnohistoric, ethnographic, and previous archaeological research, can be seen in a dynamic light. Determining the sex of child skeletal material is difficult, especially in the tropical forests of the Maya Lowlands where preservation of bone is poor. Yet the possibility that the ancient Maya used material culture to indicate the gender of children in mortuary contexts at the Dancer Household Group is realistic.

It is likely that at least one out of the four children in burial episode 3 was female in gender as signified by the red-rimmed Spondylus bivalve shell artifact associated with this individual (see Figures 4.10 and 4.11). This correlates well with the patterns at Cuello and Yaxuna and the ethnographic and ethnohistoric documentation. The larger Spondylus bivalve pendant is likely to be associated with the 5–7-year-old since the pendant was closest to her, yet no pelvises were preserved in any of the episode 3 burials. One of the other two children may also have had a female gender symbol, the smaller shell bivalve pendant. A clear association was not assigned for that artifact so it is impossible to attribute the pendant to either child.

We acknowledge that we have not addressed the male gender symbol at all. It is somewhat more problematic since white shell beads are ubiquitous in Maya burials and come in many different forms. In burial episode 3 at the Dancer Household Group, the proximity of the three shell disc beads to each other implies their use together as an adornment for one individual. Whether they were in the hair of one of the children is not clear given the poor preservation conditions.

As for burial episode 1 at the Dancer Household Group, the lack of evidence regarding gender information for the child interred in that multiple burial might also be explained in terms of the child's age. If the comparative data is any indication, this child may have already had its childhood gender symbols removed, transitioning into adult styles of dress and adornment.

Correlating the ages of the comparative archaeological data highlights an important point. At Cuello the two children with female gender ornaments were 2–4 and 8–9 years old at the time of their deaths, whereas at Yaxuna all five of the children found with female gender ornaments were in the range of 4–7 years old. At the Dancer Household Group the most likely gendered child was 5–7 years. Landa's writings were unclear as to the ages when placement and removal of the ornaments took place during the *caput sihil*. It was difficult to tell at the time of his observation whether they were placed at age 3–4 years, removed at age 3–4 years, or simply placed at some undesignated age and removed at *caput sihil*, which took place before the age of twelve. The comparative data collected thus far suggests that prior to the ethnohistoric period these symbols were worn from the age of two years at the earliest and nine years at the latest.

Chronology may also be a factor in pinpointing an understanding of the specific ages of children during practices of gender socialization. In our comparative data the Cuello sample is Preclassic in date and the Yaxuna female child burials are primarily Terminal Classic. The Dancer Household Group mirrors this pattern with child burials in both the Preclassic (burial episodes 2 and 3) and Late to Terminal Classic (burial episode 1). It is possible that the ages in which the symbols were placed and removed changed over time.

We do not propose that an indiscriminate continuity exists from the ethnohistoric record back in time to the Preclassic. Instead we support a measure of continuity in the specific practice of symbolic gender costume ornaments for children. Evidently the practice of socializing gender identities with material culture symbols did take place in the Preclassic and Late to Terminal Classic periods of Maya society. It is also possible that the ambiguities of Landa's work could be further addressed through additional archaeological research.

ACKNOWLEDGMENTS

First we thank Traci Ardren for organizing the AAA session where this work was first presented, and both Traci Ardren and Scott Hutson for their hard work as the editors of this important and timely volume. We are truly grateful for their thoughtful and valuable comments on earlier drafts of the manuscript. We especially thank the Institute of Archaeology, Belmopan, Belize, for allowing us to do this work in northwestern Belize. Funding was provided by the Programme for Belize Archaeological Project (PfBAP), the University of Texas International Education Fee Scholarship, the Dean Barbara Myers liberal arts scholarship fund, and the Frances Meskell Memorial Scholarship fund. All illustrations are courtesy of the PfBAP. We express our thanks to our friends Frank and Julie Saul for their osteological analysis and Lauren Sullivan for her ceramic analysis. Many thanks also to David Friedel and Charles Suhler for providing copies of Yaxuna field reports. Finally, we are grateful to the anonymous reviewers for their important comments on an earlier draft of the manuscript. All mistakes or omissions are our own.

REFERENCES CITED

Ardren, Traci
2002 Death Became Her: Images of Female Power from Yaxuna Burials. In *Ancient Maya Women,* ed. T. Ardren, 68–88. Walnut Creek, CA: Altamira Press.

Ariès, Philippe
1962 *Centuries of Childhood.* London: Jonathan Cape.

Bennett, Sharon
1992 Burials at Yaxuna, Yucatán. In *The Selz Foundation Yaxuna Project: Final Report of the 1991 Field Season,* ed. D. Freidel, C. Suhler, and R. Cobos P., 82–91. Dallas: Southern Methodist University, Department of Anthropology.
1993 1992 Burials from Yaxuna, Yucatán. In *The Selz Foundation Yaxuna Project: Final Report of the 1992 Field Season,* ed. C. Suhler and D. Freidel, 144–164. Dallas: Southern Methodist University Press, Department of Anthropology.
1994 The Burial Excavations at Yaxuna in 1993. In *The Selz Foundation Yaxuna Project: Final Report of the 1993 Field Season,* 89–105. Dallas: Southern Methodist University, Department of Anthropology.

Bourdieu, Pierre
1977 *Outline of a Theory of Practice.* Cambridge: Cambridge University Press.

Brokaw, Nicholas V.L., and Elizabeth P. Mallory
1993 *Vegetation of the Rio Bravo Conservation and Management Area, Belize.* Manomet, MA: Manomet Bird Observatory.

Dietler, Michael, and Ingrid Herbich
1998 *Habitus,* Techniques, Style: An Integrated Approach to the Social Understanding of Material Culture and Boundaries. In *The Archaeology of Social Boundaries,* ed. M. T. Stark, 232–263. Washington, DC: Smithsonian Institution Press.

Freidel, David
1993 Introduction: Research at Yaxuna in 1992. In *The Selz Foundation Yaxuna Project: Final Report of the 1992 Field Season,* ed. C. Suhler

and D. Freidel, i–v. Dallas: Southern Methodist University, Department of Anthropology.

Gilchrist, Roberta
1999 *Gender and Archaeology: Contesting the Past.* London: Routledge.

Guiteras H., Calixta
1960 *La familia tzotzil en la salud y en la enfermedad.* Mexico City: Tlatoani.

Hageman, Jon B., and Jon C. Lohse
2003 Heterarchy, Corporate Groups, and Late Classic Resource Management in Northwestern Belize. In *Heterarchy, Political Economy, and the Ancient Maya: The Three Rivers Region of the East-Central Yucatan Peninsula,* ed. V. L. Scarborough, N. Dunning, and F. Valdez Jr., 109–121. Tucson: University of Arizona Press.

Hammond, Gawain, and Norman Hammond
1981 Child's Play: A Distorting Factor in Archaeological Distribution. *American Antiquity* 46(3):634–636.

Hammond, Norman, ed.
1991 *Cuello: An Early Maya Community in Belize.* Cambridge: Cambridge University Press.

Joyce, Rosemary A.
1999 Social Dimensions of Pre-Classic Burials. In *Social Patterns in Pre-Classic Mesoamerica: A Symposium at Dumbarton Oaks, 9 and 10 October 1993,* ed. D. C. Grove and R. A. Joyce, 15–47. Washington, DC: Dumbarton Oaks.
2000a Girling the Girl and Boying the Boy: The Production of Adulthood in Ancient Mesoamerica. *World Archaeology* 31(3):473–483.
2000b *Gender and Power in Prehispanic Mesoamerica.* Austin: University of Texas Press.

Joyce, Rosemary A., and Julia Hendon
2000 Heterarchy, History, and Material Reality: "Communities" in Late Classic Honduras. In *The Archaeology of Communities: A New World Perspective,* ed. M. Canuto and J. Yaeger, 143–160. London: Routledge.

Landa, Diego de
[1566] 1978 *Yucatan Before and After the Conquest.* Trans. and ed. William Gates. New York: Dover Publications.

Lohse, Jon C.
2001 The Social Organization of a Late Classic Maya Community: Dos Hombres, Northwestern Belize. Ph.D. dissertation, The University of Texas at Austin.

Moore, Henrietta
1988 *Feminism and Anthropology.* Minneapolis: University of Minnesota Press.

1994 *A Passion for Difference: Essays in Anthropology and Gender.* Bloomington: Indiana University Press.

Restall, Matthew, and John F. Chuchiak IV

2002 A Reevaluation of the Authenticity of Fray Diego de Landa's *Relación de las cosas de Yucatán. Ethnohistory* 49(3):651–669.

Robin, Cynthia

1989 *Preclassic Maya Burials at Cuello, Belize.* BAR International Series 480. Oxford: British Archaeological Reports.

Robin, Cynthia, and Norman Hammond

1991 Ritual and Ideology. In *Cuello: An Early Maya Community in Belize,* ed. N. Hammond, 204–231. Cambridge: Cambridge University Press.

Saul, Frank P., and Julie Mather Saul

1991 The Preclassic Population of Cuello. In *Cuello: An Early Maya Community in Belize,* ed. N. Hammond, 134–158. Cambridge: Cambridge University Press.

Saul, Julie Mather, and Frank P. Saul

1997 The Preclassic Skeletons from Cuello. In *Bones of the Maya: Studies of Ancient Skeletons,* ed. S. L. Whittington and D. M. Reed, 28–50. Washington, DC: Smithsonian Institution Press.

2003 Interim Osteological Report, Operations 28 and 29. Manuscript on file, Department of Anthropology, University of Texas at Austin.

Sharer, Robert J.

1994 *The Ancient Maya,* 5th ed. Stanford: Stanford University Press.

1996 *Daily Life in Maya Civilization.* Westport, CT: Greenwood Press.

Sofaer Derevenski, Joanna

1994 Where are the Children? Accessing Children in the Past. *Archaeological Review from Cambridge* 13(2):7–20.

1997a Engendering Children, Engendering Archaeology. In *Invisible People and Processes: Writing Gender and Childhood into European Archaeology,* ed. J. Moore and E. Scott, 192–202. London: Leicester University Press.

1997b Linking Age and Gender as Social Variables. *Ethnographische-Archäeologische Zeitschrift* 38:485–493.

2000 Material Culture Shock: Confronting Expectations in the Material Culture of Children. In *Children and Material Culture,* ed. J. Sofaer Derevenski, 3–16. London: Routledge.

Sørensen, Marie Louise Stig

2000 *Gender Archaeology.* Cambridge: Polity Press.

Sullivan, Lauren A.

2003 Interim Ceramic Analysis Report, Operations 26, 28, and 29. Manuscript on file, Department of Anthropology, University of Texas at Austin.

Taube, Karl
2005 San Bartolo and Sacred Narrative of the Late Preclassic Maya. Paper presented at the 29th Annual Maya Meetings at Texas, Austin.

Thompson, J. Eric S.
[1954] 1970 *Maya History and Religion.* Norman: University of Oklahoma Press.

Tozzer, Alfred M., trans. and ed.
1941 *Landa's "Relación de las Cosas de Yucatán."* Papers of the Peabody Museum of American Archaeology and Ethnology, vol. 18. Cambridge: Harvard University.

Trachman, Rissa M.
2003 Household Excavations in the Dos Hombres Settlement Area: 2002 Season Preliminary Report. Manuscript on file, Department of Anthropology, University of Texas at Austin.

Trachman, Rissa M., and Fred Valdez Jr.
2001 Expressions of Childhood: Life and Death among the Ancient Maya. Paper presented at the 100th Annual Meeting of the American Anthropological Association, Washington, D.C.

Valdez, Fred, Jr., and Richard E.W. Adams
1995 The Programme for Belize Archaeological Project: An Overview of Research Goals. Manuscript on file, Mesoamerican Archaeological Research Laboratory, Austin, TX.

Welsh, W.B.M.
1988 *An Analysis of Classic Lowland Maya Burials.* BAR International Series 409. Oxford: British Archaeological Reports.

Wilkie, Laurie
2000 Not Merely Child's Play: Creating a Historical Archaeology of Children and Childhood. In *Children and Material Culture,* ed. J. Sofaer Derevenski, 100–114. London: Routledge.

Part III

CHILDHOOD IN PRACTICE

5

CHILDREN NOT AT CHUNCHUCMIL

A Relational Approach to Young Subjects

Scott R. Hutson

INTRODUCTION

If we define childhood as an interpretation of what it means to be a child, archaeological research on childhood, like all hermeneutic investigations, begins even before we initially focus our attention on the research problem. Since our own life experiences have already given us a notion of what childhood is, when we pose the question of childhood in the past we cannot avoid "pre-loading" the question with an interpretation. This interpretation often consists of the minimal assumption that children are young.[1] This starting assumption has guided the choice of what materials count as evidence of childhood. In prehistoric archaeology, commonly cited evidence of childhood includes sub-adult burials, artistic representations of people who are small (but not dwarf-like) or baby-like (in terms of body fat or limb/head proportions), poor quality artifacts presumably produced by novices, and artifacts occasionally interpreted as toys, such as figurines and miniature versions of tools.

But how can we discuss childhood at a site containing none of these forms of evidence? What if a long-running archaeological project fails to uncover anything that falls into what might be called "direct" evidence of young people—miniatures, toys, sub-adult burials, representations of youth? In such a case, can archaeologists write about childhood in the prehistoric past? These are some of the questions faced by the Pakbeh Regional Economy Program, which over the past ten years has focused on the ancient urban center of Chunchucmil and its immediate neighbors on the northwest corner of the Yucatán Peninsula, Mexico (see Figure 1.1). Although Pakbeh researchers have gathered data about subsistence (Beach 1998), commerce (Dahlin et al. 1998; Dahlin and Ardren 2002; Dahlin 2003), households (Hutson, Magnoni, and Stanton 2004), settlement patterns (Vlcek, Garza T., and Kurjack 1978; Magnoni, Hutson, and Stanton, 2002), warfare (Dahlin 2000), and ritual (Ardren and Hutson 2002), among other things, research at Chunchucmil has yet to produce direct evidence of young people.

This lack of evidence leaves two options. The first option is to ignore the topic of childhood altogether. The problem with this option recalls the problem identified two decades ago by feminist archaeologists initiating a critical archaeology of gender: we can not go further wrong than to ignore a whole class of people while waiting for evidence of their actions (Conkey and Spector 1984; Scott 1997:5; Kamp 2001). Much like engendering the past (Conkey and Gero 1991:17) or sexualizing the past (Voss and Schmidt 2000:6–7), writing children into the past should begin—*cannot help but begin,* in fact—before the "smoking gun" of direct evidence has been found. To take no stance on childhood is a stance in itself, an empty stance that silently reproduces current understandings of childhood and diverts us from asking productive and transformative questions about differences between people in the past (Conkey and Gero 1991:12).

A second problem with the idea of avoiding the topic of childhood because of the lack of evidence is that no archaeological record lacks evidence of children. Given that half of the living individuals in most prehistoric populations were under the age of twenty and perhaps a third under the age of ten, no one can deny that young people contributed to the archaeological record at Chunchucmil and elsewhere (Chamberlain 1997:249; Sofaer Derevenski 1997; Grimm 2000:53). They ate from (and probably broke some of) the pots archaeologists recover, they wore down the buildings and floors archaeologists unearth, and they contributed their labor to the households archaeologists reconstruct. The answer to the question of whether archaeologists can see the material effects of children in pre-Hispanic Mesoamerica "is clear and unequivocal: yes" (Joyce 1994). As a result, archaeologists at Chunchucmil and other places that lack direct evidence are authorized, if not obliged, to discuss young people. The abundant traces of children in fact trouble the distinction between direct and indirect forms of evidence.

The certainty that young people contributed to the archaeological record leads to the second option. The second option is to think differently about what childhood might be and what counts as evidence for it. One way of putting this strategy into practice involves methodological work: refining the approach to finding young people in the past. Such a refinement might consist of moving beyond the question, can we see young people? and asking instead, how do we approach an archaeological record to which all past actors contributed and isolate just that portion of the record for which young people were responsible?

Unfortunately, unwanted theoretical assumptions underlie this particular refinement. Any attempt to isolate the archaeological traces of young people from those of everyone else assumes that past actors can be isolated; that the human subject is an independent entity. This attempt also assumes that there is a domain of activity that is exclusively childlike and that this domain will generate the archaeological residues—the "smoking guns"—so fervently desired. These assumptions about a separate domain of childhood justify the distinction between direct and indirect evidence. But the idea that children have their own domain is precisely the kind of assumption that a study of children in the past should question. We must first ask, does childhood exist as a meaningful category of difference in the culture under study? If so, how did it come about? How is the line between childhood and other forms of subjecthood maintained?

These points about methods for finding children underscore the tight interconnection of method and theory. They also suggest that the search for new ways of identifying young people in the past requires theoretical refinement. Defining childhood in new ways or changing the questions about childhood might draw attention to previously overlooked aspects of the archaeological record. The importance of theoretical reflection—in this case the importance of keeping an open mind to unexpected perspectives on childhood—is another lesson learned from the archaeology of gender. Without critical reflection on the concept of childhood, we unwittingly allow our own unquestioned, historically particular notions of childhood to guide and shape what we learn about childhood in the past; we take for granted precisely the kind of statements that a study of childhood should challenge. This imposition of the present on the past prevents us from recognizing conceptions of childhood that are different from our own, and without knowledge of these alternative possibilities we lose potential ground from which to critique the naturalness of social formations in the present.

This chapter begins by developing a relational model of childhood that stresses the point that people develop not as independent subjects thinking their way though the world, but as nodes in an interconnected network of places, things, and other people. This model derives from post-Cartesian theories of ontology (Heidegger [1927] 1996), of practice (Bourdieu 1977), and of dwelling (Ingold 2000a, 2000b, 2000c) and resonates with a number of recent studies showing that personhood among the ancient Maya was relational and sociocentric (Monaghan 1998; Houston and Taube 2000; Gillespie 2001; Meskell and Joyce 2003). The resulting conception of childhood helps reconsider the relation between people and the built environment when discussing the renovation of architectural complexes at Chunchucmil. Following the trend in human geography that sees the spatial as always already the social (see Pred 1990; Rodman 1992), relations between people and buildings are also relations between people and people. After discussing architectural renovations, I present evidence of child's play in abandoned houses in Chunchucmil. Play in abandoned buildings foregrounds two ways in which architecture mediates relations between different actors. The first relation is between children playing in abandoned buildings and the people who lived in these buildings before abandonment. The second is between children and the elders from whom they took leave while playing in abandoned buildings. The chapter concludes with a discussion of how we might think about relations between this second pair of subjects.

APPROACHING CHILDREN

The first step in a theoretical refinement to the concept of childhood is to clarify modern understandings of childhood. The child, according to sociologist Frank Musgrove (cited in Ward 1978:vi), "was invented at the same time as the steam engine." According to Philippe Ariès (cited in James, Jenks, and Prout 1998:4), the roots of the modern concept of childhood began in mid-eighteenth-century Europe, when adults of the middle and upper classes began to think of children as a different category of being than themselves. My goal in citing these startling claims is not to preclude a deep history of childhood. In fact, as Byron Hamann argues in Chapter 8, historians have shown that early modern Europeans and their predecessors did indeed have a concept of childhood, although it was different from modern Western concepts. Rather, my goal is simply to call attention to the fact that even within the same historical tradition, the boundary between adults and children shifts over time. The fluidity of this boundary highlights the fluidity of the two categories on either side and cautions us against assuming that there is an unchanging essence to either childhood or adulthood.

Yet there are many essential understandings of children—child as angelic, child as evil, child as tabula rasa—and they are all what Allison James, Chris Jenks, and Alan Prout (1998) call "pre-sociological." In their book *Theorizing Childhood,* these authors move away from attempts to understand children by reference to an inherent essence or nature and encourage a social and phenomenological approach in which children are defined by their context in the world and their interactions with others. Children are complex beings caught up in and constituted through their relationships with people, things, and a broad spectrum of social, political, historical, and moral contexts (1998:27, 136). Thus, the exact nature of childhood cannot be specified in advance. The only certainty is that childhood will be as plural and diverse as the many worlds in which it is constructed (1998:27).

If childhood is relational, then elucidating the experience of childhood requires consideration of how children interact with people, things, and spaces. I approach these interactions from the perspective of existential phenomenology. In this perspective, interaction cannot be understood as a self-contained child coming into contact with other self-contained entities. The notion of a "self-contained child" is problematic because interactions with other people and things are said to produce the child (Dreyfus 1991). Martin Heidegger ([1927] 1996) has argued that for humans the primary form of being is not containment and detachment from the world but rather a directedness toward and involvement with it. Only when actions go wrong does a person step back from involvement with the world and begin to see oneself as separate from the world. The notion of a disengaged child contemplating entities outside the self is therefore a secondary form of being that is impoverished by the breakdown of the primary way of relating to the world. Likewise, the notion of "self-contained objects" is also problematic. In our everyday lives, things only come to be recognized as things once they are swept up in human interactions (Heidegger [1927] 1996; Latour 1983). In other words, things are entangled in and interwoven with people and gain their own complex life histories as a result of this entanglement (Heidegger 1996; Latour 1996). Insofar as people are partial products of the surroundings in which they live, it becomes difficult to separate people from the world that they inhabit.

Treating children as relational subjects highlights the idea that there is nothing inherently special about children. Thus, title of this chapter—"Children Not at Chunchucmil"—does not mean we lack evidence to talk about children at ancient Chunchucmil, but that *children are not children.* They are people. Just like adults, they are agents in interactive encounters. Thus, as the title of this book anticipates, the experience of childhood is thoroughly social. Although biological models of development help establish the range of possible experience, children's competence, confidence, knowledge, and interactions vary according to social context (Mayall 1994b:118).

In taking this position, I do not imply that there can be no difference between adults and children. Rather, I suggest that what children may lack with respect to adults—such as wisdom and economic resources—is socially constituted, not a given, and therefore infinitely variable (see also Sofaer Derevenski 1997, 2000). In some cases, children may be assessed not by what they lack but by what they uniquely possess. For example, Bill Sillar (1994) demonstrated that among the Inca, cultural perceptions of age included the belief that children were in a uniquely powerful position because of their association with fertility and their enhanced ability to communicate with the deities (see also Juan Alberto Román Berrellaza and Ximena Chávez Balderas, Chapter 9).

In reconsidering the dichotomy between children and adults, I also do not mean to suggest that children and adults are biologically identical. Rather, I imply that identity is underdetermined by biology; that age-related differences in bodies, such as height or reproductive capacity, do not set the foundation for understanding differences between people. First, biology does not fully determine the experience or meaning of childhood (Sofaer Derevenski 1997, 2000; Buchli and Lucas 2000:131), just as sex does not fully determine gender. Second, cultural assumptions about age shape our understandings of biology (James, Jenks, and Prout 1998:150–151), just as gender shapes our understandings of sex (Butler 1990).

Using Diego de Landa's *Relación de las Cosas de Yucatán,*[2] Rosemary Joyce (1994) has presented an account of childhood in Yucatán during the Contact period that resonates with the relational model developed here. After birth, young people passed through up to three stages before becoming adults. At each stage, boys and girls were actively marked by specific clothing, adornments, and bodily modifications, and participated in different rituals and contexts of training and education.

Children did not reach adulthood passively by natural processes of growth but by cultural achievement, the culmination of a long, material transformation of raw infants into socially produced agents.

Although in this model children are seen as raw material that undergoes transformation, the production of children also reproduces adulthood. Drawing analogy to Judith Butler's (1993) discussion of how alternative sexualities, although targeted by discrimination, make heterosexuality intelligible, the line that defines the limits of what is considered childish also defines and marks the limits of adulthood. In other words, the constitution of childhood is also the constitution of adulthood. Thus, the relationships in a relational model of childhood are two-way: children are formed through their relations with others just as others are formed through their relations with children. According to Anthony Giddens (1979:139), "The unfolding of childhood is not time elapsing just for the child: it is time elapsing for its parental figures, and for all other members of society; the socialization involved is not simply that of the child, but of the parents and others with whom the child is in contact, and whose conduct is influenced by the child just as the latter's is by theirs in the continuity of interaction." This quote makes clear the point that children are not powerless. They impact and influence their social environment, even when they are not intentionally attempting to do so (Buckingham 1994; Mayall 1994b:116–117; Mizoguchi 2000:142; Wilkie 2000:107).

These notions of relationality further trouble the distinction between direct and indirect evidence of children. An object that helps identify children implicitly identifies adults or other subjects. If direct means that only children were involved, then sub-adult burials, a seemingly direct form of evidence for childhood, are surely not direct because people other than children performed the burial. Likewise, artistic representations of children are also not direct since people other than children were often involved in the creation of the representation.

CHILDREN AND BUILT SPACE

Among the various archaeologists who have adopted a relational perspective, Joanna Sofaer Derevenski (2000:9) produces an eloquent summary: "Social life is not a pure construction of meaning but mutually constructed from heterogeneous materials, including bodies, technology, material culture and minds, each of which enrolls and orders the others in fluid and shifting combinations." The phrase "fluid and shifting" is worth emphasizing because it implies that the process of subjectification does not have a fixed outcome or teleology. Reflecting on the Aztecs, Rosemary Joyce (1999) showed that parents attempted to transform their offspring from raw material to the finished, adult form. Yet, as Joyce (2001) notes in her study of Formative-period burials at Tlatilco, not even death, much less the attainment of adult status, terminates the process of becoming. Human subjectivity is always emerging, always growing (Ingold 2000a:144). Of the heterogeneous materials involved in the process of subjectification at Chunchucmil, I focus first on space and then on people.

When a newborn child enters the world, its relationship with physical space is one of the most formative encounters in which it finds itself. James Gibson (1966), the pioneer of ecological psychology, proposed many decades ago that things outside of the body help infants develop a sense of physical limits. In other words, understanding of bodily existence in space is not simply "given internally by a kinesthetic sense mediated by muscle and joint receptors" (Butterworth 1995:88), but through visual, auditory, and tactile cues that come from outside the body. Since the experience of other things enables self-definition, the development of a sense of self is a product of experience in the world. But perception is not passive. Infants achieve self-perception by actively engaging their surroundings through moving, touching, sniffing, and listening. In short, learning is not the reception of sensations, it is the education of attention (Gibson 1979:254). Attention to things in the world is educated by the way those things respond to active engagement with them.

Finding a footing in the world is like fitting into a cramped space. This act of fitting presupposes a give and take between people and space. An engagement with space is thus dialogical: competence depends on establishing a rhythm with surroundings. Charles Taylor (1999) argues that dialogue and rhythm with the physical environment are like the harmony between two dance partners. Each side must accommodate the other. To become able actors, children must develop a perceptual sensitivity to the flow of everyday actions, things, and places. This sensitivity allows children not only to discern and respond to slight changes in setting, but also to determine whether the response calls for self-adjustment or allows an adjustment of the setting (Ingold 2000a:147). This ability to sense the changes in rhythm and carry oneself accordingly is precisely what Pierre Bourdieu (1977:10) refers to as practical knowledge and can be understood as a "feel for the game."

From this perspective, the built environment and lived space are fruitful archaeological avenues toward the experience of childhood. Because a child's movements are in dialogue with the physical surroundings and, following Gibson, because these physical surroundings are key to developing a sense of bodily existence, the physical surroundings, such as built environments, are engrained in the child. Insofar as the imprint of objects and places cannot be extracted from a child, built environments and children merge into a single, relational subject. Although children are born into built environments that they did not build, they incorporate those environments into their sense of self by dwelling in them and creating their place in the world through them. They have taken them up in their sense of propriety and will reproduce them when, later in life, they are entrusted with their maintenance. It is in this sense that I make the counterintuitive claim that children and their physical surroundings mutually construct each other. Architecture shapes children's sensibilities and, roughly following these sensibilities, children will later grow up and physically reshape the architecture.

The east structure of the 'Aak houselot at Chunchucmil (Figure 5.1) illustrates this point. This particular houselot, located in a dense residential neighborhood southwest of the site center, was occupied for perhaps 150 years during the latter part of the Early Classic and the early part of the Late Classic (500–650 CE) (Hutson 2004). The east structure faces an artificially raised patio with residential structures on the north, west, and south sides of the patio (Figure 5.2). For most of its history, the eastern structure consisted of a small platform that contained richly adorned burials and small compartments for the storage of ritual paraphernalia. The east structure was the ritual focus and persistent material manifestation of the identity and solidarity of the people who lived in the 'Aak group (Hutson, Magnoni, and Stanton 2004).

The eastern structure of the 'Aak group was renovated at least four times after it was originally built (Figure 5.3). This suggests that the renovations to the east structure could have occurred with the passage of each generation. When the next generations of the household renovated the building, they were not simply following a blueprint but were using their practical knowledge accumulated from childhood. Since, following Rosemary Joyce's model of childhood in Yucatán, older boys may have lived away from the homes of their parents, practical knowledge of architecture came from living both within and outside of the group compound. As Figure 5.3 shows, the renovations of the east structure respected the original position and orientation of the building, enlarging it but not beyond the bounds of the conceivable, which were inculcated over time through use and interaction.

At first glance, a disengaged, mental activity like planning the renovation of a building may seem completely unrelated to the bodily en-

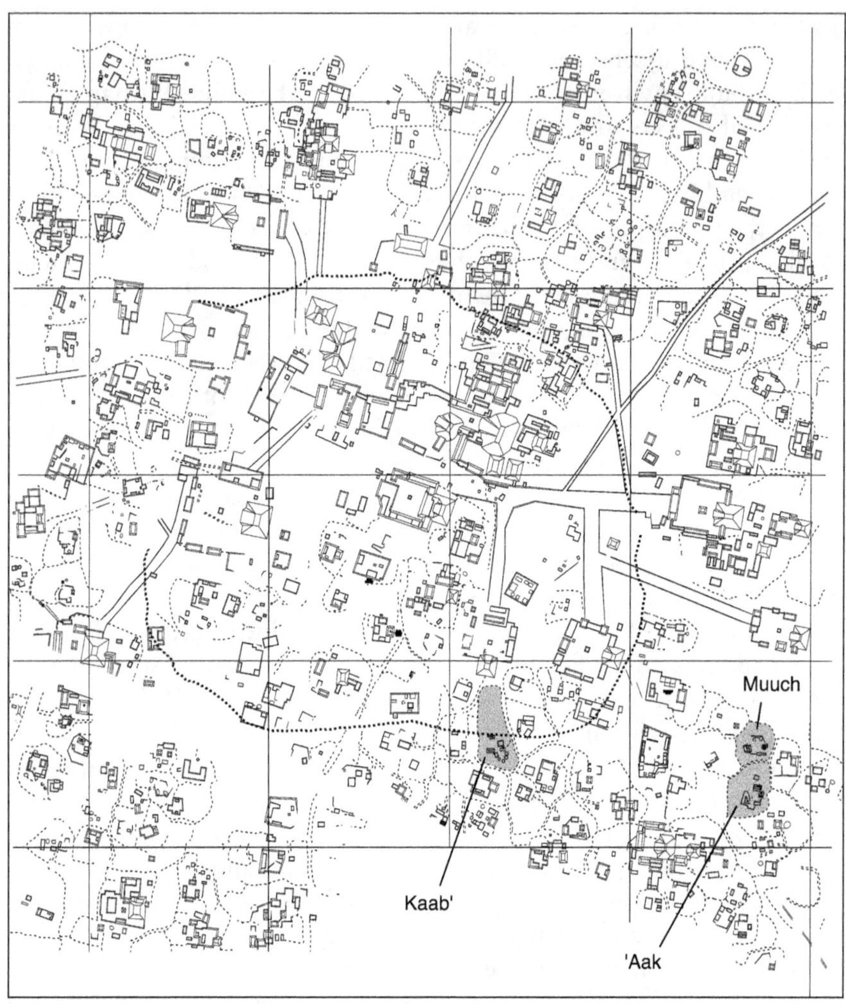

5.1: Map of central Chunchucmil with the 'Aak, Muuch, and Kaab' groups highlighted in gray. The grid is oriented to north and each grid square measures 250 x 250 meters.

gagements through which children come to be people. To paraphrase Pierre Bourdieu (1977:91), however, the mind is born of the world of objects. The subject does not appear sui generis, independent of objects, waiting to confront them. In other words, the world is the homeland of thought (Merleau Ponty 1962:24). The child's bodily interactions with the world become a basis for its cognized understanding of it (Lave 1990). Learning comes from doing, through trial and error, not by mas-

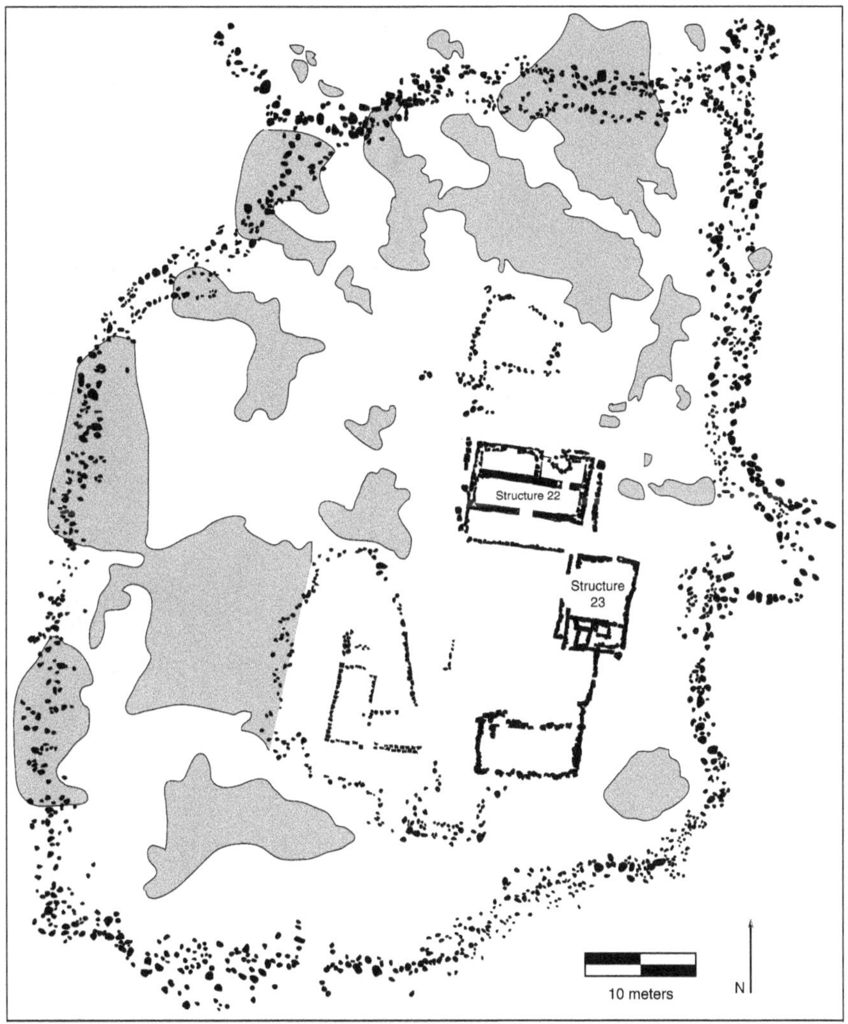

5.2: 'Aak houselot. Black dots represent stones, gray areas represent bedrock.

tering a set of rules and representations prior to practical activity (Ingold 2000b). This is not to say that people never relate to the world through abstract thoughts, concepts, and beliefs, as when drafting a blueprint for a building that does not yet exist. Yet dwelling in the world is the precondition for thinking about the world abstractly (Heidegger 1971:146–148; Ingold 2000c).

In summary, children carry with them the imprint of the built environment. When they become adults and build or renovate their own

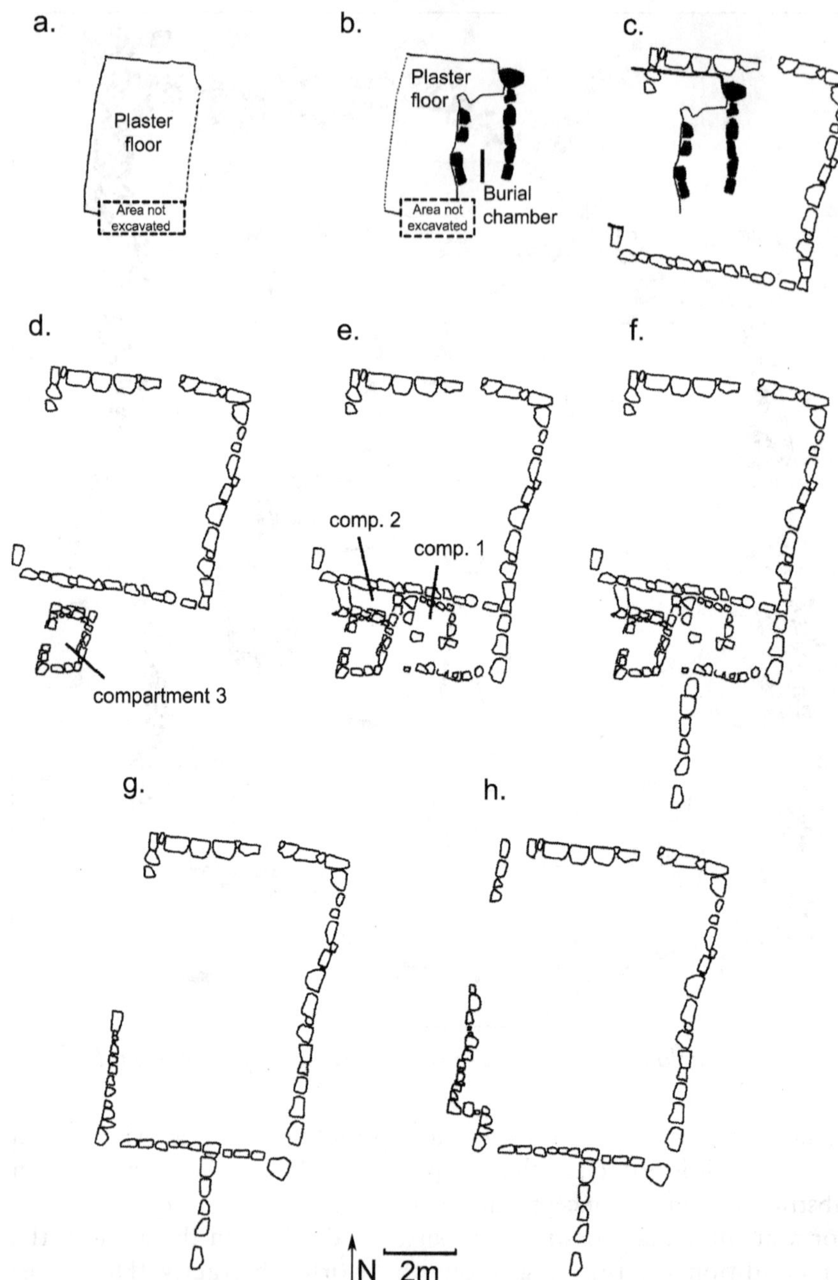

5.3: *Consecutive stages of construction in Structure 23 of the 'Aak group.*

structures, the sensibilities inculcated by the specific structures in which they first dwelled guide their work. Yet these sensibilities do not dictate the exact result: newer structures at Chunchucmil do not exactly replicate older ones. Dwelling is a skill that allows for a margin of creative improvisation; it "is flexibly responsive to ever-variable environmental conditions" (Ingold 2000a:147). At Chunchucmil, variations in environmental conditions would arise from exposure to other buildings as children began to move beyond their houselots. What differentiates children and the structures they eventually build is the extent to which their life histories are intertwined through the shared experience of inhabiting particular places. Thus, people and the outcome of their practices differ as a result of their varied knowledges and positionings (Hendon 2000).

ENCOUNTERS IN THE RUINS: POST-ABANDONMENT PLAY

Through places, children also come into dialogue with other people, both living and dead, imaginary and real. From within this humanized perspective on landscapes I introduce data that suggests children visited abandoned houses at Chunchucmil. The evidence comes from floor assemblages from the 'Aak houselots as well as the Muuch houselot, an immediate neighbor to the north of 'Aak (Figure 5.1). Both groups were gradually abandoned at the beginning of the Late Classic period. At the time of their abandonment, other residential groups, such as the Kaab' group (Magnoni 2003) located approximately 300 meters to the west (Figure 5.1), continued to be occupied.

The Muuch group floor assemblages come from Structure 13, the largest of the group's residential structures (Figure 5.4). Structure 13 consists of a 50-centimeter-high basal platform of dry core fill, which supported smooth-faced masonry walls coated with a 1-centimeter layer of plaster. In antiquity these stone walls would have been at least 1.5 meters high and capped by a beam and mortar roof. In its final stage of construction, Structure 13 consisted of three rooms: a long front room (room 1, measuring 8.2 x 2.0 meters) with a single doorway opening eastward to the Muuch group patio, a smaller room (room 2, measuring 3.4 x 2.25 meters) connected to the front room by a doorway, and a second small room (room 3, measuring 4.4 x 2.25 meters) accessible only from a back door leading to a semi-enclosed porch.

Because of excellent preservation of the plaster floors in these three rooms and the skills of the archaeological laborers from the nearby town of Kochol, we were able to isolate the five-centimeter lens of dirt lying directly on top of the floors. The rooms were gridded into blocks of

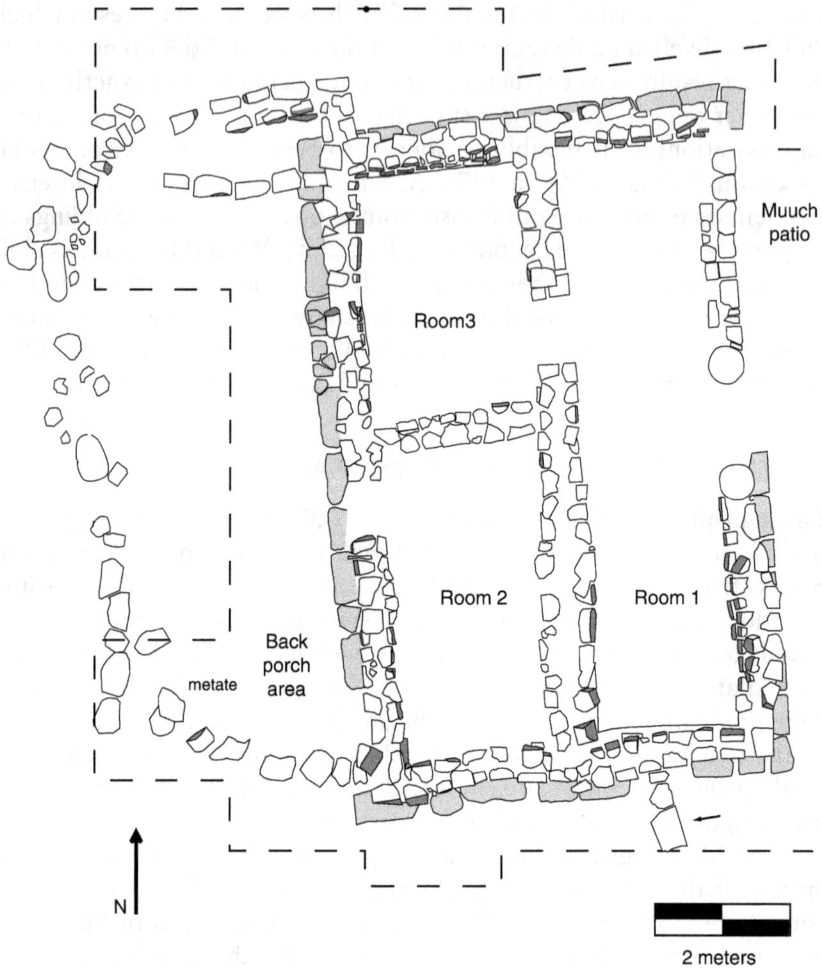

5.4: Plan view of Structure 13, Muuch group. Dotted line indicates limits of excavation. Lightly shaded stones are part of the plinth/substructural wall.

approximately seventy centimeters per side, depending on the length and width of the room, and the artifacts recovered from each block were bagged separately.[3] The sherds were counted and weighed in order to calculate the density of sherds for each block. Sherd densities for each of the blocks were then juxtaposed on a schematic representation to highlight spatial patterns of sherd distribution across the floors (Figure 5.5).

Figure 5.5 shows that relatively large concentrations of broken pottery were found on the floor of the northern end of room 3, particularly

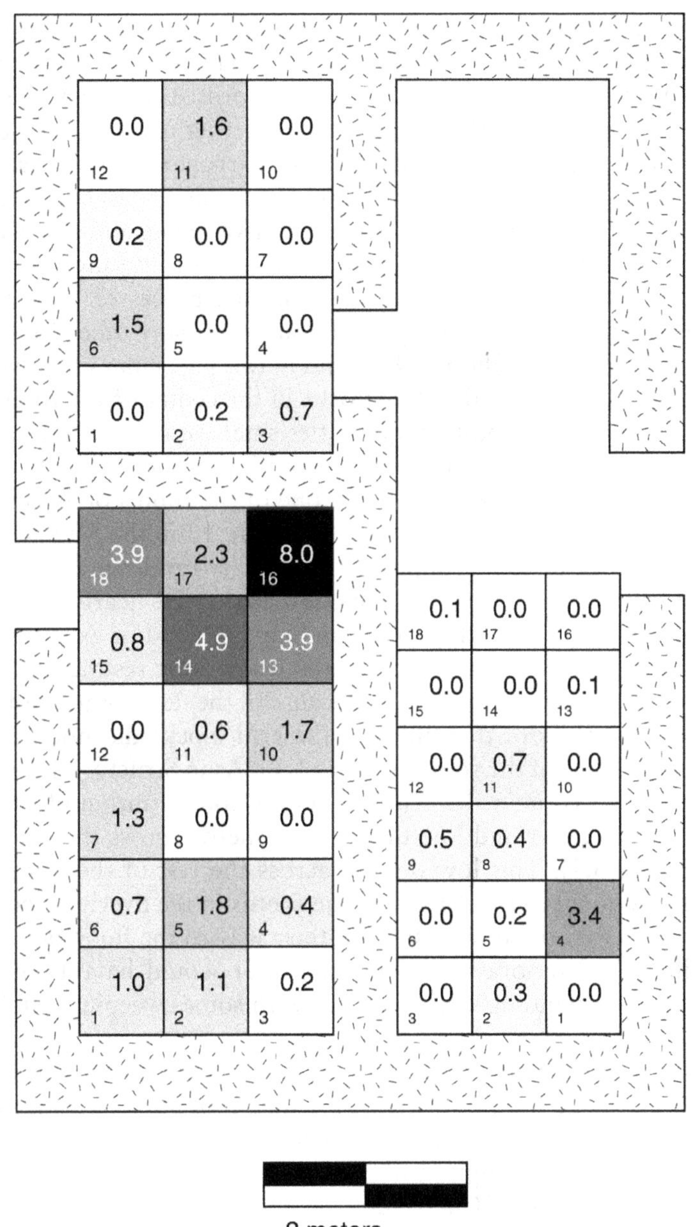

5.5: Schematic illustrations of Structure 13 showing densities of potsherds, measured in kg/m³, on the surface of the floors of rooms 1, 2, and 3. Box numbers are in southwest corner of each box. Shading represents density of sherds.

in the northeast corner. Combined, the six blocks in the northern third of this room contained 132 sherds (and one small piece of chert debitage) weighing less than a kilogram. In other words, this is a rather light concentration of small sherds. After considering a variety of possible formation processes, I concluded that this garbage is in secondary context (Hutson 2004), having accumulated in the northeast corner during the occupation of the structure as a result of sweeping and artifact traps (Hayden and Cannon 1983; Deal 1985) and then scattering to the other nearby blocks as a result of post-depositional processes. Sweeping of floors is suggested for Classic-period houses at many other Maya sites (Webster, Gonlin, and Sheets 1997) and in this particular case sweeping is supported by the fact that the blocks in the center of the room were devoid of sherds or contained quantities small enough to have arrived there by natural processes of the deterioration of the building.

A similar pattern was revealed in one of the rooms of Structure 22 of the 'Aak group (Figure 5.6). Like Structure 13 in the Muuch group, Structure 22 of the 'Aak group was the primary residence of the group. The size, floor plan, and manner of construction are nearly identical to Structure 13 of the Muuch group. The same method of excavation described earlier was used to excavate the lens of dirt resting directly on the floor in Structure 22, although because of the deterioration of floors in certain segments of the building, the grid blocks did not cover the entire dimensions of the rooms (Figure 5.7). As in Structure 13, room 3 of Structure 22 contained a relatively dense concentration of sherds in the northeast corner and low densities of sherds across the rest of the floor (Figure 5.7). This low density across the rest of the floor is approximately equal to the density of the sherds in the overlying collapse, so it appears that these sherds found their way to the floor as a part of the building's deterioration. Thus, the floor would have been swept clean while the building was occupied, with some sweepings ending up in the corner.

Room 3 of Structure 13 contained a fragment of a bivalve seashell near the center of the floor in a block that contained no other debris (block 9 in Figure 5.5). Room 3 of Structure 22 also contained a shell fragment in a nearly empty grid block close to the center of the floor (block 5 in Figure 5.7). Chert debitage and a fragment of an obsidian blade were also found in otherwise clean blocks of room 3 of Structure 22, but since these artifacts were found in the overlying collapse as well, they may have gotten there through natural processes of deposition associated with the collapse of the building. In both buildings, however, absolutely no shell was found in any of the collapse above the floor

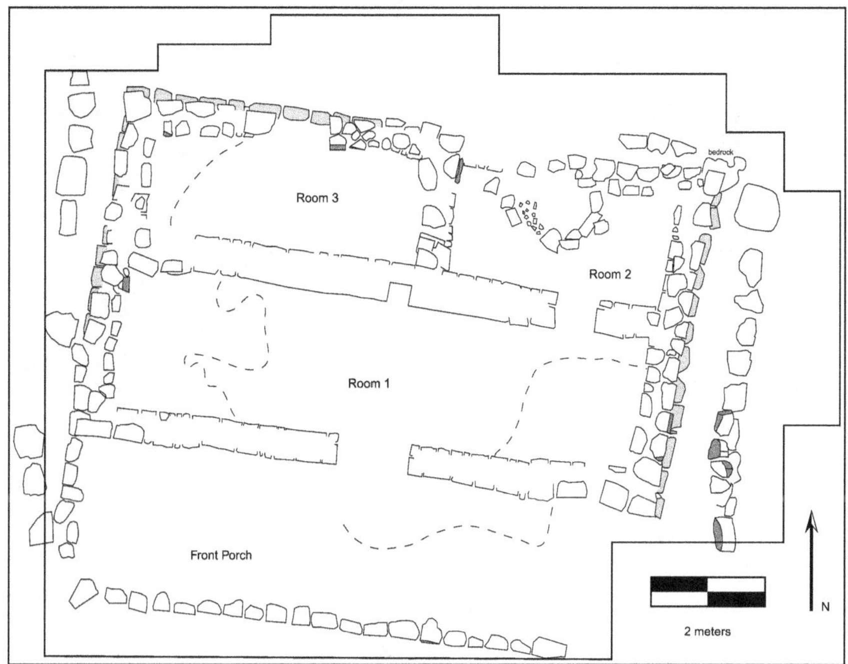

5.6: Plan view of Structure 22, 'Aak.

deposits. Finding bits of shell only on the floor suggests that shell arrived there through human processes of deposition while the walls were still standing. Yet the fact that these shell fragments were not swept into the concentrations of debris in the corners suggests that they were deposited some time after active cleaning and maintenance of the buildings had ceased. In other words, someone placed the shells there *during* or *after* the abandonment of the buildings but before the walls collapsed. I do not believe that the shell fragments were left as a cache or as part of a termination ritual (see Mock 1998) because if a lone, small, broken piece of shell were to count as a residue of a termination ritual, the definition of a termination ritual would have to be expanded to the radical point where almost everything could count as such.

Following Gawain Hammond and Norman Hammond's warning that "child's play may result in incongruous collections of objects for which a 'ritual' explanation might be adduced" (Hammond and Hammond 1981:636), I propose that children exploring the abandoned houses brought the shell fragments to their current archaeological context before the walls collapsed. Ethnoarchaeological studies have shown

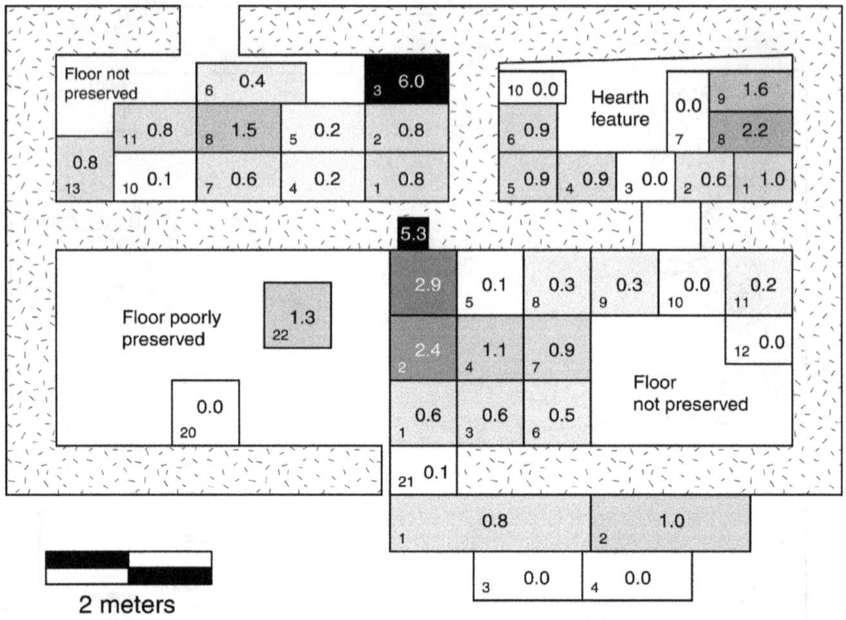

5.7: Schematic illustrations of Structure 22 showing densities of potsherds, measured in kg/m³, on the surface of the floors of rooms 1, 2, and 3. Small numbers in the lower left corners indicate box numbers.

that children profoundly modify and contribute to patterning in discarded materials (Bonnichsen 1973; Hammond and Hammond 1981; Deal 1985). Specifically, small, distinctive items are often picked up by children and redeposited far from their original context. This seems to be the case at Chunchucmil insofar as seashell fragments are small artifacts that are also quite distinctive because of their rare occurrence at the site.

Deserted places and abandoned structures are popular locations for children in Tucson, Arizona (Wilk and Schiffer 1979), in Maya villages in Highland Chiapas (Deal 1985:273), and in turn-of-the-century plantations in the American South (Wilkie 2000). Furthermore, Iona and Peter Opie (1969) write that the deepest pleasure of British children is to be away in the wastelands. Also commenting on British children, Robin Moore (1986:160–162) noted that abandoned places are particularly preferable because their roughness and state of disuse accommodate a wide variety of potentially destructive activities not sanctioned elsewhere, such as digging, throwing, building, and burning.

My purpose in bringing up the cross-cultural popularity of ruined buildings is not to suggest that there is an essence to children that conditions them to enjoy vacant lots, whether in Britain, Arizona, Chiapas, or Louisiana. Rather, I mention these examples of abandoned places to highlight key features of the relational approach to subjectivity developed earlier. First, abandoned houses are appealing because they are grounds for creative encounters with other people. Like all other lived-in spaces, ruins are caught up in the life stories of the subjects that dwelt in and around them (Basso 1996; Edmonds 1999). In this sense, places bespeak people's practices, their histories, their conflicts, their accomplishments (Rodman 1992:649). The residues of these life histories haunt abandoned places. But the meanings that haunt these places speak differently to different people (Rodman 1992:647); older neighbors who knew the former occupants of an abandoned house would have a different imagination about that house compared to younger neighbors who might be too young to have any specific recollection of the people who once lived there. Although abandoned buildings would have been intelligible to children as houses since these buildings are not too different from the structures in which the children lived, the meaning of ruined houses would have otherwise been open to children's speculation and fantasy, perhaps mixed with hearsay from elders. I suggest that the imaginary relations afforded by these abandoned buildings made them compelling places for children to visit. The abandoned places were "haunted by a residual human presence that stimulated the imagination and made it easy for the children to anthropomorphize their surroundings; to muse, to make up stories about what might have gone on there, to create a kind of local mythology from found fragments of the past" (Moore 1986:162).

A second key feature of ruined places, especially those examples cited earlier, is that they are usually beyond the supervision of elders. At Riverlake plantation in Louisiana, Laurie Wilkie (2000:110) found that children played marbles in abandoned quarters. Assuming that Riverlake's staunch Baptist community would not have approved of what was essentially a form of gambling, Wilkie concludes that children played marbles in the abandoned quarters to avoid being observed by adults. The idea of children playing among the ruins at Chunchucmil suggests that children were not only enacting imaginary relations with the past inhabitants of those ruins, but also mediating their relations with their elder guardians. From this perspective, places can be seen as resources deployed in the negotiation of personal relations: abandoned buildings serve as shields between young and old. Working from the notion of abandoned houses as secret landscapes, I conclude this chapter by attempting to move beyond the mere identification of children to consider the way relations with other people contribute to the formation of childhood subjects.

PLAY AS FORMATIVE AND TRANSFORMATIVE

Perhaps too often, the relationships seen to be most formative for the child are those between child and adult.[4] In this kind of relationship, "children are seen as the recipients of social influences, passive in social processes and the object of types of parenting" (Scott 1997:6). Children are considered lesser adults, on their way to becoming adults, and are the objects of parents' attention rather than persons in their own right (Mayall 1994a:3). But the relationship between adult and child is not totally determinate (Ward 1978; Mayall 1994a; Sillar 1994; Finlay 1997; Scott 1997; Lillehammer 2000:21; Roveland 2000; Sofaer Derevenski 2000; Wilkie 2000). Children interacting among themselves construct their own creative and innovative worlds. Iona and Peter Opie (1959) have famously documented a vast and chronologically deep world of children's lore, which circulates outside the home, beyond the influence of the family. In fact, "[a]dults were astonished and horrified that children possessed such an extensive underworld culture of their own" (Opie 1993:11–12). From this perspective, it is not difficult to attribute the unorthodox yet amateurish graffiti etched onto the plaster surfaces of the buildings' interiors at Tikal (Webster 1963; Kampen 1978; Trik and Kampen 1983) as graffiti left by children (cf. Haviland and Haviland 1995). Various writers see the world of children's lore—whether it includes playground games, television preferences, or graffiti—as a form of protest with which children actively resist and strain against the constructions of childhood that adults propose for them (Ward 1978:96; Buckingham 1994; Mayall 1994a:2–5; Scott 1997:7).

This assessment, called the "tribal child" approach, has the advantage of treating children's cultures as rich and meaningful in their own right rather than misguided, irrational, or inadequate prototypes of adult society (James, Jenks, and Prout 1998:28–29). It encourages researchers to defamiliarize children's lives and approach them with the seriousness of an anthropologist studying a distant tribe. Like all societies, children's societies contain multifaceted roles and identities, and within these societies we can imagine the circulation of "kid capital" (cf. Bourdieu 1984) and other structural inequalities.

A tribal child approach would lead to the proposition that the children at Chunchucmil who deposited the shell in the abandoned buildings were partaking in their own cultural traditions shielded from adult observation. If child's play is seen as an innovative, somewhat irreverent sphere that does not conform to adults' expectations, to what extent is this sphere resisting and straining against constructions of childhood into which adults try to mold children?

Responding to this question about child's play in ruined buildings at Chunchucmil requires attending more closely to the spatial and demographic contexts. Houselots at Chunchucmil were delimited by stone boundary walls (see Figure 5.2). Although the boundary walls likely served many purposes, they provided an effective barrier to the free circulation of small children. If the demographic profile of ancient Chunchucmil matches that of most ancient societies in which half of the population was under the age of twenty, then there would have been relatively few elders to look after the relatively numerous youths. The task of looking after the smallest children would have been aided by the stone boundary walls. The proposed demographic profile, with its relatively few adults, also implies that children may have had to make significant contributions to the daily work of the household (see Ardren, Chapter 1). If the boundary walls manifest a concern for the spatial control and containment of children and if older children are doing considerable amounts of work, then children's activities in abandoned houses could be read as an attempt to carve an independent spatial (outside the houselot) and temporal (playtime as opposed to worktime) domain.

Yet my impression is that in describing this semi-independent domain of child's play, it is not entirely appropriate to use the vocabulary of "resistance" and the traditional Weberian grammar of power—a subject acting on or against an object—often implied by such vocabulary. First, play should not be understood simply as an escape from work. Even when play involves imagination and fantasy, it also involves formative interactions between people, places, and things. These interactions can be seen as necessary experimentation with the world that familiarizes people with doxa—the culturally acceptable range of conceivable ways of being-in-the-world (Bourdieu 1977)—and prepares them for social roles. As Tim Ingold (2000b) and others note, children find their way as weavers and potters, for example, by playing at weaving and potting. Thus, play should not always be conceptualized as escape or resistance. Play is part of learning, of exploring and creating the relations that constitute one's position as a subject in and to the world. This is much like saying that play, although it may not be supervised by adults, is always in tune or in dialogue with the practices and structures of society as a whole (see Lopiparo, Chapter 6).

Yet, if *subversive* is too strong a word, the tribal child approach to play at least has *transformative* potential. This potential is best observed by recontextualizing kid cultures with their parent cultures and attending to how encounters between the two impact each other (Mayall 1994a:7–8; Scott 1997:7). This allows detection of the ways in which the innovations of playful children contribute to changes in linguistic or cultural preferences in society as a whole and how absences or abundances in "parent" cultures serve as the conditions for the possibility of innovations in kid cultures. This point of view follows remarks made earlier that children and adults share the boundary that separates them.

CONCLUSION

This chapter began with the claim that archaeologists must not only identify children in the past, but also think critically about relations between children and others and the foundational ideologies that structure these relations. I have attempted to discuss childhood as founded upon relationships with the built environment and with other people. Approaching children as relational subjects permits an understanding of how the built environment and children mutually impact each other. This approach also helps develop a model for thinking about how architecture is produced and reproduced. The built environment also mediates between children and other people. I explored this claim by looking at how and why children made use of abandoned structures at Chunchucmil. Abandoned buildings offer the imaginative possibilities of a ruined but lived-in space and opportunities for children to break away from a tightly controlled spatial landscape and a busy work schedule. Although I believe children's activities in the ruins had a vital and distinct impact on children's development, their vitality is underdetermined by tribal child theories of resistance.

ACKNOWLEDGMENTS

The data presented in this paper were gathered as part of the Pakbeh Regional Economy Program under the direction of Bruce Dahlin and Traci Ardren. For permission to operate, the Pakbeh project gives thanks to the Consejo de Arqueología of Mexico's National Institute of Anthropology and History, the INAH Centro Regional Yucatán, and the villages of Kochol and Chunchucmil. Funding for the research discussed in this chapter came from the National Science Foundation and private donors. I thank Bruce and Traci for allowing me to carry out my research under their direction. Traci receives extra thanks for including me in the original symposium that generated this chapter and the book project as a whole and for giving me the nudge I needed to refashion a line of thought whose importance extends well beyond children. In this chapter and in so many other projects I have been lucky to receive comments from Rosemary Joyce. Aline Magnoni and Travis Stanton encouraged my efforts in the early stages. Although I would like to disassociate my supporters from the shortcomings of this paper, the relational approach to which I subscribe prevents this. For better or for worse, we are all in this together.

NOTES

1. Although associating childhood with biological age is a form of biological determinism (Buchli and Lucas 2000; Sofaer Derevenski 2000), this is not necessarily a problem if the analyst is aware of the determinism inherent in such an opening assumption and is prepared to modify such assumptions if they do not fit the data.

2. Matthew Restall and John F. Chuchiak IV's (2002) examination of the original document that has been published as the *Relación* reveals that this document does not have the integrity of a book and some of it may not have been written by Landa.

3. Although most dirt from the grid units was screened in the field with a quarter-inch mesh, a five-liter sample of dirt from each unit was brought back to the lab and wet screened with 1/20-inch mesh. Results from the fine screening did not add significantly to the information obtained from the field screening.

4. More specifically, the most important adult-child relationship is often said to be that between the mother and the child. As Victor Buchli and Gavin Lucas (2000:132) note, this carries the often inappropriate consequence of placing childhood in the women's sphere, which shifts onto children the same dyadic associations—domesticity and private as opposed to worldliness and public—once reserved for women.

REFERENCES CITED

Ardren, Traci, and Scott Hutson

2002 Ancient Maya Religious Practices at Chunchucmil and Yaxuna: Using Evidence from Epigraphy and Excavation. *Pre-Columbian Art Research Institute Journal* 2(4):5–11.

Basso, Keith

1996 Wisdom Sits in Places: Landscape and Languate among the Western Apache. Albuquerque: University of New Mexico Press.

Beach, Tim
1998 Soil Constraints on Northwest Yucatan, Mexico: Pedoarchaeology and Maya Subsistence at Chunchucmil. *Geoarchaeology* 13(8): 759–791.

Bonnichsen, Robson
1973 Millie's Camp: An Experiment in Archaeology. *World Archaeology* 4:277–291.

Bourdieu, Pierre
1977 *Outline of a Theory of Practice.* Cambridge: Cambridge University Press.
1984 *Distinction: A Social Critique of the Judgment of Taste,* trans. R. Nice. Cambridge, MA: Harvard.

Buchli, Victor, and Gavin Lucas
2000 Children, Gender, and the Material Culture of Domestic Abandonment in the Late Twentieth Century. In *Children and Material Culture,* ed. J. Sofaer Derevenski, 131–138. London: Routledge.

Buckingham, David
1994 Television and the Definition of Childhood. In *Children's Childhoods: Observed and Experienced,* ed. B. Mayall, 79–96. London: Falmer.

Butler, Judith
1990 *Gender Trouble.* New York: Routledge.
1993 *Bodies that Matter.* New York: Routledge.

Butterworth, George
1995 An Ecological Perspective on the Origins of the Self. In *The Body and the Self,* ed. J. L. Bermudez, A. Marcel, and N. Eilan, 87–106. Cambridge, MA: MIT Press.

Chamberlain, Andrew T.
1997 Commentary: Missing Stages of Life—Towards the Perception of Children in Archaeology. In *Invisible People and Processes: Writing Gender and Childhood into European Archaeology,* ed. J. Moore and E. Scott, 248–250. London: Leicester University Press.

Conkey, Margaret, and Joan Gero
1991 Tensions, Pluralities and Engendering Archaeology: An Introduction to Women in Prehistory. In *Engendering Archaeology: Women and Prehistory,* ed. M. Conkey and J. Gero, 3–30. Oxford: Blackwell.

Conkey, Margaret, and Janet Spector
1984 Archaeology and the Study of Gender. In *Advances in Archaeological Method and Theory,* ed. M. B. Schiffer, 7:1–38. New York: Academic Press.

Dahlin, Bruce H.
2000 The Barricade and Abandonment of Chunchucmil: Implications for Northern Maya Warfare. *Latin American Antiquity* 11:283–298.

2003 Chunchucmil: A Complex Economy in Northwest Yucatan. *Mexicon* 25:129–138.

Dahlin, Bruce, Anthony Andrews, Tim Beach, Clara Bezanilla, Patrice Farrell, Sheryl Luzzader-Beach, and Valerie McCormick

1998 Punta Canbalam in Context: A Peripatetic Coastal Site in Northwest Campeche, Mexico. *Ancient Mesoamerica* 9:1–15.

Dahlin, Bruce, and Traci Ardren

2002 Modes of Exchange at Chunchucmil, Yucatan, Mexico. In *The Cultural Impact of Trade in Mesoamerica,* ed. M. Masson and D. Freidel. Walnut Creek, CA: Altamira.

Deal, Michael

1985 Household Pottery Dispersal in the Maya Highlands: An Ethnoarchaeological Interpretation. *Journal of Anthropological Archeology* 4:243–291.

Dreyfus, Hubert

1991 *Being-in-the-world: A Commentary on Heidegger's "Being and Time, Division I."* Cambridge: MIT Press.

Edmonds, Mark

1999 *Ancestral Geographies of the Neolithic: Landscapes, Monuments, and Memories.* London: Routledge.

Finlay, Nyree

1997 Kid Knapping: The Missing Children in Lithic Analysis. In *Invisible People and Processes: Writing Gender and Childhood into European Archaeology,* ed. J. Moore and E. Scott, 203–212. London: Leicester University Press.

Gibson, James J.

1966 *The Senses Considered as Perceptual Systems.* Boston: Houghton Mifflin.

1979 *The Ecological Approach to Visual Perception.* Boston: Houghton Mifflin.

Giddens, Anthony

1979 *Central Problems in Social Theory.* Berkeley: University of California Press.

Gillespie, Susan D.

2001 Personhood, Agency, and Mortuary Ritual: A Case Study from the Ancient Maya. *Journal of Anthropological Archaeology* 20:73–112.

Grimm, Linda

2000 Apprentice Flintknapping: Relating Material Culture and Social Practice in the Upper Paleolithic. In *Children and Material Culture,* ed. J. Sofaer Derevenski, 53–71. London: Routledge.

Hammond, Gawain, and Norman Hammond

1981 Child's Play: A Disturbance Factor in Archaeological Deposition. *American Antiquity* 46:634–636.

Haviland, William, and Anita de Laguna Haviland
1995 Glimpses of the Supernatural: Altered States of Consciousness and the Graffiti of Tikal, Guatemala. *Latin American Antiquity* 6(4):295–309.

Hayden, Brian D., and Aubrey Cannon
1983 Where the Garbage Goes: Refuse Disposal in the Maya Highlands. *Journal of Anthropological Archaeology* 2:117–163.

Heidegger, Martin
[1927] 1996 *Being and Time.* Trans. J. Stambaugh. Albany: SUNY Press.
1971 *Poetry, Language and Thought.* Trans. A. Hofstadter. New York: Harper and Row.

Hendon, Julia
2000 Having and Holding: Storage, Memory, Knowledge and Social Relations. *American Anthropologist* 102:42–53.

Houston, Stephen D., and Karl Taube
2000 An Archaeology of the Senses: Perceptual Psychology in Classic Maya Art, Writing, and Architecture. *Cambridge Archaeology Journal* 10:261–294

Hutson, Scott R.
2004 Dwelling and Subjectification at the Ancient Urban Center of Chunchucmil, Yucatan, Mexico. Ph.D. dissertation, Department of Anthropology, University of California, Berkeley.

Hutson, Scott R., Aline Magnoni, and Travis Stanton
2004 House Rules? The Practice of Social Organization at Classic-Period Chunchucmil, Yucatan, Mexico. *Ancient Mesoamerica* 15:74–92.

Ingold, Tim
2000a Ancestry, Generation, Substance, Memory, Land. In *The Perception of the Environment: Essays on Livelihood, Dwelling and Skill,* by T. Ingold, 132–152. London: Routledge.
2000b Of String Bags and Birds' Nests: Skill and the Construction of Artefacts. In *The Perception of the Environment: Essays on Livelihood, Dwelling and Skill*, by T. Ingold, 349–361. London: Routledge.
2000c Building, Dwelling, Living: How Animals and People Make Themselves at Home in the World. In *The Perception of the Environment: Essays on Livelihood, Dwelling and Skill,* T. Ingold, 172–188. London: Routledge.

James, Allison, Chris Jenks, and Alan Prout
1998 *Theorizing Childhood.* New York: Teachers College Press.

Joyce, Rosemary A.
1994 Looking for Children in Prehispanic Mesoamerica. Paper presented at the annual Meeting of the Society for American Archaeology, Anaheim, California.

1999 Girling the Girl and Boying the Boy. *World Archaeology* 31(3): 473–483.

2001 Burying the Dead at Tlatilco: Social Memory and Social Identities. In *Social Memory, Identity, and Death: Anthropological Perspectives on Mortuary Rituals,* ed. M. S. Chesson, 12–26. Arlington, VA: American Anthropological Association.

Kamp, Kathryn A.

2001 Where Have All the Children Gone? The Archaeology of Childhood. *Journal of Archaeological Method and Theory* 8:1–34.

Kampen, Michael

1978 The Graffiti of Tikal. *Estudios de Cultura Maya* 6: 155–179.

Latour, Bruno

1983 Give Me a Laboratory and I Will Raise the World. In *Science Observed: Perspectives in the Social Study of Science,* ed. K. D. Knorr-Cetina and M. Mulkay, 147–170. London: Sage.

1996 *Aramis, or, the Love of Technology.* Cambridge, MA: Harvard University Press.

Lave, Jean

1990 The Culture of Acquisition and the Practice of Understanding. In *Cultural Psychology: Essays on Comparative Human Development,* ed. J. W. Stigler, R. A. Shweder, and G. Herdt, 309–327. Cambridge: Cambridge University Press.

Lillehammer, Grete

2000 The World of Children. In *Children and Material Culture,* ed. J. Sofaer Derevenski, 17–26. London: Routledge.

Magnoni, Aline

2003 Report on the excavations at the Kaab Group. In *Pakbeh Archaeology Project Report on the 2002 Field Season,* ed. B. Dahlin and D. Mazeau. Washington, DC: Sociology/Anthropology Department, Howard University.

Magnoni, Aline, Scott Hutson, and Travis Stanton

2002 Urban Landscape Transformation and Perceptions at Chunchucmil, Yucatan. Paper presented at the 101st Annual Meetings of the American Anthropological Association, New Orleans, November 20, 2002.

Mayall, Berry

1994a Introduction. In *Children's Childhoods: Observed and Experienced,* ed. B. Mayall, 1–12. London: Falmer.

1994b Children in Action at Home and at School. In *Children's Childhoods: Observed and Experienced,* ed. B. Mayall, 114–127. London: Falmer.

Merleau Ponty, Maurice

1962 *Phenomenology of Perception,* trans. C. Smith. London: Routledge and Kegan Paul.

Meskell, Lynn, and Rosemary A. Joyce
2003 *Embodied Lives.* London: Routledge.

Mizoguchi, Koji
2000 The Child as Node of Past, Present, and Future. In *Children and Material Culture,* ed. J. Sofaer Derevenski, 141–150. London: Routledge.

Mock, Shirley Boteler, ed.
1998 *The Sowing and the Dawning. Termination, Dedication, and Transformation in the Archaeological and Ethnographic Record of Mesoamerica.* Albuquerque: University of New Mexico Press.

Monaghan, John
1998 The Person, Destiny, and the Construction of Difference in Mesoamerica. *RES* 33:137–146.

Moore, Robin C.
1986 *Childhood's Domain: Play and Place in Child Development.* London: Croom Helm.

Opie, Iona
1993 *The People in the Playground.* Oxford: Oxford University Press.

Opie, Iona, and Peter Opie
1959 *The Lore and Language of Schoolchildren.* Oxford: Oxford University Press.
1969 *Children's Games.* New York: Oxford University Press.

Pred, Alan
1990 *Making Histories and Constructing Human Geographies.* Boulder, CO: Westview Press.

Restall, Matthew, and Chuchiak, John F., IV
2002 A Reevaluation of the Authenticity of Fray Diego de Landa's *Relación de las Cosas de Yucatán. Ethnohistory* 49(3):651–669.

Rodman, Margaret
1992 Empowering Place: Multilocality and Multivocality. *American Anthropologist* 94:640–656.

Roveland, Blythe
2000 Footprints in the Clay: Upper Paleolithic Children in Ritual and Secular Contexts. In *Children and Material Culture,* ed. J. Sofaer Derevenski, 29–38. London: Routledge.

Scott, Eleanor
1997 Introduction: On the Incompleteness of Archaeological Narratives. In *Invisible People and Processes: Writing Gender and Childhood into European Archaeology,* ed. J. Moore and E. Scott, 1–14. London: Leicester University Press.

Sillar, Bill
1994 Playing with God: Cultural Perceptions of Children, Play, and Miniatures in the Andes. *Archaeological Review from Cambridge* 13(2):47–63.

Sofaer Derevenski, Joanna

1997 Engendering Children, Engendering Archaeology. In *Invisible People and Processes: Writing Gender and Childhood into European Archaeology,* ed. J. Moore and E. Scott, 192–202. London: Leicester University Press.

2000 Material Culture Shock: Confronting Expectations in the Material Culture of Children. In *Children and Material Culture,* ed. J. Sofaer Derevenski, 3–16. London: Routledge.

Taylor, Charles

1999 To Follow a Rule . . . In *Bourdieu: A Critical Reader,* ed. R. Shusterman, 29–44. Oxford: Blackwell.

Trik, Helen, and Michael Kampen

1983 *The Graffiti of Tikal.* Tikal Report No. 31. The University Museum. Philadelphia: University of Pennsylvania.

Vlcek, David, Sylvia Garza T., and Edward B. Kurjack

1978 Contemporary Maya Farming and Ancient Settlements: Some Disconcerting Evidence. In *Prehispanic Maya Agriculture,* ed. P. D. Harrison and B. L. Turner II, 211–223. Albuquerque: University of New Mexico Press.

Voss, Barbara L., and Robert A. Schmidt

2000 Archaeologies of Sexuality: An Introduction. In *Archaeologies of Sexuality,* ed. R. Schmidt and B. Voss, 1–34. London: Routledge.

Ward, Colin

1978 *The Child in the City.* New York: Pantheon.

Webster, David, Nancy Gonlin, and Payson Sheets

1997 Copan and Ceren: Two Perspectives on Ancient Mesoamerican Households. *Ancient Mesoamerica* 8:43–61.

Webster, Helen Trik

1963 Tikal Graffiti. *Expedition* 6(1):36–47.

Wilk, Richard, and Michael Schiffer

1979 The Archaeology of Vacant Lots in Tucson Arizona. *American Antiquity* 44:530–536.

Wilkie, Laurie

2000 Not Merely Child's Play: Creating a Historical Archaeology of Children and Childhood. In *Children and Material Culture,* ed. J. Sofaer Derevenski, 100–114. London: Routledge.

6

CRAFTING CHILDREN

Materiality, Social Memory, and the Reproduction of Terminal Classic House Societies in the Ulúa Valley, Honduras

Jeanne Lopiparo

Just add children and stir? Many have astutely and repeatedly pointed out that for the study of gender in archaeology, this approach to revealing and remedying past invisibilities in archaeological practice is insufficient for the investigation of multiple subjectivities in the past (Conkey and Spector 1984; Wylie 1991). As Margaret Conkey and Joan Gero (1991) argue for the study of gender, the way we conceive of or theorize children often entails changing the questions we ask, the methodologies we employ, and the models we construct to explain social processes in the past. So what is it that the study of children can uniquely contribute to our understanding of societies in the past? It is not the recovery of a missing object of study per se that is at stake. Rather, theorizing children entails questioning not only how multiple subjectivities were constructed in the past—and in current archaeological discourses—but also how children actively participated in the production and transformation of societies through the processes of structuration (Giddens 1979, 1984). We cannot assume that children were the basic building blocks of culture, replicating society. Instead, we must consider how childhood was constructed and performed through social practices marking life-cycle events and through participation in everyday and ritual activities—both within and beyond the household (cf. Joyce 1998, 2000a; Sofaer Derevenski 2000; Wilkie 2000; Kamp 2001).

The application of feminist and practice theories to archaeology has led to efforts to conceptualize and reconstruct a multivocalic past (after Rodman 1992), which was populated and constituted by diverse agents who created, reproduced, and transformed social structures through everyday practices (see, for example, Tringham 1991, 1994). Many have argued that any attempt to investigate multiple subjectivities in the past entails a change in the scale and focus of archaeological inquiry. A call for household-based studies centered in theories of practice and structuration (Bourdieu 1973, 1977; Giddens 1979, 1984) is predicated less on the top-down idea of the house as basic unit or microcosm of society but, rather, focuses more on the *work* of recreating and maintaining social structures, and advances a conception of society as heterogeneous, fluid, and always in progress.

Household-based and agency-focused studies of social and material production emphasize how structures of meaning were constituted at the microscale through everyday practices—within the context and constraints of shared history, ideas, and structures of power (see, for example, Hendon 1997, 1999; Costin 1998; Love 1999; Clark 2000; Dobres and Robb 2000; Joyce 2000a; Yaeger 2000; Robin 2002, 2003; Lopiparo 2003). This approach to household archaeology entails first, a focus on the small-scale as constitutive of society; second, an investigation of how structures of thought were embedded in and embodied through material culture and the built environment; and, third, a view of the "developmental cycles" of houses not as simple replication, but as dynamic and dependent on the "work" of agents to teach, learn, enact, and interact with their specific histories and material worlds. By considering their roles in the production of material culture and the reproduction of houses, the examination of the way that children learned and participated in daily practices in the household has the potential to provide crucial, multivocalic perspectives about the processes of structuration.

As Rosemary Joyce (1995, 1998, 2000a) has argued, the formation of ideas about personhood and social identity—the creation of social actors in ancient Mesoamerica—was an ongoing process that included the performance of life-cycle rituals through which children became engendered adults and became socialized as members of larger sociopolitical groups. It is in this regard that the concept of "house societies" described by Susan Gillespie (2000a) and Joyce (2000b) is particularly useful in linking these life-cycle rituals with the propagation and transformation of societies. Gillespie (2000b) describes membership in a house society as essentially performative and as embodied and situated in the material realm of the house. It is through the enactment of social roles and duties in the perpetuation of the interests, strategies, and subsistence of the house that one's social identity as a member is formed. Thus people made houses through their embodied practices in domestic landscapes, and houses made people in serving as mnemonics through which roles, duties, and practices were reinforced and materialized in the physical landscape.

Clearly children were instrumental in the processes of perpetuating house societies—not as "receptacles" of culture, but as active agents in its production. But how were these processes embodied through children and how might they have been embedded in material culture and the built environment and thus the archaeological record? Focusing on evidence for the domestic production of ceramics at Terminal Classic household sites in the Ulúa Valley, Honduras, I consider the processes of structuration that took place through children's participation—as audience, apprentices, producers, and consumers—in the domestic organization of craft production and in the ritual and domestic uses of household products. Through the production of material culture on the household level, fundamental ideas about aesthetics, personhood, social roles, and group and individual identity were performed by domestic groups and inscribed in media that served as mnemonics in the ongoing dialogues through which these structures of thought were reproduced and transformed. Based on the performative conceptualizations of house societies advocated by Joyce (2000b) and Gillespie (2000b), I consider these practices as instrumental in the perpetuation of household membership, shared property and prosperity, and social memory (Connerton 1989) through the discursive and nondiscursive inculcation of these ideals in children.

Paul Connerton describes the creation of social memory through commemorative ceremonies, in which non-discursive, bodily practices serve to inscribe a memory of traditions and social forms on participants involved in the performance of "prescribed bodily behaviour" (1989:72):

> Our bodies, which in commemorations stylistically re-enact an image of the past, keep the past also in an entirely effective form

> in their continuing ability to perform certain skilled actions. . . . Many forms of habitual skilled remembering illustrate a keeping of the past in mind that, without ever adverting to historical origin, nevertheless re-enacts the past in our present conduct. In habitual memory the past is, as it were, sedimented in the body. (1989:72)

Through practices of incorporation, this habitual memory is inculcated through participation in rituals and everyday, repeated practices. Participants, in turn, both inscribe and are structured by the material culture, built environments, and landscapes that are fundamental to the performance of practices of incorporation. As I will demonstrate later, the creation of, and interaction with, this material world at household sites in the Ulúa Valley included practices of inscription and incorporation at multiple scales. Habitual memory was performed and reinforced not just through ritual, but through the everyday production and interaction with material culture through which social memory was perpetuated. Evidence from the Ulúa Valley suggests that domestic production was intricately interwoven with rituals of renewal that were fundamental to social reproduction. The inscription of these practices in the material culture of the household blurs the distinction between ritual and everyday landscapes (cf. Bradley 2003). In the performance of the "skilled actions" of production in daily life, practices of incorporation were performed every day.

In this chapter, I focus in particular on one domestic industry, the production of figurines, for which recent excavations in the central alluvium of the Ulúa Valley have provided ample evidence of both production and consumption at the level of the individual household (Lopiparo 2003). These figurines and the molds used to produce them are frequently found in ritual contexts associated with the intentional destruction, reconstruction, and renovation of houses. I will consider their production and consumption as a means of propagating social memory and teaching children ways of being through ritual performances tying this material culture to the life cycles of houses and their inhabitants.

HOUSEHOLD CERAMIC PRODUCTION IN THE ULÚA VALLEY, HONDURAS: PROJECT BACKGROUND

Excavations carried out in 2001 as part of the Proyecto Arqueológico Clásico Terminal (PACT) have produced extensive evidence for household-based, fine paste ceramic production, including molds, mold-made artifacts, specialized middens, and clay preparation and firing facilities

(Lopiparo 2003). The goals of fieldwork included broad, horizontal excavations of household sites in the central alluvium of the Ulúa Valley to examine the organization of domestic activities during the Terminal Classic period; the definition and identification of evidence for household ceramic production of fine paste ceramics; the reconstruction of the scale and organization of the processes of production, interaction, and consumption; and the identification of stylistic and compositional attributes of household products.

A primary objective of the project was to investigate the preliminary evidence for small-scale ceramic production found at sites throughout the valley through the detailed documentation of the organization of household activities. In addition to the presence of ceramic molds in the collections from many sites in the valley, multiple lines of evidence for household ceramic production were identified based on excavations carried out in a pilot study at CR-132 (Lopiparo 1994, 2004; Lopiparo, Joyce, and Hendon, in press). Through the systematic examination of archived artifacts from surface collections and test excavations (undertaken as part of the 15-percent survey of the valley carried out under the Proyecto Arqueológico Sula [Henderson, Agurcia F., and Murray 1982; Henderson 1984; Pope 1985]), I identified sites with a significant Terminal Classic component and, in many cases, possible evidence for fine-paste ceramic and figurine production (in the form of molds and mold-made artifacts).

In addition to investigating the organization of ceramic production on the household level, this study sought to examine both community-level variation and integration in the organization of domestic activities. The sites were selected in order to include the range of variation in size and layout, and to include excavations of two sites that had definite evidence for production in the presence of molds in the archived collections (CR-103 and CR-132) and two sites that did not (CR-80 and CR-381). Excavations focused on sites that can be considered to have been participants in community-level social and economic interactions. The sites were in close proximity to one another (all within four square kilometers) and were clustered along the Quebrada Chasnigua in an area bounded by watercourses that separated it from sites to the south, east, and northwest (Figure 6.1).

Communities might also be defined based on the dispersed distribution of ball courts, with the assumption that these ball courts would have served as foci of community-wide interactions featuring periodic rituals and feasting (cf. Joyce 1991; J. G. Fox 1994, 1996). A cobble ball court at CR-132 is the only one in this part of the valley, and it is

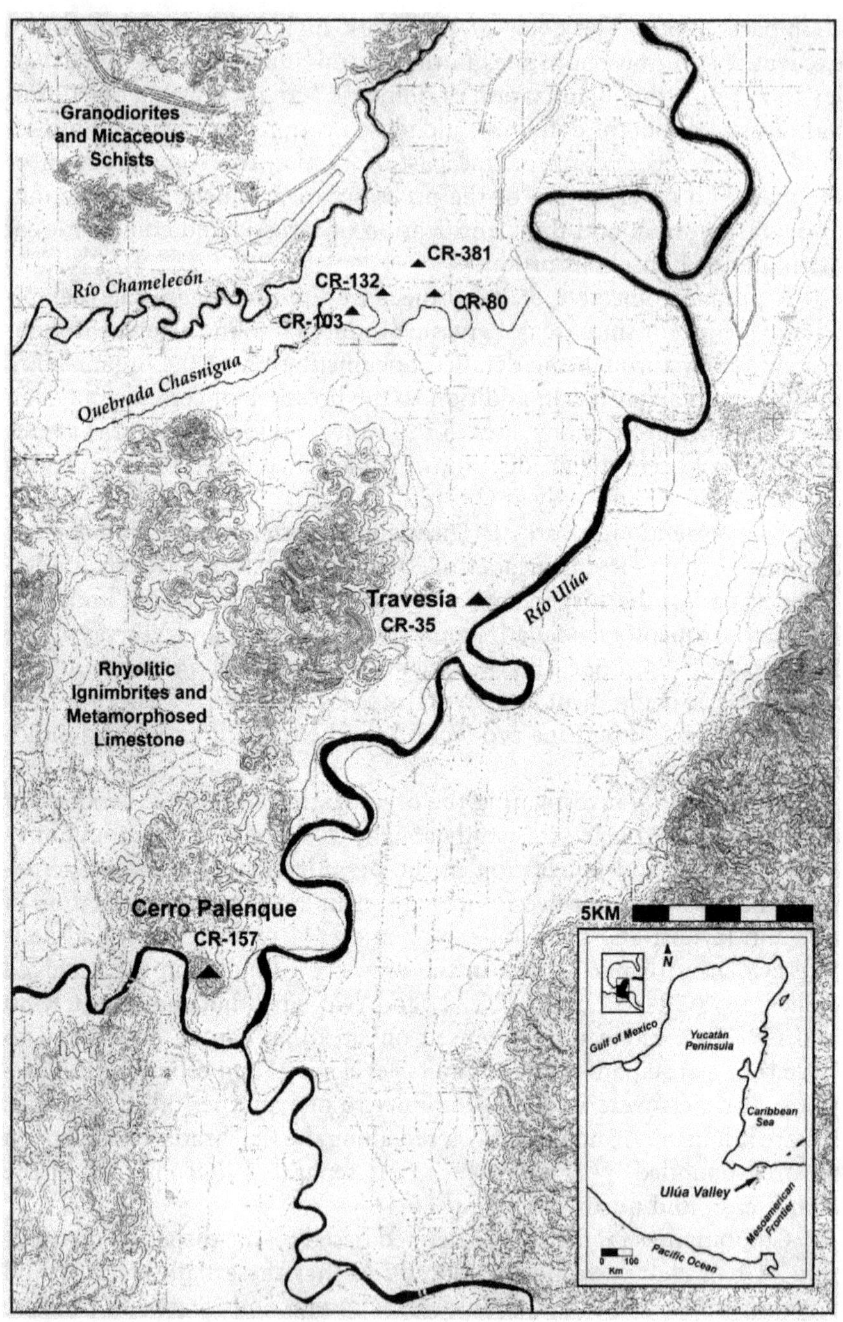

6.1: Ulúa Valley, Honduras.

unusual in its location in a dispersed settlement at a site without monumental architecture. Other ball courts are found dispersed throughout the valley, although primarily at larger centers such as Travesía and Cerro Palenque. Ball courts in the neighboring Cuyumapa drainage are dispersed among non-nucleated settlements and have been interpreted as foci for community activity (J. G. Fox 1994, 1996; Joyce and Hendon 2000). As I will discuss later, evidence for shared ritual activities at multiple scales of settlement in the Ulúa Valley, from burials in house groups to ball courts in centers, suggests social practices through which communities and social networks were integrated (Lopiparo 2003). These shared practices were in turn associated with the production of material culture, the renewal of houses, and the life cycles of people. Through these ritual cycles children became members of their houses, their communities, and societies as a whole.

EXCAVATIONS

PACT included twelve months of excavations and laboratory analysis during which broad horizontal excavations of Late through Terminal Classic occupations were carried out at three domestic sites in the central alluvium. Household sites in this area consisted of clusters of *lomas* (varying from one to about ten lomas), broad earthen rises that were built up through successive occupations over hundreds—or even thousands—of years. Occupation surfaces on lomas generally featured several small, wattle-and-daub structures arranged around a central patio. Lomas varied in size from about 500 to as much as 8,000 square meters in area and from one to three meters in height, and sites selected for excavations encompassed this range of variation. CR-103 and CR-381 were smaller sites, with fewer equally sized lomas, whereas CR-80 featured one enormous central loma surrounded by eight smaller, equally sized lomas. Areas of CR-132 had been destroyed by construction prior to excavation, but parts of five mounds remained. The Late to Terminal Classic occupations at all of the sites feature multiple renovation episodes of wattle-and-daub houses, including both floor resurfacings and periodic burning and clearing of structures associated with fill episodes, offerings, and burials.

Excavations at CR-103 and CR-381—and at CR-132 (the site excavated in the pilot project)—provided multiple lines of evidence from all stages of ceramic production (Stark 1985), including facilities for the preparation of raw materials, molds for the forming of artifacts, and multiple firing facilities found in association with middens that included

6.2: Large figurine mold from the site of CR-80.

dense concentrations of molds and mold-made artifact fragments (including multiple examples of mold-made artifacts that matched molds found at each site). At CR-80, where the much larger size of the site dictated a smaller sampling fraction in excavation, evidence for all stages of ceramic production was not recovered. The use of molds in sub-floor offerings like those found at the other sites, however, indicates that ceramic production was symbolically important here as well and might have been carried out elsewhere at the site. An unusually large figurine mold (Figure 6.2) was found in association with most of an overturned bowl in the patio of CR-80 and appears to represent ritual deposition practices. Analogous practices are indicated by a very large figurine mold recovered from the patio of CR-103 (Figure 6.3), which appears to have been a sub-floor offering associated with the latest occupation surface at the site.

Like the figurine mold found in the patio offering at CR-80, one of the large mold fragments found in front of a platform at CR-381 featured a woman carrying a vessel (Figure 6.4). Quite a few figurine fragments featuring women carrying vessels were recovered from all of the sites (Figure 6.5) and, in several cases, the vessels they are carrying appear to represent the kinds of mold-made, fine-paste vessels that we have recovered archaeologically—sometimes from ritual deposits (compare Figure 6.5 [upper left] with Figure 6.6). The presence of two of these molds in the context of deposits associated with site renovation at CR-80 and CR-381 suggests that women, the ceramic vessels and figurines they created, and the practices in which they were engaged at household sites were involved in activities fundamental to these processes of renewal. The only other figurines that depict women carrying something are those in which they are carrying babies (Figure 6.7) (cf. Willey

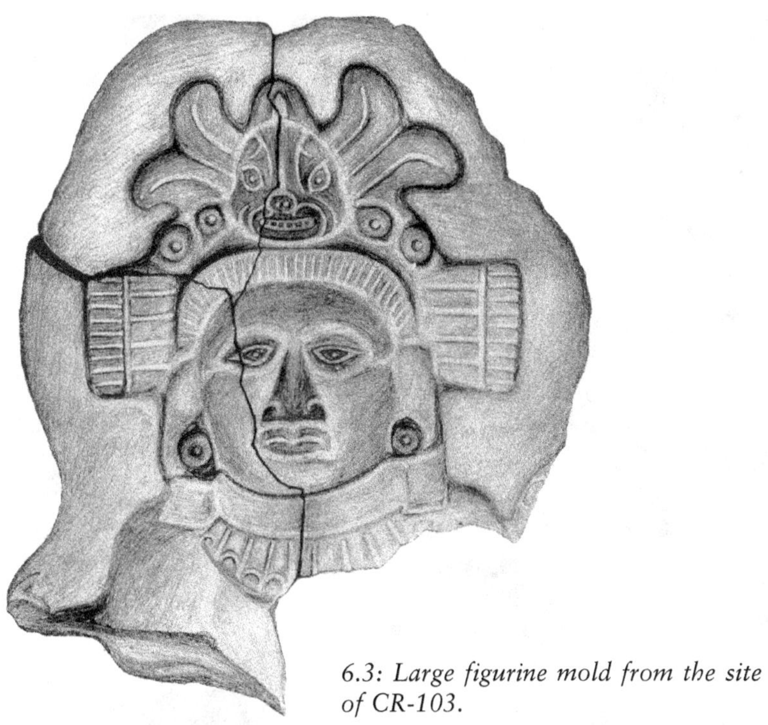

6.3: Large figurine mold from the site of CR-103.

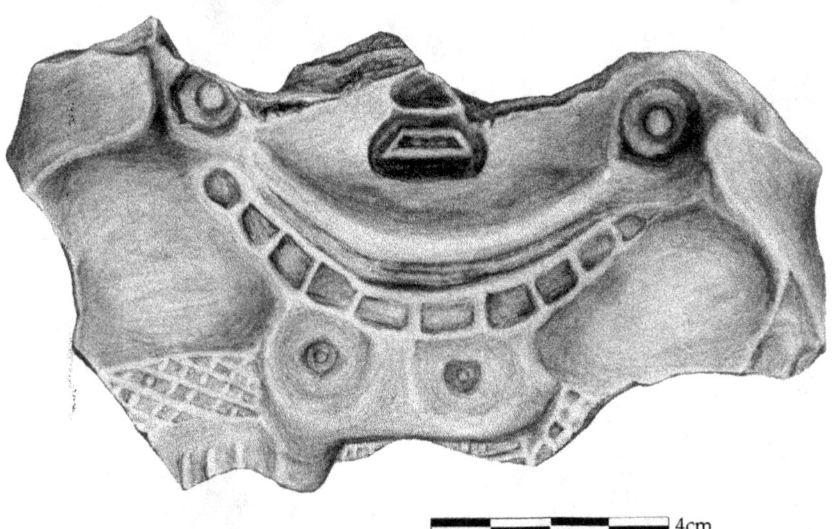

6.4: Large figurine mold from the site of CR-381.

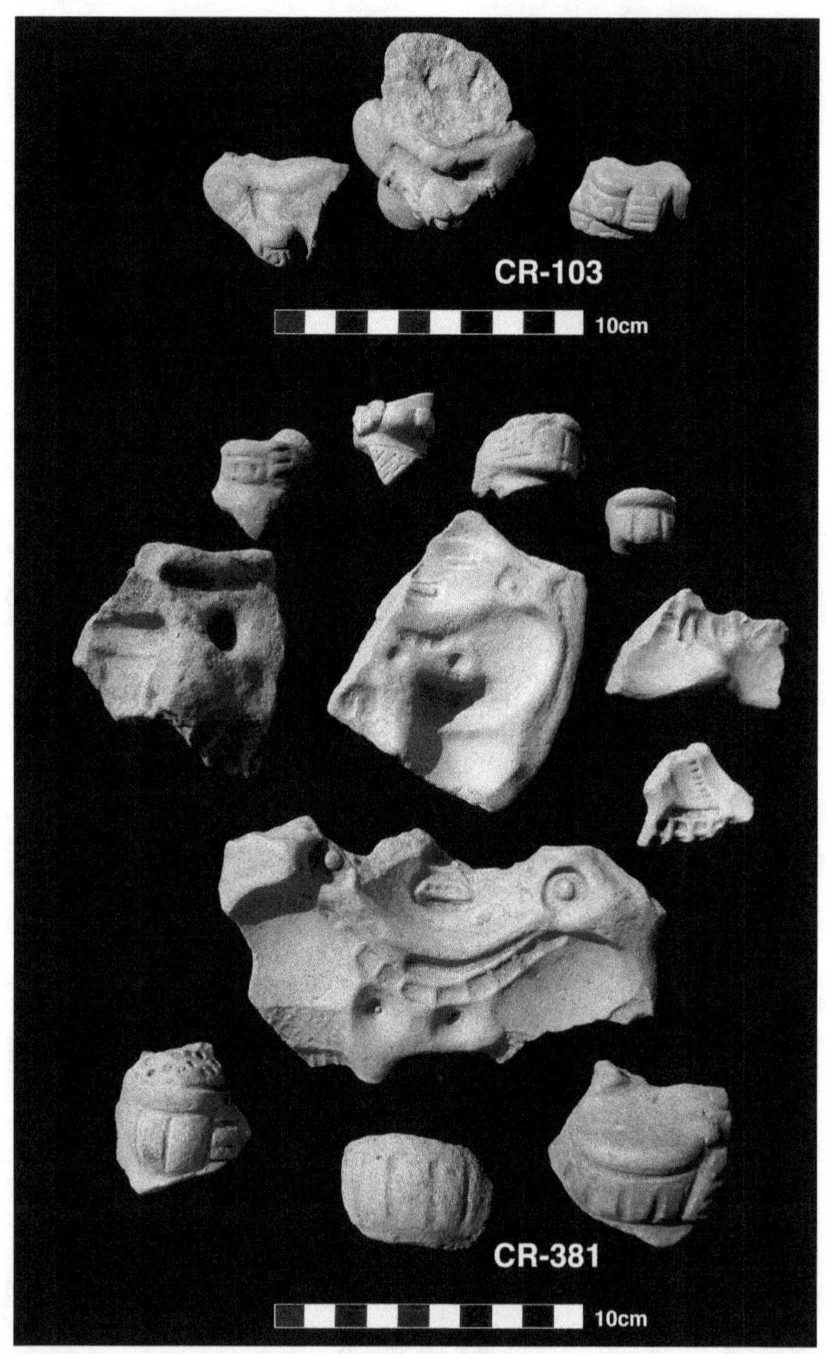

6.5: Figurine fragments from various sites featuring women carrying vessels.

6.6: Fine paste vessel similar to ceramic vessels depicted on figurines.

1972:43, fig. 24)—again suggesting connections among productive and reproductive activities.

THE LIFE CYCLES OF HOUSES AND THEIR INHABITANTS

Studies have frequently focused on the consumption of figurines through ritual (Lesure 1997; Marcus 1999), but I also would emphasize the symbolic significance and ritualized aspects of their production. In this context I consider ceramic production not just as an economic activity, but as a metaphorical means of reproduction—a crucial stage in the parallel, multiscalar life cycles that reproduce house societies, from the life cycles of domestic structures to those of people. The integral association of the life-cycle rituals of humans with those of the built environment is most apparent in the destruction and rebuilding of domestic structures frequently concomitant with burials in house floors. Other events in the life cycle, from pregnancy to birth to rites of passage, may have also involved the use of these artifacts and spaces but are not as easily identified archaeologically.

The appearance of cached or embedded figurines and molds found in association with household renewal—and, at CR-103, with the de-

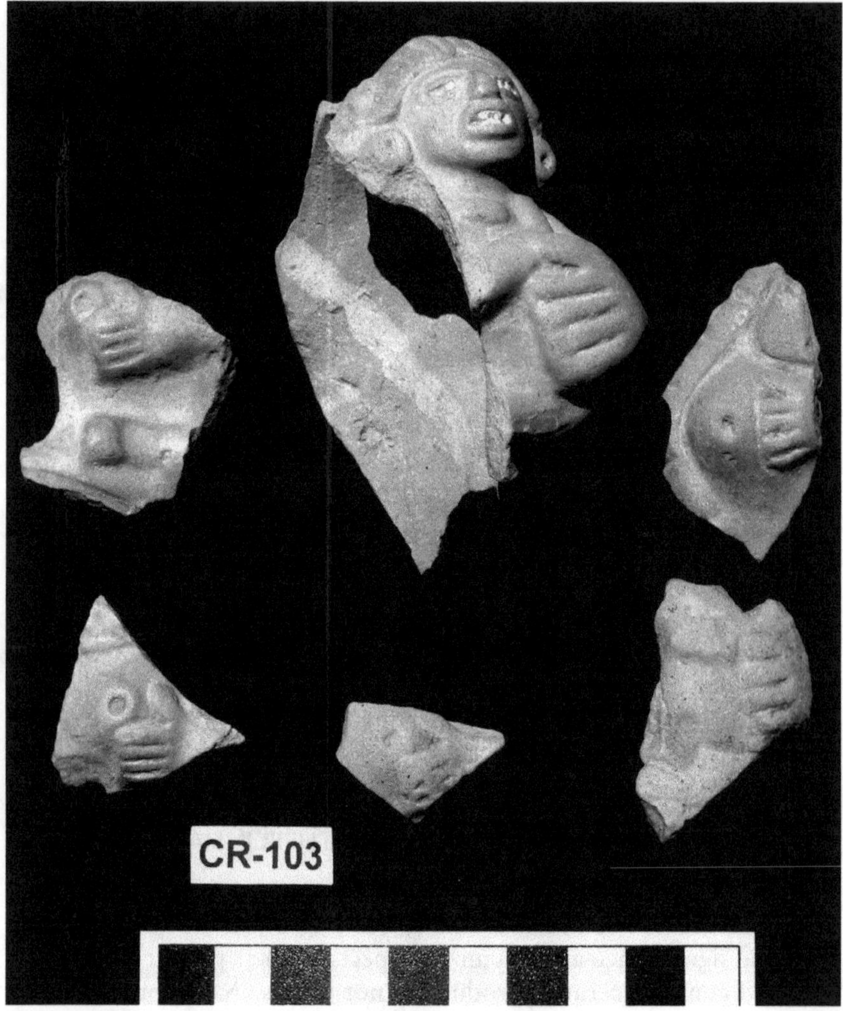

6.7: Figurines that depict women carrying babies.

struction of a possible ceramic firing facility—creates linkages not just with the symbolic significance of the consumption of figurines, but also with their production. At CR-103, four mold-made artifacts were embedded in the burned collapse of a domed, wattle-and-daub oven (Figure 6.8). The artifacts were whole and were not burned, suggesting that they were intentionally placed in the oven collapse. This oven was associated with the burning and leveling of a structure with which a burial was associated (adjacent to the house wall). Two structures on later

6.8: Mold-made artifacts embedded in the burned collapse of a domed, wattle-and-daub oven, site CR-103.

occupation surfaces were also razed in the same area of the loma. A mold for a caiman whistle deposited in association with one of these later renovation episodes—almost directly over the area of the collapsed hearth—was stylistically identical to one of the artifacts embedded in the hearth collapse (Figure 6.9).

If we consider both the interment of the dead in house floors and the associated rituals to have been integral practices in the creation of ancestors (cf. McAnany 1995, 1998; Gillespie 2000b, 2001), then these ritual practices did not represent the termination of the household; rather, they assured its rebirth or renewal. It was through the creation and sustenance of ancestors that the perpetuation and prosperity of the house was ensured. Thus the caching of ceramic artifacts and house destruction were means of renewing the house society by creating and maintaining ancestors. The Popol Vuh, a seventeenth-century Highland Maya transcription of the Quichean Maya story of creation, contains many associations of creation with sculpting, carving, grinding, and modeling (Tedlock 1996). We might make the analogous connection that the practices of all forms of crafting would have been integral to the sustenance

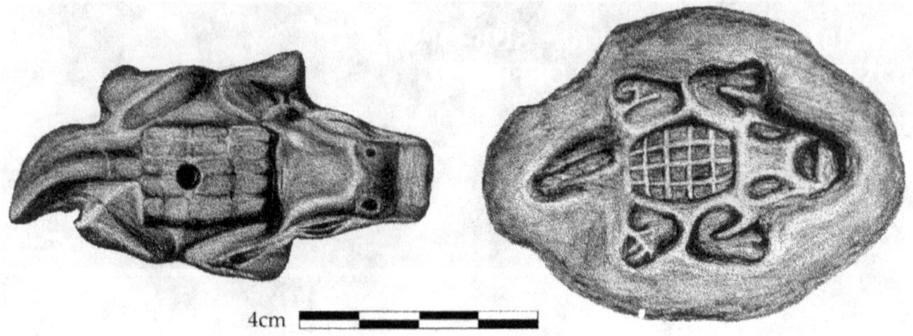

6.9: A mold for a caiman whistle deposited in association with an architectural renovation episode at CR-103.

and re-creation of houses. "Reproductive" activities therefore include not only the procreation of bodies, but also the daily practices of providing sustenance and shelter and the ritual practices of producing and sustaining ancestors who ensure prosperity and propagation of the house. The creation of figurines at the household level—and the unique association of certain figures with *specific* households—indicates that the production of these figurines in particular was an essential practice in the re-creation of that house (Lopiparo 2003). The further association of molds with transitions and renewals in the life cycles of the physical houses reinforces this significance.

THE MATERIALIZATION OF HOUSEHOLD IDENTITY

Many of the same kinds of mold-made artifacts are found at the three sites (figurines, whistles, stamps, miniature effigy vessels) and certain design categories appear at all of the sites (for example, "women carrying vessels"), but the variation in the execution of the designs is tremendous (see, for example, Figures 6.5 and 6.10). Although they are all mold-made, almost no two are alike (with the exception of cases where we were able to match molds with artifacts or document multiple artifacts from the same mold). This variety is seen in both the artifacts and the molds, indicating that although large numbers of figural artifacts were being produced, mass production clearly was not the goal. The implications of mold use for learning by children is discussed further later. The variety of artifacts with unique design elements suggests a significant role for objects made and used in life-cycle rituals in embedding imagery that is iconic of household identity.

6.10: A series of molds and mold-made artifacts showing tremendous variation in the execution of designs.

Even artifact types that have a very uniform set of design elements displayed an enormous number of variants in the site assemblage, with few or no actual repeats; despite the fact that they are all mold-made and large numbers of molds were recovered. One type of mold-made, miniature vessel features profile heads that appear to be almost glyph-like in their composition (perhaps analogous to the pseudo-glyphs found in Ulúa Polychrome pottery [Joyce 1993]). The number of variants in the execution of this design concept in the molds (Figure 6.10) suggests the possibility that this differentiation was significant and that the variation was legible to those who produced and interacted with these artifacts.

In addition to this variation within artifact types, the assemblages varied among the sites. Although several design categories were common to all of the sites, unique artifact types and designs appeared at each site. In particular, many of the ritual deposits, like those found in front of platforms, included ceramic artifacts with representations that were unusual or unique in the iconographic corpus of the sites. These include anthropomorphic figures that are similar to those categorized by Willey as "grotesques" (1972:50–54), which are believed to represent

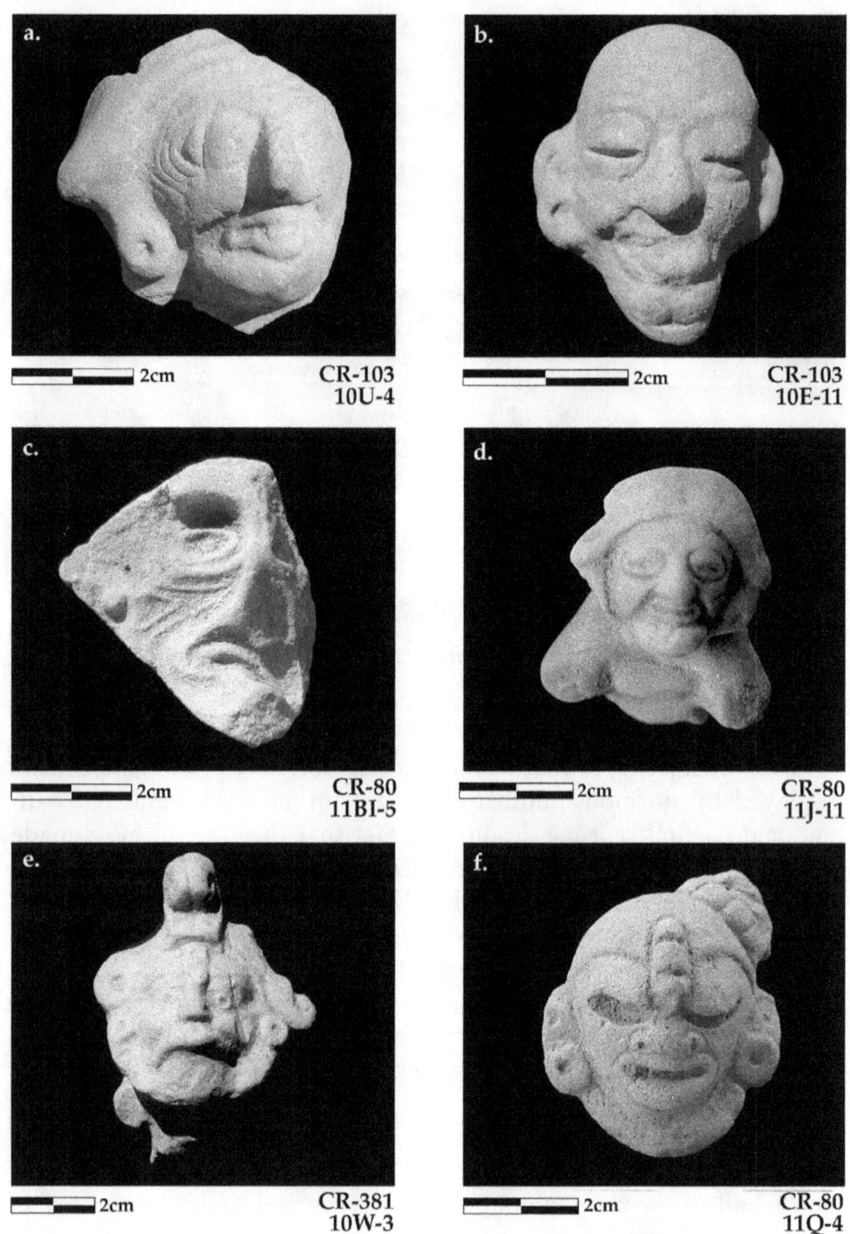

6.11: Anthropomorphic figurines and molds with representations that are unusual or unique in the iconographic corpus of Ulúa Valley sites.

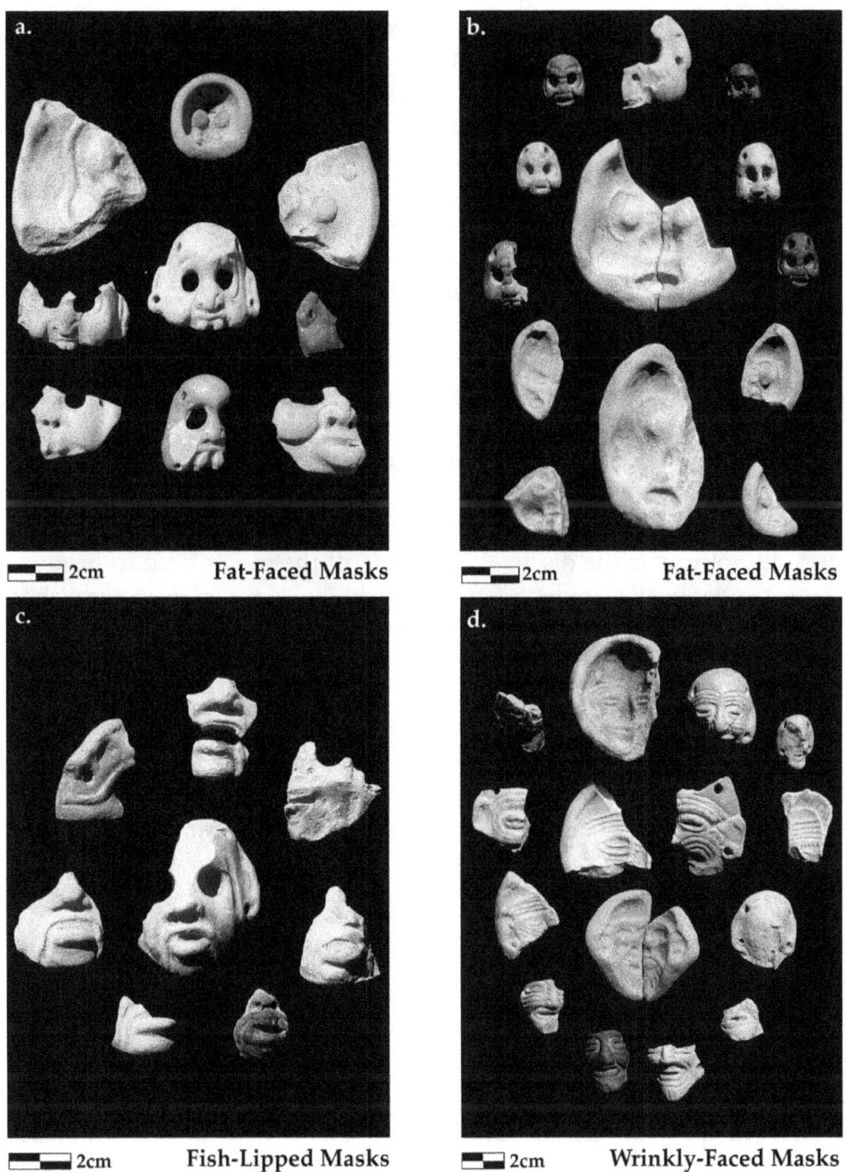

6.12: Miniature masks that include designs of aged, wrinkly, chubby, monstrous, zoomorphic, and de-fleshed or skeletal faces.

supernaturals or gods (compare, for example, Figures 6.11 and 6.12 with Willey 1972:51–53, figs. 42 and 44).

At CR-381, an artifact category was identified that is rare, if not unique, in the valley. The majority of these artifacts appear to be ornaments—pendants and beads in particular—representing a variety of miniature masks that include designs of aged, wrinkly, chubby, monstrous, zoomorphic, and de-fleshed or skeletal faces (Figures 6.12, 6.13, and 6.14). The fact that these ornaments represent masks is indicated by several features: many have hollowed eyes; they are perforated in the temples and below the ear (or through the earspools) for attachment, as if they were to be worn as masks; the backs of the masks are well-finished and flat; and several end at the top lip, like many images of people wearing masks in Maya representations in other media. In addition to masks, the pendants include representations of animals, such as deer, birds, and monkeys reclining in provocative poses.

Many examples were found of the same designs represented in masks of various sizes (ranging from about 1 to 6 centimeters) and also tiny beads representing masks and birds (probably bird masks). But perhaps most interesting is the discovery of many of the molds used to produce these pendants. Examples of these masks have never been published from excavations in the valley. With the exception of one small fragment from CR-80 and two whole miniature ceramic masks, which were found in elaborate offerings at CR-103 and which differed significantly in both their paste and designs from those recovered from CR-381, I did not find any other examples at the other sites, nor have I found any recorded for other sites in the valley. This suggests that these artifacts were produced for local, household-level consumption.

HOUSEHOLD RITUAL AND THE REPRODUCTION OF HOUSE SOCIETIES

Burials, offerings, and structural renovations in the Ulúa Valley can be understood in terms of rituals of renewal at multiple temporal and spatial scales. Throughout the life histories of these households, the cosmos were mapped onto the landscape through the renewal of and interaction with material culture and the built and natural environments (Lopiparo 2003). Burials provide one example of the creation and perpetuation of social memory through repeated practices in which notions about space and time were performed and embedded in the landscape (cf. Gillespie 2000b, 2001; Hendon 2000; Joyce 2000b; King, Chapter 7). At CR-80 a side-by-side burial beneath a house floor features two individuals who appear not to have been interred at the same time. The placement of the second burial—exactly adjacent to the first

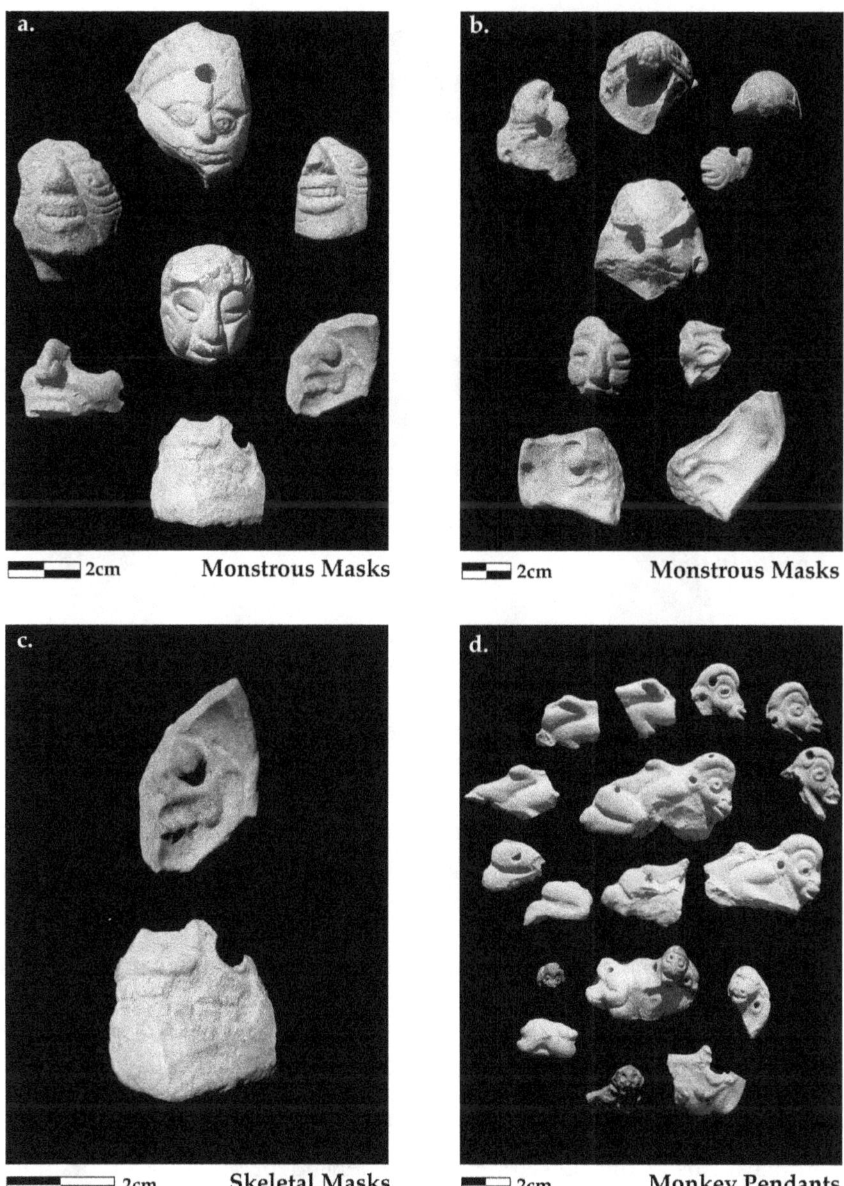

6.13: Miniature masks that include designs of aged, wrinkly, chubby, monstrous, zoomorphic, and de-fleshed or skeletal faces.

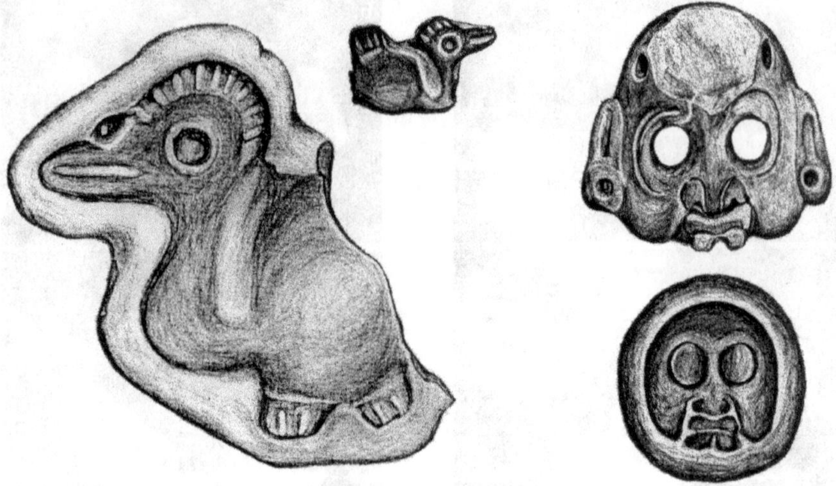

6.14: Artifacts and molds from CR-381 showing the same designs produced in multiple sizes.

and in the same position (Figure 6.15a)—suggests a formalized set of practices in the placement of burials that were very precisely maintained in the social memory of the house members. Through the rituals that accompanied the interments of house members and the renewal of houses, narratives about space, place, and time—and their significance to the life cycles of the house—were performed (Lopiparo 2003; cf. McAnany 1995, 1998; Gillespie 2000b, 2001). That these rituals frequently included distinctive molds and mold-made ceramics suggests the significant role they played in materializing the identity and social memory of the house through ritual and the reproductive value of their production.

But the placement of burials in the landscape held significance beyond the household. Burials at all three of the sites maintained the same orientation at about 24 degrees east of north, or perpendicular to it at 114 degrees east of north (Figure 6.15). The orientations of structures and platforms at the sites appear to be dependent on local factors, but the consistency of the burial orientations is both shared across all of the sites and linked to other valley-wide practices. Sites in the valley frequently have an east-of-north skew to their orientation, including the main plaza groups at the regional centers in the valley, such as Cerro Palenque, Travesía, and Currusté. The mapping of the variation of these alignments among centers revealed that the NNE-SSW axes were all

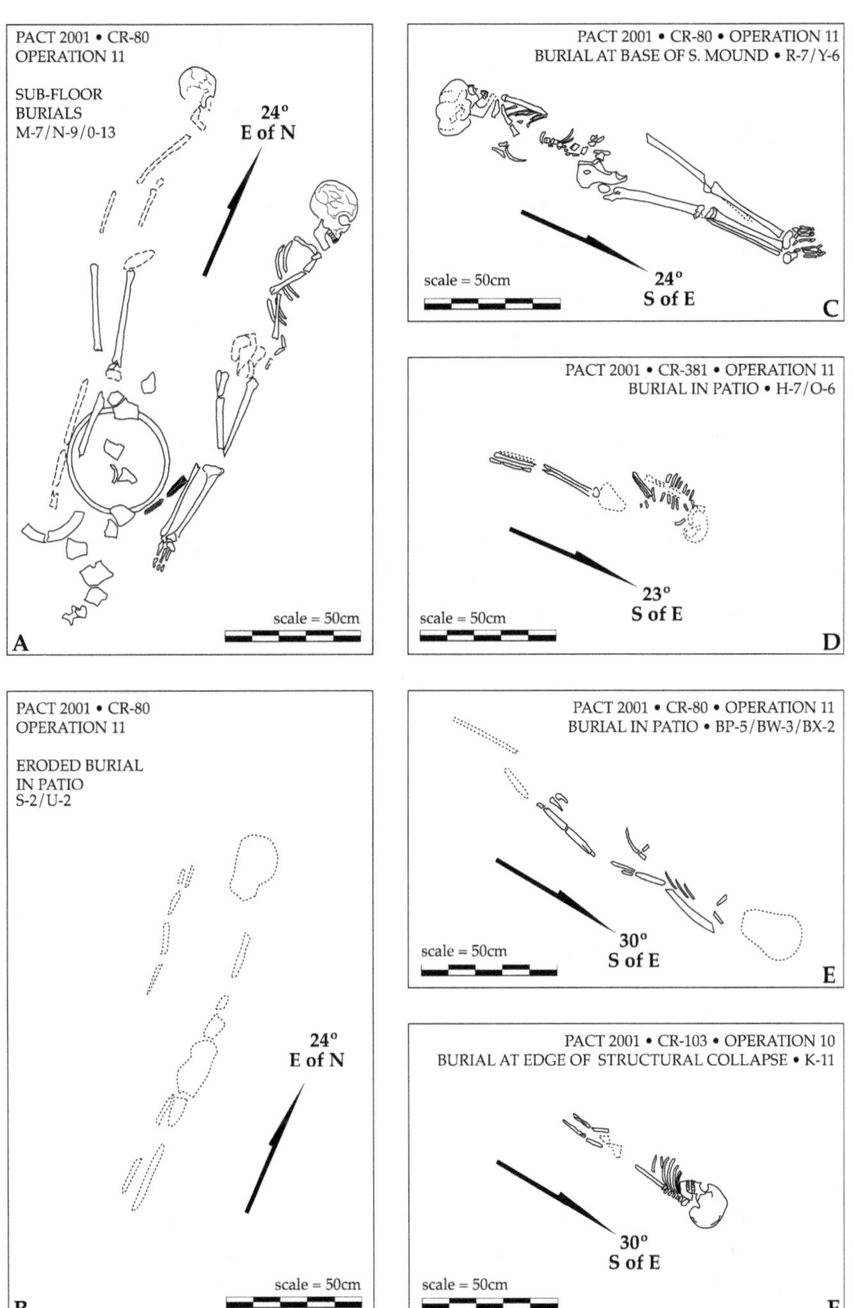

6.15: Burial placement and orientation at sites excavated in this study.

aligned with the highest mountain peak in the mountains surrounding the valley (Lopiparo 2003) (see Figure 6.16). In addition, the ESE-WNW axes would have been aligned (within a few degrees) with the sunrise on the horizon at winter solstice, a point associated with a critical moment for the renewal of the annual cycle (Aveni 2001).

This evidence suggests participation in a region-wide (or perhaps broader; see Aveni 2001) cosmology with shared conceptions of sacred landscape features, the observance of solar cycles, and the significance of their conjunction (Lopiparo 2003). This cosmology, however, was instantiated and reproduced at the household level; it was embedded in and embodied through everyday landscapes and practices. In the construction and renovation of households—and particularly in the burial of the dead associated with these renovations—geomantic referents that tied the household to broader astronomically and cosmologically significant events were maintained in the local landscape (Lopiparo 2003). The association of solstitial alignments with rituals carried out to ensure the renewal of the annual solar cycle thus was paralleled by rituals of renewal of the household and ancestors.

The renewal of the annual cycle has also been associated with ball court rituals and iconography. The association of the ballgame with the creation of this world and with the beginnings of astronomical cycles has been inferred from both ethnohistoric sources like the Popol Vuh (see Tedlock 1996) and ball court iconography at Classic Maya centers (Schele and Freidel 1990; J. W. Fox 1991; Gillespie 1991). Following this interpretation, reenactments of these events might have been critical during calendrical period–ending rituals—particularly at the winter solstice—to ensure the emergence of the sun from the underworld (cf. Gillespie 1991). It was participation in these ritual conjunctures at multiple scales that ensured the production and reproduction of the cosmos.

The presence of a ball court at CR-132 within the community of dispersed loma sites in the central alluvium suggests the enactment of ritual practices analogous to those proposed for regional centers (for example, feasting, masked dancing, and bloodletting, as suggested by Joyce [1991] for Cerro Palenque). The performance of social identities, relationships, and rights enacted through these rituals was just as critical for the definition of intra- and intercommunity relationships as it was for the perpetuation of the centers (Lopiparo 2003; cf. J. G. Fox 1994, 1996; Joyce and Hendon 2000). The differentiation of household material culture on a site-by-site basis is suggestive of other contexts in which membership in a house society would be asserted not just in household rituals, but in relationship to other neighboring sites. The

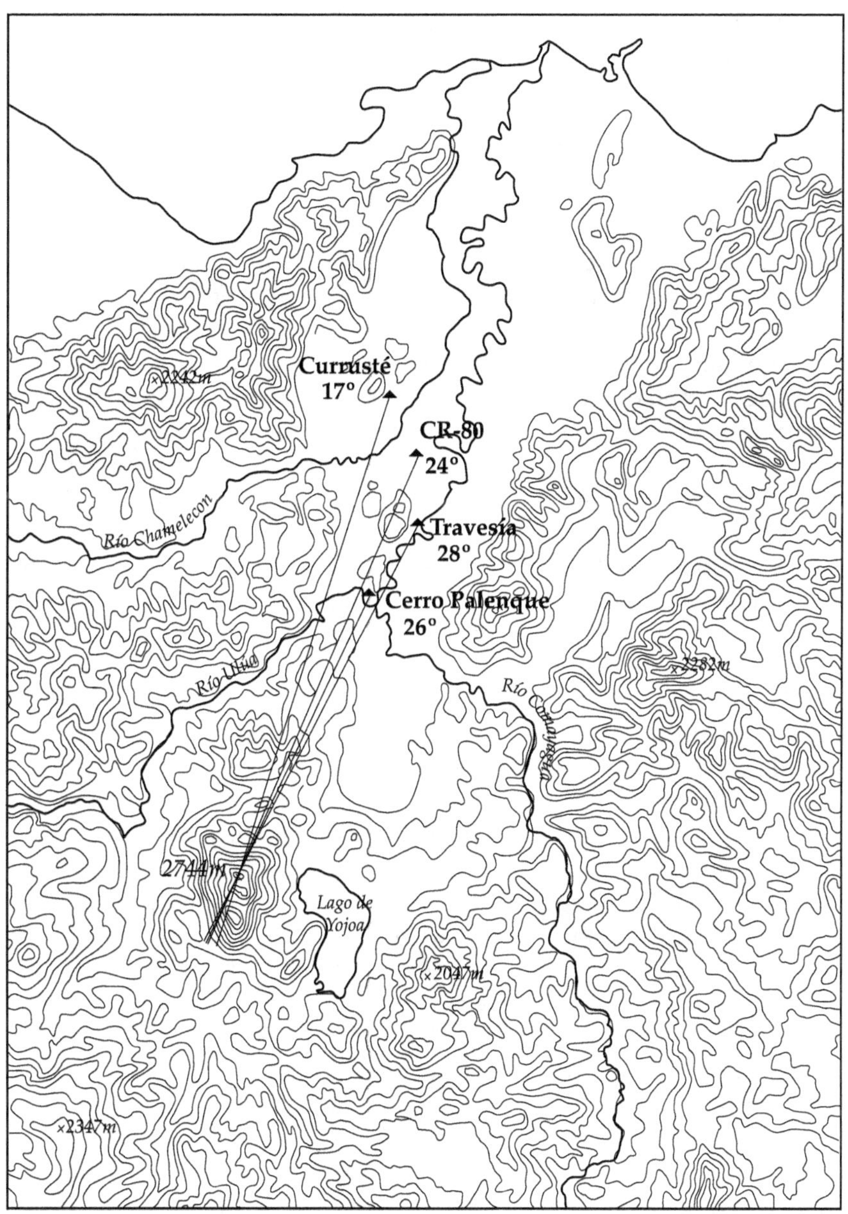

6.16: Site alignments with the highest peak in the mountains surrounding the Ulúa Valley

notion of communal ritual demarcating spatial boundaries—and the social identities affiliated with these boundaries—has an analogue in the Honduran ethnographic record in the Lenca tradition of *guancasco* (Chapman 1986). Anne Chapman describes this tradition as the visits between neighboring villages in which the patron saint of one community was paraded in a procession to the other. The formalized procession and interaction of the saints is accompanied by music, masked dancers, and elaborate offerings. Based on both ethnographic and ethnohistoric accounts, she interprets this tradition as an enactment of a "peace accord"—as a manner of affirming social alliances and the demarcation of community property. *Guancasco* provides a useful model for understanding how material culture iconic of community membership was incorporated into repeated, ritualized processional movements and how these practices of incorporation and inscription would have served as a means of demarcating social identities and boundaries (cf. Joyce 1991:132–135). Participation in or observation of such practices of incorporation would have embedded these relationships in the social memory of community members of all ages and would have entailed performances through which this memory was "sedimented in the body" (Connerton 1989:72).

By invoking acts of creation and renewal through rituals marking the conjunctures of spatial landmarks and temporal cycles, participants in rituals at multiple scales recreated the cosmos in microcosm in everyday life. Rituals of renewal on an annual basis were analogous to the types of rituals associated with the renovation of structures—such as the "death" of a house and/or one of its inhabitants—requiring ritual intercession surrounding its journey to the underworld (interment) and the subsequent renewal of the earthly world. The notions of renewal and the creation of ancestors were inherent to the perpetuation of house societies and critical to the rights, privileges, and prosperity enjoyed by members of the house (cf. King, Chapter 7). The incorporation of the life cycle of humans into the life cycle of the house society is an indication that the transformation to the status of ancestor was critical to the maintenance of the house (see also McAnany 1995, 1998; Gillespie 2000b, 2001). While the literal descent of the deceased into the underworld was marked in the domestic landscape through the practices associated with interment, the sunrise at winter solstice would commemorate this descent on an annual basis. The "apotheosis" of house members as ancestors, in turn, was marked through rituals throughout the sacred landscape in which the ancestors were propitiated in order to invoke favorable intercession in the perpetuation of everyday life.

The association of burning offerings with calendrical renewals described in the archaeological and ethnographic record (for example, Schele and Freidel 1990; Freidel, Schele, and Parker 1993) has clear parallels with the rituals associated with house renewals in the Ulúa Valley. In the following description of annual temple renovations in sixteenth-century Yucatec Maya communities, Diego de Landa documents the significance of material effigies to rituals of renewal:

> [T]hey celebrated a festival called Oc-na, meaning the "renovation of the temple," in honor of the chacs, regarded as the gods of the maize fields. . . . Each year they celebrated this festival and renewed the idols of terra cotta, and the braziers, since it was their custom for each idol to have its own little brazier for burning his incense; and if it was necessary they built a new house, or repaired the old one. ([1566] 1978:77)

This analogue to the material record of rituals of renewal at household sites in the Ulúa Valley illustrates how repeated practices centering on material culture were fundamental to practices of incorporation and inscription. It is through the repeated practices in the creation of and interaction with both sacred and mundane space that the significance of the cosmological order was reproduced and embedded in social memory. Through the demarcation of sacred space and time in such practices as the siting and orientation of architecture and the placement of burials, this order was perpetuated in the embodied experiences of agents in the past. That the performance of all rituals of house renewal was in turn associated with ceramic artifacts produced by house members suggests that these objects were powerful mnemonics in the creation and re-creation of household identity. In this regard, loma sites provide excellent examples for the diachronic observation of these practices, providing traces of how ideas about cosmic order were manifested through time in material culture and the built environment. In their hundreds—and sometimes thousands—of years of occupation, household sites in the Ulúa Valley are particularly vivid monuments to the perpetuation of social memory through production of the material realm.

CRAFTING CHILDREN AND THE CREATION OF SOCIAL MEMORY

> When a baby joins the community, with him in the circle of candles—together with his little red bag—he will have his hoe, his machete, his axe and all the tools he will need in life. These will be his playthings. A little girl will have her washing board and all

> the things she will need when she grows up. . . . The learning is done as a kind of game. When the parents do anything they always explain what it means. . . .
>
> As we grow up we have a series of obligations. Our parents teach us to be responsible; just as they have been responsible. . . . They talk to their children explaining what they have to do and what the ancestors used to do. They don't impose it as a law, but just give the example of what our ancestors have always done. This is how we all learn our small responsibilities. . . . Nearly everything we do today is based on what our ancestors did. . . . Everything that is done today, is done in memory of those who have passed on. (Menchú 1983:15–17)

In order to envision the practices through which house membership and responsibilities were inculcated in children, it is useful to consider how these ideals might have been embodied in the production of and interaction with material culture. How might children have experienced the act of crafting the figurines associated with the house and their subsequent interment as part of the dynamic life cycle of these house societies? How might multiple media—visual and auditory cues, narration and storytelling, control of the body through repeated actions and choreographed movements, and the creation and repetition of representations at multiple scales (especially miniaturization)—have combined to instill these ideas? Here I focus particularly on evidence for multiple aspects of embodied ritual practices as they relate to childhood experience, including multiple media, music, masks, miniaturization, and mimesis.

The excavated sites produced extensive evidence for the production of mold-made ceramic artifacts with human and animal figural representations and geometric motifs, including figurines, whistles, pendants, and miniature ceramic vessels. The presence of ceramic molds at all sites, the differences in designs and types of artifacts among the sites, and the incredible variation of designs within the sites indicate that certain design content might have been specifically related to the individual houses (Lopiparo 2003). So why, then, were these artifacts mold-made? The production of mold-made artifacts in this case implies that standardization was not for mass consumption and suggests that it was the precise replication of the figures that was significant (cf. Joyce 2003).

In addition, certain figures with unique and potentially distinguishing characteristics were reproduced at multiple scales and in multiple media. Figural representations of supernaturals produced in miniature masks also appear as figurines, figural incense burners, or parts of the

6.17: Figural representations of supernaturals produced in multiple media.

headdresses of other human figures (for example, Figure 6.17). Many have detailed the distinguishing treatments of heads and headdresses in Maya art (for example, Joyce 2001, 2003), demonstrating their significance in the demarcation of a range of identities from supernatural beings to social roles. Representations of "wearing" these figures, either in headdresses or as masks, indicate the assumption of a social or ritual role appropriating the characteristics, abilities, or identity of that figure. When considered in this way, the iconography takes on an almost totemic significance, with the implication that the creation of these representations and their use in domestic practices was crucial to the perpetuation of house societies and the reinforcement of household identity.

We must then consider that children would likely have participated in some capacity in domestic production industries. As is common in ethnographic examples (for example, Castegnaro de Foletti 1989), children might have been involved in many aspects of the ceramic production process with their tasks and skills varying by age and perhaps gender (Deal 1998; Crown 1999). While studies frequently cite the role of children in the performance of less skilled tasks (for example, gathering and transporting fuel, water, and clay), works that examine the processes of learning ceramic production describe the discursive and nondiscursive means through which children participate in and apprehend the conceptualization and execution of designs and knowledge about materials (DeBoer 1990; Wyckoff 1990; Crown 1999).

Jean Lave and Etienne Wenger (1991) describe how learning is situated in a "community of practice," in which an apprentice does not simply learn skills, but becomes socialized through "legitimate peripheral participation" in all aspects—both technical and social—involved in a craft. Archaeological evidence for the importance placed on household ceramic production—in the use of molds and mold-made products in the context of domestic rituals in the Ulúa Valley—demonstrates that these communities of practice reinforced knowledge about socially significant and appropriate markers of identity through repeated social practices in the domestic landscape (cf. Bowser 2000). Thus children might have learned the skills of ceramic production through peripheral participation in production processes, but they also learned about the uses of the products for the enactment of social strategies and demarcation of social identities.

Molds could also have "democratized" the processes of producing these potent representations, with more-skilled artisans creating the molds and less-skilled or inexperienced house members preparing and pressing the clay. In the processes of molding, modeling, and begetting these likenesses (after Tedlock 1996), the significance of reproducing particular figures and the significance of molding and ceramic production in general were reinforced as essential responsibilities in the formation of one's identity in the perpetuation of the house and hence as a member of the house society. These roles and responsibilities would have been repeatedly reenacted and reinforced through participation in the many rituals of renewal in which the artifacts were incorporated.

We must also examine both the content and the media of the representations for clues about the ways in which social identities were inscribed and performed through interaction with material culture. Many figural representations are molded both in the form of miniature masks (complete with perforations for attachments) and as heads for attachment onto small whistles. Both the idea of donning masks *and* the fact that unique animal and human heads were frequently grafted onto generic whistle bodies reinforces the idea of the iconic significance of the representations of these heads. Again, the notion of embodying these representations—either through wearing them as masks or by giving them sound via a whistle body—points to the possible ritual practices in which these artifacts might have been reproduced and embedded with meanings. It also points significantly to the value of these artifacts as mnemonics or lessons about the specific practices in which they were to be used, the social meanings of those practices, and their role in the perpetuation of the house.

One might then view these ceramic artifacts as condensed media or "storage devices" inscribed with meanings about social roles and practices, both in their production and in everyday and ritual practices. This notion of mnemonics raises the issues of miniaturization, of how to effectively embed and reproduce meanings in material culture, and of how children might then be taught to interact with this material culture to learn about household practices and social identities in the processes of socialization. Although it is highly unlikely that these objects were used exclusively by children, I would argue that the very nature of miniaturization—especially miniaturization of the tools of full membership and responsibilities in the house—creates a category of "plaything" through which these ideals are discursively and nondiscursively inculcated in children. To the extent that "values become condensed and enriched in miniature" (Bachelard [1958] 1992:150), miniature or "effigy" representations of objects that were fundamental to the production of social identities would have created imagery that was powerfully iconic of social ideals. It seems likely that masks and headdresses, perhaps of perishable materials, were used as ritual adornment in ways similar to those depicted in ceramic miniature. The use of miniature representations of this ritual paraphernalia and associated imagery—sometimes also as adornments in the form of pendants or beads—would have reinforced the iconic and mnemonic quality of this material culture and its embedded meanings.

The association of these objects with life-cycle events in the built environment and with the creation of ancestors through the interment of the dead and the performance of associated rituals in domestic landscapes indicates that they played a significant role in practices fundamental to the reproduction of the house. Children involved in the production and ritual use of these artifacts both inscribed and embodied the values and practices expected of house members. They not only learned the processes of clay preparation and manufacture, but also participated in and embodied social values through the ritual practices—the ornamentation, music, and movements—in which these objects were involved and for which they then became mnemonics. It was through this embodied and dialogic creation of social memory that children played a fundamental role in the reproduction of Terminal Classic house societies in the Ulúa Valley.

ACKNOWLEDGMENTS

The Proyecto Arqueológico Clásico Terminal (PACT) was carried out under the auspices of the Instituto Hondureño de Antropología e Historia. I gratefully acknowledge the support of Dra. Olga Joya and Arqla. Carmen Julia Fajardo and the invaluable assistance of Lic. Juan Alberto Durón. Generous funding for this project was provided by the Wenner Gren Foundation and the Lowie-Olson and Stahl Grants of the University of California, Berkeley. Excavations at CR-132 were carried out under the Proyecto Arqueológico Valle Inferior del Río Ulúa (PA-VIRU), directed by John S. Henderson and Rosemary A. Joyce. My research for PA-VIRU was supported by the Department of Anthropology, Phi Beta Kappa, and the Center for Latin American and Iberian Studies of Harvard University.

REFERENCES CITED

Aveni, Anthony F.

2001 *Skywatchers of Ancient Mexico,* rev. ed. Austin: University of Texas Press.

Bachelard, Gaston

[1958] 1992 *The Poetics of Space*. Trans. M. Jolas. Boston: Beacon Press.

Beaudry-Corbett, Marilyn, and Rosemary Joyce

1993 Late Classic (Late Ulúa Phase) Western Valley. In *Pottery of Prehistoric Honduras: Regional Classification and Analysis,* ed. J. S. Henderson and M. Beaudry-Corbett, 106–122. Los Angeles: UCLA Institute of Archaeology Monograph 35.

Bourdieu, Pierre

1973 The Berber House. In *Rules and Meanings: The Anthropology of Everyday Knowledge,* ed. M. Douglas, 98–110. Harmondsworth: Penguin Books.

1977 *Outline of a Theory of Practice*. Cambridge: Cambridge University Press.

Bowser, Brenda J.

2000 From Pottery to Politics: An Ethnoarchaeological Study of Political Factionalism, Ethnicity, and Domestic Pottery Style in the Ecuadorian Amazon. *Journal of Archaeological Method and Theory* 7(3):219–248.

Bradley, Richard
2003 A Life Less Ordinary: The Ritualization of the Domestic Sphere in Later Prehistoric Europe. *Cambridge Archaeological Journal* 13(1):5–23.

Castegnaro de Foletti, Alessandra
1989 *Alfarería Lenca Contemporánea de Honduras.* Tegucigalpa: Editorial Guaymuras.

Chapman, Anne
1986 *Los Hijos del Copal y la Candela: Tradición Católica de los Lencas de Honduras, Tomo II.* Mexico City: Universidad Nacional Autónoma de México and Centre D'Etudes Mexicaines et Centramericaines.

Clark, John E.
2000 Towards a Better Explanation of Hereditary Inequality: A Critical Assessment of Natural and Historic Human Agents. In *Agency in Archaeology,* ed. Marcia-Anne Dobres and J. E. Robb, 92–112. London: Routledge.

Conkey, Margaret W., and Joan M. Gero
1991 Tensions, Pluralities, and Engendering Archaeology: An Introduction to Women and Prehistory. In *Engendering Archaeology: Women and Prehistory,* ed. J. M. Gero and M. W. Conkey, 3–30. Oxford: Basil Blackwell.

Conkey, Margaret W., and Janet D. Spector
1984 Archaeology and the Study of Gender. In *Advances in Archaeological Method and Theory,* vol. 7, ed. M. B. Schiffer, 1–38. New York: Academic Press.

Connerton, Paul
1989 *How Societies Remember.* Cambridge: Cambridge University Press.

Costin, Cathy Lynne
1998 Introduction: Craft and Social Identity. In *Craft and Social Identity,* ed. C. Costin and R. P. Wright, 3–16. Washington, DC: Archaeological Papers of the American Anthropological Association Number 8.

Crown, Patricia L.
1999 Socialization in American Southwest Pottery Decoration. In *Pottery and People: A Dynamic Interaction,* ed. J. M. Skibo and G. M. Feinman, 25–43. Salt Lake City: University of Utah Press.

Deal, Michael
1998 *Pottery Ethnoarchaeology in the Central Maya Highlands.* Salt Lake City: University of Utah Press.

DeBoer, Warren R.
1990 Interaction, Imitation and Communication as Expressed in Style: The Ucayali Experience. In *The Uses of Style in Archaeology,* ed.

M. W. Conkey and C. A. Hastorf, 82–104. Cambridge: Cambridge University Press.

Dobres, Marcia-Anne, and John E. Robb

2000 Agency in Archaeology: Paradigm or Platitude? In *Agency in Archaeology,* ed. M. Dobres and J. E. Robb, 3–17. London: Routledge.

Fox, John G.

1994 Putting the Heart Back in the Court: Ballcourts and Ritual Action in Mesoamerica. Ph.D. Dissertation, Department of Anthropology, Harvard University.

1996 Playing with Power: Ballcourts and Political Ritual in Southern Mesoamerica. *Current Anthropology* 37(3):483–509.

Fox, John W.

1991 The Lords of Light Versus the Lords of Dark: The Postclassic Highland Maya Ballgame. In *The Mesoamerican Ballgame,* ed. V. L. Scarborough and D. R. Wilcox, 213–238. Tucson: University of Arizona Press.

Freidel, David, Linda Schele, and Joy Parker

1993 *Maya Cosmos: Three Thousand Years on the Shaman's Path.* New York: Quill William Morrow.

Giddens, Anthony

1979 *Central Problems in Social Theory: Action, Structure and Contradiction in Social Analysis.* Berkeley: University of California Press.

1984 *The Constitution of Society: Outline of a Theory of Structuration.* Berkeley: University of California Press.

Gillespie, Susan D.

1991 Ballgames and Boundaries. In *The Mesoamerican Ballgame,* ed. V. L. Scarborough and D. R. Wilcox, 317–345. Tucson: University of Arizona Press.

2000a Beyond Kinship: An Introduction. In *Beyond Kinship: Social and Material Reproduction in House Societies,* ed. R. A. Joyce and S. D. Gillespie, 1–21. Philadelphia: University of Pennsylvania Press.

2000b Maya "Nested Houses": The Ritual Construction of Place. In *Beyond Kinship: Social and Material Reproduction in House Societies,* ed. R. A. Joyce and S. D. Gillespie, 135–160. Philadelphia: University of Pennsylvania Press.

2001 Personhood, Agency, and Mortuary Ritual: A Case Study from the Ancient Maya. *Journal of Anthropological Archaeology* 20:73–112.

Henderson, John S., ed.

1984 *Archaeology in Northwestern Honduras: Interim Reports of the Proyecto Arqueológico Sula,* vol. 1. Ithaca: Latin American Studies Program, Cornell University.

Henderson, John S., Ricardo Agurcia F., and Thomas A. Murray
1982 El Proyecto Arqueológico Sula: Metas, Estrategias y Resultados Preliminares. *Yaxkin* 5(1–2):82–88.

Hendon, Julia A.
1997 Women's Work, Women's Space, and Women's Status among the Classic-Period Maya Elite of the Copan Valley, Honduras. In *Women in Prehistory: North America and Mesoamerica,* ed. C. Claassen and R. A. Joyce, 33–46. Philadelphia: University of Pennsylvania Press.
1999 The Pre-Classic Maya Compound as the Focus of Social Identity. In *Social Patterns in Pre-Classic Mesamerica,* ed. D. C. Grove and R. A. Joyce, 97–125. Washington, DC: Dumbarton Oaks.
2000 Having and Holding: Storage, Memory, Knowledge, and Social Relations. *American Anthropologist* 102(1):42–54.

Joyce, Rosemary A.
1991 *Cerro Palenque.* Austin: University of Texas Press.
1993 Appendix B: A Key to Ulúa Polychromes. In *Pottery of Prehistoric Honduras: Regional Classification and Analysis,* ed. J. S. Henderson and M. Beaudry-Corbett, 257–279. Los Angeles: UCLA Institute of Archaeology Monograph 35.
1995 Making Men and Women of Children: The Construction of Gender in Mesoamerican Society. Paper presented at the 94th Annual Meeting of the American Anthropological Association, Washington, DC.
1998 Performing the Body in Pre-Hispanic Central America. *RES* 33: 147–166.
2000a Girling the Girl and Boying the Boy: The Production of Adulthood in Ancient Mesoamerica. *World Archaeology* 31(3):473–483.
2000b Heirlooms and Houses: Materiality and Social Memory. In *Beyond Kinship: Social and Material Reproduction in House Societies,* ed. R. A. Joyce and S. D. Gillespie, 189–212. Philadelphia: University of Pennsylvania Press.
2001 Negotiating Sex and Gender in Classic Maya Society. In *Gender in Pre-Hispanic America,* ed. C. F. Klein, 109–141. Washington, DC: Dumbarton Oaks.
2003 Making Something of Herself: Embodiment in Life and Death at Playa de los Muertos, Honduras. *Cambridge Archaeological Journal* 13(2):248–261.

Joyce, Rosemary A., and Julie A. Hendon
2000 Heterarchy, History, and Material Reality: "Communities" in Late Classic Honduras. In *The Archaeology of Communities: A New World Perspective,* ed. M. Canuto and J. Yaeger, 143–159. London: Routledge.

Kamp, Kathryn

2001 Where Have All the Children Gone? The Archaeology of Childhood. *Journal of Archaeological Method and Theory* 8(1):1–34.

Landa, Diego de

[1566] *Yucatan Before and After the Conquest.* Trans. and ed. W. Gates.
1978 New York: Dover Publications.

Lave, Jean, and Etienne Wenger

1991 *Situated Learning: Legitimate Peripheral Practice.* Cambridge: Cambridge University Press.

Lesure, Richard G.

1997 Figurines and Social Identities in Early Sedentary Societies of Coastal Chiapas, Mexico, 1550–800 B.C. In *Women in Prehistory: North America and Mesoamerica,* ed. C. Claasen and R. A. Joyce, 227–248. Philadelphia: University of Pennsylvania Press.

Lopiparo, Jeanne

1994 Stones and Bones at Home: Reconstructing Domestic Activities from Archaeological Remains in a Terminal Classic Residence, Ulúa Valley, Honduras. Senior Honors Thesis, Department of Anthropology, Harvard University. On file at Tozzer and Widener Libraries, Harvard University, the Instituto Hondureño de Antropología e Historia, La Lima, Honduras, and El Museo de San Pedro Sula, Honduras.

2003 Household Ceramic Production and the Crafting of Society in the Terminal Classic Ulúa Valley Honduras. Ph.D. Dissertation, University of California, Berkeley.

2004 La evidencia arqueológica de la producción doméstica de las cerámicas en el Valle del Río Ulúa. In *Memoria VII Seminario de Antropología de Honduras,* ed. K. R. Ávalos, 151–160. Tegucigalpa: Instituto Hondureño de Antropología e Historia.

Lopiparo, Jeanne, Rosemary A. Joyce, and Julia Hendon

In Press Pottery Production in the Terminal Classic Ulúa Valley. In *Terminal Classic Socioeconomic Processes in the Maya Lowlands through a Ceramic Lens,* ed. S. L. López Varela and A. Foias. London: British Archaeological Reports.

Love, Michael

1999 Ideology, Material Culture, and Daily Practice in Pre-Classic Mesoamerica: A Pacific Coast Perspective. In *Social Patterns in Pre-Classic Mesoamerica,* ed. D. C. Grove and R. A. Joyce, 127–153. Washington, DC: Dumbarton Oaks.

Marcus, Joyce

1999 Men's and Women's Ritual in Formative Oaxaca. In *Social Patterns in Pre-Classic Mesoamerica,* ed. D. C. Grove and R. A. Joyce, 67–96. Washington, DC: Dumbarton Oaks.

McAnany, Patricia A.
1995 *Living with the Ancestors: Kinship and Kingship in Ancient Maya Society.* Austin: University of Texas Press.
1998 Ancestors and the Classic Maya Built Environment. In *Function and Meaning in Classic Maya Architecture,* ed. S. D. Houston, 271–298. Washington, DC: Dumbarton Oaks.

Menchú, Rigoberta
1983 *I, Rigoberta Menchú: An Indian Woman in Guatemala.* Ed. E. Burgos-Debray. London: Verso.

Pope, Kevin O.
1985 Palaeoecology of the Ulúa Valley, Honduras: An Archaeological Perspective. Ph.D. Dissertation, Stanford University.

Robin, Cynthia
2002 Outside of Houses: The Practices of Everyday Life at Chan Nohòol, Belize. *Journal of Social Archaeology* 2(2):245–268.
2003 New Directions in Classic Maya Household Archaeology. *Journal of Archaeological Research* 11(4):307–356.

Rodman, Margaret C.
1992 Empowering Place: Multilocality and Multivocality. *American Anthropologist* 94(3):640–656.

Schele, Linda, and David Freidel
1990 *A Forest of Kings: The Untold Story of the Ancient Maya.* New York: Quill William Morrow.

Sofaer Derevenski, Joanna
2000 Material Culture Shock: Confronting Expectations in the Material Culture of Children. In *Children and Material Culture,* ed. J. Sofaer Derevenski, 3–16. London: Routledge.

Stark, Barbara L.
1985 Archaeological Identification of Pottery Production Locations: Ethnoarchaeological and Archaeological Data in Mesoamerica. In *Decoding Prehistoric Ceramics,* ed. B. A. Nelson, 158–194. Carbondale: Southern Illinois University Press.

Tedlock, Dennis, trans.
1996 *Popol Vuh: The Mayan Book of the Dawn of Life,* rev. ed. New York: Simon & Schuster.

Tringham, Ruth E.
1991 Households With Faces: The Challenge of Gender in Prehistoric Architectural Remains. In *Engendering Archaeology: Women and Prehistory,* ed. J. M. Gero and M. W. Conkey, 93–131. Oxford: Blackwell.
1994 Engendered Places in Prehistory. *Gender, Place and Culture* 1:169–203.

Wilkie, Laurie
2000 Not Merely Child's Play: Creating a Historical Archaeology of Children and Childhood. In *Children and Material Culture,* ed. J. Sofaer Derevenski, 100–113. London: Routledge.

Willey, Gordon R.
1972 *The Artifacts of Altar de Sacrificios.* Papers of the Peabody Museum of Archaeology and Ethnology, Harvard University, Vol. 64, No. 1. Cambridge: Peabody Museum.

Wyckoff, Lydia L.
1990 *Designs and Factions: Politics, Religion, and Ceramics on the Hopi Third Mesa.* Albuquerque: University of New Mexico Press.

Wylie, Alison
1991 Gender Theory and the Archaeological Record: Why is There No Archaeology of Gender? In *Engendering Archaeology: Women and Prehistory,* ed. J. M. Gero and M. W. Conkey, 31–54. Oxford: Basil Blackwell.

Yaeger, Jason
2000 The Social Construction of Communities in the Classic Maya Countryside. In *The Archaeology of Communities: A New World Perspective,* ed. M. A. Canuto and J. Yaeger, 123–142. London: Routledge.

7

THE MARKING OF AGE IN ANCIENT COASTAL OAXACA

Stacie M. King

INTRODUCTION

Research on gender by feminist anthropologists during the last two decades has inspired recent theoretical and methodological work on the subject of crosscutting social identities and "intersectionality" (Moore 1993; Collins 1999; Meskell 2001). Of particular interest is how social identities differentiate individuals and groups of people, as well as how varied identities can overlap and intersect based on age, sex/gender, class, ethnic affiliation, and sexuality (Meskell 1998). As a result, archaeologists have begun to consider age-based identities in addition to social identities based on gender or status alone (see also Sofaer Derevenski 1994a, 2000; Lillehammer 1989; Moore and Scott 1997; Scott 1999; Kamp 2001). To do so, it is necessary to recognize the disjuncture between skeletal age (infants, juveniles, sub-adults, and adults) and cultural categories (children, adults), much in the same way sex and gender are separate (Sofaer Derevenski 1994b:8–10). In many circumstances, gender itself is an age-dependent category (Gilchrist 1997;

Lesick 1997:35; Lucy 1997:154; R. Joyce 2000a). Thus, recent work has sought to define childhood and adulthood (and all age-based social differences) based on emic categories using archaeological evidence specific to the culture being studied so as to develop local "cultural theories on ageing" (Lillehammer 2000:24).

Archaeological studies of childhood have focused on three primary sources of information: mortuary practices and the skeletal remains of infants and juveniles (e.g., Meskell 1994; Lucy 1997; Rega 1997; Crawford 2000; Houby-Nielsen 2000; Nagar and Eshed 2001), toys and learning (e.g., Sillar 1994; Wilkie 2000), and apprenticeship in tasks such as lithic manufacture and ceramic production (e.g., Finlay 1997; Crown 1999; Kamp et al. 1999; Grimm 2000). Historical documents and iconography that depict children are an additional line of evidence about childhood in Mesoamerica. Until now, Oaxacan archaeologists have not specifically attempted to understand childhood and age-dependent status differences (other than noting circumstances of "ascribed status" in child burials and rituals of child sacrifice), but work on figurines (e.g., Martínez López and Winter 1994; Marcus 1998, 1999) and on costuming and status symbolism in Mixtec codices (e.g., Pohl 1994; Hamann 1997) may help us to locate some of the basic markers of age difference and symbols of childhood.

In this chapter, I use two lines of evidence to consider the meaning of childhood and markers of age in ancient coastal Oaxaca. First, I discuss the figurine assemblage found in household excavations at Early Postclassic Río Viejo (Figure 1.1) and examine the connection between children and figurine use, as well as the representation of children and adults in figurines. Second, I highlight mortuary ritual in the lower Río Verde valley of coastal Oaxaca and examine the material marking gender and age in burial contexts. Mortuary practices are a promising avenue for investigating childhood in ancient coastal Oaxaca, since burial data are widely available. I examine childhood at Río Viejo by considering the *absence* of child burials and presumed spatial separation of child burials from the interior of houses where adults were buried. I draw on data from recent excavations at the site of Río Viejo, which unearthed remains of two residential neighborhoods likely pertaining to ancestors of Chatino peoples. This coastal community was connected to Highland Mixtec and Central Mexican communities of Tula, Hidalgo, and Cholula, Puebla, through long-distance networks of communication and trade in cotton and obsidian during the Early Postclassic (King 2003, n.d.).

FIGURINES FROM EARLY POSTCLASSIC RÍO VIEJO

The Operation B figurine collection includes 545 hand-modeled and mold-made fragments of figurines and whistles found in structure fill and midden contexts along with all other kinds of domestic refuse. Hand-modeled figurines were most often fashioned into small human and zoomorphic forms and were pierced for hanging as pendants. The most frequently occurring type of mold-made figurine is the combination figurine/whistle depicting a woman wearing a skirt, jewelry, and a headdress. The headdresses of these figurines were highly elaborated, with beads, feathers, intricate hair designs, and representations of birds such as turkeys and eagles. These figurines/whistles have mouthpieces on the reverse side that function both as whistles and supports for standing the figurines upright.

The Río Viejo figurine assemblage could be useful for an archaeology of childhood, especially one that considers play, learning, economic participation, apprenticeship, and the transmission of cultural knowledge from one generation to the next as part of the childhood experience and the foundation for children's social action. Elsewhere, researchers have suggested that figurines were used and perhaps made by children as toys for play (e.g., Spence 2002; Winter 2002). Based on spatial distribution, depositional context, and representational content, however, the Río Viejo assemblage can in no obvious way be linked in whole or in part to children. In the absence of clear means to connect children and figurines, I cannot interpret Río Viejo figurines as items produced by or used only by children as toys for play.

Although children might have interacted with figurines as toys, I can build strong arguments using Oaxacan ethnohistoric documents and Mexican ethnographic accounts that link figurines and figurine use to ritual action involving people of *all* ages (see also Smith 2002:105–108 for a discussion of Aztec sources). Ethnographic studies show that pre-Hispanic ceramic and stone figurines are often described by indigenous peoples to be imbued with a life-force that is symbolically linked to the earth, which was considered volatile and potentially dangerous (Parsons 1936; Sandstrom 1981; Dow 1986; Sandstrom and Sandstrom 1986; Lipp 1991; Bellas 1995; Monaghan 1995). In these accounts, figurines and *ídolos* (larger stone figures) were commonly placed on altars and offered sacrifices (Gonzalez Obregon 1912:74; Dávila Padilla 1955; Greenberg 1981; Lipp 1991; Bellas 1995), placed on the sides of paths to mark boundaries between communities (Redfield and Villa Rojas 1934; Parsons 1936; Crumrine 1964; Vogt 1969; Greenberg 1981; Lipp 1991), placed at stops in ritual processions (Greenberg 1981), set on thresholds of houses (Parsons 1936; Crumrine 1964), or placed in front of caves (Parsons 1936; Lipp 1991) to mark points of exit and entrance. They sometimes served as stand-ins for living participants in life-cycle ceremonies (Greenberg 1981). In other cases, figurines were molded into miniature versions of items being petitioned and placed as offerings (Parsons 1936). The ritual use of figurines in the Mesoamerican past has been suggested by many archaeologists in recent studies and especially linked to women, life-cycle rituals, and ancestors (e.g., Cyphers Guillén 1993; Scott 1993; Brumfiel 1996; Lesure 1997; Marcus 1998; Smith 2002). These and other examples show that figurines likely communicated powerful, yet sometimes subtle ritual messages within multiple contexts of use.

I am encouraged by the contributions of Geoffrey McCafferty and Sharisse McCafferty and also Jeanne Lopiparo (Chapters 2 and 6, respectively), in which they suggest that whistles, flutes, and sound-making objects might have been material objects used primarily by children. If we link children, play, and the ritual use of figurines, the interaction between children and figurines takes on more symbolic potency. Figurines, therefore, would provide evidence of children's social and ritual action (see Hamann, Chapter 8; Román Berrelleza and Chávez Balderas, Chapter 9). The social and ritual importance of sound and sound-making in ancient Mesoamerica is provocatively discussed by Dorothy Hosler with reference to metal bells (1994:233–248), and this discussion could appropriately be extended to clay whistles, flutes, and rattles. If children were the primary users of sound-making objects, then nearly all of the Río Viejo figurine assemblage could be connected to children. Whistles, flutes, clay bells, and clay balls used as rattles in ceramic vessel supports were all common artifacts at Río Viejo and were deposited in a variety of contexts, including those associated with adult action. These objects show a community-wide interest in sound-making associated with people of all ages.

The *use* of figurines does not provide us with the only information about the social experience of childhood. The imagery and symbolism of bodily adornment in human figurines is also a way to consider the marking of age and childhood (see Follensbee, Chapter 10). Ceramic buttons, pendants, bells, and miniature vessels found in Operation B might have served as costume ornaments that could possibly be linked to representations on figurines. These details might help us to better understand what it took to transform children's bodies into those of adults (R. Joyce 2000a; Boyd 2002:142; Fowler 2002:63–64; Robb 2002). Although the age of the individuals depicted in all of the Río Viejo figurines is rarely clear, two examples of the figurines/whistles de-

7.1: Figurine of adult and child, Operation B, Río Viejo.

pict infants. The children do not wear any clothing and are held in the arms of an adult or sub-adult (Figure 7.1). In one of these, both the child and the adult have jewelry, including ear ornaments, a necklace, and bracelets. The symbolism of these figures connects children and adults to one another in a way that is not evidenced by burial treatment at Early Postclassic Río Viejo, both in terms of burial location and bodily adornment of adult individuals. The figurines depict adults as protectors and caregivers of children with a certain amount of physical intimacy. In terms of clothing and body ornamentation, both children and adults are similarly adorned with jewelry, demonstrating that jewelry alone is not an insignia of an age-based social status. Therefore, archaeological data from figurines provide limited, yet provocative information about the role of children in ancient Oaxaca.

EARLY POSTCLASSIC MORTUARY PRACTICES AT RÍO VIEJO

Thus far, I have considered the possibility of linking the social and ritual use of figurines and the representation of children in ceramic figurines with children. Although we might speculate about the ways that children interacted with figurines, we must look elsewhere to examine the *meaning* of age differences and childhood specifically. For this reason, I focus the rest of the chapter on mortuary practices. Taken together, the combination of the figurine data and the mortuary evidence from Early Postclassic burials at Río Viejo provides a more robust evidentiary framework for considering childhood.

In 2000, portions of eleven residential structures dating to the Early Postclassic (800 to 1200 CE) were unearthed, along with a full suite of domestic artifacts and the mortuary remains of twenty-one individuals in two different residential neighborhoods (A. Joyce and King 2001). I will discuss Early Postclassic mortuary practices, drawing comparisons between the Operation B neighborhood burials and the Operation A neighborhood burials. I will also consider the entire register of lower Río Verde valley burials excavated from other sites and contexts. Roughly 175 burials spanning the Middle Formative to the Early Postclassic (400 BCE to 1200 CE) have been located and studied in the lower Río Verde region.

The lower Río Verde valley sample includes 102 burials from Late and Terminal Formative residential zones at the site of Cerro de la Cruz, reported by Arthur Joyce (1991b, 1994). In these residential zones, subfloor and sub-patio burial was common and included primary and secondary and also single and multiple individual burials of people of all ages and sexes. Burial positions were flexed or extended, and burial orientations varied but most often paralleled structure walls. The Classic-period sample includes thirty individuals recovered from test pits at the site of Río Viejo or intrusive deposits at Cerro de la Cruz (A. Joyce 1991a, 1994; Christensen 1999). In 2000 twenty-one individuals were recovered in Early Postclassic residential zones at Río Viejo. The remainder of the burial sample was recovered from contexts that have not been securely dated or the remains were highly fragmentary and therefore have not been included in this discussion.

Four Early Postclassic burials were recovered from the Operation A residential neighborhood excavated by Arthur Joyce, Laura Arnaud Bustamante, and Marc Levine (2001). These included two children buried in flexed positions outside of buildings, one adult male buried outside of a residential structure with no offerings, and two adults interred together underneath a patio.

Of the sixteen Early Postclassic burials found in the Operation B neighborhood, all were the result of primary, single individual burial events (Table 7.1). Each person was positioned similarly, in an extended

Table 7.1 Early Postclassic burials, Operation B

Burial	*Indv*	*Location*	*Sex**	*Age†*	*Orientation*	*Vessels*	*Other Offerings*
26	34	Str. 8-8	x	a	8° W of N	2	
27	35	Str. 8-8	x	a	4° E of N	0	3 obsidian blades and 1 quartz burnisher
28	36	Str. 8-8	m	a	4° W of N	3	
29	37	Str. 8-8	x	sa	7° E of N	2	
30	38	Str. 8-8	x	a	4° E of N	2	1 quartz burnisher
31	39	Str. 8-8	f?	a	4° E of N	2	
32	40	Str. 8-8	m	a	6° E of N	2	
33	41	Str. 8-8	x	a	7° E of N	2	
34	42	Str. 8-8	x	a	6° E of N	1?	
35	43	Str. 8-8	m	a	2° E of N	0	
37	45	Str. 8-8	unexc.			1	
43	52	Str. 8-7	f	a	17° E of N	3	
45	54	Str. 8-7	x	a	22° E of N	0	
46	55	Str. 8-7	m	a	9° E of N	1	5 shell pendants
50	59	Str. 8-7	x	a	12° E of N	1	
53	62	Str. 8-7	unexc.	a		2	

* x = indeterminate, m = male, f = female, unexc. = unexcavated

† a = adult, sa = sub-adult

position lying on his or her back, with arms either resting alongside the torso or with hands crossed and resting on the abdomen (Figure 7.2). Association with the Early Postclassic is based on the presence of distinctive ceramic vessels interred with most of the deceased. Ceramic debris of vessels similar to those placed in the burials was found in a midden in Operation B with a calibrated AMS radiocarbon date between 1035 and 1187 CE (2S variation, AA40040). The stratigraphic sequence of burial events, however, is difficult to discern. Earthen burial chambers or plastered floor surfaces were not present to help distinguish one burial event from another and, without any superimposition of the actual bodies, further assessment of the sequence of interment is difficult. Pathological indicators and the age-at-death profile of the individuals buried beneath the floor surfaces give no indication that the burials were the result of a single traumatic event, such as a violent massacre or an epidemic. Rather, the skeletons exhibit normal signs of aging and degenerative bony afflictions such as osteoarthritis (in the back and, in one case, the hand), osteoporosis, wear on the teeth, and antemortem tooth loss.

Eleven of the Early Postclassic burials were interred beneath the floor of Structure 8-8b. The structure is an 11 x 5 meter rectangular building in which the long axis runs east to west. The remarkable precision with which the remains were placed underneath the floor resulted in side-by-

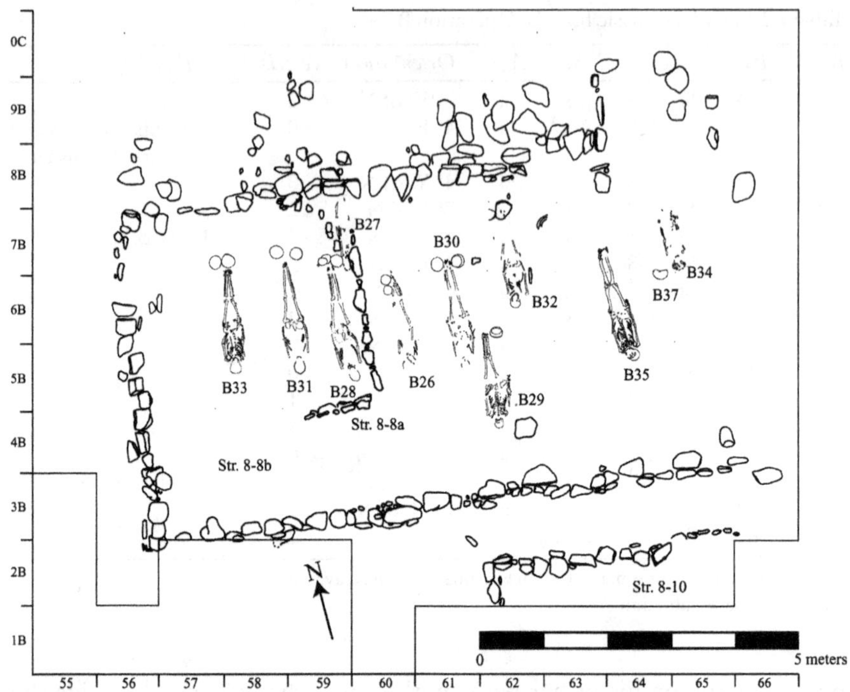

7.2: Plan of Structure 8-8b, Operation B, showing locations of Early Postclassic burials.

side interments extending nearly the entire length of the structure. The orientations of the burials paralleled the short axis of the structure walls, and all individuals were oriented north to south, with their heads to the south. Thus, the resulting distribution of burials forms a rough row of bodies across the length of the structure, as shown in Figure 7.2.

The remaining five burials were found beneath the floor of Structure 8-7. Since the structure was only partially excavated below the occupation surface, the total number of individuals buried beneath the structure may have been higher. Like Structure 8-8b, Structure 8-7 is also a rectangular building roughly 11 x 5 meters, but the long axis of this structure runs north to south. Placement of the deceased in Structure 8-7 paralleled the long axis of the building, with bodies oriented north to south and heads positioned to the south as in Structure 8-8b (Figure 7.3). If excavations had continued beneath the interior floor surface in the northernmost and southernmost sections of this structure, it is possible that auxiliary rows of burials may have been recovered.

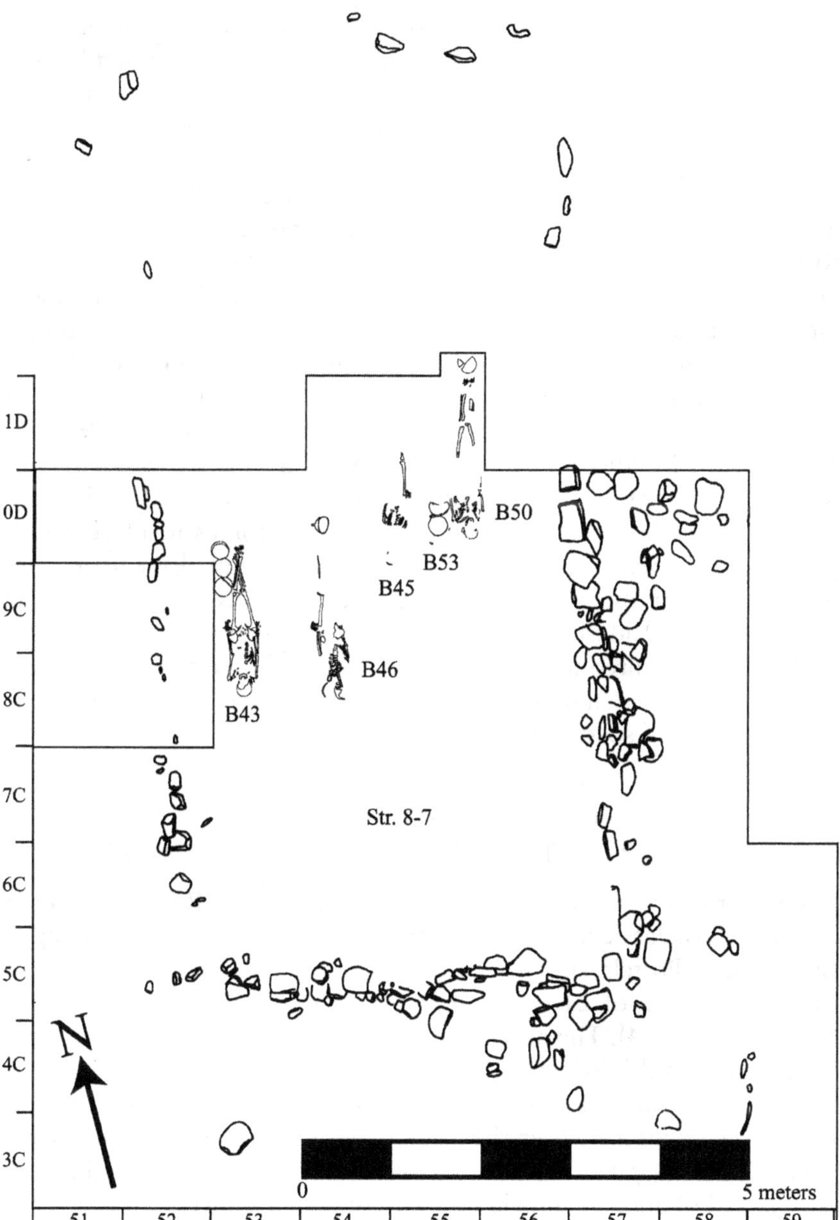

7.3: Plan of Structure 8-7, Operation B, showing locations of Early Postclassic burials.

None of the burial events disturbed the skeletal remains of individuals previously laid to rest. This shows that those still living had knowledge of the location of past burials beneath the structure floors, either by remembering where the dead had been buried or by prospecting for a location that was not already occupied. In either case, superimposition of Early Postclassic burials was purposely and carefully avoided. This practice contrasts with the evidence from earlier time periods in the lower Río Verde valley, when individuals were more often placed atop and alongside one another in complex multiple burials or in sequential and intrusive burial events (A. Joyce 1991a). In the Valley of Oaxaca, tombs were frequently reused for the burial of multiple individuals, whereas non-tomb burials typically included only one or two individuals (Whalen 1981, 1988; Martínez López, Winter, and Antonio Juárez 1995:236; Miller 1995; Middleton, Feinman, and Molina Villegas 1998). Arthur Miller (1995) argues that the addition of newly deceased individuals and "heads of household" in Valley of Oaxaca tombs involved a purposeful spatial reconfiguration of the human skeletal elements and offerings already present to emphasize connections between the newly deceased ancestor and those still living. The less formal, earthen pit burials at Río Viejo required no restructuring of burial space to accommodate the newly deceased and demonstrate a stronger preference for avoiding already occupied space rather than reconfiguring it.

CHANGE THROUGH TIME IN LOWER RÍO VERDE VALLEY MORTUARY PRACTICES

In comparison with earlier time periods in the lower Río Verde valley, the Early Postclassic mortuary practices show some significant changes. By the Early Postclassic, the residents exhibit a preference for primary single burial (19 of 21 individuals, or 90 percent) ($\chi^2 = 42.492$, $p < 0.001$) (Figure 7.4). The only burial that is not a primary single burial is the complex multiple burial located in the Operation A neighborhood. A. Joyce, Arnaud Bustamante, and Levine (2001) suggest that this complex burial might have been the result of a sacrificial ritual involving the primary burial of a tightly flexed, perhaps bundled female and secondary burial of another individual, both of which showed signs of burning. Ritual treatment might in part explain its variation from the rest of Río Viejo's Early Postclassic burials.

In addition, the Early Postclassic is the first time period in which all burials for which data are available (100 percent of 14 individuals) were positioned with their heads to the south ($\chi^2 = 34.159$, $p < 0.001$)

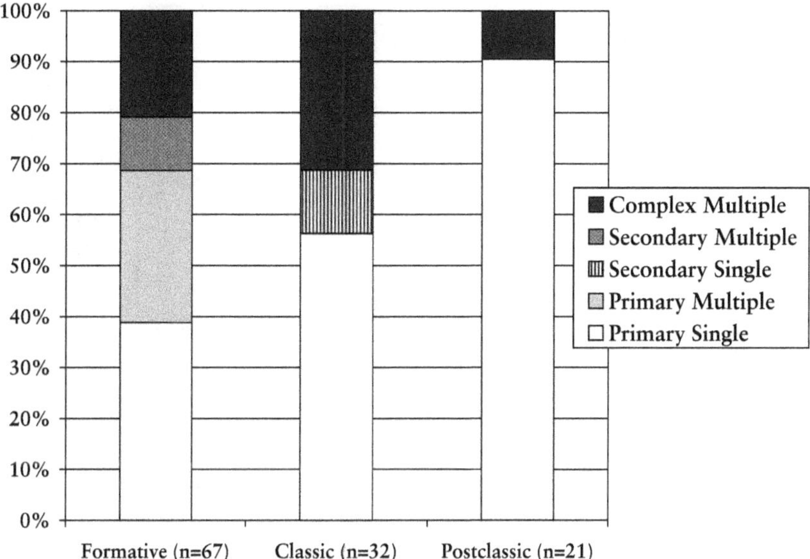

7.4: Types of burials in the lower Río Verde valley burial sample, by individual.

(Figure 7.5). In the Late and Terminal Formative, it was presumably acceptable to bury the deceased oriented in any of the four cardinal directions, preferably parallel with structure walls. By the Early Classic and Late Classic, the south and west predominated. Because the Early Classic and Late Classic have not been the focus of extensive study in the lower Verde, however, the sample sizes are quite small and have little reliable context information. For all time periods, south-facing burials were more likely to occur when individuals were placed below house floor surfaces in structure interiors (28 of 40 south-facing burials, or 70 percent) ($\chi^2 = 22.704$, $p = 0.03$), so the preference for south-facing burials during the Early Postclassic may also be related to the context preference for sub-floor burial.

Nearly all of the Operation B neighborhood Early Postclassic burials include offerings (n = 13 or 81.3 percent). In these cases, one to three ceramic vessels were placed around the feet of the deceased. The vessels are painted, differentially fired, and highly uniform with two predominant forms: high-walled and low-walled semispherical bowls. These forms in no way represent the complete range of ceramic vessel forms of the Early Postclassic, but they are also not restricted to burial contexts, since fragments of similar vessels are found throughout Early Postclassic

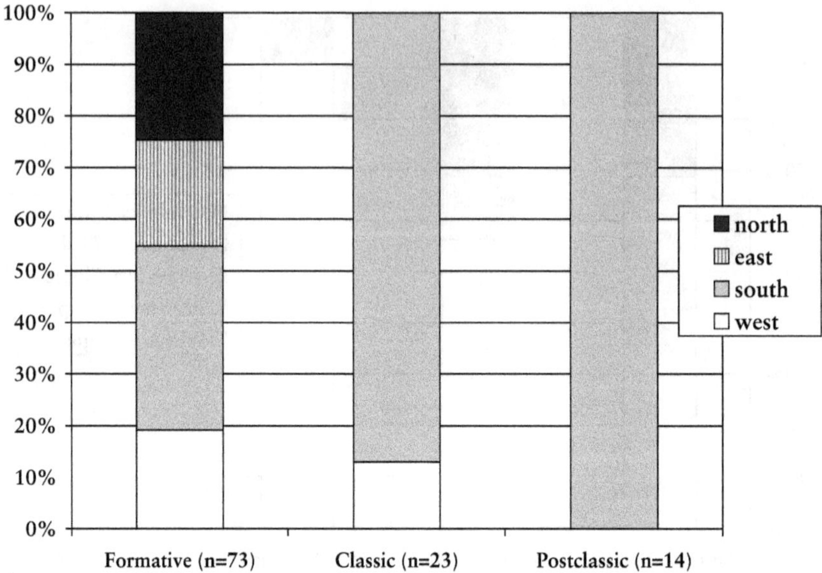

7.5: Orientation of burials in the lower Río Verde valley burial sample.

fill layers and midden deposits. Maize phytoliths were present in at least one of these vessels, demonstrating that a maize-based food was either presented to the dead or shared among participants in funerary rites, or that well-used and unwashed vessels were selected as offerings (see also R. Joyce 1999:20). Two Early Postclassic burials (Burial 27 and Burial 29) included beautifully polished quartz burnishers placed beneath the head of each person. These burnishers show evidence of extensive polishing and use wear, and were likely heavily used in pottery manufacture prior to interment with the deceased. Burial 27 additionally contained three obsidian blades, which were probably placed within the deceased individual's mouth, and yet another (Burial 46) wore a necklace of shell pendants (see Table 7.1).

The presence of offerings in the majority of Early Postclassic burials contrasts sharply with the lack of burial offerings in all earlier time periods and the Late Formative in particular, when 75 percent (70 of 93 individuals) of the deceased were buried without offerings ($\chi^2 = 16.038$, $p < 0.001$) (Figure 7.6). Burial location is also connected to the presence of offerings, such that individuals buried outside of structures were more likely to be buried without any offerings as compared to individuals interred beneath house floors. (This difference, however, is not statisti-

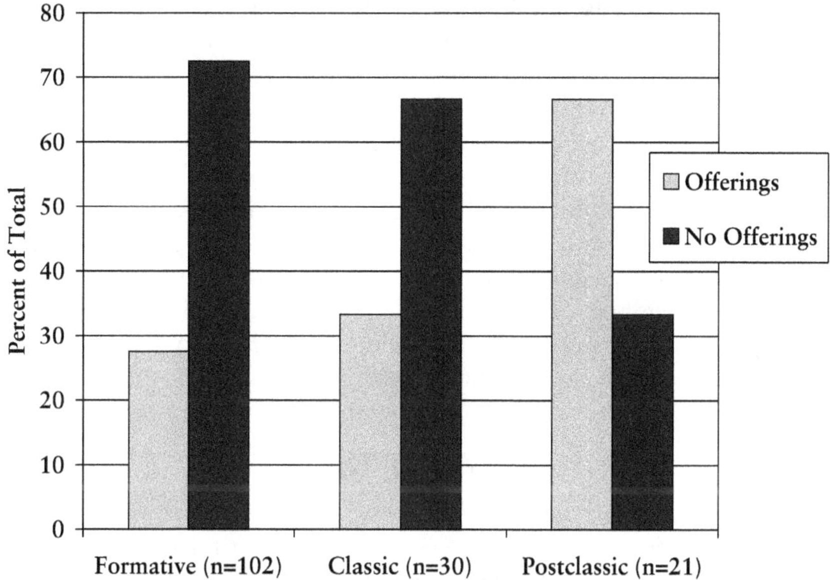

7.6: Presence of burial offerings in lower Río Verde valley burials.

cally significant.) This relationship is perhaps most clear for the Early Postclassic, where burials found underneath structure floors in Operation B almost always include offerings (14 of 16, or 81.3 percent), and the five Early Postclassic burials found outside structures in Operation A (the only Early Postclassic burials located in Operation A excavations) were buried with none. Because the two neighborhoods differed in the treatment of the dead, however, mortuary rites may not be directly comparable. Variability in mortuary practices between the neighborhoods may suggest a qualitative difference between the residents of each neighborhood, in spite of similarities in architectural design and spatial configuration, economic practices, and material culture (A. Joyce and King 2001; King 2003).

The evidence from Operation B excavations suggests that during the Early Postclassic, people customarily buried the dead below the floors of their houses. Houses were not constructed solely for the purpose of "housing" the dead but were occupied and used prior to and probably after interments. In this neighborhood, only two of the excavated structures contained burials (Structures 8-8b and 8-7), which likely marks a separation between at least two household groups. Overall similarity in the burial patterns suggests that strong community standards and traditions were in place. Because the bodies of the deceased were not elaborately decorated with costume ornaments, jewelry, or luxury items marking social differentiation, it seems that the similarity between people was emphasized more than social distinctions based on wealth, status, economic practices, or gender. On the other hand, a spatial separation exists between the locations of adult and child burials during the Early Postclassic. Only adults, including both women and men, were buried within houses, suggesting that some fundamental conceptual and social distinction separated children and adults. Perhaps only adults were considered true members of a given household or, alternatively, something special or powerful pervaded adult bodies, ancestors, or souls that required burial within the confines of architectural space.

GENDER-BASED DIFFERENCES

The mortuary data from Río Viejo give us a unique opportunity to examine the intersection between economic activities, social categories, and ritual practice as they relate to gender. Part of my interest in studying the relationships in the burial data is to connect mortuary practices to lives of the people who lived in Río Viejo and, thereby, better understand how people defined themselves vis-à-vis other communities nearby and far, other neighborhoods at the same site, and among themselves.

Traditionally, researchers have analyzed sexed individuals and their associated burial offerings to try to understand gender-based divisions of labor, status, and power, as well as gender- (and sex-) specific economic practices and social categories (e.g., Rathje 1970; Saxe 1970; Binford 1972). The faulty assumptions, however, that were often made in these studies, such as assuming the sex of an individual based on associated grave goods or interpreting grave goods as directly reflecting the wealth of those buried, have been largely exposed (Hodder 1982, 1987; McCafferty and McCafferty 1994; Arnold and Wicker 2001). In studying mortuary practices, we must be careful not to assume a direct mapping between biological sex and the cultural experience of gender and recognize that even the physiological interpretation of sex itself is culturally constructed, such that "sexed" bodies are themselves not always a stable basis on which to discuss gendered identities (Gilchrist 1999:76; Moore 1999; Sørenson 2000).

For Postclassic Mexico and the Aztec in particular, the abundant iconographic imagery and written codices support the general interpretation that an identity-related distinction was made between adult males and adult females, with males associated with images and material culture of warfare, and females associated with spinning, weaving, cooking, and child-rearing (Brumfiel 1991; McCafferty and McCafferty 1991; R. Joyce 1993, 2000b:477). Whether people of Postclassic Mexico in general actually experienced a distinction between male and female gender identities and gender roles on a daily basis or whether it was a dichotomy being represented and promoted by the producers of public media is another issue with which to contend (Hamann 1997:172; R. Joyce 2000a:184–187).

If the associations do imply a gendered division of labor, we must also recognize that divisions of labor change through time, from context to context, and throughout the lives of specific individuals (Mills 2000). In spite of the separation of male and female, the gender differences and associated roles of Postclassic Mexico seem to have been promoted as complementary and necessary rather than hierarchical and differentially valued (McCafferty and McCafferty 1988; Kellogg 1995; 1997:127; Burkhart 1997), such that women who died in childbirth, for example, were likened to male warriors who died on the battlefield (Klein 1994:141).

We must also examine the situations in Postclassic Mexico in which women's and men's roles are *not* differentiated. For example, the introduction of the carved stone "genealogical register" as a form of smaller-scale monumental art during the Oaxacan Postclassic shows the importance of marriage alliances for claiming rights and privileges (Marcus 1983; 1989:205–206). The iconography of these registers traces genealogical connections through both male and female lines. Mixtec codices and Aztec documents record numerous marital alliances in Postclassic Mexico that opportunistically emphasize maternal and paternal genealogical connections to establish or reinforce elite heritage (Spores 1974; McCafferty and McCafferty 1988; Gillespie 1989; Terraciano 2001). Although necessarily based on a distinction between maleness and femaleness, genealogies that utilize equally maternal and paternal ancestors effectively create a structural similarity between male and female, much like the parallelism in male and female images in the codices (Hamann 1997:171; Terraciano 2001).

The similarity between male and female is also represented in other situations in Oaxaca. For example, the faces of a male and female are carefully carved above the entrance to Tomb 2 at Lambityeco, presumably representing the main occupants of the tomb who Paddock, Mogor, and Lind (1968) have interpreted as a possible marriage pair. Regardless of the nature of the relationship between the two individuals, it is important to recognize that they were both presented in the same role adorning the tomb façade, and the gender reference made by the carvings was one of similarity (the same) rather than one of complementarity (separate but equal). In the Oaxaca barrio at Teotihuacan, both women and men garnered independent and equally rich burial offerings, suggesting that men and women might have enjoyed a similar status (Spence 2002).

On the coast of Oaxaca, monumental art may have changed from the Late Classic to the Early Postclassic. The Late Classic pattern of (presumably?) male persons depicted on carved stone stelae changed to include standing sculptures of females (identified on the basis of clothing and exposed breasts) during the Early Postclassic (Urcid and Joyce 1999; A. Joyce, Arnaud Bustamante, and Levine 2001). A. Joyce, Arnaud Bustamante, and Levine (2001:373) suggest that the inclusion and predominance of female figures in coastal Early Postclassic monumental art may reflect a gender ideology that allowed women greater social power. The public versions of sculptural iconography may or may not correspond to the social experience of gender and gender difference in the lives of Río Viejo residents. If it was the case that women had access to greater social power, then what were the arenas of social power for women prior to the Early Postclassic and how have they changed? How did gender difference correlate or correspond to a difference in power (James 1997:218–219; Gilchrist 1999:52)? Was women's social power unique from the social power of men, or could it be that social power in this context had no reference to gender?

The burials of Río Viejo show us that the line between male and female gender was perhaps not as sharply drawn during the coastal Early Postclassic as Postclassic Mexican iconography might suggest. At Río Viejo, all individuals were buried in nearly identical positions, in similar contexts, with similar offerings. In spite of the high number of spindle whorls and bone needle fragments found in the Río Viejo excavations, which in the iconography of Postclassic Mexico are almost exclusively associated with adult female gender identity, none were placed in burial contexts as offerings. At Early Postclassic Cholula, both men and women received spinning and weaving items as burial offerings (McCafferty and McCafferty 2000). The lack of spinning and weaving implements with *all* deceased individuals at Río Viejo may perhaps show that adult gender identities were not partitioned or that gender identities were not linked to spinning and weaving.

For all time periods on the coast of Oaxaca, variation based on sex produces no statistically significant results in the analysis of the mortuary data set. By the Early Postclassic, the people of Río Viejo chose to demonstrate the *similarity* between males and females rather than emphasize *difference* or *complementarity* between genders in mortuary practices. The burial data, rather, suggest that the gender ideology as expressed materially at Río Viejo is one in which sameness is emphasized and gender makes little difference. Perhaps in the case of Río Viejo, social roles of males and females were more non-gendered and more fluid than what is evidenced in the monumental art of Postclassic Oaxaca. Alternatively, burial contexts may not have been appropriate places to mark the distinction between male and female gender roles and the similarity in burial may simply belie marked differences between gendered adults (Kamp 2001:7; cf. Parker Pearson 1982). In either case, we must look elsewhere for supplementary positive or negative evidence for how coastal Oaxacans experienced gender.

AGE-BASED DIFFERENCES

Rather than gender, I argue that *age*-related identity was the primary identity distinction communicated through mortuary practices at Early Postclassic Río Viejo. All individuals buried inside buildings and directly below Early Postclassic house floors were above the age of seventeen (n = 20), including both males and females (Figure 7.7), and most (n = 19) are biologically mature based on skeletal markers (approximately 20–25 years of age). A normal age-at-death profile would have included nearly as many infants and juveniles as adults and certainly more than zero. Therefore, the lack of any biologically immature individuals beneath Early Postclassic house floors or in most areas outside structures suggests that cultural practices influenced the choice of burial location. If we can define a separation between adulthood and childhood on the basis of burial location and skeletal age, then the lack of individuals less than seventeen years of age buried beneath house floors may mean that these children were not yet considered full members of particular families, houses, or perhaps even the community.

The burial of children outside houses could also reflect a child's connection to multiple houses. As new members of society with parents who presumably came from different houses of origin (if Río Viejo residents practiced the kind of bilateralism widely suggested for Oaxaca), a young child's adult identification with the house of one of its parents was not already determined. The death of children before they established their house connection in practice could have foreclosed any opportunity of being part of one specific house. Children, in this case, would presumably have had the same (or greater) opportunity to be buried in open non-house spaces (as happened in the Operation A neighborhood), and the death of a child could have provided the opportunity

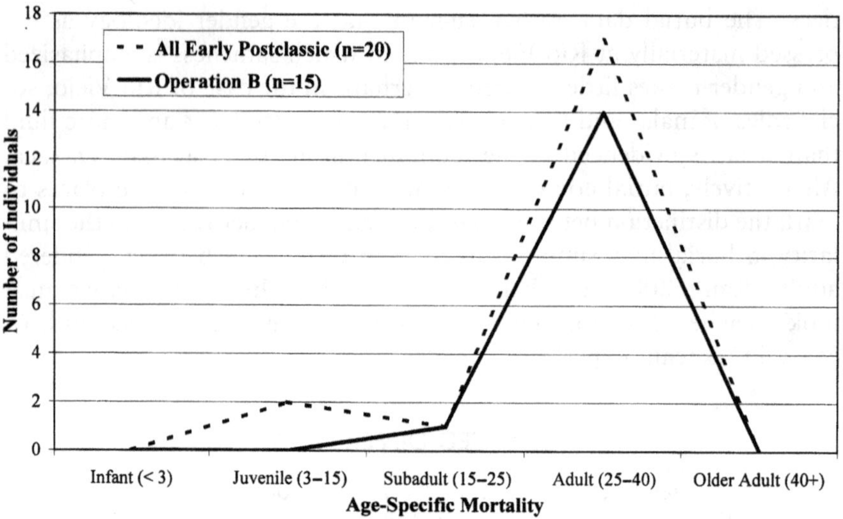

7.7: Mortality curve of Early Postclassic burials.

for larger and more diverse groups of people to celebrate, mourn, or otherwise mark a child's death.

A particular age or a social status that was connected to age was a prerequisite for burial within Early Postclassic buildings at Río Viejo. This location preference contrasts with evidence from earlier time periods in the lower Río Verde valley, with children found in the same contexts as adults, such as burials at Cerro de la Cruz and Río Viejo (A. Joyce 1991a, 1994). In Highland Oaxaca, few examples suggest that a similar age (or age-based status) was a requirement for primary burial in particular locations. The one obvious exception is the Early Formative cemetery at Santo Domingo Tomaltepec in the Valley of Oaxaca. This cemetery was located away from the residential zone and contained nearly eighty individuals, all over the age of thirteen, while infants were buried instead in residential-zone middens and near structures (Whalen 1981:table 3).

Burial practices in Highland Oaxaca tended to vary through time and from site to site, as well as within sites. Children, however, were often buried similarly to adults in locations such as tombs, patios, and underneath floor surfaces, albeit underrepresented in number and with fewer offerings (but with exceptions) (Urcid 1983; Whalen 1988; Martínez López, Winter, and Antonio Juárez 1995:234–236; Christensen 1998; Feinman, Nicholas, and Haines 2002). Marcus Winter (2002:77–78) interprets unique mortuary practices at Classic-period Monte Albán that involve infants and children buried beneath communal patio floors and in special deposits as being connected to Teotihuacan. At Río Viejo, among the burials that occurred outside of structures in the Early Postclassic Operation A neighborhood, two were children. Why did Río Viejo residents of both neighborhoods choose to exclude children from burial beneath house floors? What might this tell us about the neighborhoods, the houses, and the lives of the people who lived in and around them?

Mortuary rites create and modify ties between the deceased, the ancestors, and the living. In the case of Early Postclassic Río Viejo, burial rites were undertaken in closed spaces within the confines of a residence, suggesting that the burial was not an event of large-scale, public commemoration, but rather a smaller-scale ceremony involving household members or a ceremony defined in part by house space (R. Joyce 1999:18; A. Joyce, Arnaud Bustamante, and Levine 2001:359; Cannon 2002:192). The burial event served to create a social memory of the deceased within the home (Chesson 2001), linking the deceased by space and place to those still living (Kuijt 2001; Gillespie 2002). We have no evidence to suggest that the buildings where the dead were buried were thereafter abandoned, nor do we have evidence that residents erected altars or otherwise renovated the architectural space following the interment of a departed family member, as is evidenced at some Maya sites (Gillespie 2002:70). Although not all of the buildings crowded on this wide platform were constructed at the same time and not all buildings contained burials, residents seem to have preferred to construct new buildings, rather than renovate or architecturally modify existing structures. If residents moved following the burial of (at least) the first deceased family member, they likely did not move far. Newer buildings were added to the neighborhood in between and only a few meters away from the earlier structures. Both neighborhoods were continuously occupied for several generations, with residences clustered so tightly that architectural space was likely pre-planned and bounded.

Burial beneath house floors and within residential zones is a common practice across Mesoamerica, and most scholars have linked this sub-floor burial to ancestor worship or ancestor veneration (McAnany 1995; Gillespie 2002; Manzanilla 2002; see also Smith 2002:112 in which the lack of burials beneath house floors at Aztec sites is used to argue that Aztecs did not practice ancestor veneration). More than just providing daily access to the ancestors, however, the physical and spiritual proximity of deceased ancestors reinforced ideals about proper behavior and gave those still living access and rights to the material (and nonmaterial) property of their ancestors (Gillespie 2001, 2002). Keeping bodies in the house kept close the intangibles of status, wealth, and privilege that form individual and group identity, tying the social landscape to specific architectural spaces (Kuijt 2001:89). Standardization in mortuary ritual helps to reinforce, or is reflective of, a sense of community and generational continuity (McAnany 1995; Kuijt 2001), while at the same time the spatial location of these rites within *particular* houses differentiates one house from another and one neighborhood from another, fostering both "affinity and estrangement" at the same time (Schiller 2001:78).

It seems that by burying only those who had reached adult status underneath house floors, the residents were making a statement about what kinds of people could appropriately provide certain kinds of services to the group or deserved this kind of commemoration. Similar findings of a distinction between adult and child burial locations at Formative-period Tetimpa, Puebla, have led Gabriela Uruñuela and Patricia Plunket to a similar conclusion (2002:29). The exclusion of children from burial in houses during the Early Postclassic may suggest that children were considered "outside" of the house until a certain age-status was reached, and that their realm of physical and spiritual power was in a different, as yet undiscovered, arena. The "child's world" (Lillehammer 1989:89), at least in this one respect, was partitioned from both the world of adults and the world of adult ancestors, and children's connections to the house were most likely mediated through their associations with living and deceased adult members.

CONCLUSION

The coastal Oaxacan Early Postclassic saw a change in mortuary practices that linked only adults with houses. This evidence of social differentiation based on age is unique from Classic- and Postclassic-period sites in Oaxaca, and helps us to better understand how residents of Early Postclassic Río Viejo organized their community and experienced life and death. The mortuary evidence from coastal Oaxaca shows that the division between adult and child burial represents new ideas about belonging and house membership, and distinguishes the Early Postclassic community of Río Viejo from earlier time periods. Childhood was a stage of life during which house connections had not yet been established, and the premature death of a child required a different kind of burial treatment or ceremony.

The depiction of children in figurines reminds us, however, that we should not think of Río Viejo children as non-members of houses and therefore as separate. Children were intimately connected to adults in ways that the mortuary data do not show. Children were obviously integral parts of daily life and would have been present and active in residential social settings. What is striking is the juxtaposition between the representation of children in figurines and the separation of child burials from those of adults. Children had close connections to adults in daily patterns of interaction, but the burial patterns show that the definition of the category *child* may have had multiple meanings. Children in Early Postclassic Oaxaca might not have belonged to only one social group and may have had more fluid social positions with respect to membership in houses. The mortuary evidence from Cholula (McCafferty and McCafferty, Chapter 2) may perhaps show a similar fluidity of social position for children in that the burial patterns for children are generally more variable than those of adults.

The conclusion that Geoffrey and Sharisse McCafferty draw from the mortuary patterns at Cholula is different from (but not necessarily incompatible with) the Río Viejo evidence. They argue that children at Cholula were gradually inculcated into adult practices, given that child burial patterns increasingly conform to adult patterns with age at death. This may have also been true for Río Viejo children but, without the evidence of child burials at Río Viejo, this cannot be confirmed. The burial evidence from Río Viejo might instead show that the death of children and adults required different sets of practices and spatial standards. Rather than gradual indoctrination to norms of adult age and gender, childhood might have had its own unique social meanings, operating apart from the standardized, restricted world of adults. Children were connected and integrated into the lives of adults whose house membership was more spatially and socially segregated. The burial and figurine evidence together suggest that children were both independent and dependent in their social position, entailing multiple relations with older individuals, who themselves were parts of separate, intersecting social groups connected to particular houses.

Mortuary practices and iconography in ceramic figurines are two ways to examine childhood in ancient coastal Oaxaca. The figurine assemblage provides evidence of daily patterns of interaction between adults and children, both in terms of figurine use and representation. Although gender-based distinctions in social identity were not marked in mortuary practices at Early Postclassic Río Viejo, social distinctions based on age were expressed and created through burial location. Adults were interred beneath the floors of houses, whereas children were buried outside houses in patio space—as in the Operation A neighborhood—

or outside of residential areas in as yet undiscovered locations. These differences in burial location signal a conception of adulthood and childhood that was connected materially and socially to house membership and houses, wherein adults had connections to particular houses and children's social positions were defined without reference to a single house. Through mortuary ritual within the home, children were shown to be distinct and separate, yet intimately connected to adults, giving them multiple points of reference against which their own unique identities were formed and experienced.

ACKNOWLEDGMENTS

The Río Viejo Residence Project excavations were generously supported by the Foundation for the Advancement of Mesoamerican Studies, Inc., with Arthur Joyce; the Stahl Endowment of the Archaeological Research Facility, University of California, Berkeley; and the Lowie-Olson Fund of the Department of Anthropology, University of California, Berkeley. The subject of this chapter is one of the topics addressed in my dissertation (King 2003) and, as such, has benefited from the comments and suggestions provided by Rosemary Joyce, Christine Hastorf, and Harvey Doner. I thank Traci Ardren, Scott Hutson, and outside reviewers for insightful comments on earlier drafts of this chapter, and to the other session participants, from whom I learned so much.

REFERENCES CITED

Arnold, Bettina, and Nancy L. Wicker, eds.
2001 *Gender and the Archaeology of Death.* Walnut Creek, CA: Altamira Press.

Bellas, Monica
1995 Sacred Stones of the Mixtec. Paper presented at the Annual Mixtec Gateway, Las Vegas, NV, December 1995.

Binford, Lewis R.
1972 Mortuary Practices, Their Study and Their Potential. In *An Archaeological Perspective,* ed. L. R. Binford, 208–243. New York: Seminar Press.

Boyd, Brian
2002 Ways of Eating/Ways of Being in the Later Epipalaeolithic. In *Thinking Through the Body: Archaeologies of Corporeality,* ed. Y. Hamilakis, M. Pluciennik. and S. Tarlow, 137–152. New York: Kluwer Academic/Plenum Publishers.

Brumfiel, Elizabeth M.

1991 Weaving and Cooking: Woman's Production in Aztec Mexico. In *Engendering Archaeology: Women and Prehistory,* ed. J. M. Gero and M. W. Conkey, 224–251. Oxford: Basil Blackwell.

1996 Figurines and the Aztec State: Testing the Effectiveness of Ideological Domination. In *Gender and Archaeology,* ed. R. P. Wright, 143–166. Philadelphia: University of Pennsylvania Press.

Burkhart, Louise M.

1997 Mexica Women on the Home Front: Housework and Religion in Aztec Mexico. In *Indian Women of Early Mexico,* ed. S. Schroeder, S. Wood, and R. Haskett, 25–54. Norman: University of Oklahoma Press.

Cannon, Aubrey

2002 Spatial Narratives of Death, Memory, and Transcendence. In *The Space and Place of Death,* ed. H. Silverman and D. B. Small, 191–200. Archaeological Papers of the American Anthropological Association Number 11. Arlington: American Anthropological Association.

Chesson, Meredith S.

2001 Social Memory, Identity, and Death: An Introduction. In *Social Memory, Identity, and Death: Anthropological Perspectives on Mortuary Rituals,* ed. M. S. Chesson, 1–11. Archaeological Papers of the American Anthropological Association Number 10. Arlington: American Anthropological Association.

Christensen, Alexander F.

1998 Biological Affinity in Prehispanic Oaxaca. Ph.D. Dissertation, Department of Anthropology, Vanderbilt University, Nashville, TN.

1999 Apéndice 3: Los restos humanos. In *El Proyecto Patrones de Asentamiento del Río Verde,* ed. Arthur A. Joyce, 487–494, Informe entregado al Consejo de Arqueología y el Centro INAH Oaxaca.

Collins, Patricia Hill

1999 Moving Beyond Gender: Intersectionality and Scientific Knowledge. In *Revisioning Gender,* ed. M. M. Ferree, J. Lorder, and B. Hess, 261–284. Thousand Oaks, CA: Sage Publications.

Crawford, Sally

2000 Children, Grave Goods and Social Status in Early Anglo-Saxon England. In *Children and Material Culture,* ed. J. Sofaer Derevenski, 169–179. London: Routledge.

Crown, Patricia L.

1999 Socialization in American Southwest Pottery Decoration. In *Pottery and People: A Dynamic Interaction,* ed. J. M. Skibo and G. M. Feinman, 25–43. Salt Lake City: University of Utah Press.

Crumrine, N. Ross
1964 *The House Cross of the Mayo Indians of Sonora, Mexico: A Symbol of Ethnic Identity.* Anthropological Papers of the University of Arizona, Number 8. Tucson: University of Arizona Press.

Cyphers Guillén, Ann
1993 Women, Rituals, and Social Dynamics at Ancient Chalcatzingo. *Latin American Antiquity* 4(3):209–224.

Dávila Padilla, Fray Augustin
1955 *Historia de la fundación y discurso de la provincia de Santiago de México, de la Orden de Predicadores.* Mexico City: Editorial Academica Literaria.

Dow, James
1986 *The Shaman's Touch: Otomí Indian Symbolic Healing.* Salt Lake City: University of Utah Press.

Feinman, Gary M., Linda M. Nicholas, and Helen R. Haines
2002 Houses on a Hill: Classic Period Life at El Palmillo, Oaxaca, Mexico. *Latin American Antiquity* 13(3):251–278.

Finlay, Nyree
1997 Kid Knapping: The Missing Children in Lithic Analysis. In *Invisible People and Processes: Writing Gender and Childhood into European Archaeology,* ed. J. Moore and E. Scott, 201–212. London: Leicester University Press.

Fowler, Chris
2002 Body Parts: Personhood and Materiality in the Earlier Manx Neolithic. In *Thinking through the Body: Archaeologies of Corporeality,* ed. Y. Hamilakis, M. Pluciennik, and S. Tarlow, 47–70. New York: Kluwer Academic/Plenum Publishers.

Gilchrist, Roberta
1997 Ambivalent Bodies: Gender and Medieval Archaeology. In *Invisible People and Processes: Writing Gender and Childhood into European Archaeology,* ed. J. Moore and E. Scott, 42–58. London: Leicester University Press.
1999 *Gender and Archaeology: Contesting the Past.* London: Routledge.

Gillespie, Susan D.
1989 *The Aztec Kings: The Construction of Rulership in Mexico History.* Tucson: University of Arizona Press.
2001 Personhood, Agency, and Mortuary Ritual: A Case Study from the Ancient Maya. *Journal of Anthropological Archaeology* 20:73–112.
2002 Body and Soul among the Maya: Keeping the Spirits in Place. In *The Space and Place of Death,* ed. H. Silverman and D. B. Small, 67–78. Archaeological Papers of the American Anthropological Association No. 11. Arlington: American Anthropological Association.

Gonzalez Obregon, Luis

1912 *Procesos de indios idolatras y hechiceros.* Publicaciones del Archivo General de la Nación, vol. 3. Mexico City: Archivo General de la Nación.

Greenberg, James B.

1981 *Santiago's Sword: Chatino Peasant Religion and Economics.* Berkeley: University of California Press.

Grimm, Linda

2000 Apprentice Flintknapping: Relating Material Culture and Social Practice in the Upper Palaeolithic. In *Children and Material Culture,* ed. J. Sofaer Derevenski, 53–71. London: Routledge.

Hamann, Byron

1997 Weaving and the Iconography of Prestige: The Royal Gender Symbolism of Lord 5 Flower's/Lady 4 Rabbit's Family. In *Women in Prehistory: North America and Mesoamerica,* ed. C. Claassen and R. A. Joyce, 153–172. Philadelphia: University of Pennsylvania Press.

Hodder, Ian, ed.

1982 *Symbolic and Structural Archaeology.* Cambridge: Cambridge University Press.

1987 *The Archaeology of Contextual Meanings.* Cambridge: Cambridge University Press.

Hosler, Dorothy

1994 *The Sounds and Colors of Power: The Sacred Metallurgical Technology of Ancient West Mexico.* Cambridge: MIT Press.

Houby-Nielsen, Sanne

2000 Child Burials in Ancient Athens. In *Children and Material Culture,* ed. J. Sofaer Derevenski, 151–166. London: Routledge.

James, Jacquelyn B.

1997 What Are the Social Issues Involved in Focusing on *Difference* in the Study of Gender? *Journal of Social Issues* 53(2):213–232.

Joyce, Arthur A.

1991a Formative Period Occupation in the Lower Río Verde Valley, Oaxaca, México. Ph.D. Dissertation, Department of Anthropology, Rutgers University.

1991b Formative Period Social Change in the Lower Río Verde Valley, Oaxaca, México. *Latin American Antiquity* 2:126–150.

1994 Late Formative Community Organization and Social Complexity on the Oaxaca Coast. *Journal of Field Archaeology* 21(2):147–168.

Joyce, Arthur A., Laura Arnaud Bustamante, and Marc N. Levine

2001 Commoner Power: A Case Study from the Classic Period Collapse on the Oaxaca Coast. *Journal of Archaeological Method and Theory* 8(4):343–385.

Joyce, Arthur A., and Stacie M. King
2001 *Household Archaeology in Coastal Oaxaca, México.* Report on file with the Foundation for the Advancement of Mesoamerican Studies, Inc.

Joyce, Rosemary A.
1993 Women's Work: Images of Production and Reproduction in Prehispanic Southern Central America. *Current Anthropology* 34(3):255–271.
1999 Social Dimensions of Pre-Classic Burials. In *Social Patterns in Pre-Classic Mesoamerica,* ed. D. C. Grove and R. A. Joyce, 15–48. Washington, DC: Dumbarton Oaks.
2000a *Gender and Power in Prehispanic Mesoamerica.* Austin: University of Texas Press.
2000b Girling the Girl and Boying the Boy: The Production of Adulthood in Ancient Mesoamerica. *World Archaeology* 31(3):473–483.

Kamp, Kathryn A.
2001 Where Have All the Children Gone? The Archaeology of Childhood. *Journal of Archaeological Method and Theory* 8(1):1–34.

Kamp, Kathryn A., Nichole Timmerman, Gregg Lind, Jules Graybill, and Ian Natowsky
1999 Discovering Childhood: Using Fingerprints to Find Children in the Archaeological Record. *American Antiquity* 64(2):309–315.

Kellogg, Susan
1995 The Woman's Room: Some Aspects of Gender Relations in Tenochtitlan in the Late Pre-Hispanic Period. *Ethnohistory* 42(4):563–576.
1997 From Parallel and Equivalent to Separate but Unequal: Tenochca Mexica Women, 1500–1700. In *Indian Women of Early Mexico,* ed. S. Schroeder, S. Wood, and R. Haskett, 123–143. Norman: University of Oklahoma Press.

King, Stacie M.
2003 Social Practices and Social Organization in Ancient Coastal Oaxacan Households. Ph.D. Dissertation, Department of Anthropology, University of California, Berkeley.
n.d. Interregional Networks of the Oaxacan Early Postclassic: Connecting the Coast and the Highlands. In *Changing Cloud Formations: Late Classic/Postclassic Sociopolitical Transformations in Oaxaca, Mexico*, ed. J. Blomster and G. G. McCafferty. Forthcoming.

Klein, Cecelia F.
1994 Fighting with Femininity: Gender and War in Aztec Mexico. In *Gender Rhetorics: Postures of Dominance and Submission in History,* ed. R. C. Trexler, 107–146. Binghamton: Medieval and Renaissance Texts and Studies.

Kuijt, Ian
2001 Place, Death, and the Transmission of Social Memory in Early Agricultural Communities of the Near Eastern Pre-Pottery Neolithic. In *Social Memory, Identity, and Death: Anthropological Perspectives on Mortuary Rituals,* ed. M. S. Chesson, 80–99. Archaeological Papers of the American Anthropological Association Number 10. Arlington: American Anthropological Association.

Lesick, Kurtis S.
1997 Re-engendering Gender: Some Theoretical and Methodological Concerns on a Burgeoning Archaeological Pursuit. In *Invisible People and Processes: Writing Gender and Childhood in European Archaeology,* ed. J. Moore and E. Scott, 31–41. London: Leicester University Press.

Lesure, Richard G.
1997 Figurines and Social Identities in Early Sedentary Societies of Coastal Chiapas, Mexico, 1550–800 B.C. In *Women in Prehistory: North America and Mesoamerica,* ed. C. Claassen and R. A. Joyce, 227–248. Philadelphia: University of Pennsylvania Press.

Lillehammer, Grete
1989 A Child Is Born: The Child's World in an Archaeological Perspective. *Norwegian Archaeological Review* 22(2):89–105.
2000 The World of Children. In *Children and Material Culture,* ed. J. Sofaer Derevenski, 17–26. London: Routledge.

Lipp, Frank J.
1991 *The Mixe of Oaxaca: Religion, Ritual, and Healing.* Austin: University of Texas Press.

Lucy, S. J.
1997 Housewives, Warriors, and Slaves? Sex and Gender in Anglo-Saxon Burials. In *Invisible People and Processes: Writing Gender and Childhood into European Archaeology,* ed. J. Moore and E. Scott, 150–168. London: Leicester University Press.

Manzanilla, Linda
2002 Houses and Ancestors, Altars and Relics: Mortuary Patterns at Teotihuacan, Central Mexico. In *The Space and Place of Death,* ed. H. Silverman and D. B. Small, 55–66. Archaeological Papers of the American Anthropological Association Number 11. Arlington: American Anthropological Association.

Marcus, Joyce
1983 Changing Patterns of Stone Monuments after the Fall of Monte Albán, A.D. 600–900. In *The Cloud People: Divergent Evolution of the Zapotec and Mixtec Civilizations,* ed. K. V. Flannery and J. Marcus, 191–197. New York: Academic Press.
1989 From Centralized Systems to City-States: Possible Models for the Epiclassic. In *Mesoamerica after the Decline of Teotihuacan A.D.*

700–900, ed. R. A. Diehl and J. C. Berlo, 201–208. Washington, DC: Dumbarton Oaks.

1998 *Women's Ritual in Formative Oaxaca: Figurine-making, Divination, Death and the Ancestors.* Memoirs of the Museum of Anthropology, University of Michigan, No. 33. Ann Arbor: University of Michigan Museum of Anthropology.

1999 Men's and Women's Ritual in Formative Oaxaca. In *Social Patterns in Pre-Classic Mesoamerica,* ed. R. A. Joyce and D. C. Grove, 67–96. Washington, DC: Dumbarton Oaks.

Martínez López, Cira, and Marcus Winter

1994 *Figurillas y Silbatos de Cerámica de Monte Albán.* Contribución No. 5 del Proyecto Especial Monte Albán 1992–1994. Oaxaca: Centro INAH Oaxaca.

Martínez López, Cira, Marcus Winter, and Pedro Antonio Juárez

1995 Entierros humanos del Proyecto Especial Monte Albán. In *Entierros Humanos de Monte Albán: Dos Estudios,* ed. Marcus Winter, 79–247. Contribución No. 7 del Proyecto Especial Monte Albán 1992–1994. Oaxaca: Centro INAH Oaxaca.

McAnany, Patricia A.

1995 *Living with the Ancestors: Kinship and Kingship in Ancient Maya Society.* Austin: University of Texas Press.

McCafferty, Sharisse D., and Geoffrey G. McCafferty

1988 Powerful Women and the Myth of Male Dominance in Aztec Society. *Archaeological Review from Cambridge* 7(1):45–59.

1991 Spinning and Weaving as Female Gender Identity in Post-Classic Mexico. In *Textile Traditions of Mesoamerica and the Andes: An Anthology,* ed. M. Blum Schevill, J. C. Berlo, and E. B. Dwyer, 19–44. New York: Garland Publishing.

1994 Engendering Tomb 7 at Monte Albán: Respinning an Old Yarn. *Current Anthropology* 35(2):143–166.

2000 Textile Production in Postclassic Cholula, Mexico. *Ancient Mesoamerica* 11:39–54.

Meskell, Lynn M.

1994 Dying Young: The Experience of Death at Deir el Medina. *Archaeological Review from Cambridge* 13(2):35–45.

1998 An Archaeology of Social Relations in an Egyptian Village. *Journal of Archaeological Method and Theory* 5(3):209–243.

2001 Archaeologies of Identity. In *Archaeological Theory Today,* ed. I. Hodder, 187–213. Cambridge: Polity Press.

Middleton, William D., Gary M. Feinman, and Guillermo Molina Villegas

1998 Tomb Use and Reuse in Oaxaca, Mexico. *Ancient Mesoamerica* 9:297–307.

Miller, Arthur G.
1995 *The Painted Tombs of Oaxaca, Mexico: Living with the Dead.* Cambridge: Cambridge University Press.

Mills, Barbara J.
2000 Gender, Craft Production, and Inequality. In *Women and Men in the Prehispanic Southwest: Labor, Power, and Prestige,* ed. P. L. Crown, 301–344. Santa Fe: School of American Research Press.

Monaghan, John
1995 *The Covenants with Earth and Rain: Exchange, Sacrifice, and Revelation in Mixtec Sociality.* Norman: University of Oklahoma Press.

Moore, Henrietta L.
1993 The Differences Within and the Differences Between. In *Gendered Anthropology,* ed. T. del Valle, 193–204. New York: Routledge.
1999 Whatever Happened to Women and Men? Gender and Other Crises in Anthropology. In *Anthropological Theory Today,* ed. H. Moore, 151–171. Cambridge: Polity Press.

Moore, Jenny, and Eleanor Scott, eds.
1997 *Invisible People and Processes: Writing Gender and Childhood into European Archaeology.* London: Leicester University Press.

Nagar, Yossi, and Vered Eshed
2001 Where Are the Children? Age-dependent Burial Practices in Pequ'in. *Israel Exploration Journal* 51(1):27–35.

Paddock, John, Joseph R. Mogor, and Michael D. Lind
1968 Lambityeco Tomb 2: A Preliminary Report. *Boletín de Estudios Oaxaquenos* 25:2–24.

Parker Pearson, Michael
1982 Mortuary Practices, Society and Ideology: An Ethnoarchaeological Study. In *Symbolic and Structural Archaeology,* ed. I. Hodder, 99–113. Cambridge: Cambridge University Press.

Parsons, Elsie Clews
1936 *Mitla, Town of the Souls, and Other Zapotec-speaking Pueblos of Oaxaca, Mexico.* Chicago: University of Chicago Press.

Pohl, John M.D.
1994 *The Politics of Symbolism in the Mixtec Codices.* Vanderbilt University Publications in Anthropology No. 46. Nashville: Vanderbilt University Press.

Rathje, William L.
1970 Socio-Political Implication of Lowland Maya Burials: Methodology and Tentative Hypotheses. *World Archaeology* 1:359–375.

Redfield, Robert, and Alberto Villa Rojas
1934 *Chan Kom: A Maya Village.* Carnegie Institution of Washington, Publication 448. Washington, DC: Carnegie Institution of Washington.

Rega, Elizabeth
1997 Age, Gender, and Biological Reality in the Early Bronze Age Cemetery at Mokrin. In *Invisible People and Processes: Writing Gender and Childhood into European Archaeology,* ed. J. Moore and E. Scott, 229–247. London: Leicester University Press.

Robb, John
2002 Time and Biography: Osteobiography of the Italian Neolithic Lifespan. In *Thinking through the Body: Archaeologies of Corporeality,* ed. Y. Hamilakis, M. Pluciennik, and S. Tarlow, 153–172. New York: Kluwer Academic/Plenum Publishers.

Sandstrom, Alan R.
1981 *Traditional Curing and Crop Fertility Rituals among Otomí Indians of the Sierra de Puebla, Mexico: The Lopez Manuscripts.* Occasional Papers and Monographs, No. 3. Bloomington: Indiana University Museum.

Sandstrom, Alan R., and Pamela E. Sandstrom
1986 *Traditional Papermaking and Paper Cult Figures in Mexico.* Norman: University of Oklahoma Press.

Saxe, A. A.
1970 Social Dimensions of Mortuary Practices. Ph.D. Dissertation, Department of Anthropology, University of Michigan, Ann Arbor.

Schiller, Anne
2001 Mortuary Monuments and Social Change among the Ngaju. In *Social Memory, Identity, and Death: Anthropological Perspectives on Mortuary Rituals,* ed. M. S. Chesson, 70–79. Archaeological Papers of the American Anthropological Association, No. 10. Arlington: American Anthropological Association.

Scott, Eleanor
1999 *The Archaeology of Infancy and Infant Death.* BAR International Series 819. Oxford: Archaeopress.

Scott, Sue
1993 *Teotihuacan Mazapan Figurines and the Xipe Totec Statue: A Link Between the Basin of Mexico and the Valley of Oaxaca.* Vanderbilt University Publications in Anthropology, No. 44. Nashville: Vanderbilt University Press.

Sillar, Bill
1994 Playing with God: Cultural Perceptions of Children, Play and Miniatures in the Andes. *Archaeological Review from Cambridge* 13(2):47–63.

Smith, Michael E.
2002 Domestic Ritual at Aztec Provincial Sites in Morelos. In *Domestic Ritual in Ancient Mesoamerica,* ed. P. Plunket, 93–114. Cotsen Institute of Archaeology, Monograph 46. Los Angeles: Cotsen Institute of Archaeology, University of California.

Sofaer Derevenski, Joanna

1994a Perspectives on Children and Childhood: Editorial. *Archaeological Review from Cambridge* 13(2):1–5.

1994b Where Are the Children? Accessing Children in the Past. *Archaeological Review from Cambridge* 13(2):7–20.

Sofaer Derevenski, Joanna, ed.

2000 *Children and Material Culture.* London: Routledge.

Sørenson, Marie Louise Stig

2000 *Gender Archaeology.* Cambridge: Cambridge University Press.

Spence, Michael W.

2002 Domestic Ritual at Tlailotlacan, Teotihuacan. In *Domestic Ritual in Ancient Mesoamerica,* ed. P. Plunket, 53–66. Cotsen Institute of Archaeology, Monograph 46. Los Angeles: Cotsen Institute of Archaeology, University of California.

Spores, Ronald

1974 Marital Alliance in the Political Integration of Mixtec Kingdoms. *American Anthropologist* 76:297–311.

Terraciano, Kevin

2001 *The Mixtecs of Colonial Oaxaca: Ñudzahui History, Sixteenth through Eighteenth Centuries.* Stanford: Stanford University Press.

Urcid, Javier

1983 The Tombs and Burials from Lambityeco: A Prehistoric Community in the Valley of Oaxaca, Mexico. Master's Thesis, Department of Anthropology, University of the Americas Puebla.

Urcid, Javier, and Arthur A. Joyce

1999 Monumentos grabados y nombres calendáricos: los antiguos gobernantes de Río Viejo, Oaxaca. *Arqueología* 22:17–39.

Uruñuela, Gabriela, and Patricia Plunket

2002 Lineages and Ancestors: The Formative Mortuary Assemblages of Tetimpa, Puebla. In *Domestic Ritual in Ancient Mesoamerica,* ed. P. Plunket, 20–30. Cotsen Institute of Archaeology, Monograph 46. Los Angeles: Cotsen Institute of Archaeology, University of California.

Vogt, Evon Z.

1969 *Zinacantan: A Maya Community in the Highlands of Chiapas.* Cambridge: Harvard University Press.

Whalen, Michael E.

1981 *Excavations at Santo Domingo Tomaltepec: Evolution of a Formative Community in the Valley of Oaxaca, Mexico.* Memoirs of the Museum of Anthropology, University of Michigan, No. 12. Ann Arbor: University of Michigan Museum of Anthropology.

1988 House and Household in Formative Oaxaca. In *Household and Community in the Mesoamerican Past,* ed. R. R. Wilk and W.

Ashmore, 249–272. Albuquerque: University of New Mexico Press.

Wilkie, Laurie

2000 Not Merely Child's Play: Creating a Historical Archaeology of Children and Childhood. In *Children and Material Culture,* ed. J. Sofaer Derevenski, 100–114. London: Routledge.

Winter, Marcus

2002 Monte Albán: Mortuary Practices as Domestic Ritual and Their Relation to Community Religion. In *Domestic Ritual in Ancient Mesoamerica,* ed. P. Plunket, 67–82. Cotsen Institute of Archaeology, Monograph 46. Los Angeles: University of California.

Part IV

SACRIFICE, VIOLENCE, AND THE SANCTITY OF CHILDREN

8

CHILD MARTYRS AND MURDEROUS CHILDREN

Age and Agency in Sixteenth-Century Transatlantic Religious Conflicts

Byron Ellsworth Hamann

On the Mount of Olives, in the first century AD, Christ spoke to his disciples of intergenerational violence and the Last Days:

> The brother shall delyver up the brother to deeth, and the father the sonne: and the chyldren shall ryse agaynste theyr fathers and mothers, and shall put them to deeth. (*The Byble in Englyshe* 1540: Mark 13:12)

One and a half millennia later (ca. 1400–1650), the end of time was a pervasive concern for the many cultures of early modern Europe and its New World expansions (Reubeni [1525] 1930; Harkness 1999; Fleischer, forthcoming). Christopher Columbus, of course, undertook his journey across the Atlantic in hopes that the riches of Asia could be used to finance a New Crusade, since a Christian reconquest of Jerusalem was one of the prerequisites for the Apocalypse (Columbus [ca. 1502] 1991:65–69, 105–111; Watts 1985). Many similar attempts to bring the early modern world to an apocalyptic conclusion were further marked by the intergenerational conflict Christ foretold.

Thus in the 1490s, when the Dominican preacher Girolamo Savonarola tried to bring about an apocalyptically inspired reform of the city-republic of Florence, his teachings divided families and generations: "a great division and violent hatred had grown up in the hearts of the citizens, so that between brothers or between fathers and sons there was dissension over the question of the friar" (Guicciardini [1509] 1964:50; Weinstein 1970). Fra Girolamo focused his preaching on the training of young boys (*fanciulli*, ages 6–16) (Trexler 1974:250–251). These boys then policed the city, attacking their elders:

> 27th February [1495]. The boys were encouraged by the *Frate* to take away the baskets of *berlingozzi* [sweet Lenten cakes], and the gambling-tables, and many vain things used by women, so that no sooner did the gamblers hear that the boys of the *Frate* were coming than they fled, nor was there a single woman who dared to go out not modestly dressed. . . .
>
> 29th February [1495]. The said boys went about everywhere, along the walls of the city and to the taverns, etc., wherever they saw gatherings of people; this they did in each quarter, and if anyone had rebelled against them, he could have been in danger of his life. (Landucci [1450–1516] 1927:103)

And being attacked in turn:

> 25th May (the *Corpus Christi*) [1497]. A number of children [*fanciugli*] walked in the procession, carrying little red crosses in their hands; and because it was the order of Fra Girolamo that they should carry these red crosses, everybody hated poor Fra Girolamo, the young men [*giovani*] even more than the old ones. . . . Seeing the boys with these crosses, they said: "Here come the boys of Fra Girolamo!" And one of them approaching, snatched a little cross from one of the boys, and broke it and threw it into the river, as if he were a heathen. (Landucci [1450–1516] 1883:151; [1450–1516] 1927:121)

In the New World, where Savonarola was still remembered more than a century after his execution (Torquemada [1615] 1969, 3:594), Franciscan efforts to create a "millennial kingdom" (Phelan 1970) in the 1520s and 1530s were the cause of still more violence between young children and their parents. Fray Toribio de Benavente Motolinía described the fate of a young Christian cruelly killed by his unconverted father:

> *Y desde allí por ventana vio cómo el cruel padre tomó por los cabellos a aquel hijo Cristóbal, y le echó en el suelo dándole muy crueles coces, de los cuales fue maravilla no morir . . . y como así no pudiese matar, tomó un palo grueso de encina y diole con él*

> *muchos golpes por todo el cuerpo.* (Motolinía [1538–1541] 1969:177)
>
> [And from there through a window he saw how the cruel father took his son Cristóbal by the hair and threw him on the floor, giving him many cruel kicks, such that it was a marvel that the boy did not die . . . and because he was unable to kill the boy like this, he took a thick club and with it dealt the boy many blows over his whole body.]

And in France, where the circulation of apocalyptic plays, poems, and illustrations fomented millennial anxieties in the decades leading up to the start of the religious wars in the 1560s (Crouzet 1990, 1:182–191), a Catholic preacher in Paris quoted Deuteronomy to call on fathers to kill their Protestant siblings and children, and in the city of Toulon (see Figure 1.1) a Catholic son joined in the killing of his Calvinist father:

> If thy brother, the son of thy mother, or thy son, or thy daughter . . . entice thee secretly, saying Let us go and serve other gods . . . thou shalt surely kill him, thine hand shall be first upon him to put him to death. (Davis 1975:152)
>
> *Enumération des martyrs de la foi et de leurs tourments. . . . A Toulon . . .* François du Mas, *trainé & lapidé vif & bruslé par les enfans, ayans contraint son propre fils, le quinziesme de May 1562, à ce faire.* (Bèze [1580] 1883–1889, 3:408, 413)
>
> [Enumeration of martyrs of the faith and their torments. . . . In Toulon . . . *François du Mas,* dragged and stoned alive and burned by the children, having forced his own son, on the fifteenth of May 1562, to do this.]

On both sides of the Atlantic, then, attempts to create new socio-religious orders in the late fifteenth and sixteenth centuries were accompanied by accounts of intergenerational violence, in which fathers killed their young sons and children slaughtered their parents. Early modernity in the West (ca. 1400–1650) was a period of extreme disorder and violence, as a social order established in the eleventh and twelfth centuries was radically contested and transformed (Rabb 1975; Bartlett 1993; Moore 2000; on intergenerational conflict and social transformation see Bourdieu [1963] 1979; 1977:78; Comaroff and Comaroff 1999, 2000). And so these acts of intergenerational violence are only one of many different kinds of violent acts committed in the fifteenth, sixteenth, and seventeenth centuries. But violence, like any social action, is culturally constituted (Davis 1975:152–188; Nirenberg 1996), and so we must ask what cultural factors amplified the frequency with which accounts of murderous children and child martyrs were told and retold. For example, the Mexican martyrdom of the boy Cristóbal, quoted in its first incarnation by Motolinía earlier, was retold again by Fray Gerónimo de Mendieta ([1573–1596] 1870:236–239), Diego Muñoz Camargo ([1576–1596] 1892:244–247), and Agustin Dávila Padilla ([1596] 1625:69–74; see Trexler 1987). The city-by-city "Enumeration of martyrs of the faith and their torments," also quoted earlier, includes three other cases of adult Calvinists stoned to death by children, as do many other accounts from sixteenth-century France and Switzerland (Bèze [1580] 1883–1889, 3:412–415; Davis 1975:325). Thus the role of children as active participants in religious violence was constantly being recorded by writers on both sides of the Atlantic during the sixteenth century. This chapter asks why, in a period of such rampant and such varied sacred violence (Catholics versus Protestants, Catholic reformers versus Catholic traditionalists, Christians versus Muslims, Christians versus Jews, Christians versus Amerindians), the theme of the murderous or martyred child was so widespread.

I begin by reviewing what is known about categories of age and personhood shared throughout early modern Europe and its colonies in the New World. I will point out the widespread existence of a category of "childhood" as distinguished from "adolescence." I will then discuss European ideas about the nature of personhood at this childhood stage of life—a time of prepubescent holiness and receptivity to the divine. These ideas about childhood had existed in Europe for several centuries before the 1500s and had been institutionalized in a number of social practices uniquely controlled by children. With this background, I turn to the several accounts of child murderers and child martyrs in Motolinía's 1538–1541 *Historia de los Indios de la Nueva España.* I will read these, first, to consider how their retelling is marked by particular European ideas and even narrative precedents. I will then consider how these accounts present anomalies not present in their European models, anomalies that allow us to consider the ways in which non-European modes of thinking about the world shaped the actions of children and adults in these stories. In other words, acts of specifically indigenous agency can be recovered from an Iberian friar's narrative.

[I] CATEGORIES OF AGE AND PERSONHOOD IN EARLY MODERN EUROPE

It is unfortunate that one of the most heavily cited discussions of the category of *childhood* in the West—that of Philippe Ariès in *Centuries of Childhood*—is also one that has been heavily critiqued since its first publication in 1960. Ariès wrote about the historical origins of the connections linking commonplace twentieth-century understandings of *childhood* and the *family.* Because he produced statements like "[u]ntil the eighteenth century, adolescence was confused with childhood" and "[p]eople had no idea of what we call adolescence, and the idea was a long time in taking shape. One can catch a glimpse of it in the eighteenth century" (1962:25, 29), Ariès is often interpreted as claiming that the categories of childhood and adolescence were inventions of the eighteenth century (Ward 1978:vi; James, Jenks, and Prout 1998:4). A more extensive reading of Ariès's text, however, reveals that the absolute absence of *childhood* before the eighteenth century is not one that Ariès, or his sources, really supports. Rather—and here is a more cautious quotation—what is at issue is "the non-existence of the *modern idea* of childhood at the beginning of the seventeenth century" (1962:100, emphasis mine).

Indeed, a number of archivally based critiques of Ariès over the past three decades have shown that early modern Europeans did *not* lack the concept of childhood (Davis 1975:107–125, 305; Ladurie 1978:210–217; Christian 1981:215–222). "Rather one might say that *our* idea of childhood did not exist" (Christian 1981:218). Furthermore, research on age-associated social categories has demonstrated that throughout early modern Europe the ages of 10–14 marked a period of transition from one social category (*childhood* in various languages, based on the Latin categories of *peuris* and *infans*) to another (*adolescence* in various languages, based on the Latin category of *adolescens*).

A few examples should make this clear. Emmanuel LeRoy Ladurie (1978:215–216), writing on inquisition documents from fourteenth-century southern France, notes a separation between the categories of *puer* (2–12 years) and *adulescens* or *juvenis* (over 12 years). Richard Trexler (1974:201), writing of fifteenth-century Florence, notes a separation of *puerizia* or *fanciulezza* (childhood, under 12 or 13 years) from the older categories of *adolescente* and *giovanetto* (adolescence, ca. 13–25 years). William Christian (1981:216–217), writing about a 1449 account of an apparition in central Spain, finds a categorical separation of *niños* and *niñas* (younger than 11 or 12 years) from the older *mozas, mozuelas,* and *mozas niñas* (older than 12 years). Similar divisions existed in the twentieth century (Christian 1989:24). Richard Kagan (1990:43–44), writing on documents describing a young visionary in late-sixteenth-century Madrid, finds a distinction between female *niñas* (girls under age 10) and *doncellas* (girls ages 10–20). Juan Huarte de

San Juan's 1575 *Examen de ingenios para las ciencias* distinguishes between a younger category of *niñez* and its *niños* from a "second age" of *adolescencia*, noting however that some finish childhood (*puericia*) at age 12, some at 14, some at 16, and some at 18 ([1575] 1988:74, 78). Sebastian de Covarrubias Orozco's 1611 *Tesoro de la Lengua Castellana o Española* ([1611] 1993:439, 766, 778) similarly draws a separation between a younger category of *niño/niña* (defined in terms of the Latin *puer* and *infans*) from an older category described by *donzel/donzella* and *mozo/moza* (both defined in reference to each other and to the Latin *adolescens*). Finally, Randle Cotgrave's 1611 *A Dictionarie of the French and English Tongues* distinguishes boy/*gars/garçon* from youth/*adolescent.* Thus a number of sources, both archival and dictionary, reveal an early modern categorization that separated younger *niños, niñas,* boys, *garçons,* and *puers* from older *mozos, mozas, doncels, doncellas, adolescents,* and youths.

Despite the widespread early modern separation of the categories of *childhood* and *adolescence,* what is not clear is the exact age at which the categorical transition between childhood and adolescence took place—an ambiguity explicitly addressed in the quote from Huarte de San Juan earlier. The early modern category of adolescence was not numerically linked in the sense of the contemporary category *teenager,* whose entry and exit is marked with reference to numeric age (thirteen to nineteen). But even if it were, such unambiguous categorization would have required the practice of keeping precise annual tallies of individual ages—something that was not common in the sixteenth century (Ariès 1962:15–18, Febvre [1942] 1982:400–455). For example, it is quite common in Iberian inquisition records for witnesses to give their age as "X years, a little more or less" (poco mas o menos) (e.g., Archivo Histórico Nacional, Madrid, Inq. Leg. 550, Caja 1, No. 4, 332v, 337r, 338r, 339v, 340r). Not even the bodily changes of puberty would have provided a clear boundary marker between the categories of childhood and adolescence, since the "facts" of biology and the age-linked transformations of the body are always culturally mediated, multiple, and variable according to the individual (Butler 1993; Hutson, Chapter 5).

One important implication of this ambiguity of boundary between younger and older age categories was that the categorization of a boy or girl as a *niño* or *mozo, niña* or *moza,* was a socially negotiated interpretation. When we consider the attributes assigned to younger versus older age categories, we can see how these ambiguous age attributions were used by elders to interpret, censor, condone, and condemn certain actions. First, we will look at the attributes. A number of early modern sources suggest that preadolescent children were thought to have a privileged connection to the divine because of their inexperience and innocence. "Children were symbols of purity used by communities for intercession with God," writes William Christian (1981:216; for twentieth-century parallels, see Christian 1989:156), which may explain why children were overwhelmingly the recipients of divine visions in fifteenth-century Iberia. At the same time, in northern Italy, Dominican reformer Savonarola transformed a prior tradition of youthful religious orders into a tool for his transformation of Florence: he directed his efforts not at adolescents ages 13–24 (as had been common for earlier youthful religious orders), but at children ages 6–16 (Trexler 1974:250–252; 1980). These "'little angels' or *giovangelo* slowly became a societal ritual object, one whose correct manipulation could result in the preservation, even salvation, of the natural and civil order" (Trexler 1974:245). Finally, Michel de Montaigne, in his 1572–1574 essay "Of Solitude," demonstrates the association of children with the holy in sixteenth-century France (and perhaps the Portuguese New World as well):

> Albuquerque, viceroy in the Indies for King Manuel of Portugal, when in great peril of a shipwreck at sea, took a young boy [*jeune garçon*] upon his shoulders for this purpose alone, that in their common danger the boy's innocence might serve him as a guarantee and a recommendation to divine favor, and bring him to safety. (Montaigne 1943:175; 1998:388)

The association of children with the holy had a centuries-long history in Europe, perhaps dating as far back as the eleventh and twelfth centuries, when all of Europe's social orders, including its practices of sex and celibacy, were radically reordered (Davis 1975:104; Moore 2000:65–111). The Children's Crusade of 1212 provides one example of the perceived religious efficacy of the young in the Middle Ages; another example would be the role of groups of children, including groups with "nobody over twelve years of age," in the ritual Holy Week stoning of the walls of Jewish quarters in fourteenth-century eastern Spain, which symbolically asserted the boundary between Christian and Jewish worlds (Nirenberg 1996:207, 223–227, 248).

This centuries-long history of sacred acts whose legal legitimacy and conceptual efficacy was based on their performance by the young meant that, by the sixteenth century, children were well aware of their attributed power and undertook actions on their own that asserted their age-based agency (cf. Opie 1993 and Hutson, Chapter 5, on the deep time-depth of the child-transmitted traditions of "kid cultures"). The many murders by stoning (quoted earlier) committed by children during the French religious wars perhaps grew out of child-specific ritual stoning practices similar to those just described for eastern Spain. On a less violent note, by the 1500s children had long-established roles as prominent members of religious processions in fifteenth- and sixteenth-century Barcelona, in fifteenth-century central Iberia, in fifteenth-century Florence, and in sixteenth-century France (Trexler 1974; Christian 1981:217–220; cf. Davis 1975:97–123 on the history of adolescent-organized community spectacles in France). It is therefore not surprising that accounts of children's religious processions in Florence in the 1490s and Paris in the 1580s suggest that children were the organizers of these spectacles, again revealing that such forms of organization and action were socially acceptable—and expected?—from people of a certain age:

> *Processions à Paris, commencés par les enfants—Sur la fin de ce mois, les petits enfants, fils et filles de la ville de Paris, commencèrent à faire processions et prières publiques par la ville, allans d'église en autre, en grandes trouppes, marchans deux à deux, portans chandelles de cires ardantes en leurs mains, chantants les letanies, les VII pseaumes pénitentiaux et autres psalmes, himnes, oraisons, et priers.* (L'Estoile 1876:243–244; cf. Trexler 1980:477)
>
> [Processions in Paris, started by the children—At the end of this month [January 1589], the young children, boys and girls in the city of Paris, started to make processions and public prayers for the city, going from one church to another, in great troupes, marching two by two, holding burning wax candles in their hands, singing litanies, the seven penitential psalms and other psalms, hymns, orations, and prayers.]

Finally, in the apparitional traditions of fourteenth-, fifteenth-, and sixteenth-century Iberia, children were seen as privileged recipients of divine messages, and so were often chosen by supernatural beings (or took advantage of their privileged cultural position) to bring messages of (and thus initiate) social reform to their communities (Christian 1981).

But if the attributed holiness of preadolescent children provided such people with a powerful field for action, the unclear boundary between a *puer* and an *adolescens* meant that the elders who so often recorded the actions of the younger were also involved in judging those actions and, in so doing, performing interpretations of the ages of their participants. Again, age categories had potent associations, and in assigning otherwise ambiguous age categories, elders were able to shape the meanings of acts by younger people. The role of elder review of younger claims of access to the divine in apparition investigations demonstrates the role of intergenerational judgments most clearly. The initially skeptical investigation of the twelve-and-a-half-year-old visionary Inès in the Iberian town of Cubas (see Figure 1.1) in 1449 named her as an adolescent *moza,* not a childish *niña.* As a *moza,* her testimony and her morals could not be taken for granted: witnesses were asked if she were a "*moza* de buena fama" and if she danced at weddings like the other *mozas.* "Inès was enough of a *moza* so that she was not considered automatically innocent; hence the investigation of her behavior" (Christian 1981:216). Thus younger people could take advantage of age-attributed powers, but the legitimacy of their actions was always open to judgment by their elders.

In sum, early modern European categories of personhood made a clear conceptual separation of children and adolescents, although in practice the assignation of either category to a young person provided a field for interpretation and contestation. Furthermore, people categorized as children were thought to have particularly close contacts with the holy and could draw on several centuries' worth of traditions in undertaking specifically child-coded forms of socioreligious action (such as stoning walls and people, organizing and leading religious processions, and reporting personal visitations by the divine). In the following section, I move from these broad conceptualizations to consider how they are manifested in three tales of child martyrs and murderous children from sixteenth-century Mexico.

[II] INTERGENERATIONAL CONFLICT IN EARLY COLONIAL MEXICO

In the last section, I considered how early modern understandings of generational differences meant that children were considered to be very different people from their parents, and so had resources they could use that adults could not. And, indeed, I showed how in cases of religious conflict children could direct social action against adults (and vice versa). I argued that early modern Europeans were constantly writing about the roles of such intergenerational strife in contexts of religious conflict. Early modern Europeans were obsessed with pedagogy and were quite aware that the early training received in one's life could have a profound impact on the way one saw the world (Erasmus [1509] 1985; Castiglione [1518] 1959; Della Casa [1558] 1990; cf. Bourdieu 1977). One of the reasons the Florentine reformer Savonarola focused his attention on people younger than those previously involved in youthful religious sodalities may have been that "men who had grown up in the old corruption were incapable of reform" and so he sought to teach his recruits from as early an age as possible (Trexler 1974:250). Not surprisingly, this age-based religious indoctrination was the source of conflict within families: "Savonarolan policies . . . split families down the middle" (Trexler 1974:251). An opposite type of familial division (and a different concept of self-fashioning) is suggested in my introductory quote about the Toulon boy who joined a group of other Catholic boys in stoning his Calvinist father to death. The father (in classical Protestant fashion) had made an individualized decision to direct his soul to God in a new way, and for this he was killed by a group of Catholic boys who had been taught to live their lives according to another model of the sacred (on Protestantism and the individual care of the soul, see Greenblatt 1980:74–114).

The same types of intergenerational conflicts, deriving from different forms of sacred pedagogy and self-fashioning, can be seen in the early modern New World. In Franciscan accounts, at least, generational conflict is focused on that between young *niño* converts and elder unconverted "idolaters." The holiness of the converted *niños* is revealed in how they helped the friars root out idolatry, find hidden idols, and even proselytize on their own (Motolinía [1538–1541] 1969:174; Sahagún [1547–1579] 1938, 3:79–89; Trexler 1987), as well as in cases where these young converts came into conflict with their unconverted elders, conflicts that (at least in Franciscan retellings) often resulted in the death of one of the parties. The following paragraphs will discuss three narratives of child martyrs and murderous children from Fray Toribio de Benavente Motolinía's *Historia de los Indios de la Nueva España,* written between 1538 and 1541 and much-referenced in later sixteenth-century histories (see previous section).

The first narrative involves murderous children (*niños*) killing an elder. In the city of Tlaxcala, an indigenous priest dressed himself in the insignia of the pulque god Ometochtli and went to the marketplace of the city, chewing obsidian blades and announcing that he was the god. He was met by a group of young converts who had been taught at the Franciscan monastery. They rejected this man and his claims and told the people watching him that he was not a god, but the devil. The boys then picked up rocks and stoned the priest to death. Triumphant, they returned to the monastery and announced their victory to the friars. The friars were shocked and ordered that the boy who reported the news should be whipped for having committed murder. But the boy insisted that the friars see the slain demon. And, indeed, in the market the boys showed the friars the slain priest. Although it is not stated in the narrative, these murderous children apparently escaped punishment. The narrative's moral asserts that on seeing the powerlessness of the dead indigenous priest, many of the unconverted then "left their false beliefs, and came to be reconciled and united with God and to hear his word" (Motolinía [1538–1541] 1969:176).

This vignette has many fascinating features when viewed against the European background discussed in the last section. Like so many young children in Europe, these boys performed an act of religious violence using stones as their weapons. On the one hand, this weapon could simply be a functional parallel: stones are readily available and easily wielded by tiny hands. But on the other hand, execution by stoning was a deeply meaningful practice for cultures on both sides of the Atlantic. In the Old World, the maintenance of boundaries by stoning was a practice with an Old Testament pedigree (Exodus 19:1, 21:28–32), so the symbolic meanings of the use of rocks in holy purges may very well have been known to boys from sermons heard on both sides of the Atlantic. Stoning was also used in pre-Hispanic capital punishment in Central Mexico and was still remembered in the mid-sixteenth century by Bernardino de Sahagún's Nahua collaborators (Sahagún [1547–1579] 1950–1982, 4:104, 8:42–43, fig. 68). Indeed, Sahagún's text even records the execution by stoning of a "demon" in the marketplace by the people of Tula as part of the Quetzalcoatl-Tezcatlipoca narrative (Sahagún [1547–1579] 1950–1982, 3:27).

A second feature of this vignette is how children used their social position and resources that their age made uniquely available to them (in this case, as the beneficiaries of monastic mass-education programs for the young) to assert their power and authority against their elders. The killing of the priest represents one form of authority, and their proclamation of their success (and their apparent escape from punishment) before their Franciscan teachers represents another assertion of authority. And in their final confrontation with the friars, we see the role of conflict between children and elders over the interpretation of children's religious actions. The friars originally rejected the religiously inflected actions of the children, just as many child visionaries in Iberia were initially ignored or accused of lying (Christian 1981). Just as in those cases of child-witnessed apparitions, it is only when the children produce tangible proof of their divinely sanctioned actions that their elders provide approval.

The second narrative involves a child martyr and a murderous father. One of the lords of Tlaxcala, Acxotecatl, had sixty wives and four principal sons. He sent three of his principal sons to the Franciscan monastery to be schooled (and Christianized) but kept the fourth, his oldest, secluded in the palace. This son is described as a *niño,* age 12 to 13 years ("de edad, de doce a trece años"; Motolinía [1538–1541] 1969:176). The friars, however, soon learned of this deception, gained access to the boy, and baptized him as Cristóbal. The young convert took quickly to his instruction in Christianity, and with the new resources of his transformed worldview he began to critique his father's continued idolatry. This provided the perfect excuse for Xochipapalotzin, another wife of Acxotecatl and mother of the son second in line to the throne, to urge her husband to kill the overzealous Cristóbal (and thus place her own son Bernardino at the forefront of the succession). Perhaps Xochipapalotzin resented being attacked as an idolater by Cristóbal, who "did not stop admonishing the mother [of Bernardino] and the servants of the house to abandon idols and sins" (Motolinía [1538–1541] 1969:176–179). Xochipapalotzin's urgings finally succeeded, and the father tried repeatedly to kill his son: beating him first with a club, then throwing him in a fire, and finally taking the boy from the fire to dispatch him with a sword. The sword could not be found, however, and the boy expired on his own the following day.

The many forms of violence performed against Cristóbal will be discussed in the next section, but for now what is most important in this narrative is to consider how Cristóbal used his knowledge of Christianity in an attempt to transform the household that he should one day inherit, and how his attempts to mobilize his privileged knowledge of the religion of the colonizers against the adults of that household led one adult (Xochipapalotzin) to urge another (Cristóbal's father) to kill the boy and thus open up room for another prince, a less zealous convert, to inherit the throne. Here we can see how the conflicting goals and variable resources of children and adults are brought into a violent, deadly clash. Intrafamilial palace politics, no doubt preceding the arrival of the Franciscans, were amplified and transformed through the actions of adult friars and a child convert.

The final narrative again involves martyred children. Two years after the death of Cristóbal, a Dominican friar en route to Oaxaca asked for a few Indian boys (*niños*) to accompany him on his journey to help with his conversion efforts. Three boys volunteered to help with this conversion plan: Antonio, Juan, and Diego. Significantly, given the aforementioned association of age and sacred agency in early modern European culture, the age of these boys is highlighted with reference to Cristóbal of the previous story: "they were of the age of Cristóbal" ("eran de la edad de Cristóbal"; Motolinía [1538–1541] 1969:180). Thus both narratives of martyrdom stress the fact that the martyrs are *niños*, under age fourteen. Before they set out, the boys were warned of the potential dangers of their holy undertaking: "My children, reflect that you will have to leave your land, and go among people who still do not know God, and I believe you will see great hardships; I feel your hardships like those of my own children, and I am afraid that they may kill you on the road; therefore reflect carefully before you make a decision" (Motolinía [1538–1541] 1969:179). The boys were undeterred and even cited saintly martyrs as models for glorious emulation:

> *¿[P]ues cómo no había de haber entre tantos quien se ofreciese a tomar trabajo por servir a Dios? Nosotros estamos aparejados para ir con los padres y para recibir de buena voluntad todo trabajo por Dios; y si El fuere servido de nuestras vidas, ¿por qué no las pondremos por El? ¿No mataron a San Pedro crucificándole y degollaron a San Pablo y San Bartolomé no fue desollado a Dios?* (Motolinía [1538–1541] 1969:180)

> [How could there not have been among so many one who would offer himself to undertake hardship in order to serve God? We are ready to go with the Fathers, and to gladly receive all hardship for the love of God; and if He would be served by our lives, why should we not give them for him? Did they not crucify St. Peter, behead St. Paul, and was not St. Bartholomew flayed to death for God?]

The boys and the friar depart, and in Cuauhtinchan the boys sought out idols in peoples' houses, confiscated (stole) these images, and smashed them. Such robberies were not tolerated long: two caciques approached Juan and Antonio and clubbed them to death. Eventually, the two young bodies were found and their murderers were executed. And when the friar who allowed them to leave on their conversion mission heard of their deaths, "he remembered that which they had said to him at the time of their departure, which was: 'Now, did they not kill St. Peter and St. Paul and flay St. Bartholomew, and if they kill us will not God be doing us a very great favor?'"(Motolinía [1538–1541] 1969:181).

In this narrative, we can see the key role of religious education in shaping the self-perception and personal action of these young converts. According to Motolinía, the three volunteer to undertake this conversion journey—and we should not be too skeptical of Motolinía's claim, considering the previously discussed independent role of European children in organizing religious processions or asserting their visionary contacts with the divine. The three are clearly modeling their actions on the saintly lives (Peter, Paul, Bartholomew) they have been taught about in monastic schools. This education provided them with a specific set of perspectives from which to attack the religious practices of their elders, and it is an education that brought them into conflict with their elders, an intergenerational conflict that would cost two of them their lives.

In sum, intergenerational conflicts over issues of the sacred in New Spain have many parallels to similar intergenerational conflicts taking place at the same time in Europe and resulted in similarly tragic ends for both children and adults. In the following section, however, we will consider how this broad early modern context of struggle over the sacred took particular forms in the New World.

[III] INDIGENOUS TRADITIONS IN THE TRANSATLANTIC WORLD

Up until now, this chapter has argued that social conflicts and their representations in New Spain need to be understood as aspects of much broader, transatlantic social processes transforming people of all ages on both sides of the Atlantic. Thus conflicts between indigenous converts and indigenous traditionalists are not unlike conflicts between Catholics and Protestants in France or between the child-reformers and traditionalist adults of Florence. All of the early modern transatlantic world was caught up in revolutionary attempts to redefine the sacred, and the conflicts that resulted from these redefinitions shared basic contours.

In this final section, however, I consider the ways in which these broad, transatlantic processes and their textual representations were given specifically Amerindian features in the New World. Significantly, these Amerindian features can be recovered from European-recorded alphabetic texts. This possibility of revealing specifically Amerindian practices and understandings within European-recorded alphabetic texts has two implications. First, it suggests that European chroniclers in the New World—or at least Motolinía, on whose texts I again focus—were not simply inventing their stories or letting European-inspired models of child action overwhelm their observations in the New World. In other words, this possibility of revelation suggests that the parallels in written discourses (through which one can argue for the existence of broad transatlantic social processes) were not simply figments of the imagination created by European cultural and genre assumptions. The second implication is one that Barbara Mundy has already demonstrated in her brilliant rereading of the Map of Cortes (1998): that in order to understand European representations of the New World, one has to understand how these representations have been shaped by indigenous orders. Thus one can no longer argue, as it was fashionable to do in the 1980s and 1990s, that the colonial Other was nothing but a figment of the European imagination (Obeyesekere 1992; Ramos 1992; see critiques by Klein 1995).

My first revelation of Amerindian specificities within Motolinía considers the story of young Cristóbal and his murderous father. Again, after beating the young convert, Cristóbal's father threw him into a fire, then pulled him out, and then tried to find a sword with which to dispatch the boy. But the sword could not be found, and the boy expired the next morning. Intriguingly, this tale seems strongly inspired by a Gregory of Tours' narrative of a young Jewish convert and his would-be murderous father—a narrative first written in 585–588.

> The son of a Jewish glass-worker was studying and learning the alphabet with Christian boys. One day while the ritual of mass was being celebrated in the church of the blessed Mary, this Jewish boy approached the young boys to partake of the glorious body and blood of the Lord. After receiving the holy [Eucharist], he happily returned to his father's house. His father was working, and between embraces and kisses the boy mentioned what he had so happily received. Then his father, an enemy of Christ the Lord and his laws . . . seized the boy and threw him into the mouth of a raging furnace; he was persistent and added wood so the furnace would burn hotter. But that compassion that had once sprinkled the dew of a cloud on three Hebrew boys who had been thrown into a Chaldean furnace [Daniel 3:8–30] was not lacking. For it did not allow this boy, even though lying on a pile of coals in the middle of the fire, to be consumed in the least. When his mother heard that the father had evidently decided to incinerate their son, she hurried to save him. (Gregory of Tours 1988:29–30)

The boy was removed from the fire unscathed, reporting a vision of Mary as his protectress. The father was then thrown into the furnace and killed, and the son and mother were "baptized in the waters of salvation" (Gregory of Tours 1988:31).

The conversion, the furnace that does not kill: the parallels between the two stories are strong, and they lead to the question of whether poor Cristóbal ever lived at all or was simply a figment of Motolinía's imagination. This constructivist interpretation, however, is insufficient. It is of course probable that Gregory of Tours' narrative was in Motolinía's mind as he wrote this story, for this tale was known in early modern Europe (Grenaille 1642). But the allusions to Gregory's story in

Motolinía's tale should not surprise us, nor should they be grounds for rejecting the tale of Cristóbal as a mere fantasy. After all, storytelling, indeed all communication, is made possible through quotation, through the shaping of observations to the contours of culturally prescribed genre forms (Bakhtin 1981, 1990; Davis 1987). But despite the fact that all of our narrations are always based on other narrations, we are still able to improvise, to use known forms and genres to describe new phenomena. Significantly, Motolinía's account of Cristóbal does not involve a miraculous salvation from the fire: the boy is pulled out so that he can be killed by another method, and in the end dies on his own. In addition, the intricate palace politics recorded by Motolinía have no parallels in the tale of Gregory of Tours. So although it is probable that the retelling of Cristóbal's death is based on familiarity with an early medieval story, it also seems clear that this story was simply used as a frame for which to retell a much different event.

That Motolinía's tale is faithful to actual events is further suggested by a detail not found in the medieval tale, a detail that suggests in killing his son, Cristóbal's father was following specifically Central Mexican cultural constructions of violence. Cristóbal is beaten, thrown in the fire, and then removed for a final execution by sword. Such surface-burning before a bladed death is recorded in other sixteenth-century accounts of pre-Hispanic Central Mexican sacrificial techniques (Sahagún [1547–1579] 1950–1982, 2:115). Unfortunately, as Javier Urcid observes, the first step would not be osteologically recorded in the archaeological record, so we will be unable to find pre-Hispanic material remains to corroborate colonial memories of this method of sacrifice (Urcid n.d.; López Lujan, Neff, and Sugiyama 2000:225).We can say, however, that this method differed significantly from early modern European uses of fire in execution, which was employed to burn people alive or to reduce a body to ashes after it had been killed by some other method (commonly hanging or strangulation) (Landucci [1450–1516] 1927:142–143; Weinstein 1970:288; Foucault 1977:3–31; Tedlock 1993). Indeed, Motolinía himself remarks on this two-step Central Mexican burning/cutting sacrifice earlier in his *Historia,* but if he realized the connection between that account of sacrifice and his own account of the death of Cristóbal, he does not make that fact clear (Motolinía [1538–1541] 1969:34). I am not saying that we need to consider Cristóbal's death to have been an attempt at sacrifice. Rather, I am arguing that his death should be understood as an example of how culturally specific understandings of sacred violence shape acts of violence in other contexts.

My second revelation of Amerindian specificities within Motolinía considers a tale in many ways the inverse of the one I just related: instead of a younger convert being killed by an elder traditionalist, Motolinía's tale of the stoning death of the priest of Ometochtli involves the killing of an elder traditionalist by the stones of younger converts. One curious detail of Motolinía's retelling involves the seeming confusion of the priest in a god's costume with the god (or the demon) that he represents. Motolinía begins his narrative by stressing that the priest is merely dressed in the costume of the god:

> *vestido de ciertas insignas de un ídolo o demonio* Umotochtli, *y [ser] su ministro, se llamaba* umetoch cocoya . . . *salió al tianguez o mercado.* (Motolinía [1538–1541] 1969:174)
>
> [dressed in the costume of an idol or demon *Umotochtli,* and being his priest, he was called *umetoch cotoya* . . . he went to the tianguez or marketplace.]
>
> *vínose para ellos aquel mal demonio, o que traía sus vestiduras, y comenzó de reñir a los niños y mostrarse muy bravo, diciéndoles: "que presto se morirían todos."* (Motolinía [1538–1541] 1969:175)
>
> [the wicked demon, or he who was wearing his clothing, approached them and started to upbraid the boys and acted very brave, telling them "that soon they would all die."]

The young converts, however, react to this impersonation in a curious way. They constantly assert that they are facing not a man in costume but an actual demon.

> *Y como viesen tanta gente tras el demonio, preguntaron qué era aquello, y respondieron unos indios diciendo: "nuestro dios Umothotli"; los niños dijeron: "no es dios sino diablo, que os miente y engaña."* (Motolinía [1538–1541] 1969:175)
>
> [And as they saw so many people behind the demon, they asked what it was, and some Indians responded saying "Our god Umothotli"; the boys said, "He is not a god but the devil, who is lying to and deceiving you."]
>
> *A lo cual algunos de los grandecilos que tuvieron más ánimo le respondieron: "que él era el mentiroso, y que no le tenían ningún temor porque él no era dios sino diablo, y malo y engeñador."* (Motolinía [1538–1541] 1969:175)

> [To this some of the older boys who had more spirit replied "that he was the liar, and that they had no fear of him because he was not God but a devil, and evil and deceiver."]

> *"Echemos de aquí este diablo, que Dios nos ayudará"; y diciendo esto tiróle con la piedra, y luego acudieron todos los otros. (Motolinía [1538–1541] 1969:175)*

> ["Let us drive from here this devil, God will help us"; and saying this he threw the stone at him [the impersonator], and then all the others did likewise.]

Motolinía even comments on this seeming confusion of the boys, who thought that killing a man in costume involved the killing of the devil himself:

> *Acabada la lid y contienda, no parecía que habían muerto hombre sino al mismo demonio. . . . Vanse los niños muy regocijados para el monasterio y entran diciendo cómo habían muerto al diablo. Los friales no los entendían bien, hasta que el intérprete les dijo cómo habían muerto a uno que traía vestidas las insignias del demonio.* (Motolinía [1538–1541] 1969:175)

> [The fight and conflict ended, it did not seem that they had killed a man but rather the devil himself. . . . The boys left elated for the friary, and entered saying that they had killed the devil. The friars did not understand them well until the interpreter told them that the boys had killed someone who was dressed in the insignia of the demon.]

> *Y luego el maestro mandábale azotar diciéndole: "que cómo había hecho tal cosa, y había muerto hombre?" El muchacho respondió, "que no habían muerto hombre sino demonio."* (Motolinía [1538–1541] 1969:175–176)

> [And then the master gave orders that the boy be whipped, saying to him, "How could you have done such a thing, and killed a man?" The boy responded, "that they had not killed a man but a demon."]

But in the end, Motolinía's tale asserts that the being under the stones was, in fact, only a man in costume:

> *Y no vieron sino un gran montón de piedras, y descubriendo y quitando de ellas vieron cómo el muerto estaba vestido del pontifical del diablo, y tan feo como el mismo demoino.* (Motolinía [1538–1541] 1969:176)

> [And they saw nothing but a great pile of rocks, and searching and removing them they saw that the dead man was clothed in the robes of the devil, and was as ugly as the demon himself.]

In this account, Motolinía and the friars always stress that the boys kill a man in costume; in contrast, the boys assert that they have killed an actual demon—an assertion that causes some confusion among their friar-teachers. Such a merger of representation and represented, however, was a key conceptual feature of indigenous Central Mexican religion. People costumed as the gods were understood to be the gods. The impersonator who became the literal incarnation of the god was called the *teixiptla,* a key feature of Central Mexican (indeed, pan-Mesoamerican) religion that has been extensively discussed by Arild Hvidtfeldt (working with sixteenth-century alphabetic sources from Central Mexico [1958]), John Monaghan (working with twentieth-century ethnographies [2000]), and Stephen Houston and David Stuart (who demonstrate the pre-Hispanic genealogy of these beliefs through decipherments of Classic Maya hieroglyphs [Houston and Stuart 1996, 1998; Stuart 1996]). Thus, when the boys called the god-costumed priest the devil, they were importing indigenous understandings of sacred performance into their new Christian framework. As Fernando Cervantes (1994) has shown, such mergers of the devil with indigenous religious beliefs from before the conquest were an important feature of the spiritual topography of sixteenth-century New Spain. Thus, by carefully reading Motolinía's account and considering how he presents the different reactions of the *niños* and the friars (and how he describes the costumed priest), we can see the complex merger of Old and New World ideas of the sacred. And we can appreciate Motolinía's detailed narration of the event, which allows us five centuries later to understand the conceptual complexities of this murder.

The previous paragraphs have argued that Motolinía's accounts, as products of colonial Mexico, need to be contextualized both as part of a broader early modern transatlantic world as well as within pre-Hispanic Amerindian traditions. I will therefore end this excavation of indigenous traditions from European-authored texts by considering how Motolinía's accounts of child martyrs and murderous children, so similar to accounts from the Old World, may also be shaped by pre-Hispanic Mesoamerican ideas about age and agency.

As I argued earlier, early modern Europeans distinguished a category of *childhood* from a category of *adolescence* and distinguished a category of *adolescence* from a category of *adulthood* (Davis 1975:97–

123). In contrast, indigenous Mesoamerican models of age and personhood for centuries have focused on a series of three prepuberty stages of maturation and formation, at whose conclusion the child was finally considered an adult and possibly something even more profound: an actual human being (see Ardren, Chapter 1; Joyce, Chapter 11). Rosemary Joyce's study of Mesoamerican age categories argued that colonial documents on sixteenth-century Central Mexicans revealed a series of specific manipulations of young people's bodies at birth, at age 4, at age 7 or 8, and at age 12 (Joyce 2000:475–480). This series of bodily manipulations socialized youngsters into humans through three age grades (or "stages of being") of roughly four years each (0–4, 4–8, 8–12) (see also Clendinnen 1991:189–192). That a radical change in being occurred at the end of this series of socializations is supported by sixteenth-century linguistic data from Central Mexico. Nahuatl age terminology, although it divided prepubescents into a number of types (see Román Berrelleza and Chávez Balderas, Chapter 9), lacked gender-specific forms. Only at puberty were young Nahuatl-speakers described with specifically male and female terminologies, a dichotomy that would mark age categories for the rest of their lives (López Austin 1988, 1:285–290). Only after a dozen years of socialization was the "boying" and "girling" of newborns complete; only then could they be described as gendered humans (cf. Joyce 2000:474)

The division of prepubescence into a series of grades, culminating in the attainment of adult status, is documented across Mesoamerican time and space. Rosemary Joyce noted divisions similar to those of the sixteenth-century Mexicans in Colonial documents describing the sixteenth-century Yucatec Maya (Joyce, Chapter 11). Traci Ardren (Chapter 1) and Rebecca Storey and Patricia McAnany (Chapter 3) note that a similar age structuring—from birth to 3–4, from 3–4 to 9, and from 9 to 12–13—was a feature of Zinacanteco Maya socialization in the twentieth century (citing Vogt 1970). Ardren also cites Storey's archaeological observation of similar age patterning in child burials over a thousand years earlier at the Classic Maya site of Copan. And in this volume, Storey and McAnany (Chapter 3) have found even earlier evidence for the tripartite treatment of child burials in Late Formative K'axob (400 BC to AD 250). In sum, evidence from twentieth-century ethnography, sixteenth-century texts, and pre-Hispanic archaeology suggests that the staged formation of "not-yet-fully-human" youngsters into fully formed adult humans by age 12 or 13 is part of "the *longue durée* of Mesoamerican civilization" (Ardren, Chapter 1; Joyce, Chapter 11; but see King, Chapter 7).

For both indigenous Mesoamericans and early modern Europeans then, a prepubescent stage of childhood was marked off from the stage of being that followed it. We also have evidence that suggests that fourteenth-, fifteenth-, and sixteenth-century Central Mexicans, like their European contemporaries, attributed a certain level of holiness to children that was lost as they grew up. As Román Berrelleza and Chávez Balderas (Chapter 9) discuss, memories of the importance of young children in pre-Hispanic sacrifices were repeatedly recorded in colonial-era sources from Central Mexico. Colonial sources often note that children 6–7 or younger were preferred sacrificial victims (Román Berrelleza 1993:138). These colonial memories are corroborated by the pre-Hispanic archaeological evidence discussed in Chapter 9. Of the forty-two children sacrificed as part of Offering No. 48 in the Great Temple of Tenochtitlan, all were ages 3–7 with ages 4, 5, and 6 being most heavily represented (Román Berrelleza 1993:138–139). Of the thirty sacrificed children found at the bottom of the staircase of Ehécatl-Quetzalcóatl at Tlatelolco, twenty were age 7 or younger, one was 9, and one was 10. The remaining victims included one 18-year-old, two 20-year-olds, and the rest were "adults" (Guillem 1999:335). Alphabetic and osteological evidence for the sacrifice of children in pre-Hispanic rituals, then, suggests that young people in the earliest age grades were the most sacred. Perhaps, as Joyce (Chapter 11) suggests, very young children whose substances had not yet been fully transformed by human socialization still retained the integrity of the precious materials from which the gods had shaped them into newborns. Indeed, there may even be a lexical category for these young victims: Alfredo López Austin's linguistic studies reveal that Nahuatl distinguished "children under 6" (*pipil, conepil, conetl*) from "children over 6" (*piltontli, piltzintli*) (López Austin 1988, 1:287).

How does all of this enrich our readings of Motolinía's tales of child martyrs and murderous children? First, we should note the contrastive meanings that "from 12 to 13 years" (Motolinía [1538–1541] 1969:176) had in early modern European traditions versus in contemporary Central Mexican traditions. Whereas the early modern European model, which contrasts childhood from adolescence, allowed young people to retain their sacred qualities up to the doorway of adolescence (remember that Huarte de San Juan observed that childhood [*puericia*] ended for some at 12, some at 14, some at 16, and some at 18; [1575] 1988:74, 78), Central Mexican models of childhood sacredness, as evidenced by the age of sacrificial victims, weighted young people's sacredness toward the earliest stages of their multi-step socialization process.

Preferred sacrificial victims were not teenagers, nor were they *piltontli* or *piltzintli* ("children over 6"). They were children 6 and under. Thus, from a Mesoamerican perspective, the reason that 12- and 13-year-old boys were so prominent in the violent clashes of religious transformation in colonial Mexico may not have been because they were still children and thus considered imbued with sacred qualities. Rather, their prominence may have been because these *niños* saw themselves as having passed beyond the borders of childhood and into the status of fully formed adults, true humans (cf. Ardren, Chapter 1, on Aj Wosal). Perhaps one of the reasons that the Tlaxcalan *niño* Cristóbal took such a forceful approach in attacking the "idolatry" of his father and other household members is because, although in terms of age he was attacking his "elders," in terms of age category he was asserting his authority against fellow adults.

[IV] CONCLUSIONS

The goals of this chapter were both thematically focused and conceptually wide. Thematically, I aimed to describe the age-associated categories of personhood in early modern Europe and its colonial extensions. What were the categories of personhood used to describe different life stages in early modern Europe? What were the different qualities ascribed to these different life stages? How did these differential qualities of age allow certain individuals to undertake certain forms of action not permissible (or at least not interpretable in the same ways) for persons of other ages? Finally, how did understandings of those attributes and actions shape the ways in which such actions were observed, recorded, interpreted, and sanctioned (or condemned)?

In exploring the connections between categorization, the practices authorized by certain categorizations, and the ways in which such practices were textually described, I looked not simply at events on the European peninsula, but at events in European colonies in the New World. Too often, as Tamar Herzog has lamented, studies of the early modern world treat the Old World and the New as separate spheres, or at best combine primary source research in one area with mere dabbling in secondary source information from the other (Herzog 2003:230–231). This study considered sixteenth-century texts from both sides of the Atlantic and argued that reading such texts side by side reveals the extent to which people of all ages on both sides of the Atlantic were caught up in the same broad social processes—in this case, radical reconceptualizations of the role of the sacred in daily life.

In addition, although this transatlantic study sought to read accounts of the conflicts of indigenous conversion efforts in the New World alongside accounts of similar conversion conflicts in the Old, I was also aware of the long history of New World societies before the arrival of the Europeans. Thus, after considering the similarities of sacred conflict that joined converts and traditionalists on both sides of the Atlantic, I examined how these transatlantic social transformations were uniquely refracted by New World people. I demonstrated how a knowledge of indigenous ideas about the sacred, and indigenous conceptualizations of age categories, can help us better understand the ways in which accounts of intergenerational religious violence in the New World digress from their European parallels and narrative models. A consideration of transatlantic social processes need not, therefore, ignore the particular ways in which these broad social processes are realized in particular places and in the differential actions of particular generations (Elias [1939] 2000:385, 431–432, 462; Wolf 1982; Sahlins 1988).

ACKNOWLEDGMENTS

I thank Scott Hutson and Traci Ardren for inviting me to contribute to this volume, and express my appreciation for comments on earlier drafts of this essay from Tamar Herzog, Scott Hutson, and Matthew Restall. The translations from Motolinía, Bèze, and L'Estoile are my own; thanks to Tamar Herzog for checking my French translations.

REFERENCES CITED

Archivo Histórico Nacional, Madrid, Inq.

1540–1571 "Processo del Promotor Fiscal del Sancto Officio de la Inquisición de Valencia Contra Don Sancho de Cardona, Almirante de Aragon, Vezino de Valencia." Archivo Histórico Nacional, Madrid. Ing. Leg. 550, Caja 1, No. 4.

Ariès, Philippe

1962 *Centuries of Childhood.* London: Jonathan Cape.

Bakhtin, Mikhail

1981 Discourse and the Novel. In *The Dialogic Imagination,* ed. M. Holquist, 259–422. Austin: University of Texas Press.

1990 *Speech Genres and Other Late Essays,* trans. V. W. McGee and ed. C. Emerson and M. Holquist. Austin: University of Texas Press.

Bartlett, Robert

1993 *The Making of Europe: Conquest, Colonization, and Cultural Change 950–1350.* Princeton: Princeton University Press.

Bèze, Theodore de

[1580] 1883–1889 *Histoire Ecclésiastique des Églises Réformées au Royaume de France, ed. nouvelle avec commentaire, notice bibliographique et table des faits et des noms properes* 3 vols., ed. G. Baum and E. Cunitz. Paris: Librairie Fischbacher.

Bourdieu, Pierre

[1963] 1979 The Disenchantment of the World. In *Algeria 1960,* by Pierre Bourdieu, 1–94. Cambridge: Cambridge University Press.

1977 *Outline of a Theory of Practice.* Cambridge: Cambridge University Press.

Butler, Judith

1993 *Bodies that Matter: On the Discursive Limits of "Sex."* New York: Routledge.

The Byble in Englyshe

1540 Second edition. London: Rychard Grafton.

Castiglione, Baldesar

[1518] 1959 *The Book of the Courtier.* Trans. C. S. Singleton. New York: Anchor.

Cervantes, Fernando

1994 *The Devil in the New World.* New Haven: Yale University Press.

Christian, William

1981 *Apparitions in Late Medieval and Renaissance Spain.* Princeton: Princeton University Press.

1989 *Person and God in a Spanish Valley.* Princeton: Princeton University Press.

Clendinnen, Inga

1991 *Aztecs: An Interpretation.* Cambridge: Cambridge University Press.

Columbus, Christopher

[ca. 1502] 1991 *The Libro de las Profecías of Christopher Columbus.* Trans. and ed. D. C. West and A. Kling. Gainesville: University of Florida Press.

Comaroff, Jean, and John Comaroff

1999 Occult Economies and the Violence of Abstraction: Notes from the South African Postcolony. *American Ethnologist* 26(2):279–303.

2000 Millennial Capitalism: First Thoughts on a Second Coming. *Public Culture* 12(2):291–343.

Cotgrave, Randle

1611 *A Dictionarie of the French and English Tongues.* London: Adam Islip.

Covarrubias Orozco, Sebastian de

[1611] 1993 *Tesoro de la Lengua Castellana o Española.* Madrid: Editorial Castilia.

Crouzet, Denis
1990 *Les Guerriers de Dieu: La Violence au Temps des Troubles de Religion vers 1525–vers 1610,* 2 vols. Mayenne: Floch.

Dávila Padilla, Augustin
[1596] 1625 *Historia de la Fundación y Discurso de la Provincia de Santiago de Mexico,* 2nd ed. Brussels: Iuan de Meerbeque.

Davis, Natalie Zemon
1975 *Society and Culture in Early Modern France.* Stanford: Stanford University Press.
1987 *Fiction in the Archives: Pardon Tales and Their Tellers in Sixteenth-Century France.* Stanford: Stanford University Press.

Della Casa, Giovanni
[1558] 1990 *Galateo.* Trans. K. Eisenbichler and K. R. Bartlett. Toronto: Centre for Reformation and Renaissance Studies.

Elias, Norbert
[1939] 2000 *The Civilizing Process.* Oxford: Blackwell.

Erasmus, Desideradus
[1509] 1985 "De Pueris Instituendis/A Declamation on the Subject of Early Liberal Education for Children." In *Collected Works of Erasmus, Literary and Educational Writings,* vol. 4, ed. Craig R. Thompson, 297–346. Toronto: University of Toronto Press.

Febvre, Lucien
[1942] 1982 *The Problem of Unbelief in the 16th Century: The Religion of Rabelais.* Cambridge: Harvard University Press.

Fleischer, Cornell
n.d. *A Mediterranean Apocalypse: Imperialism and Prophecy, 1453–1550.* Stanford: Stanford University Press. Forthcoming.

Foucault, Michel
1977 *Discipline and Punish: The Birth of the Prison.* New York: Pantheon.

Greenblatt, Stephen
1980 *Renaissance Self-Fashioning: From More to Shakespeare.* Chicago: University of Chicago Press.

Gregory of Tours
1988 *The Glory of the Martyrs.* Liverpool: Liverpool University Press.

Grenaille, François de
1642 *L'Honneste garçon, ou l'Art de bien élever la noblesse à la vertu, aux sciences et à tons les exercises convenables à sa condition.* Paris: T. Quinet.

Guicciardini, Francesco
[1509] 1964 "The History of Florence." In *Guicciardini: History of Italy and History of Florence,* trans. C. Grayson and ed. J. R. Hale, 1–84. New York: Washington Square Press.

Guillem, Salvador
1999 *Ofrendas a Ehécatl-Quetzalcoatl en México-Tlatelolco.* Mexico: INAH, Colección Científica.

Harkness, Deborah E.
1999 *John Dee's Conversations with Angels: Cabala, Alchemy, and the End of Nature.* Cambridge: Cambridge University Press.

Herzog, Tamar
2003 *Defining Nations: Immigrants and Citizens in Early Modern Spain and Spanish America.* New Haven: Yale University Press.

Houston, Stephen, and David Stuart
1996 Of Gods, Glyphs, and Kings: Divinity and Rulership among the Classic Maya. *Antiquity* 70:289–312.
1998 The Ancient Maya Self: Personhood and Portraiture in the Classic Period. *RES* 33:73–101.

Huarte de San Juan, Juan
[1575] 1988 *Examen de Ingenios para las Ciencias.* Barcelona: Promociones y Publicaciones Universitarias, S.A.

Hvidtfeldt, Arild
1958 *Teotl and Ixiptlatli: Some Central Conceptions in Ancient Mexican Religion.* Copenhagen: Munksgaard.

James, Allison, Chris Jenks, and Alan Prout
1998 *Theorizing Childhood.* New York: Teachers College Press.

Joyce, Rosemary
2000 Girling the Girl and Boying the Boy: The Production of Adulthood in Ancient Mesoamerica. *World Archaeology* 31(3):473–483.

Kagan, Richard
1990 *Lucrecia's Dreams: Politics and Prophecy in Sixteenth-Century Spain.* Berkeley: University of California Press.

Klein, Cecelia
1995 Wild Woman in Colonial Mexico: An Encounter of European and Aztec Concepts of the Other. In *Reframing the Renaissance,* ed. C. Farrago, 245–263. New Haven: Yale University Press.

Ladurie, Emmanuel LeRoy
1978 *Montaillou: The Promised Land of Error.* New York: Vintage Books.

Landucci, Luca
[1450–1516] 1883 *Diario Fiorentino dal 1450 al 1516,* ed. J. del Badia. Florence: G. C. Sansoni.
[1450–1516] 1927 *A Florentine Diary from 1450 to 1516,* trans. A. de Rosen Jervis. London: J. M. Dent and Sons.

L'Estoile, Pierre de
1876 *Mémoires-Journeaux, Tome Troisième Journal de Henri III 1587–89*. Paris: Librairie des Bibliophiles.

López Austin, Alfredo
1988 *The Human Body and Ideology: Concepts of the Ancient Nahuas*, 2 vols. Salt Lake City: University of Utah Press.

López Lujan, Leonardo, Hector Neff, and Saburo Sugiyama
2000 The 9-Xi Vase: A Classic Thin Orange Vessel Found at Tenochtitlán. In *Mesoamerica's Classic Heritage: From Teotihuacan to the Aztecs*, ed. D. Carrasco, L. Jones, and S. Sessions, 219–249. Boulder: University Press of Colorado.

Mendieta, Fray Gerónimo de
[1573–1596] 1870 *Historia Eclesiástica Indiana*. Mexico: Antigua Libreria.

Monaghan, John
2000 Theology and History in the Study of Mesoamerican Religions. In *Supplement to the Handbook of Middle American Indians*, Volume 6: *Ethnology*, ed. J. Monaghan, 24–49. Austin: University of Texas Press.

Montaigne, Michel de
1943 *The Complete Essays of Montaigne*. Stanford: Stanford University Press.
1998 *Essais de Michel de Montaigne*, ed. A. Tournon. Paris: Nationale Éditions.

Moore, Robert Ian
2000 *The First European Revolution*. Oxford: Blackwell.

Motolinía, Fray Toribio de Benavente
[1538–1541] 1969 *Historia de los Indios de la Nueva España*. Mexico: Editorial Porrua.

Mundy, Barbara
1998 Mapping the Aztec Capital: The 1524 Nuremberg Map of Tenochtitlán, Its Sources and Meanings. *Imago Mundi* 50:11–33

Muñoz Camargo, Diego
[1576–1596] 1892 *Historia de Tlaxcala*. Mexico: Oficina Tip. De la Secretaria de Fomento.

Nirenberg, David
1996 *Communities of Violence: Persecution of Minorities in the Middle Ages*. Princeton: Princeton University Press.

Obeyesekere, Gananath
1992 *The Apotheosis of Captain Cook: European Mythmaking in the Pacific*. Princeton: Princeton University Press.

Opie, Iona

1993 *The People in the Playground.* Oxford: Oxford University Press.

Phelan, John Leddy

1970 *The Millennial Kingdom of the Franciscans in the New World.* Berkeley: University of California Press.

Rabb, Theodore

1975 *The Struggle for Stability in Early Modern Europe.* Oxford: Oxford University Press.

Ramos, Gabriela

1992 Política Eclesiástica y Extirpación de la Idolatría: Discursos y Silencios en Torno al Taqui Onqoy. *Revista Andina* 10(1):147–169.

Reubeni, David

[1525] 1930 Diary 1522–1525. In *Jewish Travellers in the Middle Ages: 19 First-hand Accounts,* ed. E. N. Adler, 251–328. London: Routledge.

Román Berrelleza, Juan Alberto

1993 Offering 48 of the Templo Mayor: A Case of Child Sacrifice. In *The Aztec Templo Mayor,* ed. E. H. Boone, 131–144. Washington, DC: Dumbarton Oaks.

Sahagún, Bernardino de

[1547–1579] 1938 *Historia General de las Cosas de Nueva España,* 5 vols. Mexico: P. Robredo.

[1547–1579] 1950–1982 *Florentine Codex: General History of the Things of New Spain,* 13 vols. Ed. and trans. A.J.D. Anderson and C. E. Dibble. Salt Lake City: University of Utah Press; and Santa Fe: School of American Research.

Sahlins, Marshall

1988 Cosmologies of Capitalism: The Trans-Pacific Sector of "the World System." *Proceedings of the British Academy* 74:1–51.

Stuart, David

1996 Kings of Stone: A Consideration of Stelae in Ancient Maya Ritual and Representation. *RES* 29/30:148–171.

Tedlock, Dennis

1993 Torture in the Archives: Mayans Meet Europeans. *American Anthropologist* 95(1):139–152.

Torquemada, Juan de

[1615] 1969 *Monarquia Indiana,* 3 vols. Mexico: Editorial Porrua.

Trexler, Richard

1974 Ritual in Florence: Adolescence and Salvation in the Renaissance. In *The Pursuit of Holiness in Late Medieval and Renaissance Religion,* ed. H. Oberman and C. Trinkaus, 200–264. Leiden: Brill.

1980 *Public Life in Renaissance Florence.* New York: Academic Press.

1987 From the Mouths of Babes: Christianization by Children in 16th Century New Spain. In *Church and Community 1200–1600: Studies in the History of Florence and New Spain,* ed. R. Trexler, 549–573. Rome: Edizioni di Storia e Letteratura.

Urcid, Javier

n.d. Convenio con la Madre Tierra: La Muerte Ritual entre los Mexicas. Manuscript.

Vogt, Evon

1970 *The Zinacantecos of Mexico: A Modern Maya Way of Life.* New York: Holt, Reinhart, and Winston.

Ward, Colin

1978 *The Child in the City.* New York: Pantheon.

Watts, Pauline Moffitt

1985 On the Spiritual Origins of Christopher Columbus's "Enterprise of the Indies." *American Historical Review* 90(1):73–102.

Weinstein, Donald

1970 *Savonarola and Florence: Prophecy and Patriotism in the Renaissance.* Princeton: Princeton University Press.

Wolf, Eric

1982 *Europe and the People without History.* Berkeley: University of California Press.

9

THE ROLE OF CHILDREN IN THE RITUAL PRACTICES OF THE GREAT TEMPLE OF TENOCHTITLAN AND THE GREAT TEMPLE OF TLATELOLCO

Juan Alberto Román Berrelleza

Ximena Chávez Balderas

INTRODUCTION

References to children are particularly scarce in the specialized literature of Mesoamerica. What were the roles of children in ancient societies? The apparent absence of this group in the archaeological record can be explained by several factors: taphonomy, complex and selective ritual practices, and researchers' preconceived notions concerning children's relevance. When Kathryn Kamp (2001:1) asks, where have all the children gone? she answers that they are apparently "invisible" as a result of methodological factors. It is possible that some researchers do not consider this group relevant to studies of economics, politics, or religion, since a child is visualized as not yet an adult, and the child is only learning and waiting for an opportunity to reach maturity in order to become part of oral and written history.

Nevertheless, recent research shows that in spite of the factors that make children invisible to archaeological researchers, a detailed and careful analysis that considers them a relevant group within social dynamics will render valuable results. This is true of the research led by Billie Follensbee (Chapter 10), who through the study of anthropomorphic figurines provides evidence that small children, besides being the major sacrificial victims in Olmec culture, are fundamental to gaining insight into the social dynamics of the group.

Kamp suggests (2001:3) that although a connection often exists between biologically young people and those considered to be children, childhood cannot be reduced to biology. The age categories of our particular society, those employed analytically to define age ranges in osteology, or those used in other societies, present or past, are social *constructions* that we must be conscious of to render a more precise interpretation of the archaeological record (Hamann, Chapter 8, addresses the concept of *childhood* in the Occidental world).

In the Central Plateau of Mexico during the late Postclassic period, the concept of childhood was quite different from our present view. As a result of a detailed study undertaken by Alfredo López Austin (1988: 320–329), we know that childhood was not considered a uniform period. López Austin divides childhood into the following stages: (1) intrauterine life (before birth); (2) lactation; (3) pre-speech; (4) speaking but less than six years old; and (5) six years and older.

Given López Austin's study and multiple lines of additional evidence, it is possible to understand quite precisely the way childhood was conceptualized in the late Postclassic, which in turn enables us to reassess its role within social dynamics (Figure 9.1). In some cases, archaeological, historical, and osteological evidence can be used to complement one another. An example of this situation is the archaeological contexts excavated by the Proyecto Templo Mayor (Great Temple Project), directed by Eduardo Matos Moctezuma. The Proyecto Templo Mayor focuses on the sacred buildings of Tenochtitlan, ancient capital of the Aztecs, and Tlatelolco, its sister city (Figure 1.1). New data from the Proyecto, when interpreted with the aid of historical information, allow us to corroborate the reasons why children were chosen to play the role of sacrificial victims in rituals that opened communication between humans and the divine realm.

CHILDHOOD FROM THE POINT OF VIEW OF THE MEXICAS

Before referring to the participation of children in the cosmovision and, therefore, in ritual practices, it is important to characterize briefly some salient features in the Mexica conception of child development. As noted by López Austin (1988:322–324), childhood was a period when indi-

*9.1: A couple, husband and wife, with two children. A snake with two faces is situated between the calendric names of the man and the woman (*Codex Borgia, *1993:60; photo by Germán Zúñiga/Proyecto Templo Mayor).*

viduals were subject to great dangers, both natural and supernatural. This is constantly reflected in the work of Sahagún (1997), who mentions the ease with which children were harmed by sorcerers and other supernatural beings. Given the health conditions of that time, Sahagún's statement about children's vulnerability could also refer to the ease with which diseases infected them. Childhood was a period of formation, of certain limitations, and of purity; this last aspect aided communication with the gods. Communication between gods and children began when children were not yet born. In the intrauterine life, the fetus was ensouled with the *tonalli,* the anima of one of the entities central to Mexica cosmology. This soul was housed in the head and was strengthened with the ritual bath (López Austin 1988:223–241; McKeever Furst 1995:178). From the moment of birth the child as well as the new mother were the subjects of various rites. During the four days between birth and the ritual bath/naming ceremony, a fire was kept in the house of the new mother in order to maintain the good fortune of the newborn (Sahagún 1997:250). As a reference to the central activities that the child would

*9.2: The Chichihuauhcuahco, a foster tree that feeds children who died before being linked to maize (*Codex Vaticanus A, *f. 3v; drawing by Enrique Vázquez).*

undertake as an adult, a segment of the umbilical cord was buried near the hearth if the newborn was a girl, or buried in the battlefield if the newborn was a boy (Sahagún 1997:384). It was believed that an infant's date of birth and the date of the ritual bath would influence some aspects of her/his life. In the case of an unlucky date of birth, the date of the ritual bath and naming ceremony could be postponed until the conditions were more favorable (Sahagún 1997:250–253). Children not yet weaned were a special group and possessed the highest purity, which is reflected in the funerary patterns. They received special treatment and were buried in a location distinct from the rest of the population. This type of separation, according to van Gennep (1960:152–153), relates to the fact that if small children died before becoming adults, they would not receive adult burial treatment.

Children were incorporated into the next stages of personhood through the feeding process (López Austin 1988:358). When a child was not yet linked to maize, after her/his death s/he would go to Chichihuauhcuahco, where a foster tree would feed her/him (Figure 9.2). Mercedes Garza (1997:125) locates this place as a subregion of Tlalocan, the resting place of those who died of water-related causes.

After this stage, the development of the child is amply portrayed in sources like the *Florentine Codex* and the *Codex Mendoza.* A child was presented to the temple at an early age and later was sent to one of the priestly or secular schools in order to develop abilities crucial for the later stages of his life.

CHILDREN IN RITUAL PRACTICES: HISTORICAL EVIDENCE

Besides the information on children's developmental cycles, historical sources describe the participation of children in the ritual sphere. Communication with the realm of gods was one of the main aspects of pre-

*9.3: Tlaloc, the god of the rain, and Lord of the Tlalocan (*Codex Borgia, *1993:25; photo by Germán Zúñiga/Proyecto Templo Mayor).*

Hispanic cosmovision. A key component of communication between the natural and supernatural worlds was the elaboration of intricate rituals such as offerings, sacrifices, and funerals. Offerings and sacrifices were celebrated during periodic festivities following a calendar or as part of special or extraordinary occasions not dictated by the calendar. These rituals could be propitiatory or could acknowledge the fulfillment of a previous petition. Bertina Olmedo and Carlos González (1986:49) and Leonardo López Luján (1993:103) mention that the main reasons for placing offerings in religious buildings were to mark the construction or extension of existing buildings, to celebrate scheduled festivities, to commemorate the ascent of an individual to the highest level in the social hierarchy, to perform a ritual prior to the setting out of merchants, and to observe funerals of important persons.

Of special relevance are the petitions made to Tlaloc, god of rain (Figure 9.3), who could provide water to nurture crops or send floods to destroy the harvest. This deity was assisted by the *tlaloques,* considered to be "ministers of small body" and dwellers of the hills. Hills were considered to be water containers from which rains emanated (Broda

2001). Droughts, lethal for harvests, were linked to the anger of Tlaloc's ministers.

An important aspect of scheduled festivities was their association with the gods of rain and maize, a logical fact if one considers the importance of agriculture in the subsistence of the Mexicas. Sahagún notes that these celebrations, where child sacrifice was undertaken, took place in the solar calendar's first four 20-day periods (*veintenas*)—*atlcahualo* (beginning in mid-February), *tlacaxipehualiztli* (beginning in early March), *tozoztontli* (beginning in late March), and *huey tozoztli* (beginning in mid-April). Other sources mention rain- and maize-based celebrations held during *atemoztli* (beginning in mid-December) and *izcalli* (beginning in late January). In Central Mexico, these periods lasted from the dry season until the arrival of torrential rains. Based on these descriptions, the importance of the wind-water-maize complex is highlighted. This complex is fundamental to understanding the archaeological finds of the Great Temples of Tenochtitlan and Tlatelolco.

Fray Diego de Durán's (1995, 1:285–286) account of the 20-day period of *atemoztli,* "the descent of water," is quite illustrative. During this time, people requested that the rain arrive in spring and they pretended that "a child descended from heaven on that day and was named water." Sahagún (1997:147) adds that the people announced the arrival of the *tlaloques* when the water ran down the hills. In the 20-day period called *izcalli,* a ritual symbolizing growth featured an analogy between maize and children. As part of a growth metaphor, children were pulled by their necks, ears, noses, and feet in order to "stretch them during nursing." Two hills where rains were believed to originate, Tlaloc and Matlacueye, were also commemorated as part of this festivity. During these celebrations a boy and a girl were sacrificed in honor of such hills, concurrent with the sowing time (Durán 1995:289). Another relevant festivity was held in the 20-day period *huey tozoztli,* when the hill Tlaloc was commemorated in the presence of the highest rulers of that time. While ritual music played, a six- or seven-year-old boy was sacrificed by the priests of Tlaloc and his blood was used as an offering. A final festival in honor of the *tlaloques* took place during the first 20-day period, *atlcahualo* (Sahagún 1997:98). Two children with double cowlicks were chosen for sacrifice. This distinguishing trait is a suggestive aspect if we consider that the head housed the *tonalli* and that spiral as well as helical forms, such as cowlicks, were associated with the movement of one plane of the universe with respect to the other. The sacrifice took place in the hills and in a vortex of a lake near Pantitlán. The vortex was probably related to the cowlicks. Children to be sacrificed were richly dressed and taken to the hills where a vigil was kept; if the children cried this was considered a good sign since the tears augured rain. The analogy between tears and rain is demonstrated in ceramic vessels called Tlaloc braziers, which have been found in large quantities in the excavations of the Great Temple in Tenochtitlan. This type of propitiatory ceremony could be extraordinary and was practiced during emergent situations not predicted by the calendar. During the dry season, for example, they could be held to counteract supernatural effects over rains and consequently on the harvest (Román Berrelleza 1990). This aspect will be addressed again later.

CHILDREN IN MEXICA RITUAL PRACTICES: ARCHAEOLOGICAL EVIDENCE

Within the Proyecto Templo Mayor, numerous excavations have been undertaken in the ceremonial zones of the cities of Tenochtitlan and Tlatelolco (Figure 9.4). The recovered evidence provides complementary insights on ritual life. One of the main forms of communication between this world and that of the gods is by means of oblations. The

*9.4: The Great Temple of Tenochtitlan (*Codex Durán, *1995:30; photo by Germán Zúñiga/Proyecto Templo Mayor).*

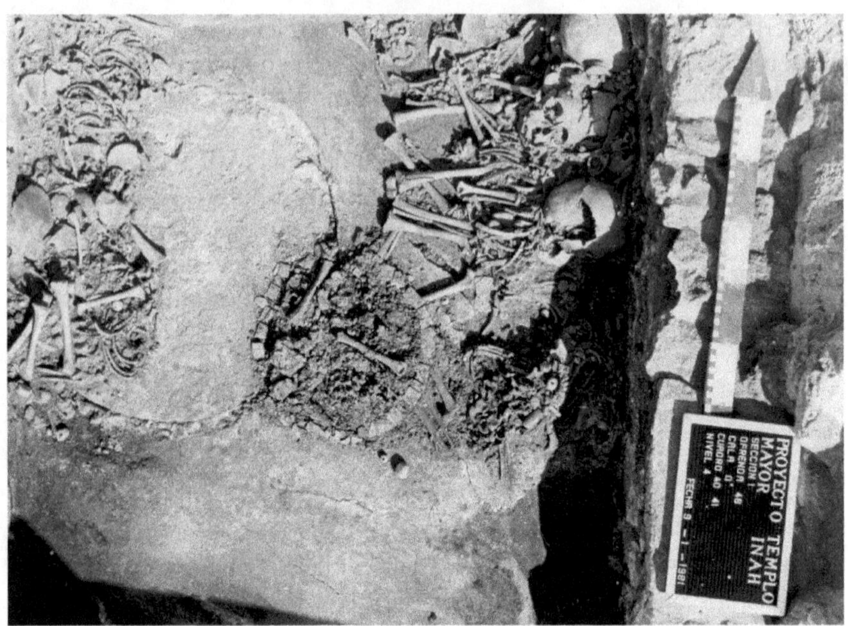

9.5: Excavation of Offering 48. Close-up from the fourth excavation level (photo by Juan Alberto Román/Proyecto Templo Mayor).

material expression of this act, linked to a sacred space and other ritual acts, is the offering (López Luján 1993:52). This offering was the sacrifice of an inert object or a living being to propitiate, or as a kind of payment to, the supernatural beings (Nagao 1985:1). Two archaeological contexts have given us further understanding of the ceremonies directed to deities related to rain and fertility: Offering No. 48 in the Great Temple in Tenochtitlan and the findings at the foot of the staircases of the Ehécatl-Quetzalcóatl Temple in Tlatelolco. As we will see, the character of the offerings and sacrifices made at these two sites matches the symbolism and sacred connotations appropriate to the deities of these two places.

Offering No. 48 in the Great Temple of Tenochtitlan (Figure 9.5) was found on a small altar in the northwest corner of the temple dedicated to Tlaloc, over the platform corresponding to the main façade of the Great Temple in what has been called stage IVb. This platform was built around 1469 CE, during the reign of the sixth Mexica tlatoani, Axayácatl (Matos 1989:37, 50). Forty-two children were placed inside a rectangular container made of stone blocks, measuring 1.70 meters in length, 1.10 meters in width, and 0.69 meter in depth. Associated with the skeletons were eleven sculptures in the shape of vases with the image of the god Tlaloc, two disks made of turquoise with wooden bases, numerous greenstone beads, blue pigment, and a fragment of an obsidian blade. Various natural objects such as two carved shells, a seashell, squash residues, and fragments of wood and copal were also found.

At Tlatelolco, the skeletons of forty-one sacrificed persons, thirty of which were children, were found at the bottom of the staircase of the main façade of Temple R, which was dedicated to the cult of Ehécatl-Quetzalcóatl. The skeletons were deposited as part of two types of offerings. The first type consisted of clay pots of globular shape containing skeletons of children. Associated with them were various objects, including copper rattles, conch and other seashells, obsidian blades, wooden residues, blue pigment, and animal bones. In many cases, pottery in the shape of zoomorphic and anthropomorphic representations as well as clay objects such as flat earthen bowls, dishes, and vases were placed outside the globular pots. In the second type of offering, infants, youngsters, and adults were placed directly on the ground, accompanied by objects and materials similar to the ones described previously.

OSTEOLOGICAL ANALYSES: RECENT RESULTS

Osteological investigation of the bones from these offerings consisted of the analysis of paleopathologies and DNA. These analyses corroborated numerous aspects of the historical sources and introduced new details not described historically, particularly in reference to the gender of the individuals and their health conditions.

Paleopathology

The analysis of teeth revealed simple, acute, and chronic caries and several cases of enamel hypoplasia. The causes of this syndrome may be hereditary, localized trauma, or metabolic systemic stress such as malnourishment, which is the most probable origin in pre-Hispanic populations (Goodman et al. 1984; Skinner and Goodman 1992). Another ailment reported for this sample was gingivitis, resulting from poor oral hygiene, accumulation of dental plaque, trauma, dental calculus, and chronic and acute caries. This lesion was detected by the morphoscopic observation of the altered anatomy of the affected region. Severe cases of both enamel hypoplasia and gingivitis resulted in the loss of the affected teeth. Based on the values obtained for each of the ailments present in this study, the more common diseases are the ones related to alterations

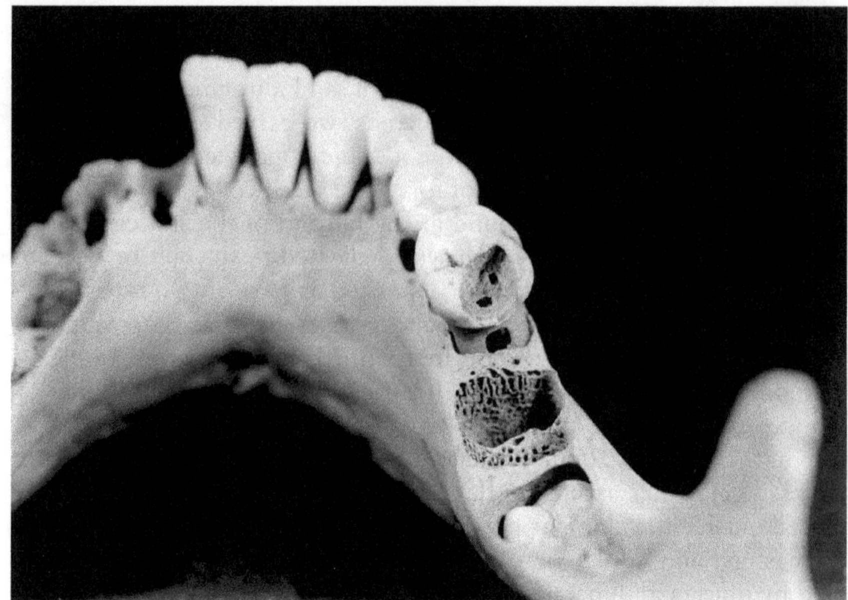

9.6: Mandible (infantile) with third-degree caries affecting the pulp cavity. The bone shows the traces of an infection (photo by Juan Alberto Román/ Proyecto Templo Mayor).

in the development of teeth structure, mainly represented by enamel hypoplasia (localized in the fringe of the dental crown), which was found in thirty-six persons. Lesions found in dental tissue were second among tooth anomalies. The most common lesion of this sort is incipient or first degree caries (Caries A), encountered in twenty-seven individuals. Second and third degree caries (Figure 9.6) (Caries B and C, respectively) were found in a lesser proportion. The decrease in these last ailments can be explained by the loss of teeth as a result of the substitution of permanent teeth for deciduous teeth. Dental calculus was present in eighteen subjects.

Another common pathology was porotic hyperostosis (Figure 9.7). This lesion of spongy appearance, which also affects the roof of the ocular orbits, is associated with malnutrition, especially iron-deficiency anemia. This disorder was present in more than 50 percent of the sample. When talking of paleopathologies, we must bear in mind that they are not merely descriptions of osteological characteristics but also indicators of undernourishment and the low quality of everyday life these children endured.

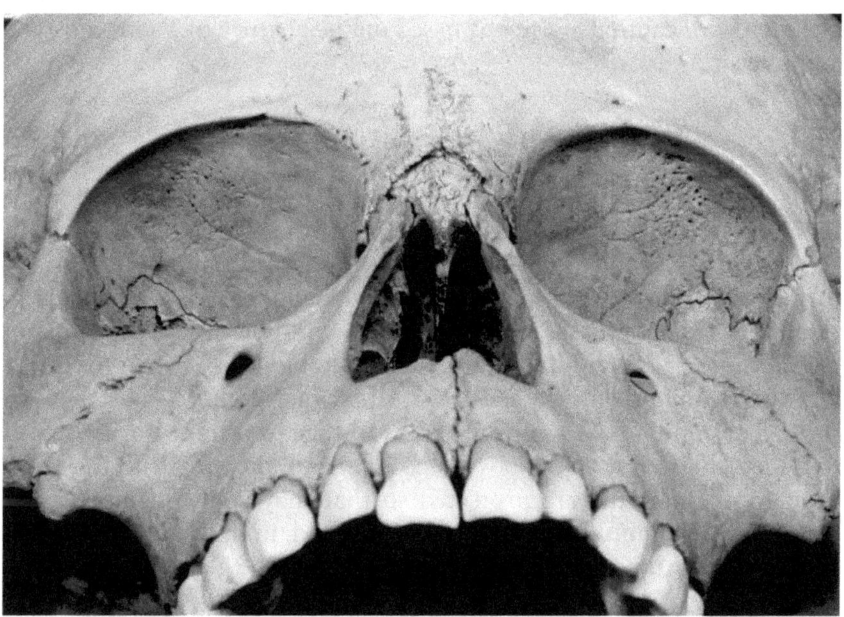

9.7: Cribra orbitalia, a lesion in the ocular orbit, caused by iron-deficiency anemia. Skull (infantile) from Tlatelolco (photo by Juan Alberto Román/ Proyecto Templo Mayor).

DNA Analysis

Molecular techniques based on Polymerase Chain Reaction (PCR) amplification of segments of the single-copy amelogenin gene, using ancient DNA recovered from archaeological human remains, allow for reliable sex identification of infantile or fragmentary skeletons (Faerman et al. 1995; Stone, Pääbo, and Stoneking 1996). This analysis was carried out in the samples coming from Tlatelolco by an interdisciplinary team of the Faculty of Sciences at the Universidad Nacional Autónoma de Mexico in the laboratory of Dr. Torre Blanco. Ancient DNA was extracted from the ribs and vertebrae of each individual, taking the necessary precautions to avoid contamination, such as UV irradiation, and using the necessary controls to detect contamination. Samples were pulverized and the procedures were carried out under a laminar flow cabinet. DNA was amplified and sequenced. The results show that because of the presence of amplified products of the Y chromosome, twenty-nine children and six adults were males. In only one case were products of this type absent, therefore indicating a female child. This information must be taken with caution, since it is based on the absence of Y-chromosome amplified products.

CONCLUSIONS

Bringing together historical, archaeological, and osteological information helps establish a fuller understanding of the role children played in the cosmovision and ritual life of ancient Tenochtitlan. Given this information we can infer aspects such as why children were sacrificed in ceremonies leading up to the rainy season and how the special characteristics of certain children made them suitable for sacrifice to Tlaloc and the *tlaloques*. In reference to the first question, we must bear in mind that childhood was conceived as a stage of utmost purity, which provided children with the possibility of communicating with the gods. Therefore, children were protected so that they could maintain their capacity for communication with the gods and, in this manner, successfully secure the favors that the Mexica asked of the gods (López Austin 1988, 1:324).

The offerings at Tlatelolco confirm that children were sacrificed to Tlaloc as part of an attempt to secure favors. In the particular case of the individuals found in Tlatelolco, we must remember that they were associated with the temple of the god of wind, Ehécatl-Quetzalcóatl. This deity was equal to a *tlaloque,* since the wind proclaimed the arrival of the rain. The Tlatelolco offering has been interpreted by Salvador Guilliem (1999) as the product of an extraordinary ceremony around 1454 to 1457 CE, perhaps motivated by a famine exacerbated by adverse climatic conditions, based on historical sources. All the analyzed individuals come from offering contexts localized in buildings dedicated to worship of these deities. In all cases, the conclusion reached was that these sacrifices were carried out to honor gods such as the ones mentioned previously, with the intention of asking for rain during prolonged droughts, or other petitions related to natural phenomena, or as payment for granted favors.

The DNA analysis adds new details about the characteristics of children sacrificed to Tlaloc. The dominance of Y-chromosome products shows a preference for males as sacrificial victims. The preference for male subjects lies in the analogy between the sacrificed individuals and the assistants of Tlaloc, in the case of Tenochtitlan, and of the god of the wind, in the case of Tlatelolco. Children sacrificed to the gods of rain were supposed to be living representations of these deities (*ixiptla*) and, as mentioned in the sources, assistants of Tlaloc. Since the deities were male and the sacrificed children were representations of the deities, it makes sense that mostly male children were sacrificed.

On the other hand, health conditions must have played a crucial role in explaining why the children found in the two offerings were seen as suitable candidates for sacrifice. In pre-Hispanic times diseases and ailments were often attributed to the gods. A wide variety of forces and divine beings were capable of inducing morbid states (Ortiz de Montellano 1993:158–195). The reasons for losing one's health were varied. It could be related to a violation of some divine rule on the part of humans. As a consequence, a god might unleash a certain type of punishment related to the violation, and such punishments might involve illness. One could only recover from a sickness through petitions, prayers, penance, and sacrifices directed to the god causing the sickness because that god had the capacity to confer both health and illness according to his will (Pérez Tamayo 1988:35–36). This concept is particularly relevant, since one pre-Hispanic belief was that certain deities were the originators of specific diseases. Thus, reproachful behavior motivated the gods such as Tlaloc, his *tlaloques,* Xipe-Tótec, Xochiquetzal, Chalchiuhtlicue, Chicomecóatl, Tezcatlipoca, and Quetzalcóatl to inflict the miscreant with gout, cripplement, leprosy, mange, or facial paralysis (López Austin 1975:32; Sahagún 1997:49–51). Sahagún mentions that such deities were also the patrons of these diseases.

In addition to reproachful behavior, virtuous behavior also attracted the attention of the gods. People who were struck by lightning, drowned in rivers or lagoons, or who died a water-related death were said to have been singled out by Tlaloc and Chalchiuhtlicue, who chose these victims as their servants.

Another factor that might cause disease and was attributed to the gods was determined by the date of birth of the individuals. Being born on an unlucky day in the *tonalpohualli,* the 260-day divinatory calendar, could increase the possibility of contracting certain morbid states (López Austin 1975:32).

It is worth mentioning that the children in our skeletal sample had indications of poor health. Although children may not have committed the reproachful behaviors that brought about disease and other afflictions, children with disease may have been seen as candidates for sacrifice because their diseases matched those governed by Tlaloc and his assistants. At this point it is appropriate to comment that the *tlaloques* were patrons of certain diseases associated with water. The results of our osteological analyses indicate that the subjects had mainly dental ailments. Having a condition or disease governed by the *tlaloques,* however, would not necessarily be the reason why the person was chosen for sacrifice. It is possible that for the more severe conditions this was the case, but with respect to the rest of the sample we are drawn toward other explanations. From an odontological point of view, most dental ailments encountered in the analysis—mainly caries and periodontal processes—may reflect precarious health, for these pathologies are infection foci at a systemic level. Michael Newman and Anthony Goodman (1989) suggest that a dental pathology may generate other pathologies in organs and systems located in the periphery of the buccal cavity, or even distant from it. Among the most important pathologies related to the airways are rhinopharyngitis, laryngitis, and even some lung and ear (otitis) infections. Other diseases may affect the digestive system, causing gastritis, ulcers, and diarrhea. Severe cases may cause cerebral abscesses and osteomyelitis (Newman and Goodman 1989:247), or cause various articular illnesses such as rheumatoid arthritis. Within this clinical scenario, there is no doubt that the buccal cavity is relevant to more severe conditions at an organismic level. During the analysis, we became aware of a correspondence between the illnesses attributed to the gods of rain in pre-Hispanic times and the illnesses recently identified in the Templo Mayor archaeological samples.

In conclusion, we suggest that if individuals sacrificed to certain gods are found to have maladies of which those gods are patrons, these individuals were selected for sacrifice precisely because their maladies matched those with which the gods were affiliated. Yet to be considered appropriate for sacrifice, individuals had to comply with other requirements, such as having the double cowlick, being born under the appropriate calendrical sign (Sahagún 1997), having the appropriate age, or behaving in a way that would provoke the gods. As Traci Ardren (Chapter 1) mentions, children are depositories of power and sacred knowledge; ethnographic and historic records corroborate this condition. The present work adds to other studies that highlight the importance of children in the cosmovision and ritual life of the Mexica. Children's closeness to purity and to certain deities was important to achieve communication with the divine world and secure a vital asset for the rest of the population, the arrival of the rain.

REFERENCES CITED

Broda, Johanna

2001 Ritos Mexicas en los Cerros de la Cuenca: los Sacrificios de Niños. In *La Montaña en el Paisaje Ritual,* ed. J. Broda, S. Iwaniszewski, and A. Miranda Montero, 295–317. Mexico: Conaculta, INAH.

Durán, Fray Diego de
1995 *Historia de las Indias de la Nueva España e Islas de Tierra Firme.* Mexico: Conaculta, Cien de México.

Faerman, Marina, Dvora Filon, Gila Kahila, Charles L. Greenblatt, Patricia Smith, and Ariella Oppenheim
1995 Sex Identification of Archaeological Human Remains Based on Amplification of the X and Y Amelogenin Alleles. *Gene* 167:327–332.

Garza, Mercedes
1997 El Perro como Símbolo Religioso entre los Mayas y los Nahuas. *Estudios de Cultura Náhuatl* 27:111–133.

Goodman, Alan, Debra L. Martin, George J. Armelagos, and George Clark
1984 Health Changes at Dickinson Mounds, Illinois. In *Paleopathology at the Origins of Agriculture,* ed. M. N. Cohen and G. Armelagos, 271–305. Orlando: Academic Press.

Guilliem, Salvador
1999 *Ofrendas a Ehécatl-Quetzalcóatl en México Tlatelolco.* Mexico: INAH, Colección Científica.

Kamp, Kathryn A.
2001 Where Have All the Children Gone? The Archaeology of Childhood. *Journal of Archaeological Method and Theory* 8:1–34.

López Austin, Alfredo
1975 *Textos de Medicina Náhuatl.* Mexico: UNAM.
1988 *Cuerpo Humano e Ideología,* vol. 1. Mexico: UNAM–IIH.

López Luján, Leonardo.
1993 *Las Ofrendas del Templo Mayor de Tenochtitlan.* Mexico: INAH.

Matos Moctezuma, Eduardo
1989 *Guía Oficial Templo Mayor.* Mexico: INAH/Salvat.

McKeever Furst, Jill
1995 *The Natural History of the Soul in Ancient México.* New Haven: Yale University Press.

Nagao, Debra
1985 *Mexica Buried Offerings: A Historical and Contextual Analysis.* Oxford: BAR.

Newman, Michael, and Anthony Goodman
1989 Oral and Dental Infections. In *Anaerobic Infections in Humans,* ed. S. Finegold and L. George, 234–259. San Diego: Academic Press.

Olmedo, Bertina, and Carlos González
1986 Presencia del Estilo Mezcala en el Templo Mayor, una Clasificación de Piezas Antropomorfas. Tesis de licenciatura de arqueología, ENAH, México.

Ortiz de Montellano, Bernard
1993 *Medicina, Salud y Nutrición Aztecas.* Mexico: Siglo XXI Editores.

Pérez Tamayo, Ruy
1988 *El Concepto de Enfermedad.* Mexico: UNAM–Facultad de Medicina, CONACYT-FCE.

Román Berrelleza, Juan
1990 *El Sacrificio de Niños en el Templo Mayor.* Mexico: INAH/GV Editores, Asociación de Amigos del Templo Mayor.

Sahagún, Fray Bernardino
1997 *Historia General de las Cosas de la Nueva España.* Mexico: Editorial Porrúa.

Skinner, Mark, and Alan Goodman
1992 Anthropological Uses of Developmental Defects of Enamel. In *Skeletal Biology of Past Peoples: Research Methods,* ed. S. R. Saunders and M. A. Katzenberg, 153–174. New York: Wiley-Liss.

Stone, Anne C., George R. Milner, Svante Pääbo, and Mark Stoneking
1996 Sex Determination of Ancient Human Skeletons Using DNA. *American Journal of Physical Anthropology* 99(2):231–238.

van Gennep, Arnold
1960 *The Rites of Passage.* Chicago: University Press of Chicago.

10
THE CHILD AND THE CHILDLIKE IN OLMEC ART AND ARCHAEOLOGY

Billie Follensbee

At first mention, the role of children among the Gulf Coast Olmec might appear to be a well-explored topic. After all, the "Olmec baby-face" is one of the most frequently used descriptive terms in the study of Olmec sculpture, and virtually every exhibit on Olmec art includes examples of the "Olmec hollow baby figures." Closer examination, however, reveals that these appearances are quite deceiving. The term *baby face*[1] actually refers to a distinctive type of facial configuration that appears as often on adult figures and supernatural figures as on diminutive images. The "Olmec hollow baby figures" actually have a relatively minor presence on the Gulf Coast; these figures were made predominantly by early Central Mexican peoples who were once thought of as Olmec but are now recognized as a fully distinct culture (see, for example, Grove 1993:83–111).[2] Until recently, in fact, only meager attention has been paid to the appearance and role of human children among the Olmec. Further, most of this discussion has focused on the relevance of the children to adult images, such as the debates on whether the childlike figures on Olmec thrones represent sacrifices (e.g., Stirling 1940:324–326) or high-status heirs (e.g., Bernal 1969:58). The lack of discussion about children is not necessarily because of lack of interest, but much more likely the result of how difficult it is to identify children among the Olmec.

Although the task of isolating and understanding children in the remains of any ancient culture is difficult, finding children in Gulf Coast Olmec material culture is especially problematic. Because the Olmec are a very ancient Mesoamerican people from the Formative period, flourishing from approximately 1200 to 300 BCE, scholars do not have the ethnographic or ethnohistoric resources available for the Olmec as they do for the Aztec and the Maya. There are also relatively few extant Olmec and Epi-Olmec hieroglyphs and, even for these, the current translations and their relevance to the Gulf Coast Olmec are disputed.[3] And, because the Olmec were located in a tropical rainforest environment with heavily acidic soils, osteological and other perishable remains are meager and rare; generally, only the most durable of Gulf Coast material culture survives.[4] The bulk of relevant primary information about Olmec children, therefore, survives only in what are most plentiful among Olmec remains: sculpted images.

Unfortunately, identifying children in Olmec sculpture is difficult. Olmec stone sculpture is noted for the stylization of its figures; although they are relatively naturalistic, their physical forms are often blocky and somewhat ambiguous. This physical ambiguity thwarts clear understanding of specific aspects of the human imagery, including such basics as gender and age. More than fifty figures that are childlike in form or scale have been identified in small and large Olmec stone sculptures, but the great variety among them suggests that some diminutive images may not represent children but perhaps fetuses, dwarfs, supernaturals, supporting relatives, or ancestor/patron spirits. Preliminary to discussions of children in the sculpture, therefore, is identifying which of these images actually represent children; the key to identifying children lies in isolating the Olmec cultural signifiers of children and childhood.

Part of the solution to this enigma can be found through the study of a common, but often overlooked, form of Olmec sculpture: the small, solid, handmade ceramic figurines, which are generally much more physically naturalistic than Olmec stone sculpture. In my previous research, the systematic analysis of 1,539 identifiably human, Formative-period figurine fragments, collected in the early archaeological explorations of the Gulf Coast Olmec sites of San Lorenzo, La Venta, and Tres Zapotes (Figure 1.1), has proven useful in clarifying other aspects of Olmec sculpture. Through the examination of physical traits, subtle stylizations, garments, and accoutrements on these figures, the more idiosyncratic Olmec cultural signifiers of sex, gender, and social status have been isolated. This knowledge, in turn, has made it possible to identify the more ambiguous male and female Olmec stone images, as well as figures that were apparently made intentionally ambiguous (Follensbee 2000). The humble ceramic figurines, I contend, also hold the key to understanding representations of children in Olmec imagery, as their naturalism provides the opportunity to clarify the physical traits and adornments that are associated with childhood.

THE CERAMIC FIGURINES

Previous classifications of Gulf Coast Olmec figurines focused heavily on the heads to create primary figurine typologies. Since over 99 percent of the heads are separated from the bodies, these typologies are inadequate for systematic studies of more body-specific traits such as sex or age.[5] A few heads do show sunken cheeks and prominent cheekbones suggesting advanced age, as confirmed on a rare, nearly complete figurine of an elderly woman from La Venta (Figure 10.1). A small number of other heads show sunken cheeks as well as emphasized facial hair, which together are commonly used to indicate men of advanced age in Mesoamerican depictions.[6] Beyond these few examples, the heads do not clearly represent other age distinctions. Because most heads and bodies are separated, it is also not possible to identify which specific facial features and hairstyles might be cultural indicators of age grades. The figurine bodies, however, show more promise in determining age distinctions.[7]

As justifiably noted by most previous scholars, the majority of the figurine bodies appear to be anatomically consistent with young, adult females (e.g., Drucker 1943:76–86; 1952:132–141; Weiant 1943:98–99), and more in-depth study of the bodies reveals that both the head and the body features show consistent patterns of form that vary little among these three sites and that are consistent in these patterns from the Early Formative (Initial Olmec phase, 1200 BCE) through the Late Formative period (Epi-Olmec phase, 100 CE[8]).[9] Thus, a useful classification system may be based on a close analysis of the body forms, followed by close analysis of garments and adornments. Although the majority of the figurines appear to be adults, understanding the depiction of adult sexed and gendered imagery is useful in identifying depictions of children and distinguishing them from adult dwarf figures.

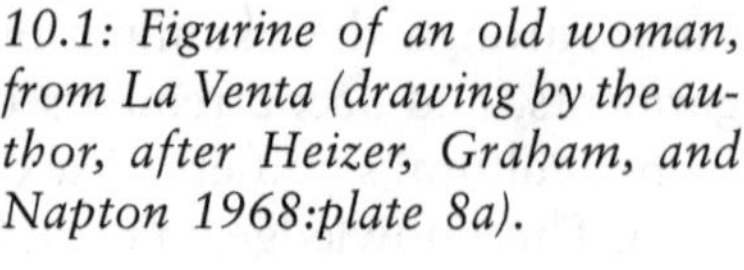

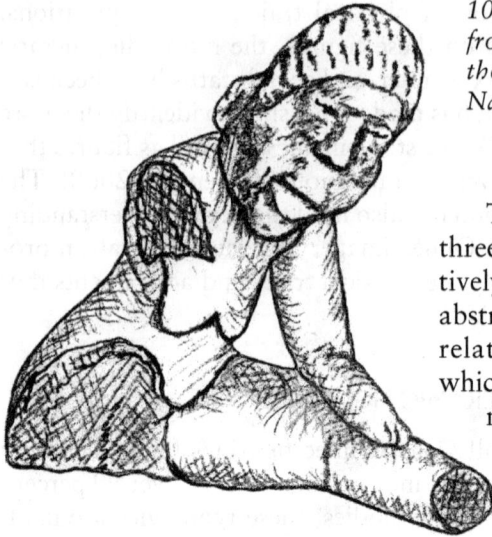

10.1: Figurine of an old woman, from La Venta (drawing by the author, after Heizer, Graham, and Napton 1968:plate 8a).

The figurines readily fall into three general categories: the relatively naturalistic, the somewhat abstracted, and the grotesque. The relatively naturalistic figurines, which are those closest in form to natural human anatomy, are the most prevalent type, making up roughly 92 percent of the sample; most of these are identifiably female. Although pubic genitalia is rare in all forms of Olmec sculpture, these figurines do show other clear, consistent secondary sexual characteristics. The most obviously sexed images are those with prominent female breasts. Some of these figurine bodies show women of advanced age with flaccid, sagging breasts (Figure 10.1); others, with large, distended bellies and especially full breasts, are clearly meant to portray adult, pregnant females, simultaneously indicating the beginning of another human life in the potential new child.

Meanwhile, slender, non-pregnant figurines with similarly pronounced breasts display other consistent, sexed physical characteristics, including pinched waists that start just below the breasts, lower torsos that slope out to flaring hips, and wide thighs that taper sharply to the lower legs (Figure 10.2). When nude, these figures also often have shapely buttocks with pronounced cleavage and a clearly indicated Y or triangular shape at the pubic area—a feature widely recognized by scholars as an almost universal female sex indicator, appearing on ancient female ceramic figurines throughout Mesoamerica and around the world.

An interesting aspect revealed by this study was that large breasts are actually an unusual trait among Olmec figurines. In most figures, the breasts are indicated by small, pointy protrusions, by a rounded undulation, or often simply by an edge or a line in rounded W shape under an only slightly modulated chest area (Figure 10.2).[10] That breasts are represented this way on adult female figures should not be surpris-

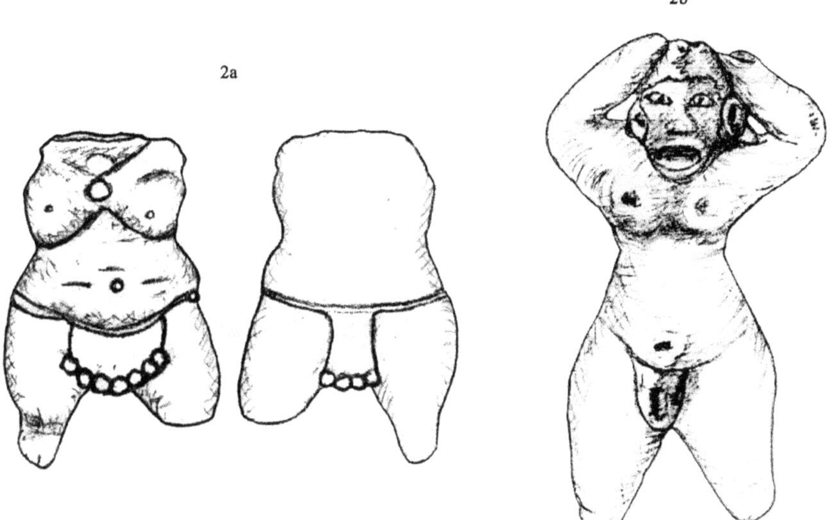

10.2: (a) Figurine of a woman wearing a pubic apron with both front and back pendant flaps, from La Venta (drawing by the author); (b) Figurine of a woman wearing a pubic apron, from La Venta (drawing by the author, after Piña Chan 1989:60). (Figures not to scale.)

ing, however, as other Mesoamerican cultures often indicated adult female breasts rather minimally in their sculpture, even obscuring the breasts completely under clothing. Instead of breasts, it is the aforementioned characteristics—the slender, pinched waist; the sloping torso and flaring hips; the wide, tapering limbs; the pubic Y or triangle; and the rounded W-shaped line underneath the breast—that the Olmec emphasized much more as primary indicators of femaleness.[11]

About 90 percent of these figurines are nude, although most also have extended limbs that would have facilitated the addition of perishable garments.[12] Nevertheless, about 10 percent wear molded-on garments, and these show strong patterns. The most common garment on the female figures is the loincloth apron, or pubic apron—an article of clothing that appears frequently on Formative figurines throughout Mesoamerica. This simple pubic covering consists of a low-slung belt across the hips, which may or may not be beaded, with a free-hanging flap in the front and sometimes another free-hanging flap in the back (Figure 10.2). Another common garment is the low-slung skirt; however, unlike many later Mesoamerican cultures, Olmec female figurines wear short as well as long skirts. Female figures also wear capes, vests,

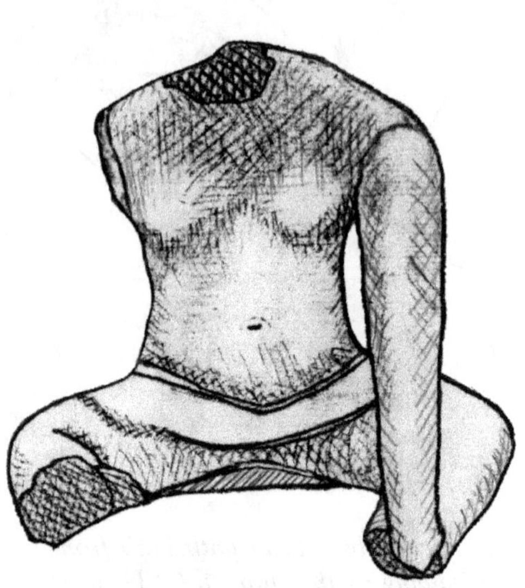

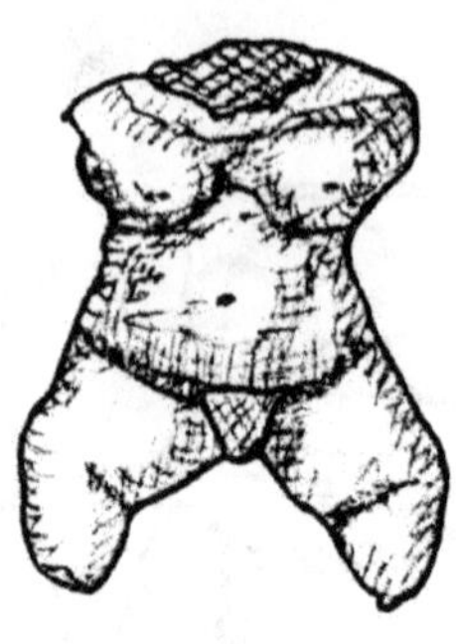

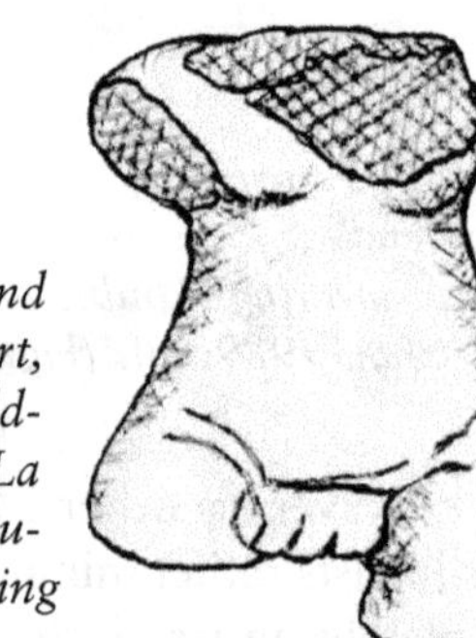

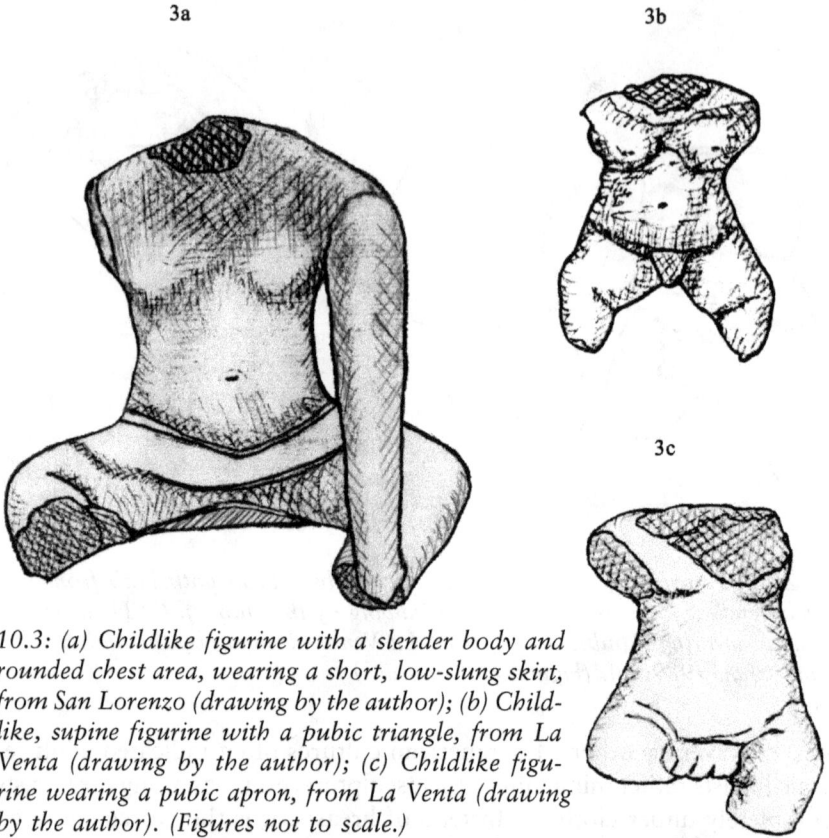

10.3: (a) Childlike figurine with a slender body and rounded chest area, wearing a short, low-slung skirt, from San Lorenzo (drawing by the author); (b) Childlike, supine figurine with a pubic triangle, from La Venta (drawing by the author); (c) Childlike figurine wearing a pubic apron, from La Venta (drawing by the author). (Figures not to scale.)

tunics, pectoral ornaments, necklaces, low-slung beaded belts, and earspools that often have pendant pieces.

Armed with these identifications of adult characteristics and garb, it is possible to discern childlike figures among this group, and some images do appear to represent children (Figure 10.3). As discussed previously, modest breasts are common on adult female figures; however, some figures with slightly rounded chest areas also have slender, more generalized bodies and only a slight indication of a pinched waist. Others have tubby bodies with the small, fleshy breasts associated with baby fat and only slight pinching underneath the chest. These figures also display pubic Ys or triangles and/or wear garments that clearly identify them as female. Although some of these figures could simply represent chunky adults, most of these almost certainly depict female children. Poses vary widely among Olmec figurines, but those that may be babies

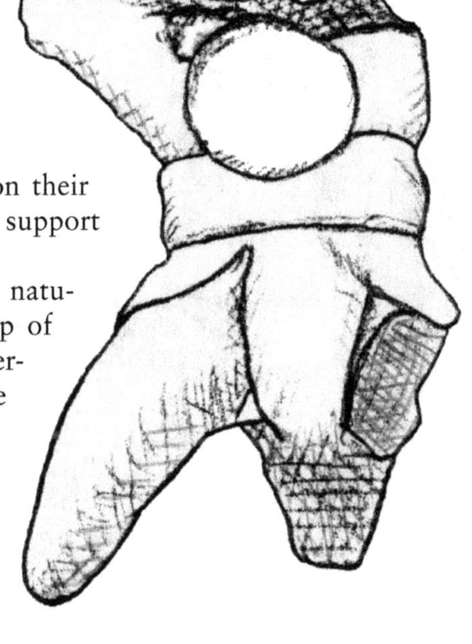

10.4: Tripod male figurine with a light bulb–shaped body, wearing a wrapped loincloth and backflap skirt (drawing by the author, after Coe 1980:figure 305).

frequently appear to be lying on their backs, a position that helps to support their identification as infants.[13]

In contrast to the relatively naturalistic figurines, another group of figurines, representing about 4 percent of these assemblages, is more abstracted (Figure 10.4). The bodies of these figures are much more geometric, taking the form of cylinders or flat rectangles or, in the case of tripod figures, they have smoothly light bulb–shaped bodies, likely in part to accommodate the rear leg support. All of these invariably have completely smooth chests and torsos, with no undulations or demarcations. In addition to the significantly different bodies, these figures wear complex garments that are strongly consistent with male-gendered garments of later Mesoamerican cultures, such as the male loincloth. These male loincloths differ clearly from the female loincloth apron; they may or may not have a pendant flap in front, but they clearly wrap underneath the groin. The Olmec male loincloth is also worn with a wide or multilayered belt that is placed high on the waist, as compared to the female, low-slung apron belt. Like the more naturalistic images, these figures may wear capes, vests, pectoral ornaments, earspools, and necklaces or tied fillets around the neck; however, given the other strong body and garment contrasts, these more abstracted figures likely represent male images. Unfortunately, the strong stylization of the bodies and the heavy clothing of these figures obscure any possible distinctions in relative body development.

The last group of figurines, representing the last 4 percent of the total sample, is the compact-bodied grotesques group. Some of these are heavily abstracted, aberrant figures with exaggerated or misshapen forms, but others appear to be naturalistic, pudgy humans.[14] Most of

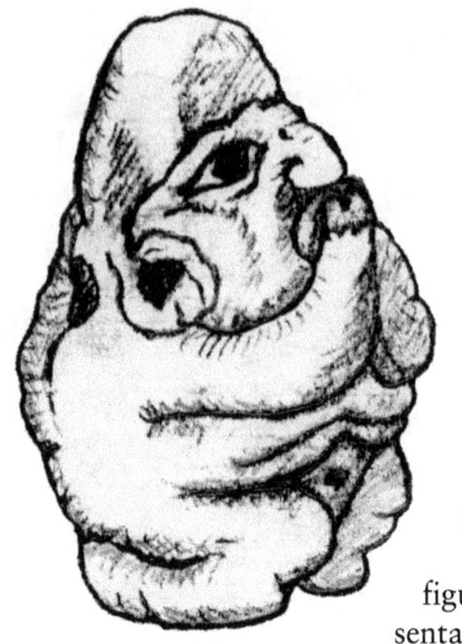

10.5: Grotesque baby figurine, from La Venta (drawing by the author).

the more naturalistic figures are nude and some that have legs drawn up to the body may represent tubby babies (Figure 10.5).[15] Other figures, however, wear skirts or pubic aprons and display pinched waists, flaring hips, and/or pronounced, protruding breasts. Such characteristics serve to identify these figures as adult female dwarfs, rather than children.

Overall, this study of the ceramic figurines indicates that probable representations of babies and juveniles make up only a small portion of the total ceramic figurine assemblage—about 3 percent.[16] Nevertheless, as it is also widely acknowledged that young adult females make up the vast majority of Formative-period handmade figurines, the fact that children are represented in the assemblage at all is significant, especially considering that they appear about as frequently as male figurines and more frequently than figurines portraying the elderly.[17] As the figurines were recovered predominantly from secondary deposits of household refuse and fill dirt,[18] their primary context is unclear; however, their representation does indicate a recognition of children, and the depiction of some with adult-like garb suggests that certain children may have held importance as individuals. Further, these identifications of children among the figurines also provide solid, useful clues for identifying children in other forms of Olmec sculpture.

Although there are only a few large ceramic figures collected from Gulf Coast Olmec sites,[19] these sculptures are particularly useful in confirming hypotheses formed using data gathered from the small figurines. Not only do these larger figures use the same stylizations as the figurines, but they also often display clear genitalia. In the group of five nude figures reported to be from La Venta that are displayed in Mexico's National Museum of Anthropology and History, the hourglass figures of two young adult females contrast strongly with the form of a headless, hollow baby figure (Figure 10.6). This baby figure is smoothly bulb-shaped, like male ceramic figurines, and it shows tiny but clear

10.6: Headless large, hollow figure of a baby boy, from La Venta (drawing by the author).

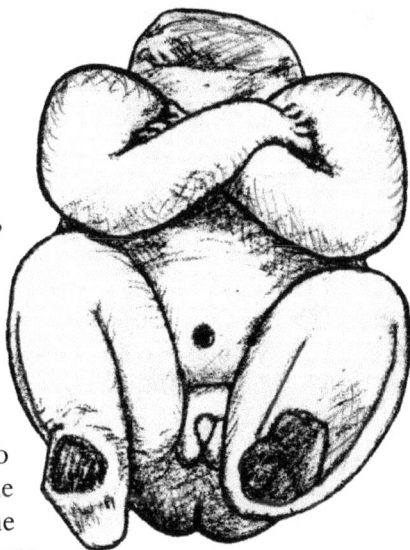

male genitalia; its arms are crossed and its legs are drawn up in a crouch, a pose similar to those assumed by the small ceramic baby figurines. In contrast, two twin-like toddler figures show clear female genitalia (Figure 10.7). These not only have baby-like faces and expressions and tubby, baby-like bodies, but also the fleshy chests, slight pinching at the waist, and flaring hips seen in some of the childlike small ceramic figurines (Figures 10.3b and 10.3c). Unfortunately, the specific context of these La Venta figures was not recorded, so their purpose and meaning is unclear, but such prominent depictions as these would support the contention that children could hold some kind of autonomous importance in Olmec culture.[20]

SMALL STONE FIGURES

At least thirty-seven provenienced, small-scale, stone human images have been collected from Gulf Coast Olmec sites. Although some of these images are naturalistic, the bulk of them appear to be the classic Olmec figures often called "baby-faces," because they are depicted with stylized,

10.7: Hollow ceramic figure of a toddler girl, one of a pair of twin figures, from La Venta (drawing by the author).

frowning faces that resemble that of a howling baby.[21] As mentioned previously, the "baby-faces" should not be confused with actual images of babies, because most of these figures are slender, stylized, formulaic images of adult males and females. Of the provenienced Olmec greenstone figures, only five actually display compacted, childlike bodies.

Study of these five figures reveals that two have the mixed, grotesque features that identify them as representations of a common Olmec dwarf-like supernatural: figure 2 from La Venta Offering #3 and figure 10 from La Venta Offering 1943-M (Drucker 1952:plate 50, figure 10; Drucker, Heizer, and Squier 1959:plate 26, figure 1, bottom). The remaining three figures—La Venta figures 8, 9, and 11 from Offering 1943-M—appear definitively to represent children (Figure 10.8). Figures 8 and 9 have stylized facial features like the formulaic adult "baby-faces," but they also have very large heads and infantile, chubby bodies. They also have pubic triangles, which clearly indicate that they are female. The figures hold their hands forward somewhat like paws, suggesting a subtle association with Olmec animal-human supernaturals.[22] The relatively wide separation of the limbs from the body also indicates that the figures may have been adorned with additional garments, and this hypothesis is bolstered by the figures' drilled earholes, which are common in Olmec greenstone figures and clearly meant for the addition of separate earspools. Such elite ear ornamentation suggests that these depictions of children, and

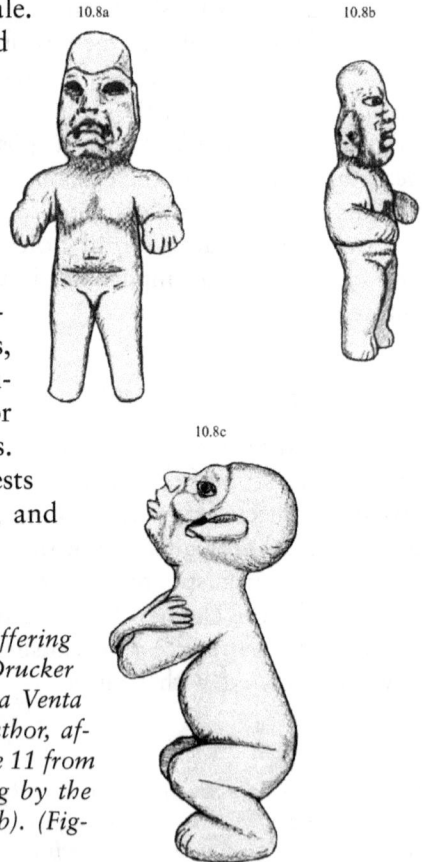

10.8a

10.8b

10.8c

10.8: (a) Figure 8 from La Venta Offering 1943-M (drawing by the author, after Drucker 1952:plate 50a); (b) Figure 9 from La Venta Offering 1943-M (drawing by the author, after Drucker 1952:plate 50b); (c) Figure 11 from La Venta Offering 1943-M (drawing by the author, after Drucker 1952:plate 51b). (Figures not to scale.)

thus some Olmec children, may have possessed high status in Olmec society.

Figure 11 from La Venta Offering 1943-M is a relatively naturalistic image of a young baby,[23] with a baby-like, corpulent body and a large head (Figure 10.8c). The figure's arms are crossed, like those of the aforementioned hollow ceramic male baby, and its legs are flexed into a crouch, similar to the poses of both large and small ceramic depictions of babies. Like the small ceramic figurines, however, there is no clear indication of gender on this larger stone figure. As on the small jade figures of children, this figure has drilled holes in its ears for the addition of elite ear ornamentation.

Perhaps even more interesting than these childlike depictions is that all three figures were recovered from the same deposit, La Venta Offering 1943-M, which was apparently an offering cache in the top clay cover of an important burial mound, Mound A-3. Furthermore, the cache was placed just one meter south of a possible child burial in that mound. (The child burials will be discussed in more detail later in this chapter.) Taken in context, these sculptures are additional evidence that children may have held importance as individuals in Olmec culture because they were depicted in sculpture, and in the high-status greenstone medium, and because they were likely being depicted as elite individuals, as they wore earspools. These depictions may have been used as a commemorative offering for the child in the associated burial, suggesting also that the deceased child may have held considerable social status.[24]

LARGE STONE IMAGES

In Gulf Coast Olmec large stone sculpture, 215 provenienced anthropomorphic images exist and, of these, at least 61 are childlike in scale or proportions. Over half of these—32—are relief figures on stelae or thrones that contrast in size with the primary figures of the scene depicted.[25] These images have normal adult proportions and often wear elaborate, elite regalia, and they are frequently referred to as supporting relatives, supernaturals, or ancestor spirits (Table 10.1). In other Mesoamerican cultures, children may have been depicted as miniaturized adults;[26] however, several factors indicate that these Olmec figures do not represent children, but that they are more likely small-scale representations of adults with different social status than the primary subject(s) of the sculpture, or that they are representations of beings of another realm (Figures 10.9 and 10.10).

Unlike in other Mesoamerican images, Olmec small-scale figures are not only smaller than the primary figures, but they are clearly separated from the main action of the scene. Whereas the primary figures sit or stand firmly on a groundline, one type of diminutive figure may float behind or around the primary figures, or it may hover horizontally above the main scene (Figure 10.9). This type of figure also sometimes wears a supernatural mask. Because these figures are differentiated by size, are shown with supernatural paraphernalia, and have the ability to float above the space occupied by the earthbound human figures, the definition of these figures as otherworldly beings, such as ancestors or other supernaturals, is well founded. The other type of small-scale adult figures—those that do not float about the scene (Figure 10.10)—are still unlikely to portray children, as their size difference is not the most important difference in depiction. These images are not placed in the same panel as the larger figures but appear in a separated area or panel or even on a separate side of the sculpture. They are also depicted in much lower relief than the main figures. The combination of the marked difference in scale, the separation of the figures from the main action of the scene, and the much lower level of relief suggests a difference in social status.

Table 10.1: Diminutive Images in Large Stone Olmec Sculpture: Ancestor/Supernaturals and Supporting Relatives/Allies

Monument	*No.*	*Difference in Depiction*	*Pose*	*Status**	*Role*	*Sex*	*Age**
SL Mon. 14	2	yes (relief, panels)	seated	S	SR/A	1 F, 1 Amb	Ad
LV Stela 2	6	yes (relief)	floating behind	S	A/S	6 M	Ad
LV Stela 3	6	yes (relief)	floating behind	S	A/S	1F, 3M, 2 Amb	Ad
LV Stela 5	1	no	floating above	S	A/S	1 F	Ad
LV Altar 3	4	yes (relief, panels)	standing, seated	S	SR/A	1F, 2M, 1Amb	Ad
LV Altar 4	2	yes (relief, panels)	seated	S	SR/A	1 M, 1 Amb	Ad
LV Altar 5	4 (large)	yes (relief, panels)	seated	S	SR/A	2 F, 2 M	Ad
LV Altar 7	6	yes (relief, panels)	standing	S	SR/A	4F, 2 Amb	Ad
TZ Stela D[†]	1	no	floating above	S	A/S	1 Amb	Ad

* S = Subordinate, Ad = Adult

[†]Although it could be argued that this monument may postdate the Gulf Coast Olmec, it is clearly an Olmec-related sculpture that follows Olmec conventions.

KEY:

Monument	*Status*	*Role*	*Sex*
SL = San Lorenzo	S = Subordinate	A/S = Ancestor/Supernatural	M = Male
LV = La Venta	P = Primary	SR/A = Supporting Relative/Ally	F = Female
TZ = Tres Zapotes		AH = Autonomous Human	Amb = Ambiguous
LL = Las Limas		DH = Dependent Human	
LdZ = Loma del Zapote		ASN = Autonomous Supernatural	
CdM = Cruz del Milagro		DSN = Dependent Supernatural	

10.9: La Venta Stela 3 (drawing by the author).

The fact that they stand or sit firmly on a groundline further suggests that they are human rather than supernatural. Finally, confirming that such small-scale figures most likely represent adults rather than children is that some of them are juxtaposed to figures of children in the same scene, as on the throne known as La Venta Altar 5. Unlike the adult figures, these child figures have relatively childlike proportions.[27] The definition of these small-scale adult figures as images of mature, supporting relatives or allies is, therefore, also probably correct.

Of the other twenty-nine childlike images in large Olmec sculpture, fourteen exhibit the combination of features consistent with dwarfism portrayed in the ceramic and small stone figures (Table 10.2). These figures have compact proportions but adult female or male body features, as well as common adult hairstyles and garb. In addition, six of these fourteen figures display supernatural facial features, supernatural-associated headdresses and other garb, and/or unusual characteristics; thus, these images clearly represent supernatural beings.[28] Because of their strong stylization, however, it is unclear whether these childlike images are meant to portray supernaturalized dwarfs, supernaturalized children, or simply compact-bodied supernaturals.

Ten of the remaining fifteen images are representations that more clearly represent children or child supernaturals (Table 10.3). In these scenes, children are portrayed as the object, rather than the subject, of the image.[29] Six of these ten—three in high relief and three sculptures in-the-round—are portrayed in the same manner as on the front of La Venta Altar 5 (Figure 10.10): a seated, full-size figure extends its forearms

10.10a

10.10b

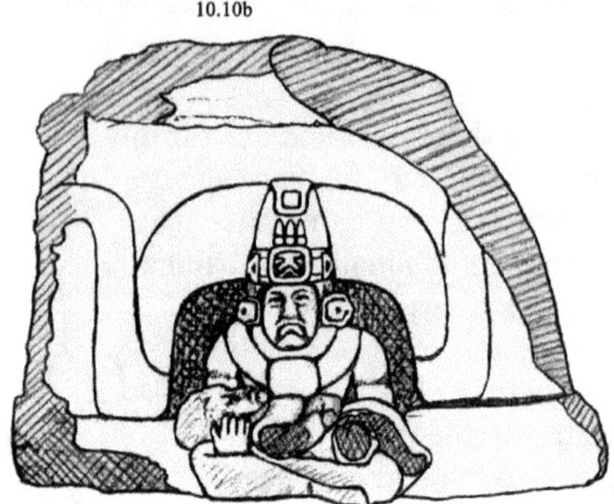

10.10c

10.10: La Venta Altar 5: (a) right side; (b) front; (c) left side (drawings by the author).

Table 10.2: Diminutive Images in Large Stone Olmec Sculpture: Dwarfs

Monument	*No.*	*Pose*	*Status*	*Role*	*Sex*	*Age*
SL Mon. 18	2	standing	primary	AH	2 F	Dwarfs
LdZ Mon. 2	2	standing	primary	AH	2 F	Dwarfs
SL Mon. 41	1	standing(?)	primary	ASN	1 Amb	Supernatural
SL Mon. 52	1	seated	primary	ASN	1 M	Supernatural
SL Anthro. Column	1	seated(?)	primary	ASN	1 Amb	Supernatural
LV Mon. 5	1	kneeling	primary	AH	1 F	Dwarf
LV Mon. 65	1	contorted	primary	AH	1 F	Dwarf
LV Mon. 70	1	seated	primary	ASN	1 F (4 faces)	Supernatural
LV Mon. 72	1	seated	primary	AH	1 F	Dwarf
LV Mon. 74	1	seated	primary	SN	1 Amb	Supernatural
TZ Mon. M*	1	seated	primary	SN	1 M	Supernatural
Alvarado Stela*	1	seated	primary	AH	1 F	Dwarf

* Although it could be argued that this monument may postdate the Gulf Coast Olmec, it is clearly an Olmec-related sculpture that follows Olmec conventions.

Table 10.3: Diminutive Images in Large Stone Olmec Sculpture: Adolescents and Children

Monument	*No.*	*Pose*	*Status*	*Role*	*Sex*	*Age*
LV Altar 5, front	1	limp, supine on lap	S	DH/DSN?	Amb	Child
LV Altar 5, sides	4 (small)	struggling	S	DSN	Amb	Children
LV Altar 2	1	limp, supine on lap	S	DH/DSN?	Amb	Child
SL Mon. 12	1	limp, supine on lap	S	DH/DSN?	Amb	Child
SL Mon. 20	1	limp, supine on lap	S	DH/DSN?	Amb	Child
SL Cat 13-385	1	limp, supine on lap	S	DH/DSN?	Amb	Child
LL Mon. 1, Fig. 1	1	seated	P	AH	M	Adolescent
LL Mon. 1, Fig. 2	1	limp, supine on lap	S	DH/DSN?	M	Child
LdZ Mons. 8 & 9	2	kneeling	P	AH	M	Adolescents
CdM Mon. 1	1	seated	P	AH	F	Adolescent
LdZ Mon. 11	1	seated	P	AH	F	Adolescent

forward and its open palms upward to hold out a limp baby. On La Venta Altar 5, the contrast between the motionless child on the front and the four child figures on the sides is quite revealing. On each side are the images of a man and a woman, each restraining a grimacing, wildly struggling toddler. It is clear that these frantic children understand that they will have the same fate as the now-lifeless child on the front of the throne. Altogether, these ten images—the six limp babies and the four toddlers in relief on the sides of the La Venta Altar 5—are most likely portrayals of child sacrifice, in which the children served as offerings related to these monuments, apparently for accession to power.[30]

Another important aspect to note is that the last example of this type of image, Las Limas Monument 1 (Figure 10.11), portrays a youth as

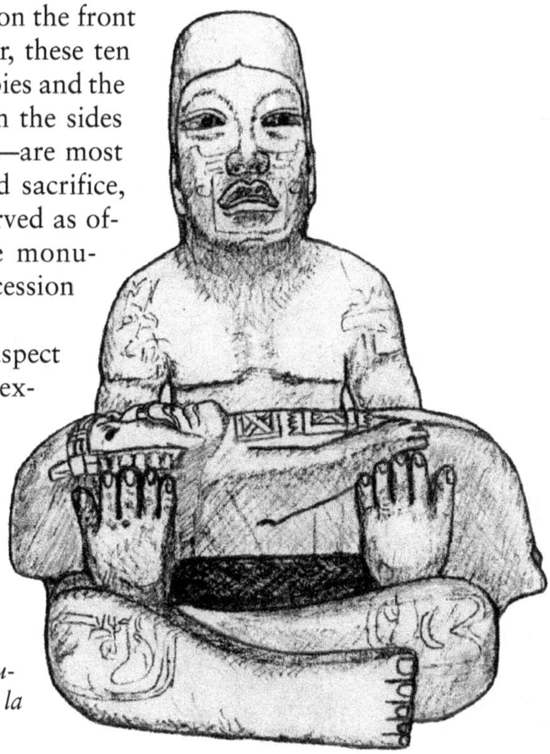

10.11: Las Limas Monument 1 (drawing by the author, after Benson and de la Fuente 1996:171).

well as a baby. One of the last five images in this study, the main figure is an adolescent male, as indicated by the male-style, wrapped loincloth visible on the back of the figure and the comparatively youthful face and straight, slender body. As large stone Olmec sculpture in-the-round typically portrays mature males with fleshy, squared pectorals, the chest of this figure also suggests that this is a youthful male; its pectorals are squared, but quite flat. Like the adult figures holding children, this youth offers in his open arms a limp baby figure; however, this child has markedly supernatural features.[31] Because the well-preserved images of baby sacrifice figures (mainly, the La Venta Altar 5 reliefs) also display slightly supernaturalized features, such supernaturalism may be associated with child sacrifice as well as with accession to power.[32] In any event, Las Limas Monument 1 illustrates a baby used as an object juxtaposed to the figure of an autonomous youth who assumes a position—seated and offering a child sacrifice—that is otherwise only assumed by figures of very high status. The youth is therefore likely being depicted as conducting the ritual in which he will accede to a high level of social status and power.

The last four childlike images might also be identified as illustrations of high-status adolescents.[33] Loma del Zapote Monuments 8 and 9 (Figure 10.12) are twin-like figures that display compact but slender bodies and youthful faces. Although their rigid pectoral garments obscure part of their chests, the unusual smoothness above and below indicates a youthful chest akin to that of Las Limas Monument 1. In addition, their elaborate headdresses and clothing, which include wrapped loincloths, also identify them as elite males. Although they were recovered in a

10.12: Monuments 8 and 9, from Loma del Zapote (drawing by the author, after Pacheco, in Vela 1996:figure 15).

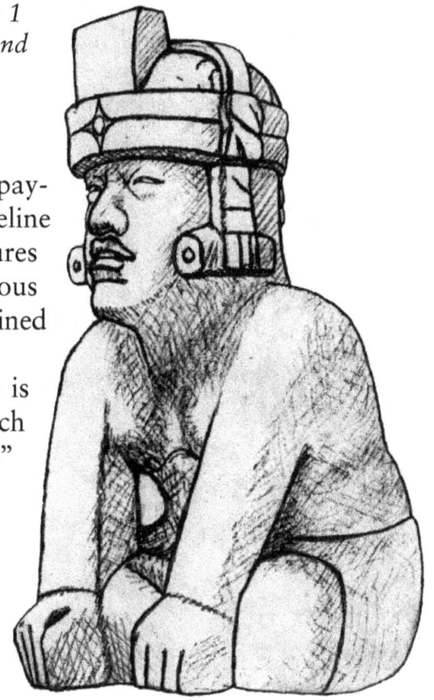

10.13: Cruz del Milagro Monument 1 (drawing by the author, after Benson and de la Fuente 1996:167).

scene in which they appeared to be paying homage to two supernatural feline sculptures, it is clear that these figures represent two important, autonomous male juveniles who had already attained high status at a young age.[34]

The third figure in this group is Cruz del Milagro Monument 1, which is often referred to as "The Prince" (Figure 10.13). As demonstrated in previous research, however, close analysis of this sculpture leads to a revised identification as a female. The figure has small, rounded breasts visible on each side of the chest, as well as a rounded, W-shaped delineation below them and a torso that flares out gently at the hips. In addition, it wears the female skirt, which is short and low-slung on the hips, as well as a headdress and ear ornaments that are consistent with Olmec female adornment. These physical features and garments confirm that this sculpture should be renamed "The Princess."[35] Stocky bodies and oversized heads are not uncommon in Olmec sculpture in-the-round, but the particularly youthful facial features and the modest, but clear, physical features of Monument 1 appear to depict a female adolescent elite.

Finally, Loma del Zapote Monument 11, also known as the Ejido de Xochiltepec Torso, is the most recently discovered Olmec sculpture that may represent an adolescent. This slender figure lacks its head, lower arms, and lower legs, but it displays a number of features that reveal its age, gender, and status (Figure 10.14).[36] The monument's chest, unfortunately somewhat obscured by a thick, sleeveless tunic or shirt, does protrude in a slightly mounded form. Given Olmec sculptural conventions, this modest chest and a very pinched waist emphasized with a rope cummerbund[37] indicate that the figure is possibly a young female. This identification is supported by the consistently female garments of a knee-length skirt topped with a free-hanging, ornamented apron flap,

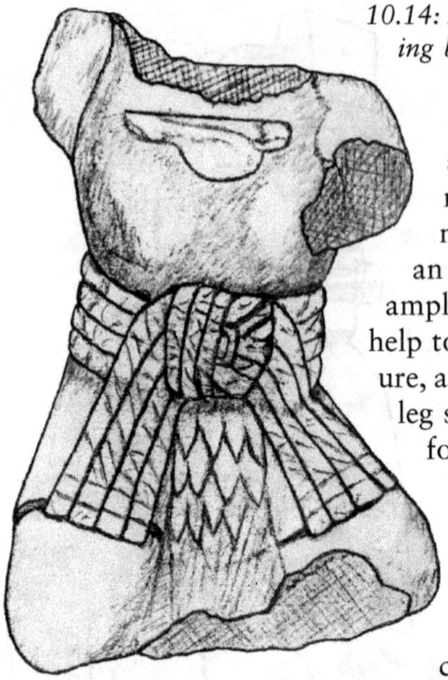

10.14: Loma del Zapote Monument 11 (drawing by the author).

as well as a "spoon" pectoral ornament, which is associated with female depictions and may represent an elite weaving tool.[38] The unusually ample garments of Monument 11 also help to confirm the elite status of the figure, and its pose, seated with an extended leg so that it must be placed on a platform, has also been interpreted as a pose of high status and power.[39]

ARCHAEOLOGICAL DATA

Studies of Gulf Coast archaeological excavations of burials and offerings serve to support the hypotheses that some children served as honored, high-status members of Olmec culture, while others served as objects of sacrifice. Excavations at the site of San Lorenzo have produced samples of the burned bones of children (Cyphers 1997:176) and cannibalized, juvenile human bones (Coe and Diehl 1980:386), and excavations in the anaerobic springs at El Manatí have revealed amazingly well-preserved, elaborate offerings incorporating the disarticulated bones of young infants or fetuses, including carved infant crania (Rodriguez and Ortiz 1994:40–41). These findings confirm the likelihood of child sacrifice among the Olmec cultures.[40]

In contrast, excavations in the central section of La Venta's Complex A, an area of elite graves and elaborate buried offerings, have revealed several burials and deposits that may be the graves of elite children. Among these is the most famous elite tomb found at La Venta: Tomb A, or the Basalt Log Tomb, found in Mound A-2. Although only a few splinters of bone survived within the swamp muck that covered the limestone slab floor, excavators Matthew Stirling and Philip Drucker determined from these bone fragments, along with the size of the burials, their associated cinnabar stains, and the presence of children's deciduous teeth, that the tomb contained "the remains of two bundle burials . . . probably of juveniles" (Drucker 1952:23–26; see also Stirling and Stirling 1942:640). These burials included rich offerings of obsidian, hematite, and jade ornaments and figures. The layout of these objects is not well recorded, but among them were two squared, jade earspools of about 7 centimeters in diameter, but with rather small stem holes of 1.2 centimeters. Current studies by Rosemary Joyce have established that most Mesoamerican earspools have a maximum shaft diameter of about 2.4 centimeters, and this size is stable over time. She equates this dimension with the final size of the adult earspool shaft inserted in a hole that was produced and enlarged over the life of the child (Joyce 2001:114–115; 2003; Rosemary Joyce, personal communication, 2002–2003; Meskell and Joyce 2003). Of earspools found in assemblages, Joyce identifies those with smaller shaft diameters as likely having been used early in the process of widening the pierced hole, during childhood. Thus, the small-shaft earspools of La Venta Tomb A were likely adornments for a young elite and therefore are consistent with the other findings of the tomb that indicate that this was the burial of two elite juveniles.

In addition, the two children of Tomb A apparently also merited sacrifices, because in the southwest corner of the tomb, a burned human skullcap was placed beside a pottery vessel offering (Stirling and Stirling 1942:641). The practice of giving elite Gulf Coast Olmec juveniles very rich burials is consistent with practices in other parts of Formative-period Mesoamerica, as Paul Tolstoy (1989) noted for Tlatilco and Joyce (1999b) documented for several early Maya regions.[41]

In Mound A-3 of this same sacred complex, another elite child burial was found (Drucker 1952:72–73). Designated as Offering 1943-L/ "Tomb D," these remains contained no surviving bone matter but included small jade earspools measuring 3.7 centimeters on the exterior with a 1.2-centimeter interior hole, along with pendants laid out as if they had adorned a small body. These items were placed, along with a jade disk and a few beads, within a small, 30 x 50 centimeter, rectangular layer of cinnabar, ranging from 22 to 25 centimeters thick, with a ceramic vessel just outside the main deposit. Found just one meter south of this burial was the cache of offerings that included the three previously discussed jade figures of children.

In addition, the Northeast Platform of this ceremonial precinct contained Offerings 5, 6, and 7 (Drucker, Heizer, and Squier 1959:162–174 and figures 41, 44, and 45).[42] Each of these deposits consisted of a layer stained with cinnabar, within which miniature jade earspools and other small ornaments were laid out as if adorning a small body.

Offering #5, the most elaborate of these deposits, was laid out in a 69 x 33 centimeter rectangle of cinnabar, outlined by eight small chunks

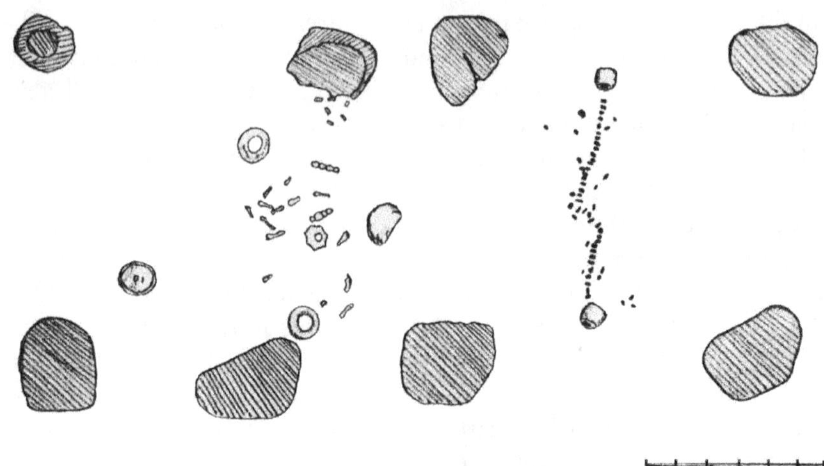

10.15: Offering #5, Northeast Platform, La Venta, Tabasco, with scale in inches (drawing by the author, after Drucker, Heizer, and Squier 1959:163, figure 41).

of volcanic tuff (Figure 10.15). The recovered cache consisted of numerous tiny jade ornaments, including miniature earspools (2.9 to 3.2 centimeters in outer diameter with a 1- to 1.4-centimeter hole diameter), pendant beads, and a dark green masquette, also less than 3 centimeters in diameter. Included among numerous tiny ornaments was a roughly clamshell-shaped pectoral ornament, 3.8 centimeters across the widest point, as well as a belt consisting of two 2-centimeter anchor beads and 95 very tiny jade beads. These jade ornaments are miniatures of the large clamshell-shaped pectoral ornaments and beaded belts found in other La Venta burials.

Offering #6 was laid out in a larger cinnabar rectangle of approximately 69 x 76 centimeters. Although not nearly as elaborate as Offering #5, among the offering's miniature jade ornaments were earspools measuring 2.5 centimeters in outer diameter with a 1- to 1.1-centimeter hole diameter, along with 3.8-centimeter "jaguar fang" pendant pieces that had been cut from another pair of earspools and two 1.8-centimeter tubular pendant beads. The deposit also included two tiny masquettes, each less than 2.5 centimeters across; a possible hair tube about 3 centimeters long; and another belt of tiny beads anchored by two larger beads measuring less than 2.5 centimeters across. Because beaded belts are only associated with female Olmec figurines, and earspools with pendant ornaments are more often associated with female images than male, this type of ornamentation might indicate that Offerings #5 and #6 were the graves of female children.

Offering #7, the simplest of the three deposits, consisted of a roughly oval, 38 x 33 centimeter area of cinnabar. Within this area was a pair of small, earspool-like ornaments 4.2 centimeters in outer diameter with a 1.6-centimeter hole diameter and two tubular beads about 3 centimeters in length, which may have served as ear ornament pendants. Among the other jade objects in this deposit were a tiny, 2.5-centimeter jade clamshell pendant and a jade masquette less than 5 centimeters in diameter. Although Offering #7 does include possible pendant ear ornaments, these ornaments are not definitive alone; therefore, the gender of the owner remains ambiguous.[43]

Although these three deposits, as well as "Tomb D," are consistent with elite burials at La Venta, excavators Philip Drucker, Robert Heizer, and Robert Squier designated these as "pseudo-burials" or offerings, rejecting the idea that they were actual burials because of the lack of bone material[44] and the very small spatial layout of the deposits.[45] What the excavators did not consider, however, was the possibility that these were the graves of elite juveniles. Given the generally poor preservation of bone material in the acidic soil of La Venta graves and the absence of any protective enclosures around these deposits, a lack of preservation for the soft bone of children would not be surprising. Overall, the most simple and logical explanation is that the Northeast Platform served as a cemetery for the burials of elite children, likely of a very young age.[46]

CONCLUSIONS

In sum, the surviving Gulf Coast depictions, offerings, deposits, and burials illustrate that children are present and visible in the material remains of the Olmec. Various sculptural depictions and archaeological evidence indicate that some boys and girls were powerless pawns in Olmec society, serving as ritual human sacrifices. It is quite possible that adult sacrifice also took place, but the existing evidence seems to indicate that small children were the main victims in Olmec culture. This isolation of children for human sacrifice indicates that early childhood, at least in this case, was a recognized cultural category separate from adulthood. Further, portrayals of childlike supernaturals, and of supernatural traits or paraphernalia on images of otherwise fully human children, indicate that young, specifically childlike beings played roles in Olmec mythology and religious ritual.[47] Unfortunately, the actual human children in reenactments of these religious scenarios were likely recognized and valued only as objects for ritual sacrifice, apparently serving as vehicles of legitimization for accession to power.

As attested by markedly different portrayals in Olmec stone sculpture and by elaborate burials, however, other Olmec children, both male and female, undoubtedly enjoyed elite positions. The evidence also indicates that the high social status of these children was apparently not heavily influenced by factors such as sex, gender, age, or personal agency; elite status was ascribed to some children while they were still far too young to have earned their positions, suggesting that inherited status existed in the Formative period. This also suggests that significant social stratification had been established in Olmec society, at least in their major centers. Bolstering such hypotheses of lineal power are the large stone depictions and rich burials of elite young adolescents, who apparently were already participating in society as autonomous and powerful individuals.

Although initially it may be difficult to identify children in Gulf Coast Olmec material culture, this chapter illustrates that isolating Olmec children and the roles they played is not only possible, but quite important to understanding Olmec society. The recognition that children were apparently the main Olmec sacrifices is informative for Olmec religion, ritual, and mythology. That some children served as sacrifices, whereas others of about the same age served as elites, carries implications for our understanding of the Olmec socialization process and of Olmec social categorization. Further, recognizing that some children were raised to the level of elites while very young and that some elites gained power while still adolescents assists in our understanding of Olmec political organization and social stratification. As such, continued investigation of children in Olmec civilization is definitely warranted. Whether the children were powerful or powerless, they were clearly an important component of that society, and they are intrinsic to our overall comprehension of Olmec culture.

ACKNOWLEDGMENTS

In gratitude I acknowledge Traci Ardren, for her encouragement to explore this new topic; Rosemary Joyce, whose active, critical commentary has helped me greatly in testing, re-evaluating, and refining these hypotheses; and the Smithsonian Ethnology Archives and the Yale Peabody Museum Archives, for their generosity in allowing me to examine their collections. This essay is dedicated to the memory of Dr.

Mark Sandler, a wonderful teacher, an invaluable mentor, and a true role model.

NOTES

1. This term was apparently first coined by Suzannah and George Vaillant in 1934, interestingly, to distinguish the more naturalistic faces from the more typically stylized faces of hollow ceramic grave figures from Gualupita in Central Mexico (1934:50). Previously, Olmec grimacing faces had been equated with the snarl of a feline (Saville 1929:268, 284), but upon comparison to these hollow baby figures, the facial configuration came to be associated with both crying babies and snarling felines (e.g., Covarrubias 1957:56–57).

2. Jeffrey Blomster challenges this widely held contention but acknowledges that the current paucity of intact, contextualized hollow baby figures prevents this situation from being clarified (2002:191–192).

3. See, for example, Justeson and Kaufman 1993; Macri and Stark 1993; and Anderson 1993.

4. An exception to the poor preservation of perishable Olmec material culture exists in the offerings found at the recently rediscovered site of El Manatí (Rodríguez and Ortiz 1994), discussed later in this chapter.

5. For a review of previous typologies and a complete discussion of my analysis of the figurines for sexed and gendered traits, garments, and accouterments, see Follensbee 2000:26–89.

6. A few of the larger, hollow-figure heads also appear to depict babies, as explained in the discussion of Gulf Coast hollow baby figures.

7. These hand-formed Olmec figurines tend to vary considerably in size, ranging from approximately three to over twenty centimeters in total height, but relative size cannot be taken as reliable in distinguishing status, gender, age, or other such factors. No obvious patterns in body features, garments, or accouterments correspond to these size differences.

8. For a cogent discussion of Olmec cultural continuity beyond the Terminal Olmec phase, see Pool 2000:137–153.

9. This consistency is especially apparent in Philip Drucker's analyses, where he creates very complex categories only to acknowledge at the end of his analyses that the figurines were relatively homogenous in their forms and patterns (1943:76–86; 1952:132–141; see also Weiant 1943:98–99, Follensbee 2000:26–34). This homogeneity is also clearly the case for the figurines excavated by Michael Coe and Richard Diehl at San Lorenzo; see my discussion (Follensbee 2000:32–33) and their illustrations (Coe and Diehl 1980:259–279). Figurines made in Olmec hinterland sites, such as La Joya, also appear to show great consistency in the patterns of body types and forms through time, throughout the Formative period (Philip Arnold III, personal communication, 2001).

10. The fact that figurines had unaccentuated breasts, but were identifiably female, was also noted by the early excavators (Drucker 1943:76–86; 1952:132–141; Weiant 1943:98–99).

11. Studies of provenienced Formative-period figurines from other parts of Mesoamerica show striking correlations with these patterns of sexed body forms, including studies of figurines from Central Mexico (e.g., Vaillant and Vaillant 1934; Cyphers Guillén 1989), the Oaxaca area (e.g., Marcus 1998), the Mazatan region of Coastal Chiapas (e.g., Lesure 1997), and the Maya area (e.g., Joyce 1993). For a more complete discussion of such comparisons, see Follensbee 2000:59–65).

12. For further discussion of the possibility of clothing on Olmec sculptures, see Follensbee 2000:42, 83–84, 149–151, 350–351, 365, 383, and 386.

13. One of these babies appears to be strapped to a cradleboard, but an adult figure strapped to a similar backboard suggests that these might instead represent funerary biers. Surprisingly, no certain patterns of pose are associated exclusively with a specific gender or age—unlike the case with some other Formative-period figurine assemblages (e.g., Agurcia Fasquelle 1977:16 and figure 15; Rosemary Joyce, personal communication, 2002–2003; see also Agurcia Fasquelle 1978:221–240). Among Gulf Coast Formative figurines, both young and old, male and female figurines appear to assume all of the different identifiable poses, with females frequently assuming a pose previously believed to signify male authority—seated with legs crossed tailor-fashion (Follensbee 2000:36–50).

14. This study of children has modified some of the conclusions of my dissertation. After this extension of my research, I have re-identified as babies some of the figurines that I previously identified as probable dwarfs (see Follensbee 2000:41 and figure 16C).

15. Some of these figures also have holes at the back of the head, indicating they were suspended on cords (Follensbee 2000:41–42, 76–80); such suspended figures of babies are known in other Mesoamerican figurine assemblages. Unlike in the other assemblages, however, there are no known Gulf Coast Olmec small ceramic representations of women holding infants. Yet, as Rosemary Joyce notes, figures meant for suspension would still represent dependent images, as they would hang on other bodies (Joyce, personal communication, 2002–2003).

16. With the provenienced hollow baby figure fragments added, this percentage rises to about 4 percent of the total assemblage of provenienced Gulf Coast ceramic figures.

17. One possible explanation for the paucity of figures showing youth and old age might be the existence of "social age grades." In such systems, young individuals who pass a milestone ritual could be placed, regardless of actual age, into an adult social age group. These individuals would be portrayed as adults in sculpture from that point on, and the manner of their portrayal would not change until they passed menopause, death, or some other milestone that would re-categorize them as more elderly or ancestral/

supernatural. Age-grade systems of this type were well known in other Mesoamerican cultures. Among Maya elites, for example, children could become social adults well before puberty and even in early childhood (Joyce 2000:120–156).

18. For discussion, see Follensbee 2000:26–28.

19. Many arm and leg fragments, and some head fragments, of large, hollow figures were collected from the Gulf Coast sites in the archaeological investigations. Because of their very chubby appearance, many were likely parts of child figures, but the fragments are inconclusive by themselves. These fragments, however, serve to help confirm the authenticity of the nearly complete examples of hollow figures reported to be from La Venta, which bear the same type of limbs (see Follensbee 2000:55–58).

20. For a fuller discussion, see Follensbee 2000:55–58.

21. See note 1. Like the ceramic figurines, the greenstone figurines vary from naturalistic to very stylized; however, they are often much more difficult to sex than ceramic figurines (see Follensbee 2000:90–152, 456–463).

22. One other archaeologically recovered Olmec image exhibits similar features: the well-known jade figurine excavated at Cerro de las Mesas (Drucker 1955:31–32). This figure is sometimes called a dwarf, but its baby-like face, its open-mouthed crying expression, and its childlike proportions indicate that Philip Drucker's conclusion, that it represents an infant, is more likely correct. Because this figure was recovered in a large "heirloom cache" of Olmec jades at this Epi- or Post-Olmec site, however, its use, meaning, and importance are not discernible beyond the acknowledgment that elite images of children were produced.

23. This is one of a number of figures that Carolyn Tate and Gordon Bendersky claimed represent newborns or fetuses (Tate 1995:62; Tate and Bendersky 1999), and represents their only example recovered archaeologically from an Olmec site. As the sculpture's features match traits associated with baby images that were identified in the small and large ceramic sculpture, the results of this study concur with Tate and Bendersky's identification of the figure as an infant.

24. Juan Alberto Román Berrelleza and Ximena Chávez Balderas (Chapter 9) note that elite offerings also sometimes accompany sacrificed individuals in Mesoamerica. Unlike the contexts they cite, however, there are no indications that this burial represents a sacrifice, nor are there indications that the other child burials discussed in this essay represent sacrifices.

25. Important to note is that the different types of Olmec large stone sculpture differ in their depiction of female sexed features. On low-relief and incised sculpture, the pinched waist and flaring hips are key female sexed features, and breasts are usually only minimally defined or obscured. On Olmec large wooden or stone sculpture in-the-round, however, the bodies show only minimal pinching, if any, and instead modest but clearly depicted, rounded breasts are shown, sometimes with a rounded W line underneath. These representations contrast markedly with the male chests, which

are flatter, angular forms that are straight on the bottom. For a more detailed discussion, see Follensbee 2000:153–455, 456–460.

26. This is common, for example, on Maya stelae, as discussed in Joyce 2000:122–132.

27. As discussed later in this chapter, some scholars have called these figures dwarfs, but their body proportions and features fit more correctly into the category of Olmec child figures than into the category of Olmec dwarf figures.

28. La Venta Monument 5 and the two figures on San Lorenzo Monument 18 also have what may be supernatural mouths, but they otherwise show normal adult dwarf features.

29. Los Idolos Monument 16 could also represent this type of monument (see Follensbee 2000:436–437). Los Idolos, however, is not well established as an Olmec site, and this monument shows numerous non-Olmec attributes suggesting that this could be another type of representation, even a mother-and-child image.

30. The adults on these monuments display identifiable gender, but the toddlers show no sexed or gendered features, suggesting that this type of identification was considered unimportant in the depiction of sacrifices, and this emphasizes their objectification. For a complete discussion of the gender identifications of the figures and the purpose and meaning of this monument, see Follensbee 1998 or Follensbee 2000:260–267.

31. Because there is a line around the face, it is possible that this represents a human child who wears a supernatural mask and headdress.

32. Some of the limp baby figures also appear to display supernatural facial features, but because they are heavily mutilated, this is difficult to claim with certainty. As discussed in this study, supernaturalized features also appear on many other types of figures associated with ritual, power, and/or rulership, including dwarfs and adults. The supernatural baby figure is often interpreted as an Olmec god of rain. This is consistent with the rain gods of later Mesoamerican cultures, which often had childlike assistants and demanded child sacrifices. The "baby face" grimace here might also relate to how crying children were considered a fortuitous sign for rain in later cultures (Follensbee 1998, 2000; see also Román Berrelleza and Chávez Balderas, Chapter 9).

33. Three additional figures could also represent adolescent males, as they display similarly smooth, youthful human bodies; these are La Venta Monument 31 and possibly 73, as well as Laguna de los Cerros Monument 3. The bodies of these mutilated, headless figures, however, are more generalized than those included in this study, and they are also similar in form and pose to La Venta Monuments 9, 10, and 75, which portray supernaturals with similarly generalized bodies. It is possible that these figures have generalized bodies because they were meant to be engendered by the addition of clothing; alternatively, all of these may be supernaturals that represent partly human adolescents, partly supernatural creatures. Unfortunately, further in-

formation would be necessary to clarify these ambiguities. For further discussion of these figures, see Follensbee 2000:341–344, 350–351, 364–365, 368–369, and 421–423.

34. See also Follensbee 2000:314–317. A figure similar in proportions and pose to these figures is San Martín Pajapán Monument 1; however, this figure is much more stylized and so heavily clothed that it is not possible to confirm whether it represents a juvenile human.

35. For a more detailed explanation, see Follensbee 2000:321–325.

36. Please note that my identification of this figure has been modified since the writing of my dissertation (Follensbee 2000:318–320).

37. The figure's pinched waist is particularly apparent when viewing the figure from the back (see Cyphers 1995:figure 16).

38. See Follensbee 2003, 2004.

39. For further discussion of this pose, see Follensbee 2000:320.

40. Similar finds of possible child sacrifice—as well as elite child burials—have been reported for the Olmec-related sites of Teopantecuanitlán (Niederberger 1996:102) and Chalcatzingo (Grove 1984:67; Fash 1987:90–91).

41. See also note 40. Studies of other Formative-period cultures might suggest that juveniles did not wear ear ornaments (e.g., Joyce 1999a:481), but this was apparently not the case among the Olmec, as indicated not only by these burials, but also by the three Olmec small stone figures of children discussed earlier in this chapter. These figures were carved with holes in their earlobes, which could only have been meant for the addition of ear ornaments. Joyce also suggests that earspools and beaded belts were interregionally recognized badges of status (Joyce 1999b), which would confirm the elite status of the children in these tombs. For further discussion of these objects in Olmec iconography and graves, see Follensbee 2000:34–53 and 462–463.

42. Also buried in this platform were five deposits of pottery. It is possible that these were associated offerings or that they indicate other burials within the platform.

43. Although masquettes are not definitively known as a gender indicator for the Olmec, Joyce notes that small masquettes were a notable costume ornament for Formative-period graves of young females at Tlatilco (Joyce 2000:31).

44. Scholars have questioned the necessity of the presence of actual bones in Mesoamerican deposits in order to classify a deposit as a grave. Marshall Becker, for example, has suggested that Maya graves, secondary burials, and burials of offerings were part of a larger, more fluid and complex Mesoamerican category honoring deceased individuals (Becker 1992:185–196; Rosemary Joyce, personal communication, 2002–2003). Thus, the case may be made that a deposit of only these elite miniature ornaments could have sufficed as a sort of "grave."

45. The excavators also state that these deposits are too undisturbed for the ornaments to have been laid out on actual corpses (Drucker, Heizer, and

Squier 1959:162). The photographs and drawings of the objects in situ, however, show that the ornaments were not found in as perfect an arrangement as claimed (1959: figures 41, 44, and 45; see also Figure 10.15). Although the earspools were found roughly parallel to each other, these are also the heaviest objects and the most likely to have fallen down evenly, especially if only laid on a body or in a headdress. Further, the other ornaments around the heads were scattered and sometimes turned upside-down, as if they had fallen off a body. And each of the beaded belts in Offerings 5 and 6 forms a curved, snaky pattern, as if they were laid across a convex form that disintegrated. The type of slight disarray seen in each of the La Venta deposits is, in fact, also evident in other Formative-period graves, such as Chalcatzingo Burials 39 and 40, which were found with skeletal matter intact (Merry de Morales 1987:100–101).

46. The special treatment, as well as the elaborate ornamentation of these children (see note 40), suggests that they may have been placed into a higher-than-normal "social age grade" (see note 17), possibly because of elite birth. For a comparative example, Joyce notes that Classic-period, elite Maya children as young as six years old were known to have attained fully adult social status (Joyce 2000:124).

47. Also bolstering this hypothesis is the possibility that the aforementioned elite children had gained adult social status (see notes 17 and 46).

REFERENCES CITED

Agurcia Fasquelle, Ricardo

1977 The Playa de los Muertos Figurines. M.A. thesis, Department of Antropology, Tulane University.

1978 Las Figurillas de Playa de los Muertos, Honduras. *Yaxkin* 2(4): 221–240.

Anderson, Lloyd B.

1993 *The Writing System of La Mojarra and Associated Monuments.* 2 vols. 2nd ed. Washington, DC: Ecological Linguistics.

Becker, Marshall J.

1992 Burials as Caches, Caches as Burials: A New Interpretation of the Meaning of Ritual Deposits Among the Classic Period Lowland Maya. In *New Theories on the Ancient Maya,* ed. E. C. Danien and R. J. Sharer, 185–196. University Museum Monograph 77. Philadelphia, PA: The University Museum, University of Pennsylvania.

Benson, Elizabeth P., and Beatriz de la Fuente, eds.

1996 *Olmec Art of Ancient Mexico.* Washington, DC: National Gallery of Art.

Bernal, Ignacio

1969 *The Olmec World.* Berkeley: University of California Press.

Blomster, Jeffrey P.
2002 What and Where Is Olmec Style? Regional perspectives on hollow figurines in Early Formative Mesoamerica. *Ancient Mesoamerica* 13 (2002):171–195.

Coe, Michael D., and Richard A. Diehl
1980 *In the Land of the Olmec, vol. 1: The Archaeology of San Lorenzo Tenochtitlan.* Austin: University of Texas Press.

Covarrubias, Miguel
1957 *Indian Art of Mexico and Central America.* New York, NY: Alfred A. Knopf.

Cyphers Guillén, Ann
1989 Cultos y Cuentos: Reflexiones en Torno a las Figurillas de Chalcatzingo, Morelos. In *El Preclásico o Formativo: Avances y Perspectivas,* ed. M. Carmona, 207–221. Mexico: Consejo Nacional Para la Cultura y las Artes.
1995 *Descifrando los Misterios de la Cultura Olmeca: Una Exposición Museográfica de los Resultados del Proyecto Archeológico San Lorenzo Tenochtitlán 1990–1994.* Mexico: Universidad Nacional Autónoma de México.

Cyphers, Ann, coord.
1997 *Población, Subsistencia, y Medio Ambiente en San Lorenzo Tenochtitlán.* Mexico: Universidad Nacional Autónoma de México, Instituto de Investigaciones Antropológicas.

Drucker, Philip.
1943 *Ceramic Sequences at Tres Zapotes, Veracruz, Mexico.* Smithsonian Institution Bureau of American Ethnology, Bulletin 140. Washington, DC: United States Government Printing Office.
1952 *La Venta, Tabasco: A study of Olmec Ceramics and Art.* Smithsonian Institution Bureau of American Ethnology, Bulletin 153. Washington, DC: United States Government Printing Office.
1955 *The Cerro de las Mesas Offering of Jade and Other Materials.* Smithsonian Institution Bureau of American Ethnology, Bulletin 157. Washington, DC: United States Government Printing Office.

Drucker, Philip, Robert F. Heizer, and Robert Squier
1959 *Excavations at La Venta, Tabasco 1955.* Smithsonian Institution Bureau of American Ethnology, Bulletin 170. Washington, DC: United States Government Printing Office.

Fash, William, Jr.
1987 The Altar and Associated Features. In *Ancient Chalcatzingo*, edited by David C. Grove, pp. 82–94. Austin: University of Texas Press.

Follensbee, Billie J. A.
1998 Slaughter of the Innocents? The Evidence for Infant Human Sacrifice Among the Gulf Coast Olmec. Paper presented at the An-

nual Meeting of the Society for American Archaeology, Seattle, March 27, 1998.

2000 Sex and Gender in Olmec Art and Archaeology. Ph.D. dissertation, Department of Art History and Archaeology, University of Maryland, College Park, 2000.

2003 Presentation of Research: The Importance of Weaving in Gulf Coast Formative Period Cultures. In *Dumbarton Oaks Bi-Annual Report 2003*. Washington, DC: Dumbarton Oaks.

2004 Fiber Technology and Weaving in Formative Period Gulf Coast Cultures. Paper presented at the Annual Meeting of the Society for American Archaeology, Montreal, April 3, 2004.

Grove, David C., editor

1984 *Chalcatzingo: Excavations on the Olmec Frontier*. London: Thames and Hudson Ltd.

1987 *Ancient Chalcatzingo*. Austin: University of Texas Press.

1993 "Olmec" Horizons in Formative Period Mesoamerica: Diffusion or Social Evolution? In *Latin American Horizons*, edited by D. S. Rice, pp. 83–111. Washington, DC: Dumbarton Oaks Research Library and Collections.

Heizer, Robert F., John A. Graham, and Lewis K. Napton.

1968 The 1968 Investigations at La Venta. In *Papers on Mesoamerican Archaeology. Contributions of the University of California Archaeological Research Facility,* No. 5. Berkeley: University of California Archaeological Research Facility, Department of Anthropology.

Joyce, Rosemary A.

1993 Women's Work: Images of Production and Reproduction in Pre-Hispanic Southern Central America. *Current Anthropology* 3: 255–274.

1999a Girling the Girl and Boying the Boy: The Production of Adulthood in Ancient Mesoamerica. *World Archaeology* 31(3): 473–483.

1999b Social Dimensions of Pre-Classic Burials. In *Social Patterns in Pre-Classic Mesoamerica*, edited by D. C. Grove and R. A. Joyce, pp. 15–47. Washington, DC: Dumbarton Oaks.

2000 *Gender and Power in Prehispanic Mesoamerica.* Austin: University of Texas Press.

2001 Negotiating Sex and Gender in Classic Maya Society. In *Gender in Pre-Hispanic America*, edited by C. Klein, pp. 109–141. Washington, DC: Dumbarton Oaks.

2003 Concrete Memories: Fragments of the Past in the Classic Maya Present (500–1000 AD). In *Archaeologies of Memory*, edited by R. Van Dyke and S. Alcock, pp. 104–125. Malden, MA: Blackwell.

Justeson, John S., and Terrence Kaufman.

1993 A Decipherment of Epi-Olmec Hieroglyphic Writing. *Science* (19 March): 1703–1710.

Lesure, Richard G.

1997 Figurines and Social Identities in Early Sedentary Societies of Coastal Chiapas, Mexico, 1550–800 B.C. In *Women in Prehistory: North America and Mesoamerica*, edited by C. Claassen and R. A. Joyce, pp. 227–248. Philadephia: University of Pennsylvania Press.

Macri, Martha J., and Laura M. Stark.

1993 *A Sign Catalog of the La Mojarra Script*. Pre-Columbian Art Research Institute Monograph 5. San Francisco: Pre-Columbian Art Research Institute.

Marcus, Joyce.

1998 *Women's Ritual in Formative Oaxaca: Figurine-making, Divination, Death and the Ancestors*. Ann Arbor: University of Michigan.

Merry de Morales, Marcia.

1987 Chalcatzingo Burials as Indicators of Social Ranking. In *Ancient Chalcatzingo*, edited by D. C. Grove, pp. 95–113. Austin: University of Texas Press.

Meskell, Lynn M., and Rosemary A. Joyce

2003 *Embodied Lives: Figuring Ancient Egypt and the Classic Maya*. London: Routledge.

Niederberger, Christine

1996 Olmec Horizon Guerrero. In *Olmec Art of Ancient Mexico*, edited by E. P. Benson and B. de la Fuente, pp. 95–103. Washington, DC: National Gallery of Art.

Piña Chan, Roman.

1989 *The Olmec: Mother Culture of Mesoamerica*, edited by L. Laurencich Minelli. New York: Rizzoli International Publications, Inc.

Pool, Christopher A.

2000 From Olmec to Epi-Olmec at Tres Zapotes, Veracruz, Mexico. In *Olmec Art and Archaeology in Mesoamerica*, edited by J. E. Clark and M. E. Pye, pp. 137–153. Washington, DC: Trustees of the National Gallery of Art, Washington.

Rodriguez, María del Carmen, and Ponciano Ortiz.

1994 *El Manatí: Un Espacio Sagrado Olmeca*. Xalapa, Veracruz: Instituto Nacional de Antropología e Historia.

Saville, Marshall H.

1929 Votive Axes from Ancient Mexico, Part I. *Indian Notes*, October 1929: 266–299.

Stirling, Matthew W.

1940 Great Stone Faces of the Mexican Jungle. *The National Geographic Magazine* 78 (3): 309–334.

Stirling, Marion, and Matthew Stirling.

1942 Finding Jewels of Jade in a Mexican Swamp. *The National Geographic Magazine* 82(5): 635–658.

Tate, Carolyn E.
1995 Art in Olmec Culture. In *The Olmec World: Ritual and Rulership*, pp. 47–68. Princeton, NJ: The Art Museum.

Tate, Carolyn, and Gordon Bendersky.
1999 Olmec Sculptures of the Human Fetus. *Perspectives in Biology and Medicine* 42(3): 303–332.

Tolstoy, Paul.
1989 Coapexco and Tlatilco: Sites with Olmec Materials in the Basin of Mexico. In *Regional Perspectives on the Olmec*, edited by R. J. Sharer and D. C. Grove, pp. 85–121. Cambridge and London: Cambridge University Press.

Vaillant, Suzannah B. and George C. Vaillant.
1934 Excavations at Gualupita. In *Anthropological Papers of the American Museum of Natural History, 35, part 1*. New York, NY: American Museum of Natural History.

Vela, Enrique, editor
1996 *Olmecs: Special Edition, Arqueología Méxicana*. Mexico: Editorial Raices/Instituto Nacional de Antropología e Historia.

Weiant, Clarence Wolsey.
1943 *An Introduction to the Ceramics of Tres Zapotes, Veracruz, Mexico*. Smithsonian Institution Bureau of American Ethnology, Bulletin 157. Washington, DC: United States Government Printing Office.

Part V

CONCLUSION

11

WHERE WE ALL BEGIN

Archaeologies of Childhood in the Mesoamerican Past

Rosemary A. Joyce

What is our subject when we set out to do an archaeology of children? My initial attempt to draw together some of my own thoughts on this topic in 1994 was titled "Looking for Children in Prehispanic Mesoamerica." Taking the commonsense stance that we already are describing the effects of young people as past social agents in every archaeological situation, I suggested that we need to be careful not to rush ahead "looking for children" and assume that young people in the past formed one, or even several, definite categorical groups. I suggested that the ability to identify physical traces of young people is not a proxy for understanding the cultural construct "childhood" (Joyce 1994). I argued that even when archaeologists can identify direct evidence of the presence of children—such as studies of fingerprints on pottery (Kamp 1999)—we simultaneously, and perhaps more significantly, provide powerful sources of information about the intersection between culturally specific practices that are the means through which lived experience is transformed into the commonalities that categorical terms—like "child"—imply (Joyce 1994).

Stacie King (Chapter 7) notes that archaeologists interested in children or childhood in the past have taken advantage of the same four lines of evidence, one of which is available only in literate societies or those with an abundant visual culture. These lines of evidence are found in the Mesoamerican cases under discussion here and, predictably, form the methodological framework of these analyses: mortuary remains (the subject of discussion by Follensbee, King, McCafferty and McCafferty, Román Berrelleza and Chávez Balderas, Storey and McAnany, and Trachman and Valdez); material culture of play and childhood enculturation, including "toys" (central to Lopiparo's paper and also considered by McCafferty and McCafferty); evidence of the processes of learning adult tasks (another focus of Lopiparo's discussion); and visual and textual representations of children or childhood (most thoroughly considered by Follensbee). How they are used by different analysts illustrates the range of approaches marked by the search for children or childhood in the distant past.

In the comments that follow, I highlight the different ways these lines of evidence are used by the contributors to this volume. But I do so while teasing out a somewhat different series of connections that I think represent the real promise of this research for archaeology as a field. These other connections run from discussion of the way an ongoing flow of life, individual experiences of biological maturation, was divided into stages and coordinated across populations, to the practices through which children learned how to be adults and in the process recreated the societies into which they were born. Groups of similar-aged young people in many of the Mesoamerican societies discussed shared experiences distinct from those of other age groups and these experiences contributed centrally to their development as adult subjects. The enjoyable experiences such groups of children shared helped shape their orientations as adults, coloring the transition to adult responsibilities simultaneously enforced in life cycle rituals and infused in the material culture of play.

The nostalgia of Mesoamerican adults for childhood is critical to our interpretation of visual representations of the young, always likely represented from the perspective of adults. The repeated representation of children as dependent on adults and as small copies of adults that confounds many attempts to use visual materials to talk about childhood can be seen less as a reflection of the truth of childhood in ancient Mesoamerica and more as the adult's retrospective reflection on his or her experience. Mesoamerican materials, not surprisingly, are more informative about relations between people than about any assumed categories of people. But it is still not only possible, but also necessary, to consider the agency of the young people who became Mesoamerican adults, to ask whether elders always controlled so well the lives and actions of the young, and to consider how the actions of children affected the sites we explore today.

AGE AND CHANGE IN MESOAMERICAN LIVES

Rebecca Storey and Patricia McAnany present a compelling analysis of an early Maya burial population including twenty-six individuals who died before they reached adulthood (defined by them as under the age of fifteen). They note that the proportion of young people in the archaeological sample is lower than demographic models would lead us to expect. Using the changing biological status of young people to define age groups that might have been socially recognized in the K'axob community, Storey and McAnany explore what are also experiential differences during childhood: the period before children could walk, the toddler years (ages 1–3) that in this community may have preceded weaning, a period of young childhood after weaning (ages 4–9), and the last stage of childhood when children might have neared puberty and social adulthood (represented by two sub-adults ages 11–13). They find that regularities in burial treatment emerge when they are examined by age class, a situation also noted by Rissa Trachman and Fred Valdez in their analysis of child burials at Dos Hombres, Belize.

Although based on biological landmarks, these stages also correspond well to the points of transformation in the lives of Mesoamerican children that I have identified, based on sixteenth-century ethnohistoric documents from Central Mexico and Yucatán (Joyce 1994, 2001). The Mexica sequence of life-cycle rituals illustrated in the *Codex Mendoza* and described in the works of Sahagún is well known and has provided material for many analyses of age and gender (Brumfiel 1991; Clendinnen 1991; McCafferty and McCafferty 1991; Calnek 1992; Serra Puche and Durand 1998; Joyce 2000a, 2001:145–153). Mexica childhood, based on these sources, was divided into a series of phases. From birth to age 3 or 4, children were little differentiated, subject to no discipline or training, and wore undifferentiated haircuts. Their adult destiny was marked symbolically by the provision of miniature tools and costume, and their bodies were prepared for distinctive adult ornaments differentiating between priestly and secular careers. Between about age 4 and 8, Mexica children were subject to the beginnings of training in adult tasks and wore parts of the adult costume. By the end of this period, they had received the ear perforations that would eventually accommodate adult earspools, were subject to physical discipline, and were initiated into key aspects of ritual practice, notably ceremonial drinking. By age thirteen, following continued practice of their adult tasks, boys and girls had adopted a long, flowing haircut and were using full, adult clothing that distinguished between male and female. Transition to full adult status was accompanied by the use of earspools and adult hairstyles.

An indication that such stages were not specific to the Central Mexican people but were part of wider Mesoamerican conceptions of childhood in the sixteenth century is provided by the much less detailed work of the Spanish priest Diego de Landa (1941), the *Relación de las cosas de Yucatan*, describing the life of the Maya of Yucatán (Joyce 2001:120–123), also discussed by Trachman and Valdez. According to this source, Yucatec Maya children's development also was subdivided into intervals with transitions marked by rituals and changes in practices of dress, work, and participation in ritual. From four to five days after birth, following their first bath, through the first three years of life, children were provided with gender-specific ornaments but otherwise wore no adult clothing (Landa 1941:102). At about age three, children underwent a ritual called "second birth" in Yucatec (*caput sihil*) that was compared to Christian baptism (1941:102–106). At this ritual, children participated in ritual for the first time and were disciplined by their elders, also apparently for the first time. Children ages 4–5, who would have recently gone through this ritual, reportedly began to wear versions of adult clothing and began to use the name they had inherited from their fathers (1941:125, 129). The ritual of second birth was a prerequisite for marriage and was supposedly carried out at the latest by age twelve (1941:102).

Several features appear to be common to these two sixteenth-century accounts, suggesting some dimensions of a possible model of late Mesoamerican concepts of childhood. Postclassic Yucatec Maya and Mexica societies both saw major breaks in development marked by ritual at age 3 to 4 and age 12 to 13. Before age 3 to 4, children were not expected to participate in ritual, were not subject to formal training, nor were they subjected to formal discipline. Among both Mexica and Maya, the young adult period inaugurated at age 12 to 13 included formal training in—and at least for males residence at—institutions outside the residential compound. Between these two marked breaks in development, late pre-Hispanic Mexica and Maya children participated in rituals that reinforced their adult obligations of labor and duty.

REPRODUCING SOCIETY BY PRODUCING ADULTS

Geoffrey and Sharisse McCafferty make the critical point that cultural transmission is effected through the social experiences of children. The efforts expended through rituals directed at coordinating children's experiences and introducing them to adult life in late Mesoamerica underscore this point. Jeanne Lopiparo takes the questions of how children were effective agents in the reproduction of culture, and how they learned to reproduce their own specific social structures, as her central focus. She employs as evidence the material remains of household-based production of small ceramic vessels and artifacts consumed at the household level in periodic rituals, distinguished by unique iconographies. The incorporation of social values by young children learning the craft of ceramic production would have been a powerful way for adults to shape the attitudes of the young.

Although studies of pottery have long argued for the identification of evidence of young apprentices at work in assemblages from workshop sites (e.g., Crown 1999), Lopiparo goes further. Not just suggesting that we can see the imperfect products of learners and thus infer the presence of children, Lopiparo argues rather that through engagement in learning a craft, children would simultaneously learn what it was to be a proper person in their society. In the specific case she discusses, the reproduction of social structure was advanced as well by the specific content of the images molded into figurines and vessels. Her argument notably provides a rationale for the use of molds in what is otherwise a puzzling context, small-scale production for local consumption. Lopiparo's paper illustrates that we need not look for a specific material culture of children to find material culture that speaks to the experience of childhood.

Sharisse and Geoffrey McCafferty draw attention to the lack of explicit archaeological discussion of the experiences and social actions of what must have been about half of most ancient populations. In their view, this is not to be explained as the result of a lack of evidence for children and their experiences. Using mortuary data from Cholula and juxtaposing it to sixteenth-century colonial texts, they weave together the undeniable evidence of the existence of children with inferences that can be drawn about the nature of childhood.

In the process, the McCaffertys pinpoint a recurring difficulty for all analyses that attempt to deal with the specific, historically situated experiences of different people without assuming that those people were distinguished from the population as a whole, and thus seen as an identity group (not merely an archaeologically identifiable group). In other words, because we can stratify an ancient burial population by age, are we justified in assuming that people of like age shared experiences and social positioning distinctive from that of others of different ages? As Stacie King notes, much as progress in the archaeology of gender has involved a recognition that there cannot be a presumed universal cultural meaning to sexual variation, so the archaeology of childhood must involve a critical awareness that age differences may have been differentially recognized within different societies.

Viewing the mortuary population as a sample of boys and girls "interrupted" in the process of childhood development into adults, the McCaffertys go far in the direction of tracing a history of childhood, rather than merely documenting the already self-evident presence of children. Immediately striking is the disparity they document in the presence of young individuals in domestic burials and the Great Pyramid complex. In the latter location, most of those buried were adults (in this analysis meaning individuals over the age of twenty-one). In contrast, the majority of those recovered from burials associated with the house structure they discuss were children, half of them under a year in age. This echoes Storey and McAnany's analysis of burials at K'axob, where over time, as the nature of buildings at the locations sampled changed, shifting from more residential to other uses, the proportion of juveniles buried in these locations declined.

Comparing the treatment of individuals of similar age in the two different settings at Cholula, the McCaffertys note that children in the Great Pyramid were buried without grave goods, whereas even some of the very young individuals in the house compound were accompanied by objects, including possible items of value. Comparing the burials of young persons in both locations with those of adults from the Great Pyramid (since only one adult was identified in the house sample), they identify some patterns suggestive of gradual transformation of childhood practices into those of adulthood, particularly in the steady increase in seated flexed position with age.

Stacie King's discussion of Early Postclassic society at Río Viejo, Oaxaca, takes the emphasis on childhood, rather than children, to the ultimate extreme. Were the purpose of our analyses to find children, King could not be included in our discussion or this volume: the mortuary data she reports on include no burials of individuals younger than sub-adult (17–19 years old). But by reminding us that it is incontrovertible that the ancient population was composed of mixed ages—and that perhaps half of the individuals living at any one time were children—King shows that the absence of younger people from the formal burial contexts within the houses she excavated is actually evidence of a marked break in age-related identities. This is of course also implicit in the other analyses of burial populations in this volume that demonstrate segregation of age groups in specific locations (Román Berrelleza and Chávez Balderas) or differences in proportion of adults and subadults in residential and non-residential locations (Storey and McAnany; McCafferty and McCafferty). But King's example underlines the fact that this sort of difference may reflect ideas changing over time, or differing between societies, about the strength of age-related difference as a basis for identity.

CHILDREN'S WORLDS AND SUBJECTIVITY

The Río Viejo population of adult burials is extraordinarily uniform and so, like the somewhat different sample from Cholula, King's mortuary evidence leads her to propose that adulthood was a time of maximal uniformity of practice and perhaps of identity (at least, that is, the kinds of idealized identities that survivors inscribe in burials). Importantly, King shows that this practice of exclusive burial of adults in Early Postclassic Río Viejo developed in a society that had previously buried individuals of mixed ages in the same locations. She thus suggests that here we see the historical development of a notion of a "child's world" separate from that of adults, a shift within local historical traditions from emphases on corporate groups including individuals of multiple ages to hierarchies of age-based difference within residential groups. How would such a changed conception of the identities of young people—emphasizing their difference from elders within their own house groups—have influenced the lives and experiences of those Early Postclassic people?

Scott Hutson begins his analysis from a position not unlike that occupied by King. At Chunchucmil, as at Río Viejo, none of the generally accepted clear evidentiary bases for discussing children have been found: no child burials, no images of children, and no material culture of childhood (after Sofaer Derevenski 2000). His suggestion that archaeologists interrogate aspects of the material world that children must have experienced (the standing, but abandoned architecture of ancient Chunchucmil), with a self-conscious attention to the possible distinctive characteristics of children's experience of these spaces, could lead archaeologists to a generally more positive assessment of their ability to talk about children in the past. Emphasizing theories of learning in childhood that foreground experience with the real material stuff of the world, Hutson echoes points made by Lopiparo in her study of children's engagement with the process and products of household-based craft production.

Hutson suggests that bits of shell in two rooms at Chunchuchmil may have made their way into abandoned rooms as a result of child's play. Following an approach pioneered in an early landmark consideration in Maya archaeology of children's effects on the archaeological record (Hammond and Hammond 1981), Hutson shows that the application of careful analysis of site formation processes may indeed allow us to identify the presence of children and the exercise of their agency. His intriguing argument underlines the potential of thinking about the child's experience of the built environment as independent of that of adults.

Marginal spaces like the abandoned rooms at Chunchuchmil, not otherwise subject to regular adult use, were open to colonization by sub-adults who could create, at least temporarily, a "child's world" in them. Following Laurie Wilkie (2000), Hutson suggests that children may be motivated to seek out such interstitial places in order to escape the control of adults and to pursue relations among themselves that are equally important for the formation of their subjectivity as the adult-child relations normally foregrounded in archaeology.

The significance of children's interactions with each other must always be kept in mind when thinking about childhood in Mesoamerica, as Trachman and Valdez also note. The institutionalized rites of passage that I discussed for the Mexica and Yucatec Maya (Joyce 1994, 2000a, 2001) had as one of their effects the coordination of the experience of an age-related cohort. The passage of such cohorts through residential institutions in young adulthood—the Houses of Youths of the Mexica and the young men's houses of Yucatán—also demonstrably constituted a set of social bonds between individuals of the same age and status through their regular interaction apart from the wider adult population (Joyce 2000a, 2000b, 2001). The images adult informants provided, in texts and visual representations, of their own experiences as children in such places are dominated by descriptions of pleasurable activities, such as playing games, dancing, and singing, expressing a nostalgia for youth that must have been significant for Mesoamerican adult subjectivity.

THE MATERIAL WORLD OF CHILDHOOD

Although proposing that there was a separate "child's world" in Early Postclassic Río Viejo, King is disinclined to take the step of identifying a material culture of childhood in the abundant assemblages she recovered from around the houses she discusses. Similar reluctance is often expressed by archaeologists interested in talking about childhood. We have been warned that it is only with the modern era that a definite life stage with its own material culture of toys took shape in Europe. And, of course, we should not assume there will be objects made specifically for young people to use.

But nor should we assume there will not be. My review of the sixteenth-century texts providing accounts of the shaping of childhood among the Mexica of Central Mexico and the Yucatec Maya demonstrated that periodically, young people were the subject of household-based ceremonies effecting transitions from one age status to another (Joyce 1994). What I have emphasized less in subsequent publications (Joyce 2000a, 2001; Meskell and Joyce 2003) is the fact that texts about these life-cycle rituals routinely describe specific material culture of childhood. If we need a warrant to consider some of the objects in our archaeological assemblages as potentially of special use by young people, these late texts would seem to provide it.

Some forms of material culture of childhood can be identified because some practices in the life cycle would have required them to be used at young ages. The identification of body ornaments as media through which the social status of children was transformed led me to examine earspools from this perspective (Joyce 2002, 2003a, 2003b). Because the hole pierced in the ear must be successively widened to eventually allow larger diameter earspools to be inserted, we can explore whether, in any particular archaeological assemblage, we find evidence of a range of earspools from small to large. If so, we may be able to suggest that the smaller diameters were worn by individuals at an early stage in the widening of ear piercings, which could represent younger people, as in the La Venta burials Billie Follensbee mentions.

Other possible material media of childhood can be identified from the sixteenth-century texts. Both the Maya and Mexica sources describe buildings that were settings for the training of juveniles on the verge of full social adulthood. Despite the fact that this would seem to offer precisely what we normally cannot define—a spatial location exclusive to one social group—there is almost no mention in the archaeological record of the possibility that excavated or surveyed buildings might represent such facilities (but see Joyce 2000b). Most aspects of childhood described in the sixteenth century, however, imply no such restricted settings. Instead, these ceremonies were held in the courtyards of residences and in the exterior plazas attached to temples. In neither case were these spaces exclusively used for such rituals. Nonetheless, these are sites where we should expect that the ceremonial marking of life stages was taking place, and we should examine the artifacts and features recovered in these settings for any evidence of rituals aimed at childhood transitions.

The spatial segregation of children's burials at La Venta, suggested by Follensbee, and in some other Mesoamerican archaeological sites, such as the Oaxacan Classic sites mentioned by King, provides another opportunity to identify possible material culture of childhood. For Cholula, the McCaffertys identify whistles and flutes, more common in the burials of young people than in those of adults, as possible "toys" or at least candidates for a distinctive material culture of childhood. It is interesting in this context to note the argument made by Lopiparo, in her discussion of children's participation in the production of musical instruments adorned with residential group– or community-specific images, that by using such instruments children may have been mimetically giving voice to fundamental conceptions about relations between humans and supernatural beings: learning in the guise of play.

The Mexica and Maya sources make clear that rituals of childhood involved the use of material goods. Many of these would not necessarily be distinctive. But the Mexica sources refer explicitly to some items, including small drinking vessels that were scaled down for young participants in rites. Miniature ceramic vessels are a constant, low-frequency part of assemblages in many areas of Mesoamerica. In assemblages from Honduras's Ulúa Valley, including those discussed by Lopiparo, miniatures are executed in the forms and decorative treatment of the more common large open bowls and necked jars, forms whose shapes suggest use in transporting, pouring, and drinking liquids. If the sixteenth-century documents are any guide, then an important part of the participation of children in rites of passage that marked the beginning of adult discipline, labor, and religious practice was accomplishment of at least token ritual drinking. Small-scale drinking vessels, like those discussed by Lopiparo, should be considered potential correlates of such actions. Mentioned in descriptions of Mexica ritual are other scaled-down materials: miniature spears, shields, and spinning tools offered to recently born infants. These might also have physical representation in archaeological assemblages.

Lopiparo argues that miniaturization may in fact be a predictable approach to creating a material culture of childhood in those situations where objects are intended to be used to introduce children to practices of the society they are expected to reproduce as adults. She suggests that miniaturization "creates a category of 'plaything' through which these ideals are discursively and non-discursively inculcated in children," reinforcing mnemonic and iconic properties inherent in all things by producing material culture scaled so that children can experience it phenomenologically with their smaller bodies and from their distinct physical perspectives.

SEEING CHILDREN, SEEING ADULTS

Billie Follensbee takes up another line of evidence, one that King identifies as not uniformly available for archaeologists interested in childhood: the representation of the child and what Follensbee terms "the childlike" in visual culture. She touches on a central issue for anyone who wants to use Mesoamerican representations as evidence for an archaeology of children: Mesoamerican imagery includes a wide range of small figures; therefore, one cannot necessarily assume that small people are also young people.

Follensbee relies on a systematic study of a large group of figurines as a basis to potentially clarify what physical features might be markers of child status in Gulf Coast Olmec art. The approach requires the assumption that the makers of these images were motivated to represent physical differences between children and adults and the further assumption that a marked child category existed. If we consider the latter assumption the main hypothesis, then we can see Follensbee's work as testing a null hypothesis that no categorical division between childhood and adulthood was systematically recognized and represented. As with any such test, failure to find distinctive child representations would not prove they did not exist; and the discovery of stable sets of characteristics that appear to differentiate children could always be a result of some other, correlated, representational category. But these problems are not unique to the attempt to identify representations of children.

Like many others analyzing assemblages of Formative period figurines, Follensbee is able to point to a specific iconography of advanced age, marked by wrinkled skin and sunken cheeks, showing that age is one of the dimensions of personhood at issue for Gulf Coast Olmec artisans. But she notes that youth is less obviously marked, except in the case of infants on cradleboards (which she notes might actually represent bodies of the dead). Instead, she identifies possible juvenile females based on the use of costumes typical of figurines with the body type she has defined for adult females, in the absence of the diagnostic "hourglass-type" figure that is her diagnostic adult feature. Extending this model of representation of physical traits of childhood to other forms of visual culture, including monumental art, Follensbee concludes that some children were important in Olmec society, especially certain elite children.

Examples of securely identified representations of youths in other Mesoamerican societies underline the conclusion that select young people may have enjoyed the same status as older individuals in some Mesoamerican societies. But the successful identification of young people in these cases sets in sharp relief the initial distinction I drew between seeking children and creating an archaeology of childhood. If the reason that we can "see" some children is because they are essentially being presented as small-scale adults, then arguably we have not identified evidence of childhood. Hutson, in the opening comments in his chapter, characterizes similar "methodological refinement" as "potentially misleading" because we assume there is a domain of the child occupied by children, conceived of as universally distinct from adults.

Relations between children and adults are important for understanding not only visual representation, but also practices for which no discursive evidence is available. Storey and McAnany draw attention to the probability that the secondary burials of very young children at K'axob resulted from the preservation by surviving family and community members of the bodies of these prematurely dead, who at K'axob were most often ultimately laid to rest with primary adult burials (family groups and, especially, women). They note that scattering of skeletal elements of the very young, related to the secondary interment of defleshed bodies, cannot be taken as an indication of lack of respect, and draw attention to the presence of offerings in examples of scattered secondary burials at K'axob. Their suggestion is that the treatment of the youthful dead is a consequence of the attachments between the young and older members of their social group (cf. Meskell 1994).

Follensbee sharply underlines the distinction between identifying young individuals (who may not inform us about a specific experiential realm of children) and tracing evidence of culturally situated distinctive experiences of childhood when she draws attention to the only unequivocably identifiable children in Olmec archaeology: those selectively buried in sites such as Laguna El Manatí, commonly described as sacrificial offerings. Very young infants, these children are assumed to have been identified categorically as appropriate for offering to the gods. Clearly there is a process of abstraction of an age-related category from the general population involved in the separate disposal of these infants, but it is possible that we have too hastily leapt to the conclusion that early Mesoamericans engaged in wholesale child sacrifice (Joyce 2003c). The example illustrates a significant dilemma facing archaeologists interested in understanding childhood: if we assume from the outset that the patterns we see are accounted for primarily by age, then we may well miss other aspects of the intersectionality of identities that are the causes of these groupings.

In the case of infants abstracted for specialized disposal in ritual settings, their interpretation as sacrificial victims is solidly grounded in post-conquest interpretations of Mexica texts. But as represented in the detailed data reported by Juan Alberto Román Berrelleza and Ximena Chávez Balderas from Tenochtitlan and Tlatelolco, in actual Mexica practice it was not just any children that were ultimately laid to rest in ritual precincts. Drawing on work based on textual sources written immediately after the Spanish conquest, they note that childhood was described as a time of great danger. They relate these discursive descriptions to actual conditions of health that routinely led to high infant and early childhood mortality, an experience of the young also documented by Rebecca Storey (1992, 1997) in her pathbreaking studies of children buried at Classic Maya Copan.

Román Berrelleza and Chávez Balderas identify a group of young children buried in a single event at a temple dedicated to Tlaloc. Their analysis suggests that these children suffered from poor health before being selected for ritual disposal. They suggest that suffering from specific diseases may have singled out these children as appropriate for offering to this deity. Given the indications in Mexica texts that young children were considered to be materially distinct from adults and composed of precious substances worked by the gods and entrusted to humans (Joyce 2000a), we might consider whether our notion of sacrifice quite describes the return of not-yet-fully human young people to the realm that their diseases showed they had not fully abandoned. From our perspective, children are just young versions of adults. From the perspective of ancient Mesoamericans, children, especially very young children, may have often been something quite distinct.

Here, it is worthwhile to recall the observations Storey and McAnany make concerning some of the predictable demographic realities of life in ancient Mesoamerica. As they put it, "all juvenile mortality is premature mortality . . . but some losses are more predictable than others." The very young, under the age of five, would have been at relatively high risk of death, but children ages five and above, having lived through the risky early years, would be expected to survive. A fundamental distinction in attitudes toward the very young might well be expected in this case, not unlike the kinds of maternal attitudes explored by Nancy Scheper-Hughes (1992) in her ethnographic study, *Death Without Weeping.*

CHILDHOOD AGENCY

Román Berrelleza and Chávez Balderas note that many researchers fail to consider children because they are not considered relevant in political, economic, or religious explanations of social relations, raising an issue that Traci Ardren frames as central to the study of childhood: how do children feature as social agents in our models? Lopiparo addresses this question head-on: the agency of children is both identifiable and indispensable for social models. Using an approach grounded in the theoretical works of Pierre Bourdieu and Antony Giddens, she suggests that archaeologists consider how "fundamental ideas about aesthetics, personhood, social roles, and group and individual identity were performed by domestic groups—and inscribed in media that served as mnemonics in the ongoing dialogues through which these structures of thought were reproduced and transformed," arguing that everyday practices were "instrumental in the perpetuation of household membership, shared property and prosperity, and social memory—through the discursive and nondiscursive inculcation of these ideals in children." Hutson pursues similar arguments, noting that children and adults are bound in social relations so that each forms the other, a point substantively illustrated by Lopiparo's richly grounded analysis. The social agency of children is thus unavoidable, and all that archaeologists do when they fail to consider it is inadvertently perpetuate uninterrogated naturalized assumptions.

Byron Hamann's account of the role of the young in the early colonial campaigns of European missionaries to change the nature of Mesoamerican society vividly illustrates the power that children have in the reproduction of society through a discussion of their refusal to recapitulate the past in early colonial Mesoamerica. The deliberate production of a generational rift in regard to religion was a strategy of conquest based in a specific European theory of the holiness of children. But it was effective because children are, in any society, the guarantors of continuity or, if they will it, the agents of change. Hamann's argument that cultural conventions attributing a state of holiness to children in early modern Europe would have been a resource for children to exercise agency suggests that we try to consider how Mesoamerican young people might have built on the specific qualities attributed to them to create spheres of action in ancient Mesoamerica whose effects could well have been profound.

CONCLUSION

The papers gathered in this book employ three different terms—children, childhood, and young people—that signify different, productively complementary, perspectives for approaching the complex topics of the early lives of human subjects. The status of being a child is commonsensically associated with youth in something of the same way that gender is associated with biological sex. So from one perspective, the questions we must ask deal with the identification of differences and continuities in the experiences of people of different ages. It is thus no accident that bioarchaeologists are among the leaders in raising awareness of childhood as a topic of investigation in Mesoamerica.

Mortuary analyses promise the potential of defining the kinds of social breaks in development that are marked by life-cycle rituals, and they simultaneously provide information about the specific experiences of specific individuals. Mortuary studies, consequently, have potential to call attention to categorical identification between different individuals resulting from the way they were treated by survivors, and differences in practices related to the individuation of each person during their own life course and in their social relations.

The way that childhood and its stages are socially construed will vary with different theories of development and in the presence of different experiences of mortality. The experience of mortality of infants (whose deaths may have been more expected) and older children (whose deaths would have been less common and therefore more disruptive) would have influenced the way survivors, who would include both adults and children, regarded these categories of young people. Our discussions of practices of differential disposition of infants, including ritual death and burial, need to take into account the way that very young children were viewed, perhaps not even as completely human. The death of very young people may have been viewed differently from the deaths of older children, who would have clearly been integrated into the living human community.

Concern with the integration of children into society brings into focus the different emphases that arise if we take as our goal understanding childhood or locating children. Understanding childhood requires approaching childhood as relational. Relations with adults are foregrounded in much of the material we have available for analysis, most of which is produced by adults. A complementary perspective would attempt to understand the experience of childhood from the perspective of the child.

This brings us back to the discussion of children's participation in practices that socialize them and, through that process, reproduce society. Material practices that discipline young people will exist in tension with practices that in studies of adulthood we might call resistance. Where children are concerned, however, we have as a resource an alternative concept, that of play.

Play, in contrast to resistance, introduces the idea of noncompliance with discipline that is a means of simultaneously learning the rules and testing the limits. Play is certainly not limited to what children do, but it is an important human capacity for those learning how to be in particular societies. Play can encompass things that adults see as opposed, both the unstructured and the formally constrained. Children playing outside the formal control of elders and children participating in making pottery figurines and miniature objects can both be seen as engaging in pleasurable activity.

Although there is a tendency, given the recent Western notion of childhood as leisure, to see children's labor as the *end* of childhood, I think we might consider whether one of the major differences between adulthood and childhood may be the degree of pleasure children can derive from carrying out tasks that adults view as work. Children, we might suggest, are learners who enjoy doing a wider range of things than adults routinely manage to do.

Kathryn Kamp's (2001) query, "Where have all the children gone?" echoes as a call for archaeologists to think through the social past more fully. With this collection, Mesoamerican archaeologists have set an agenda that should spread throughout our discipline. By tacking back and forth between the recognition of age-specific experience by young people, the representation of children in works of art, the traces of actions we can think of as "play" typical of children as developing subjects, and the social practices that marked stages of childhood and through which young social subjects—children—were transformed, we have here the beginnings of a rich exploration of an archaeology of childhood that truly is fundamental to any understanding of the perpetuation of society. The perspectives employed here no doubt will continue to be debated, and issues overlooked by these authors will undoubtedly be identified in the future. But these authors conclusively demonstrate that children are good to think: they have transformative potential for our understanding of the material remains of past worlds. The questions raised by an archaeology of childhood should resonate with each of us: this is, after all, the one place from which we all come.

ACKNOWLEDGMENTS

I thank Traci Ardren for her generous invitation to participate in the AAA session that gave rise to this book. When Elizabeth Chilton, Blythe Roveland, and Martin Wobst invited me to present ideas they had heard sketchily referred to at a roundtable at the University of Massachusetts, Amherst, as part of a session on childhood for the 1994 SAA meetings in Anaheim, I doubt they knew what a critical contribution they were making by encouraging me to continue to think about the apparently undetectable children of the past. Jeanne Lopiparo has pushed me to think more deeply about these issues, getting me past an archaeology of the adult imposition of discipline on children to some baby steps in thinking about children's experience.

REFERENCES CITED

Brumfiel, Elizabeth M.

1991 Weaving and Cooking: Women's Production in Aztec Mexico. In *Engendering Archaeology*, ed. J. Gero and M. Conkey, 224–251. Oxford: Basil Blackwell.

Calnek, Edward E.

1992 The Ethnographic Context of the Third Part of the *Codex Mendoza*. In *The Codex Mendoza, Volume 1: Interpretation*, ed. F. Berdan and P. Anawalt, 81–91. Berkeley: University of California Press.

Clendinnen, Inga

1991 *Aztecs: An Interpretation*. Cambridge: Cambridge University Press.

Crown, Patricia L.

1999 Socialization in American Southwest Pottery Decoration. In *Pottery and People: A Dynamic Interaction*, ed J. M. Skibo and G. M. Feinman, 25–43. Salt Lake City: University of Utah Press.

Hammond, Gawain, and Norman Hammond

1981 Child's Play: A Disturbance Factor in Archaeological Deposition. *American Antiquity* 46:634–636.

Joyce, Rosemary A.

1994 Looking for Children in Prehispanic Mesoamerica. Paper presented in the symposium "The Archaeology of Childhood" (Elizabeth Chilton and Martin Wobst, organizers). 59th Annual Meeting of the Society for American Archaeology, Anaheim, CA.

2000a Girling the Girl and Boying the Boy: The Production of Adulthood in Ancient Mesoamerica. *World Archaeology* 31:473–483.

2000b A Precolumbian Gaze: Male Sexuality Among the Ancient Maya. In *Archaeologies of Sexuality,* ed. B. Voss and R. Schmidt, 263–283. London: Routledge.

2001 *Gender and Power in Prehispanic Mesoamerica.* Austin: University of Texas Press.

2002 Beauty, Sexuality, Body Ornamentation, and Gender in Ancient Mesoamerica. In *In Pursuit of Gender,* ed S. Nelson and M. Rosen-Ayalon, 81–92. Walnut Creek: Altamira Press.

2003a Concrete Memories: Fragments of the Past in the Classic Maya Present (500–1000). In *Archaeologies of Memory,* ed. R. Van Dyke and S. Alcock, 104–125. Malden, MA: Blackwell.

2003b Making Something of Herself: Embodiment in Life and Death at Playa de los Muertos, Honduras. *Cambridge Archaeological Journal* 13:248–261.

2003c Las Raíces de la Tradición Funeraria Maya en Prácticas Mesoamericanas del Período Formativo. In *Antropología de la eternidad: La muerte en la cultura Maya,* ed. A. Ciudad Ruiz, M. H. Ruz Sosa y M. J. Iglesias Ponce de León, 7–34. Madrid: Sociedad Española de Estudios Mayas.

Kamp, Kathryn

1999 Discovering Childhood: Using Fingerprints to Find Children in the Archaeological Record. *American Antiquity* 64:309–315.

2001 Where Have All the Children Gone? The Archaeology of Childhood. *Journal of Archaeological Method and Theory* 8:1–34.

Landa, Diego de

[1566] *Landa's "Relación de las cosas de Yucatan."* Trans. A. M. Tozzer.

1941 Peabody Museum Papers, 18. Cambridge: Peabody Museum of Archaeology and Ethnology, Harvard University.

McCafferty, Sharisse D., and Geoffrey G. McCafferty

1991 Spinning and Weaving as Female Gender Identity in Post-Classic Mexico. In *Textile Traditions of Mesoamerica and the Andes,* ed. J. C. Berlo, M. Schevill and E. B. Dwyer, 19–44. New York: Garland.

Meskell, Lynn M.

1994 Dying Young: The Experience of Death at Deir el Medina. *Archaeological Review from Cambridge* 13:35–45.

Meskell, Lynn M., and Rosemary A. Joyce

2003 *Embodied Lives: Figuring Ancient Egypt and the Classic Maya.* London: Routledge.

Scheper-Hughes, Nancy

1992 *Death Without Weeping: The Violence of Everyday Life in Brazil.* Berkeley: University of California Press.

Serra Puche, M. C., and K. R. Durand

1998 Las Mujeres de Xochitecatl. *Arqueologia Mexicana* 5 (29):20–27.

Sofaer Derevenski, Joanna
2000 Material Culture Shock: Confronting Expectations in the Material Culture of Children. In *Children and Material Culture,* ed J. Sofaer Derevenski, 3–16. London: Routledge.

Storey, Rebecca
1992 The Children of Copan: Issues in Paleopathology and Paleodemography. *Ancient Mesoamerica* 3:161–167.
1997 Individual Frailty, Children of Privilege, and Stress in Late Classic Copán. In *Bones of the Maya: Studies of Ancient Skeletons,* ed. S. L. Whittington and D. M. Reed, 116–126. Washington, DC: Smithsonian Institution Press.

Wilkie, Laurie
2000 Not Merely Child's Play: Creating a Historical Archaeology of Children and Childhood. In *Children and Material Culture,* ed. J. Sofaer Derevenski, 100–114. London: Routledge.

INDEX

www.ingramcontent.com/pod-product-compliance
Lightning Source LLC
Chambersburg PA
CBHW060026030426
42334CB00019B/2196

* 9 7 8 1 6 0 7 3 2 4 6 3 8 *